ROMANCE

*Generic Transformation
from Chrétien de Troyes to Cervantes*

ROMANCE

Generic Transformation
from Chrétien de Troyes to Cervantes

Edited
and with an introduction
by
Kevin Brownlee
and
Marina Scordilis Brownlee

Published for Dartmouth College
by University Press of New England
Hanover and London, 1985

University Press of New England

Brandeis University
Brown University
Clark University
University of Connecticut
Dartmouth College
University of New Hampshire
University of Rhode Island
Tufts University
University of Vermont

LIBRARY OF CONGRESS CATALOGING IN PUBLICATION DATA
Main entry under title:

Romance : generic transformation from Chrétien de Troyes to Cervantes.

Based on the proceedings of the Second Dartmouth Colloquium on Medieval and Early Modern Romance Literatures, held in Hanover, N.H., in Sept., 1982.
Bibliography: p.
1. Romances—History and criticism—Congresses. I. Brownlee, Kevin. II. Brownlee, Marina Scordilis. III. Dartmouth Colloquium on Medieval and Early Modern Romance Literatures (2nd : 1982)
PN663.R66 1985   809.1'3   84-40581
ISBN 0-87451-338-3

CONTENTS

PREFACE

The present volume results from the second Dartmouth Colloquium on Medieval and Early Modern Romance Literatures, held in Hanover in September 1982. As such it reflects the methodological orientation of the Colloquium series as a whole. This orientation is simultaneously historical and theoretical, combining an awareness of new critical approaches with a commitment to close readings of individual literary texts. Each Dartmouth Colloquium seeks to examine a key literary question within the context of the European Romance literatures in their continuity and gradual evolution from the Middle Ages to the early modern period. Our goal is to provide a forum for scholarly interaction that transcends the limitations imposed by conventional periodization on the one hand and linguistico-literary "nationalism" on the other. It is our hope that such interaction will result in the growth of historical literary studies across the boundaries that have obscured continuities in form and concept while at the same time rendering difficult the appreciation of real change. Such growth was certainly the result of the first Colloquium (1981), out of which grew the important study *Mimesis: From Mirror to Method, Augustine to Descartes* (Hanover, N.H.: UP of New England, 1982). By choosing to focus the second Colloquium on the problematics of genre, we sought to bring a similar historical perspective to bear on an issue of literary theory that has itself changed radically over time and continues to preoccupy contemporary critics. From our point of view, the most effective way to accomplish this necessarily involves a rigorous grounding in a particular literary corpus, a self-conscious attention to the specificity of textual *realia*. Thus our decision was to study the question of genre as process by focusing on the romance and its development during the formative centuries of the vernacular literatures of France, Italy, and Spain.

The romance genre has been one of the most protean and long-lived in Western European literature. Beginning with its emergence as an identifiable generic system in twelfth-century France, the romance underwent (in response to changing historico-literary milieux) a series of transformations which may be said to culminate in works as disparate as *Don Quijote* and *L'Astrée*. Romance thus provides a privileged locus for study of the nature and function of literary genre as well as the dynamics of generic transformation. At the same time, the importance and complexity of the romance genre as such call for special treatment. The present collection of essays attempts to respond to this double challenge by presenting a coherent treatment of romance on its own terms, taking into account the formal and thematic heterogeneity that is built into the genre. Our intended audience is equally heterogeneous: students and scholars, comparatists and literary historians, philologists and literary theorists.

It is a pleasure to acknowledge the many people whose generous help has been essential to the successful completion of this volume. First and foremost is the exemplary collaborative effort of the distinguished scholars who participated in the Colloquium. It has been exciting indeed to work with such a group. We wish to give special thanks to our colleagues John Lyons, Stephen Nichols, and Nancy Vickers, fellow members of the Dartmouth Study Group in Medieval and Early Modern Romance Literatures, for their many important contributions to this project. Suzanne Coonley, formerly of the Comparative Literature program at Dartmouth, provided invaluable organizational help for the Colloquium as well as for the volume in its initial stages. We have greatly appreciated the meticulous typing of Terry Viens, the careful proofreading of Elise Morse, and the excellent copyediting of Barbara Flanagan.

The Ramon Guthrie Fund provided the primary financial support for the Colloquium. Ramon Guthrie himself—by his example and by the values he embodied—provided inspiration for the entire enterprise represented by this volume. It is to the memory of this distinguished poet, professor of romance languages, and intellectual mentor for generations of Dartmouth students and colleagues that we dedicate this book.

We are grateful to the Dartmouth College Faculty Research Committee for having funded our work at important stages. Finally, we would like to thank David McLaughlin, president of Dartmouth College, for his presence at the Colloquium and his support of our collective intellectual endeavor.

Hanover, New Hampshire   *Kevin Brownlee*
                                          Marina Scordilis Brownlee

In memoriam Ramon Guthrie (1896–1973)

INTRODUCTION

The purpose of this volume is to examine the nature and function of the generic entity that is romance. The approach is consciously and rigorously textual, involving detailed analyses of specific romances. While theoretical questions are necessarily investigated, these investigations eschew mere abstraction and focus always on concrete textual loci.

A twofold presupposition determines our approach. First, romance—and, more generally, any literary genre—has no meaningful existence as a static category. Rather, it is a question of genre as process: the functional literary life of romance involves a series of generic transformations over time resulting in a kind of dynamic continuum. Our second presupposition is a necessary complement to the first: an insistence on the fundamental importance of history to an understanding of genre. Romance is thus conceived as inextricably bound up with a complex, evolving, historical situation. On the one hand, this means a constant interchange between a given romance text and its literary environment, past and present. Seemingly alien generic discourses and constructs are again and again remotivated in terms of and integrated into a continually transformed and transforming romance generic system. On the other hand, the evolving identity of the romance genre reflects—indeed, results from—a dialectic with social and political history involving issues as diverse as inscribed ideology, sociolinguistic hierarchization, and readership. It goes without saying that social and literary history "interact" in any given romance text.

Within the broad contours of our overall perspective, the individual essays display a wide diversity of procedure and methodology. While this kind of pluralism is characteristic of any collective enterprise, it is particularly appropriate to an anthology concerned precisely with the striking diversity among specific textual embodiments of a continually changing generic system. Different romances in different historico-literary contexts call above all for methodological heterogeneity. The way in which Chrétien de Troyes's romances thematize their generic status differs radically from, for example, the "spiritual poetics" of the *Queste del Saint Graal*.

It must be stressed, however, that we consider the textual focus of our volume to be a necessary complement to the exciting developments in genre theory that have taken place over the last quarter century. Indeed, the importance of these theoretical developments as the context in which we concentrate on textual *realia* necessitates a brief overview.

In a very real sense, Northrop Frye's *Anatomy of Criticism* (1957)[1] initiated a new era in genre criticism. Frye reopened the question of the theoretical status of literary genre by demonstrating the fundamental inadequacy of the canonical taxonomic triad: drama/epic/lyric. On the one hand, Frye argues that these three terms are employed with such imprecision as to render them practically meaningless as conceptual categories. On the other hand, Frye stresses that literary texts are not monolithic structures and thus cannot be categorized reductionistically. A new approach is therefore required since "the purpose of criticism by genres is not so much to classify as to clarify . . . traditions and affinities, thereby bringing out a large number of literary relationships that would not be noticed as long as there were no context established for them" (247).

The core of Frye's new approach to genre study is his theory of modes, which in turn is built on the Aristotelian differentiation of literary types according to the hero's potential: "Fictions may be classified, not morally, but by the hero's power of action, which may be greater than ours, less, or roughly the same" (33). From this principle, Frye advances five basic literary modes:

> 1) If superior in kind both to other men and to the environment of other men, the hero is a divine being, and the story about him will be a myth; 2) If superior in degree to other men and to his environment, the hero is the typical hero of romance, whose actions are marvelous but who is himself identified as a human being; 3) If superior in degree to other men but not to his natural environment, the hero is a leader. . . . This is the hero of the "high mimetic" mode, of most epic and tragedy; 4) If superior neither to other men nor to his environment, the hero is one of us . . . the hero of the "low mimetic" mode, of most comedy and of realistic fiction; 5) If inferior in power or intelligence to ourselves . . . the hero belongs to the ironic mode. (33–34)

The analytical effectiveness of Frye's model theory is greatly increased by his assertion that several modes may coexist in the same text: "while one mode constitutes the underlying tonality of a work of fiction, any or all of the other four may simultaneously be present. Much of our sense of subtlety of great literature comes from this modal counterpoint" (50–51).

It is important to stress that Frye's approach is fundamentally transhistorical, in the sense that he projects a largely cyclical view of literary history. He conceives of modes as "epochs" in the diachronic progression of a given national literature. In the context of the five-part modal progression, Frye observes that "European fiction, during the last fifteen centuries, has steadily moved its center of gravity down the list" (34). Political, economic, and religious factors are the agents of such changes from one predominant mode to another.

Finally, Frye posits this modal approach as the conceptual wedge which makes meaningful interpretation of even temporally remote literature possible: "through such modal analysis we may come to realize that the two essential facts about a work of art, that it is contemporary with its own time and that it is contemporary with ours, are not opposed but complementary facts" (51).

Ten years after the appearance of *Anatomy of Criticism*, E. D. Hirsch reexamined genre theory from the perspective of hermeneutics.[2] Hirsch leveled several important criticisms against Frye's methodology. First, he challenged Frye's concept of genre as being too exclusively constitutive. For Hirsch, the heuristic function of genre is at least as important as its constitutive function: "If we believe that 'genres' are constitutive rather than arbitrary and heuristic, then we have made a serious mistake and have also set up a barrier to valid interpretation" (110–11).

Second, Hirsch rejects the notion of genre as a transhistorical, cyclical construct, focusing rather on diachronic specificity. He asserts that "if traditional genres really were specific concepts that constrained a speaker and an interpreter, then new types could obviously not arise" (109). The validity of this perception is dramatically demonstrated, for example, by the sixteenth-century "*romanzi* polemic"—the romance being a form which Aristotle had obviously never envisioned. Moreover, in Hirsch's view the critic's attention should be focused not on traditional generic classifications but on microtextual units—"vocabulary range, syntactical patterns, formulaic invariants," and so on (80). In this way, a meaningful distinction between the *novella* of Cervantes and Borges may be formulated.

Hirsch's overall approach to genre stems from the principle of the so-called hermeneutic circle, or the fundamental interdependence of part and whole. An important reciprocity is at issue here: the whole can be adequately represented and understood only through an examination of its parts, and the individual parts generate meaning only when considered collectively. As a logical corollary, "all understanding of verbal meaning is necessarily genre-bound" (76), that is, it is only with reference to a context that a literary text—or even a sentence—can be evaluated. A further corollary is that genre is inextricably linked to the creative process itself, forming a kind of perpetually changing system of expectations. As Hirsch remarks, "No one would invent or understand a new type of meaning unless he were capable of perceiving analogies and making novel subsumptions under previously known types" (105). Literary works deviate from recognizable norms while necessarily maintaining perceptible generic markers or systems of expectations. In so doing, genre is equally heuristic and constitutive in nature and function.

Tzvetan Todorov[3] considers genre from the perspective of speech act theory, viewing literary discourse(s) in the broader context of linguistic discourse(s). Todorov thus formulates the global proposition that "a genre, literary or otherwise, is nothing but a codification of discursive properties" (162). This ostensibly simple equivalence, however, immediately raises two fundamental issues: (1) the definition of the relevant discursive properties and (2) the problem of how these discursive properties become codified. In response to the first question, Todorov considers a "discursive property" to be any linguistico-literary feature which consensus by readership has identified as a defining generic trait:

> . . . tragedy is opposed to comedy by thematic elements; the suspense narrative differs from the classic detective novel by the fitting together of its plot; finally, autobiography is distinguished from the novel in that the author claims to recount facts rather than construct fictions. (162)

In answer to the second question, Todorov further refines his definition of genre according to historical context and the wide range of possibilities which the axis of history implies. Unlike earlier taxonomic theorists who viewed genre as comprising a set of unchanging "Platonic ideals," Todorov perceives genre as being culturally determined: "genres, like any other institution, reveal the constitutive traits of the society to which they belong" (163). It is, more precisely, the intersection of a given historical actuality with a given discursive potentiality which produces the codification of genre. Hence genre is not in itself either a purely discursive or a purely historical fact, but rather the liminal space or point of contact which fuses a selected poetics and a particular historical moment. The specific range of literary possibilities which a given society chooses to actualize will therefore vary markedly from one epoch to another. By the same token, however, a continuum of organicity ensures that in the face of individual creativity the socioverbal contract will be maintained: writers will, in a recognizable way, adhere to "models of writing" which will elicit a predictable "horizon of expectations"[4] in their readers. Were this not the case, genres would lose their communicative function (for both author and reader) as response-inviting structures of a particular kind, thereby forfeiting not only their own existence but the possibility for literary communication itself.

Gérard Genette's approach to genre theory is essentially that of a structuralist.[5] He is above all concerned with establishing a taxonomic system of transhistorical and translinguistic generic "distinctive features." His extended historical survey of genre criticism from Plato and Aristotle to the late twentieth century serves as a prelude to and a justification of a new formulation of the status of literary genre in ahistorical terms. The fundamental distinction for Genette's inquiry into the history of genre theory is that between modes of enunciation (which he views as a linguistic category) and thematic content (an essentially literary category). After elaborately demonstrating the fundamental and frequently misunderstood difference between these two sets of categories, Genette combines them in a kind of neo-Aristotelian grid which takes into account the minimum number of generic distinctive features. By adding "formal" elements as a third (but not necessarily final) category, Genette arrives at a new taxonomic system. The various combinations of these three qualitatively different criteria will serve to identify, describe, and trace the development of the *realia* of different literary genres inscribed, historically, in the production and reception of specific texts.

Genette's overriding concern is that his taxonomic grid be both accurate and "effective," that is, that it be able to account for the maximum number of historical and potential generic subgroupings. Thus the theoretical open-endedness of Genette's system is a function of its transhistorical aspirations. On the other hand, Genette's attempt to be resolutely nonhierarchical with regard to the modal, thematic, and formal elements whose intersections identify generic categories (*Introduction* 83) leads him back into history. The set of "constants" proposed by Genette both "indicates the background against which the evolution of literature as system takes place and determines, to a large degree, something like the stock of generic possibilities from which this evolution chooses" (*Introduction* 83). Genette's theoretical enterprise focuses on the constitutive elements of genre and their permutations. But his is a deductive system and is thus based on "the empirical study of genres . . . as socio-historical institutions" (*Introduction* 85). At the same time, the study of any specific genre becomes the province of the literary historian. For if Genette's "architext" identifies a given combination of generic distinctive features, genre as such can exist only in specific and "coherent" historical contexts. The relevance of this notion to the present volume is obvious: the necessary counterpart to the poetician's theoretical concern with romance as transhistorical supercategory is a detailed investigation of the literarily functional role genre in a corpus of romance texts.

Maria Corti's analysis of generic systems involves a semiotics deeply informed by an awareness of history.[6] She clearly articulates the important diachronic factor which determines the way in which individual texts as well as entire genres express and transform themselves:

> The correlation of messages and codes is a profitable critical-semiological operation because the insertion of the single text or hypersign in its rightful place in the evolution of a genre clarifies its individual qualities, its dosages of originality and convention; at the same time it also sheds light on the process of literary communication through the evolution of contents and forms both in themselves and in relation to historical-social contexts. (125)

Putting this critical perspective to the test, Corti observes that generic codes either are canonized or are transformed by individual writers in one of two directions. Writers may "transform the codes from the inside or . . . corrode and subvert them to the point of destroying them" (125).

Corti elaborates four possible vehicles of generic transformation. First, the genre may be internally transformed; for example, a secondary (recessive) constitutive element in one era may replace a primary (dominant) element in another. This type of change is thus infrageneric. Second, there exists an intergeneric phenomenon whereby entire genre systems may change from serving one purpose to serving another: "It is not only genres that change but their own hierarchy, which is differently constituted from one era to another" (134). Third, literary displacement can occur in eras of broad-based literary movements:

When large artistic and cultural developments take place—for example that of the Baroque or of Romanticism—a kind of density is produced in the literature that renders it more homogeneous, as if it were nourished equally in all its parts. In such cases literary genres, while preserving their autonomous structures, are displaced coaxially in a certain direction as if a unifying spiritual principle had intervened. This phenomenon touches both codes and individual messages. (134)

Fourth, genre can be displaced "when a great writer causes a crisis in the constitutive laws of the genre, of its codification" (136). The notable generic deviance achieved by Ariosto and Cervantes illustrates this type of change. Ariosto, "without abandoning the chivalric genre, rises in the literary hierarchy to the same nobility as the lyric" (137). Likewise, although with increased generic complexity, "Cervantes has deliberately set side by side, without annihilating them, the typical traits of the various genres in a subversive mixture of codes—a death knell for the chivalric genre" (137).

Finally, Corti addresses the phenomenon of generic "restorations and recoveries"—that is, remotivated genres: "The reassumption of a literary genre of the past can take place when the opposite phenomenon, that is, its rejection, ceases to be artistically active, productive, or significant in the system" (139). Such revival is, moreover, never a mere reduplication but a genuine remotivation, a new permutation which evolves as the product of a new diachronic situation.

The recent trend which views the historicization of genre as functional literary construct was, paradoxically, perceived some forty years ago by Mikhail Bakhtin.[7] However, owing to the accidents of politics and history, some of Bakhtin's most important theoretical works did not see the light of day until the 1970s. While contemporaries in the 1930s were regarding genre taxonomically (in a wholly constitutive manner), Bakhtin saw genre as a fluid—sociohistorical—function of language.

Bakhtin understood language as a polysemous and ever-changing medium:

Language—like the living concrete environment in which the consciousness of the verbal artist lives—is never unitary. It is unitary only as an abstract grammatical system of normative forms, taken in isolation from the concrete, ideological conceptualizations that fill it, and in isolation from the uninterrupted process of historical becoming that is characteristic of all living language. (288)

As a function of sociohistorical change there arise within

an abstractly unitary national language a multitude of concrete worlds, a multitude of bounded verbal-ideological and social belief systems; within these various systems (identical in the abstract) are elements of language filled with various semantic and axiological contents and each with its own different sound. (288)

Literary genres correspond to these various "concrete worlds," each one "knit together with specific points of view, specific approaches, forms of thinking, nuances" (289), and so on.

Bakhtin makes a further distinction between "high" and "low" genres. The former preclude any depiction or valorization of contemporary reality; "events and heroes receive their value and grandeur precisely through . . . association with the past" (18). The discourse of the "high" genres is authoritative, "official," since it aims at perpetuating hierarchical authority formulated in the past. The "low" genres, on the other hand—especially the novel—are "associated with the eternally living element of unofficial language and unofficial thought (holiday forms, familiar speech, profanation)" (20).

At a given point in time, the "high" genres (which exhibit a kind of artificial, oversimplifying "Ptolemaic language consciousness") are confronted by the polysemous "Galilean language consciousness" which Bakhtin privileges as "novelistic." The medieval and early modern period is singled out by Bakhtin as a prime example of such sociohistorically motivated generic exploration and transformation:

> The era of the Renaissance and Protestantism, which destroyed the verbal and ideological centralization of the Middle Ages, was an era of great astronomical, mathematical and geographical discoveries, an era that destroyed the finitude of mathematical quantity, which shifted the boundaries of the old geographical world—such an era could find adequate expression only through a Galilean language consciousness. (415)

With Fredric Jameson's "dialectical" approach to genre theory, our brief survey comes full circle.[8] Jameson focuses squarely on the specifics of the romance genre to investigate the problematics of literary genre in general. Northrop Frye serves as a key point of departure, as Jameson modifies the transhistorical aspect of Frye's concept of romance as mode. Jameson's goal is to make "a genuinely *historical* account of romance possible." This involves, somewhat paradoxically, the recognition that a mode is, by definition, not period-specific, that it is a "particular type of literary discourse . . . not bound to the conventions of a given age, nor indissolubly linked to a given type of verbal artifact, but rather persists as a temptation and a mode of expression across a whole range of historical periods, seeming to offer

itself, if only intermittently, as a formal possibility which can be re-
vived and renewed" ("Magical Narratives" 142). The history of romance therefore involves a series of transformations, as different social and literary codes are pressed into service under the changing
constraints of historical evolution. The principal area of Jameson's
"empirical" investigation is thus a series of detailed textual analyses
of particular romances in all the specificity of their various historical
contexts.

The theoretical basis for Jameson's readings is a systematic refor-
mulation of genre criticims as such. Three variable terms are posited,
and the relationship among them is characterized as a "permuta-
tional scheme . . . a *combinatoire*." First is the "individual work itself" and second, "the intertextual sequence into which it is inserted
through the ideal construction of a progression of forms" ("Magical
Narratives" 157). It is important, in this connection, to stress Jameson's concept of genre as *system:* "the notion of system . . . presup-
poses a series of synchronic states, in which the various existent
genres are related to each other only by difference, constellations
which shift and rearrange themselves ceaselessly as certain genres
fall into neglect, or as new ones emerge unexpectedly and force the
older, traditional generic system to redefine itself in order to accommodate them" ("Magical Narratives" 152). The relationship between
a specific literary text and the generic system(s) in which it participates thus involves "two basic elements [that] are wholly distinct in
nature from each other." The latter must be understood as "consti-
tuting something like an environment for the [former], which
emerges into a world in which the genres form a given determinate
relationship among themselves, and which then seeks to define itself
in terms of that relationship" ("Magical Narratives" 153).

The third term in Jameson's theoretical *combinatoire* is, not sur-
prisingly, history, "that series of concrete historical situations within
which the individual works were realized" ("Magical Narratives"
157). This third component is, for Jameson, the crucial one: historical
changes produce literary changes—both in generic systems and in
individual works—but the converse is not true. Jameson's system is
thus self-consciously hierarchical, with history playing the key causal
role: "the historical moment blocks off a certain number of formal
possibilities which had been available in earlier situations, all the
while opening up certain determinate new ones, which may or may
not then come into being" ("Magical Narratives" 158). Jameson's
ultimate purpose in treating genre theory in terms of a permuta-

tional scheme is to reveal "not the causes behind a given form, but rather the *conditions of possibility* of its existence" ("Magical Narratives" 158). On the one hand, this involves taking into account the synchronic relationship between a particular literary text and its immediate historical situation. On the other hand, there is the equally important diachronic perspective in which a given historical situation is perceived as a moment in an ongoing continuum, thus allowing specific realizations of generic forms to be evaluated in the context of other, radically different sets of generic possibilities tied to other sociohistorical moments.

In the case of romance, this double perspective means that Jameson gives special attention to the birth of the genre in the vernacular literature of medieval Europe. Historical context is essential here, for twelfth-century France, in Jameson's view, generated romance as a distinctive generic form to resolve an ideological contradiction: the feudal nobility's new self-awareness as a universal class and its residual sense of a binomial opposition with worthy forces of evil (an essentially epic construct). For Jameson, however, twelfth-century romance is only a first step: "this vision of a realm of magic superimposed on the earthly, purely social world, clearly outlive[d] the particular historical and ideological contradiction which it was invented to resolve, thereby furnishing material for other quite different symbolic uses as the form itself [was] adapted to . . . varying historical situations" (161). The persistence of romance thus necessarily involves a set of changing problems related to the changing historico-literary environment. To study the evolution of this genre is to study the phenomenon of generic transformation itself.

The privileged status of romance in the context of genre studies has been an important feature of recent theoretical work. For all the differences between them, Frye shares Jameson's evaluation of the importance of romance as a special generic case:

> Romance is the structural core of all fiction: being directly descended from folktale, it brings us closer than any other aspect of literature to the sense of fiction, considered as a whole, as the epic of the creature, man's vision of his own life as a quest.[9]

The essays in this volume examine particular examples of the evolution of the romance genre from its inception, with Chrétien de Troyes in the late twelfth century, to its culmination with Cervantes's *Don Quijote* in the early seventeenth century. For reasons of historical coherence we have restricted our primary focus to the romance vernacular literatures of continental Europe. The ground-breaking work of literary theorists from a variety of schools has provided us with the orientations behind our specific studies: the relation between genre and history, the primacy of the individual text, the constancy of generic transformation in the history of romance.

Cesare Segre undertakes a historical typology of the medieval romance in terms of Bakhtinian genre theory. This involves, first, a twofold critique, a modification of Bakhtin's theoretical system to make it capable of handling the medieval romance on its own terms. Segre is, of course, highly aware of the value of Bakhtin's distinction between the " 'two stylistic lines in the European novel,' the first monoglot, the second heteroglot, the first abstract/idealizing, the second polyphonic in the social sense" (27).[10] The problem with regard to medieval literature is Bakhtin's anachronistic hierarchization in this context. To privilege the second line at the expense of the first means to valorize medieval "polyphony" over medieval narrative. Segre dehierarchizes the Bakhtinian model to focus on the dynamic interaction between narrative structure and polyphonic content in the development of the medieval romance.

Similarly, Bakhtin's methodological orientation involves an anachronistically exclusive focus on the linguistic manifestations (polyphony) of what both he and Segre see as the central problem of genre study: the multiple relations between writer and subject matter. Segre therefore analyzes the "author-character dialectic" (29) in the medieval romance in terms of "structural heterogeneity." The most fruitful avenues of approach (determined by the diachronic status of the "evolving" genre) prove to be discourse analysis, narrative syntax, perspectivism and point of view, the inscribed reader, and textual intercalation (involving "registral polyphony").

Segre thus establishes the necessity of a diachronic perspective for serious consideration of the problematics of literary genre in general and of the medieval romance in particular. It is the entire historico-literary context that determines at once the functional generic form itself and the most effective critical approach to this form. Segre suggests, then, that—especially in the case of the medieval romance—generic continuity means generic transformation. In this context, Segre's application of the Bakhtinian notion of the chronotope to twelfth- and thirteenth-century French and Provençal romance is of primary importance; it provides a theoretical construct that can take into account both the "deep structure" of a particular romance (*Le Bel Inconnu, Partenopeus de Blois, Perceval,* and *Flamenca* receive special attention) and the dynamic evolution of the genre itself.

In the context of Segre's "historicization" of the Bakhtinian system, Stephen G. Nichols sees "multivoicedness" as the fundamental generic trait of medieval romance as opposed to earlier "monologic" narrative genres both in Latin and in the vernacular. Nichols applies Bakhtin's theoretical binome to the literary production of twelfth-century France to analyze the genesis of romance as a new generic category. Primary attention is given to the pivotal *Roman d'Enéas* (c. 1160), one of the so-called romances of antiquity, normally regarded as a kind of hybrid genre midway between epic and the courtly romance epitomized, for example, by Chrétien de Troyes. Focusing on narrative dynamics and on the author/protagonist/reader configuration, Nichols explores how the *Enéas* simultaneously embodies and suppresses the inescapably double perspective involved in a romance treatment of the problematics of love. His point of departure is the Augustinian model: a monologic Christian narrative configuration which allows the discourse of desire (as manifested in the *Aeneid*) to be recovered by and rewritten as part of the "discourse of metanoia" used in the *Confessions*. While operative in Old French hagiography (such as the *Vie de Saint Alexis*), the Augustinian model is programmatically undermined by the new kinds of generic constraints at work in the *Roman d'Enéas,* which thus rewrites the *Aeneid* both as such and as "contained" by the *Confessions*. The *Enéas* carefully uses the Augustinian strategy but in a secular context in which discourse is no longer guaranteed by transcendence. In the case of both Enéas and Lavinia, the official (controlled) discourse of love is ironized by textual traces of a radically different discourse which valorizes desire as such. The attempt in the *Enéas* to impose "a monologic censorship on the incipient dialogism of romance" (61) has important consequences for "our understanding of the transformation of romance from at least a potentially didactic genre, in its early stages, to a pseudo- or even an antididactic genre" (52).

Douglas Kelly focuses on Chrétien de Troyes (fl. c. 1170–81) to arrive at a functional definition of romance as a generic—indeed, as a literary—category. The central questions are how romance conveys meaning and what kind of meaning it privileges. Kelly analyzes both Chrétien's textually inscribed readers and his extratextual or historical readers. At issue is the relationship between the formal and the semantic aspects of romance, between marvelous narrative itself and what such narrative celebrates, its *san*. Twelfth- and thirteenth-century critics of Chrétien's romances contrast their formal perfection and profound aesthetic appeal with a deep-structure "vanity." In all cases the "truth" of romance subject matter is in question, either in terms of historical authenticity (Jehan Bodel) or Christian moral values (the *Vies des pères* and the like). Chrétien's "nonhistorical" Arthurian romance world valorizes, even idealizes, an emergent aristocratic "tradition parallel to but still largely distinct from that of Christianity" (78). *Chevalerie* and *clergie* (clerkliness) here collaborate in the service of a refined system of courtliness in which secular love is privileged. The status of this idealized courtly system is ultimately a function of the perspective of the audience, determined to a large degree by social class. For the ecclesiastical order it is vanity. For the aristocratic order it is a self-evident "truth," reflecting the aristocracy's own beliefs and aspirations. The meaning, the *san* produced by romance, thus depends on a set of period- and audience-specific values. This for Kelly is an "idiosyncratic feature of romance which makes it a distinct class of writings" (86). Yet this very historical specificity provides Kelly with a means of characterizing romance synchronically, as a general literary category: "the endless attempt to achieve a given society's vision of order and truth, a truth which, as Chrétien's own romances make explicit, is ultimately a *misterium*—a union of mystery and significance" (87), which only the narrative discourse of romance can adequately articulate. Implicit in Kelly's formulation is the notion that romance, by definition, involves a continuing series of transformations with regard to its functional system of generic features.

This phenomenon of generic transformation as an inherent part of romance is explicitly addressed in Nancy Freeman-Regalado's study of *La Queste del Saint Graal* (c. 1225–30). The very structure of the *Queste* involves the combination and interaction of two seemingly disparate generic and discursive modes: Arthurian narrative and religious thematic commentary. A variety of interrelated transformations are operative. Freeman-Regalado begins by investigating the ways in which the *Queste* simultaneously recalls, reinforces, and undermines the constructs—"the motifs and values" (93)—of earlier chivalric romance. Programmatic shifts in narrative action (playing on the reader's generic *horizon d'attente*) result in an implicit moral and religious redefinition of the Arthurian world, which thus acquires a spiritual dimension.

Freeman-Regalado goes on to analyze the explicit elaboration of this spiritualization, distinguishing between two different interpretive procedures in the *Queste*. *Fabula* involves a mode of commentary

whose form and content differ radically from those of the primary
story line. The use of extensive allegorical exegesis to systematically
reinterpret Arthurian narrative marks a striking and unique innovation in thirteenth-century vernacular literary practice. Furthermore, unlike its Latin models, the *Queste* involves an allegorical discourse directed not at its readers but at its characters. "Allegorizing
thus feeds into the narrative structure of romance, altering its course"
(102). *Figura* involves the establishment of "analogies between juxtaposed narratives to derive thematic commentary" (98). The
Queste repeatedly remotivates Arthurian material in terms of typological Christian narratives. Galaad is simultaneously a type of Christ
and the culmination of Solomon's lineage. The romance world thus
"acquires spiritual meaning not only by being interpreted in religious terms but also by being transformed into the endpoint, the
final *signifié,* of figural typology" (103). That this process escapes
religious orthodoxy results from the fact that both *figura* and *fabula*
serve to represent a fictional world of spiritual revelation within the
context of the *Queste* as a whole. For this latter is not a doctrinal or
didactic treatise but a new kind of romance—perceived as such by
contemporary readers. The *Queste*'s "polyvalent" discourse embodies
a high spiritual seriousness which confers a "mythological dimension" on the motifs of Arthurian chivalry. And the "truth" of these
myths remains inseparable from the language and the stories that
express them (111).

When viewed in tandem with the *Queste,* Guillaume de Lorris's
nearly contemporary *Roman de la Rose* (c. 1225–30) appears as the
other extreme among the early-thirteenth-century transformations of
twelfth-century courtly-chivalric romance models. Guillaume's generic innovation is striking: the conflation of amorous lyric *matière*
and quest-narrative procedure in a first-person structure whose courtliness (both as behavioral and as verbal code) has displaced chivalry.
Jean de Meun's continuation and completion (c. 1270–75) of Guillaume's apparently unfinished romance takes this process one step
further. Indeed, Jean's *Rose* self-consciously thematizes generic transformation as such. Kevin Brownlee investigates this thematization in
terms of Jean's simultaneous articulation and *dépassement* of the
limits of romance, as embodied by Guillaume's poem.

To this end, K. Brownlee concentrates on the two strategic textual
loci where Guillaume and his *Romance* are treated explicitly in
Jean's conjoined *Rose:* Amors's speech near the midpoint and
Genius's speech near the end. Amors redefines and reduces the im-

portance of Guillaume's courtly romance world at the diegetic level: Guillaume qua lover-protagonist ceases to function as privileged internal addressee, while Guillaume qua poet-narrator is explicitly displaced (within the fiction of the poem) by Jean de Meun. Genius deals with Guillaume de Lorris's *Romance* as written object, as *écriture*. Indeed, his elaborate critique of Guillaume involves a consistent program of textual citation and deformation. This critique explicitly condemns the courtly "value system" inherent in Guillaume's *Rose,* judging it "inadequate according to a standard external to Guillaume de Lorris's poetic world" (121). In effect, the character Genius emerges as an inscribed poet-figure whose philosophico-poetic discourse in a pseudo-Chartrian mode is radically opposed to the courtly discourse of Guillaume de Lorris. At the same time, however, Genius writes Guillaume's *Romance* back into Jean's conjoined *Rose* text at a point when the earlier work seemed to have been superseded. Genius and Guillaume thus appear to embody the two *cas limites* for romance as a generic and a discursive category. It is, however, the dialectical interaction between them that produces meaning within the larger containing structure of Jean's *Rose.* For Jean's expansion of the limits of romance has resulted in a new kind of generic entity: the vernacular poetic *summa.*

In the wake of Jean de Meun's extremely influential achievement, late medieval French literature was characterized by an extraordinary series of generic experiments and innovations. In this context, Karl D. Uitti examines new departures in romance composition in fourteenth- and fifteenth-century France. His focus is one of the period's most generically problematic texts, Antoine de la Sale's *Jehan de Saintré* (1456). Acknowledging the lack of any critical consensus as to its generic status, Uitti adopts as his point of departure the one generally accepted notion that "there is something essentially true to life in [the *Saintré*] and, consequently, something not characteristically 'medieval'" (136).

Uitti's detailed analysis of the *Saintré* concentrates on its narrative structure, on its use and "disjunction" of chivalric codes, and on its key intertextual relation to Jean Froissart's "Arthurian" romance *Méliador* (c. 1365–80). As a result, the *Saintré* is shown to participate, with a profound literary self-consciousness, in the dynamic and continually evolving tradition of the medieval French romance. Indeed "Antoine de la Sale rewrites Froissart in a fashion quite analogous to that great chronicler's replication-in-transformation of the tradition issued from the *Romance of the Rose*" (137).

Uitti singles out the "celebration and practice of *restoration*" (137) (that is, the repeated deconstruction, recodification, and renewal of a profoundly coherent literary code) as a primary defining feature of romance as generic process. Thus, Uitti argues that what has been perceived as a surprising "modernity" (the *Saintré*'s ostensibly "realistic" presentation) in fact constitutes an "extraordinary fidelity to quintessentially medieval poetic procedures" (137).

This perceived realism, moreover, is shown by Uitti to be only apparent, inauthentic, if one situates the narrated events in their actual historical context. De la Sale manipulates the pseudohistorical discourse of Froissart—the romantic fictionalization of history—by effecting precisely the opposite procedure, by defictionalizing it. He offers instead an analysis and proof of the insufficiency or inoperativeness of mythic paradigms of behavior.

Seeing the *Jehan de Saintré* as a precursor of the "modern psychological novel," a kind of antecedent to the *Princesse de Clèves,* Uitti defines its generic transformation and innovation as the "remotivating and conjoining anew [of] the very ideas of writing and adventure" (150).

Edward Morris investigates the status of romance in a very different context: the prose narratives of Rabelais. In Morris's view, Rabelais simultaneously utilizes the romance tradition as an important "generic subtext" and systematically experiments with "nontraditional" sign systems to articulate the (transformed) romance constructs that are functional in his own text. Morris focuses on *Pantagruel,* particularly chapter 16 in the original 1532 edition. A variety of Rabelaisian alternatives to the standard semiotics of romance composition are considered in sequence. Each involves the use of a different set of signs and codes to deform and to parody, to re-present and to remotivate the "normative" writing of romance.

Writing in numerals, in which Rabelais indulges liberally, is one manifestation of this alternative romance composition. Writing by means of mystic Pythagorean figures (intended to elucidate the inadequacy of mere words) is another instance. A further type of alternative writing is "invisible writing," which is so subtle as to be decipherable by only the most discerning of readers. Finally, there is the kind of writing, demonstrated by the anonymous poetess, which dispenses entirely with vowels.

At the root of these alternative modes of expression for Rabelais is an illustration of the limitations of old forms (and the manifold possibilities of new forms) of romance composition. Morris traces these boundaries in terms of the spatial limits of the text, its graphic space. In addition to studying *Pantagruel* as "a written place," he details the literary innovations of numerous characters who are themselves authors of one kind or another: Gargantua, Panurge, the anonymous poetess, and Pantagruel himself.

The point of Rabelais's programmatic literary experiment is to adapt romance to new (Renaissance) contexts, given the outmoded nature of old (medieval) contexts. Morris sums up the inherently problematic nature of this enterprise by asking if, for sixteenth-century French literature, there is "perhaps no such thing as written romance, only unwritten romance or invisibly written romance" (175).

In an important sense, literary history confirms Rabelais's perception of the fragility of romance qua functional generic system in the context of the French Renaissance. Indeed, as Segre puts it, "there is a hiatus in the development of the French romance . . . from the middle of the fifteenth to the middle of the sixteenth century" (38). While an overall generic continuity most certainly prevails, there is a geographico-literary shift. The extraordinary vitality characteristic of vernacular romance from its inception is, during the Renaissance, most strikingly evident in Italy and in Spain. Indeed, the Italian Renaissance romance was a dominant literary form whose relation to its social context was particularly dynamic. On the one hand, it was immensely popular. On the other hand, it was relentlessly being scrutinized and analyzed to determine the source of its remarkable popularity as well as its effects on society.

Of central importance in the analysis of reader response to romance in the Italian Renaissance is the neo-Aristotelian controversy which dominated European literary academies during the second half of the sixteenth century. Because of the unprecedented success of Ariosto's *Orlando Furioso* (1516–32) and because of the rediscovery and translation into Italian of Aristotle's *Poetics* (1549), the romance genre was criticized, both per se and in terms of epic, on moral and on aesthetic grounds. The advocates of romance, chief among them Torquato Tasso, saw it as being potentially as legitimate a genre as epic. Those who deemed romance to be unsatisfactory, on the other hand, called for a wholesale rejection of the genre and a return to the writing of Virgilian epic.

Addressing this romance/epic controversy, David Quint examines the generic transformation effected by Tasso in the *Gerusalemme liberata* (1575) vis-à-vis his chivalric romance *Rinaldo* (1562) as well as Boiardo's *Orlando innamorato* (pub. 1495). While romance had traditionally valorized adventure for its own sake and epic had offered a teleological, providential system, Tasso effected a radical change in the generic intent of both romance and epic by treating voyages of discovery as events which raised the adventures of romance to the level of the epic quest.

Milton, Quint argues, reverses this process, deflating Satan from the status of epic voyager to that of chance romance adventurer.

Quint situates these generic changes in a socioeconomic context, juxtaposing epic as the aristocratic genre par excellence to romance, which he identifies as the genre of the bourgeoisie, concerned primarily with commercial trading ventures. Camões's *Os Lusíadas* (1572) exemplifies the bourgeois concern for the economically motivated voyage of discovery. Milton, highly critical of such superficially veiled lucrative aspirations in the *Lusíadas,* recasts Vasco da Gama's voyage as Satan's voyage, undermining the latter's epic dimension and reducing him to a romance adventurer cum commercial traveler in book 2 of *Paradise Lost* (1667).

"The failure of aristocratic ideology and literary forms to describe a reality that was increasingly pervaded by early capitalism" is at the root of the great popularity which the romance genre enjoyed during the Renaissance, in Quint's view. "As a bourgeois reading public began to command the literary marketplace, epic was doomed and romance had to adapt quickly to survive. A late flowering of courtly and pastoral prose romances proved to be a dead end. The future for romance, as epic had already intimated, lay with the new world of money and materiality—and with the novel" (196).

While Quint explores the rise of romance in Italy and Portugal, Harry Sieber explores its decline, the nature of the reading public, and shifts in reader demand in Spain.

In defining "the reader," Sieber cautions against the frequent temptation to ascribe generic changes to "a few isolated though well-publicized, major happenings" (213), as is so often the case in "official" literary history.

The literary corpus which forms the focus of Sieber's study is the chivalric romance in Spain in the sixteenth century and the very dramatic generic shift which occurred with the introduction of the picaresque. The unprecedented and insatiable desire for romances which characterized the first half of the century faded very markedly during the second half. Numerous critics have sought to account for this sudden change in taste on the part of Spain's literary public. Was this phenomenon the result of Charles V's abdication in 1555 or the defeat of the Armada in 1588? Moreover, what new need did picaresque fulfill that romance no longer did?

Sieber attributes the waning interest in romance to a complex series of circumstances, among them demographic expansion and accelerating urbanization, a shift in migration patterns within Spain, and the lack of any new Hispanic frontier to be conquered after the 1550s.

Despite Philip II's European campaigns, the exemplary heroic confrontations celebrated in romance could not maintain their "literary credibility." It was instead the picaresque, initiated in 1554 with *Lazarillo de Tormes,* which replaced romance as the dominant narrative genre in Spain.

Sieber establishes a direct link between the rejection of romance and the acceptance of the picaresque in the social climate of the times. Namely, the picaresque novel signals a shift in narrative authority from the distant anonymous authorship of romance biographical narrative to the immediacy of a new type of named autobiographical author figure. This generic innovation implied a temporal and spatial transformation as well. No longer situated in a temporally and spatially remote Middle Ages, the picaresque dealt with the contemporary urban centers of Seville, Toledo, and Madrid, replete with "recognizable geographical landmarks and street names" (216).

This "fiction of immediacy," as Sieber terms it, was accommodated by Cervantes into the world of chivalric romance in the figure of Don Quijote. "Cervantes's choice of an old man to fill the role of knight-errant, however ridiculous it seemed at the time, is strangely emblematic of the end of the genre's career" (217).

While, as Sieber and Quint both affirm, the *Quijote* signaled the end of the romance genre, it relied heavily on the controversial text which initiated the romance polemic of the Renaissance neo-Aristotelians, Ariosto's *Orlando Furioso.* Cervantes's programmatic remotivation of the *Furioso* is the subject of Marina Scordilis Brownlee's essay.

The lengthy dispute which grew out of the rediscovery of Aristotle's *Poetics* in Renaissance Italy and Spain resulted in two polemical factions among literary theorists, the so-called Ancients, who denigrated romance, and the Moderns, who saw it as a legitimate genre worthy of the same serious consideration as the classical, "canonical" genres.

Cervantes, in the *Quijote,* addresses himself to this academic

debate in the encounter between the Canon of Toledo and Don
Quijote near the end of part 1. The Canon is a proponent of the
Moderns, which has contributed to the assumption that Cervantes
himself was a staunch advocate of neo-Aristotelian theory and practice. There is, however, a consistently skeptical countercurrent to this
attitude concerning neo-Aristotelian doctrine, expressed in generic,
structural, and characterological parallels shared by the *Quijote* and
the *Furioso,* which M. S. Brownlee considers. Paradoxically, we see
Cervantes simultaneously criticizing the neo-Aristotelian controversy
and dealing the death blow to chivalric romance by valorizing the
Furioso per se, thereby affirming the primacy of artistic freedom
(235).

Of all the dimensions of human experience explored by the romance genre, eros is by far the most essential. Its articulation, proliferation, and prolongation, however, find expression in a very wide
range of possibilities. Ruth El Saffar's essay focuses on the all-
important function of eros in the context of generic transformation:
"from pastoral romance to parody of romance to quest romance"
(250) in the development of Cervantes's career as a writer. The
movement from romance to novel and back to romance, from *La
Galatea* (1585) to the *Quijote* (1605, 1615) to the *Persiles* (pub.
1617), constitutes one of the enduring enigmas of Cervantine criticism. How are we to interpret Cervantes's return to the so-called
naive and idealizing form of romance in the *Persiles* after the elaborate devaluation of romance which is at issue in the *Quijote?*

In his perpetual attempt to reconcile fantasy and reality, Cervantes
embraces and thereafter rejects escapist fantasy, the kind of writing
which provides an environment of wish fulfillment totally unrelated
to the everyday world of empirical reality. This kind of romance has
as its prime concern eros in all of its possible manifestations. Part 1
of the *Quijote,* as El Saffar shows, is an illustration of the irreconcila-
bility of escapist romance and empirical reality. Part 2, therefore, like
the remaining works of Cervantes, attempts to bridge this existential
gap by moving toward an exploration of quest romance.

In quest romance, eros is subservient to the bonds of marriage,
leading the privileged protagonist into and out of the dream world
of pure fantasy. This dual perspective on romance which Cervantes
offers is both emblematized and concretized by the Cervantine image
of the androgyne.

Eros similarly serves as the focus of Louise Horowitz's investigation of the key problem of identity in Honoré d'Urfé's great prose

romance *L'Astrée* (pub. 1607–27). Taking the device of disguise as a constant feature of romance composition (particularly during the Renaissance), this essay reveals d'Urfé's original remotivation of it.

The characters who populate *L'Astrée,* in fact, represent a multiple series of transformations: "Once knights, then shepherds, now transvestites—so goes the movement of the principal episodes in *L'Astrée"* (254).

At the root of the work's numerous tales exists a constant tension between the theoretical systems and the practical realities of love. The traditional values of "honnête amitié" are juxtaposed with scenes of pure eroticism designed to subvert these values. What is at issue in these myriad tales of eroticism generated by disguised identities (men dressed as women, women as men—with the inevitable resulting confusions, attractions, and ambiguities) is, moreover, a mark of d'Urfé's originality. For unlike the traditional expression of eros as gender-specific, *L'Astrée* establishes a gender-free, androgynous system which refuses to relate sexuality to gender.

In his afterword, Ralph Cohen addresses the problematics of genre theory as such, stressing its necessarily ambiguous nature: "A theory of genre . . . attempts to characterize the processes of continuity and discontinuity, and its language is inevitably ambiguous" (269). Part of the reason for the ambiguity of definition which Cohen identifies is "the confusion of mode with genre . . . a confusion that conflates the abstract with the empirical" (270). To illustrate his point, he turns to an example from eighteenth-century English literature, the case of *Joseph Andrews,* which Fielding himself refers to as " 'a comic epic in prose,' " a hybrid "combination of structures from several different genres" (271).

The paramount importance of the genre/mode dichotomy is further illustrated by Cohen in "The Ballad of George Barnwell," which underwent a series of multiple transformations: from poem to short prose to drama to novel.

Taking as his point of departure Maria Corti's description of the two normative categories of genre theory, " 'those of an abstract, atemporal, deductive nature and those of a historic, diachronic, inductive nature' " (266), Cohen calls for a form of genre theory and criticism based on two inseparable criteria. The first is a question of periodization; namely, much of contemporary genre theory simply grafts on all literary epochs the concerns peculiar only to current author/text/reader relations. This type of anachronistic reading leads to serious hermeneutic distortions. Thus, Cohen's second criterion, a logical and necessary corollary of the first, is that any contemporary genre theory must account for a given text as part of a literary corpus which constitutes a synchronic as well as a diachronic system of meaning.

Notes

[1] Northrop Frye, *Anatomy of Criticism* (Princeton: Princeton UP, 1957). For an important analysis of the state of both Anglo-American and European genre theory before Frye, see René Wellek and Austin Warren, *Theory of Literature* (New York: Harcourt, 1942), esp. ch. 17, "Literary Genres" 226–37.

[2] E. D. Hirsch, Jr., *Validity in Interpretation* (New Haven: Yale UP, 1967).

[3] Tzvetan Todorov, "The Origin of Genres," *New Literary History* 8 (1976): 159–70. See also Tzvetan Todorov, *Les Genres du discours* (Paris: Sueil, 1978), ch. 3 of which is a reworking of the earlier article.

[4] For the notion of the generic "horizon of expectations," see Hans Robert Jauss, "Theory of Genres and Mediaeval Literature," *Toward an Aesthetic of Reception,* ed. Hans Robert Jauss (Minneapolis: U of Minnesota P, 1982), 76–109, translated from *Grundriss der Romanischen Literaturen des Mittelalters,* vol. 6 (Heidelberg: Winter, 1972).

[5] Gérard Genette, *Introduction à l'architexte* (Paris: Seuil, 1979). See also Gérard Genette, "Genres, 'types,' modes," *Poétique* 32 (1977): 389–421.

[6] Maria Corti, *An Introduction to Literary Semiotics* (Bloomington: Indiana UP, 1978), a translation of *Principi della communicazione letteraria,* 1976.

[7] Mikhail Bakhtin, *The Dialogic Imagination: Four Essays,* trans. Caryl Emerson and Michael Holquist, ed. Michael Holquist (Austin: U of Texas P, 1981). See also Tzvetan Todorov, *Mikhaïl Bakhtine: Le principe dialogique* (Paris: Seuil, 1981).

[8] Fredric Jameson, "Magical Narratives: Romance as Genre," *New Literary History* 7 (1975): 135–63. See Fredric Jameson, *The Political Unconscious: Narrative as a Socially Symbolic Act* (Ithaca, N.Y.: Cornell UP, 1981), esp. ch. 2, "Magical Narratives: On the Dialectical Use of Genre Criticism" 103–50.

[9] Northrop Frye, *The Secular Scripture: A Study of the Structure of Romance* (Cambridge: Harvard UP, 1976) 15.

[10] Subsequent references in the Introduction are to page numbers in this book.

WHAT BAKHTIN LEFT UNSAID
The Case of the Medieval Romance

Cesare Segre

I

Mikhail Bakhtin's contribution to the theory of the novel is of fundamental importance. His field of inquiry, of course, involves both theory and history. If at times, following Blanckenburg and Hegel, he defines the nature of the novel with respect to the epic, elsewhere he retraces its prehistory and history from Greek times to the advent of the *roman bourgeois.*

In this historical tableau there is nonetheless a vast hiatus corresponding precisely to the medieval romance, which is our concern here. A rather cursory survey of the medieval romance can be found in Bakhtin's "Forms of Time" (sec. 5): one passes in six or seven pages from *Tristan* to Wolfram von Eschenbach's *Parzival* and the *Divine Comedy,* from the *Roman de la Rose* to *Piers the Plowman.* There are also, here and there, some perfunctory allusions to the *dit d'avantures* (Bakhtin, "Epic and Novel" 1), *Aucassin et Nicolette,* the *Mule sans bride,* and the *Roland comique* (Bakhtin, *Rabelais* 15). These latter seem to indicate an inattentive or perhaps incomplete study of the subject. Indeed, Bakhtin, influenced more by German than by French culture, is more precise and comprehensive when he speaks of Wolfram's *Parzival.* In any case, scarcity of information is not the basic reason for Bakhtin's limited treatment of medieval romance.

It is, rather, that for Bahktin, theory and history exist on two different levels: although noteworthy and suggestive, his historical inquiries are always subordinated to theory, which in turn is subordinated to criticism. His admirable studies of Dostoievsky (*Problems*) and Rabelais (*Rabelais*) in fact constitute the culmination of his work. This is confirmed by the chronology of Bakhtin's corpus: the important volume on Dostoievsky appears before the writing of the historical essays, which do not seem to have been conceived of as anything but props.[1]

II

We must first identify Bakhtin's notion of the novel's defining features. The following is an early statement:

> I find three basic characteristics that fundamentally distinguish the novel in principle from other genres: (1) its stylistic three-dimensionality, which is linked with the multi-languaged consciousness realized in the novel; (2) the radical change it effects in the temporal coordinates of the literary image; (3) the new zone opened by the novel for structuring literary images, namely, the zone of maximal contact with the present (with contemporary reality) in all its openendedness. ("Epic and Novel" 11)

We recognize the theme of several of Bakhtin's fundamental writings, but we are hard put to find here the most significant traits of the medieval French and Provençal romance. Moreover, Bakhtin's characterization, like all definitions of genres, can be charged with a lack of historicity.

We find a more plastic, more malleable character in other assertions. Bakhtin says, for example, that "the novel comes into contact with the spontaneity of the inconclusive present; this is what keeps the genre from congealing" ("Epic and Novel" 27). But it would be easy to demonstrate that Bakhtin is thinking not of the novel's past but of its future; he is thinking not of its codification but of its transformations. Bakhtin has in fact constructed his idea of the novel on the basis of a literary evolution beginning with Rabelais and leading to Dostoievsky, and his work on earlier periods constitutes a series of excursuses on the novel's prehistory, the goal of which is to identify the first appearances of the tendencies, processes, and procedures which, after having been exploited to excess by Rabelais, were not to coalesce into an organic whole until Cervantes.

III

The date of the birth of the modern novel has been determined with variations of as much as centuries. The most recent dating, by Hegel, would coincide with the eighteenth-century English novel or more precisely, as Curtius feels, with Fielding's *Tom Jones*. Other critics go back to *Don Quijote* (Heine) or to the *Amadís de Gaula* (Menéndez Pelayo); still others identify the point of departure as even earlier, with the *Jehan de Saintré* (Kristeva), Boccaccio's *Fiammetta* (actually a model for the Spanish sentimental romance), or Dante's *Vita Nuova*. And we must add those who go back to the Arthurian prose romances. The *romanistes,* on the other hand, find it quite legitimate to consider as the first representatives of the genre the Old French *romans d'antiquité* and above all the romances of Chrétien de Troyes. Are they not already defined as *romans* by their authors and their contemporaries?

But if one chooses to rely on the term *roman,* other problems arise. The term at first indicated translations from the Latin, or narrative texts in general, given the preference of translators for narrative. It is difficult to include the *Roman de Renart* and the *Roman de la Rose* in the history of the novel, and it is still more difficult in the case of such texts as the *Roman des Ailes* or the translations of the *Disticha Catonis*. One might even go so far as to agree with historians of the term, such as Voelker, that the meaning of the word *roman* has been progressively restricted and that the term can be meaningfully applied only to the type of text for which it was invented at the end of the twelfth century.[2]

The French term *roman* of course designates a more heterogeneous group than the works that English distinguishes by the terms "novel" and "romance," at the same time expanding the definition with the terms "fiction" and "narrative." But the distinction between "romance" and "novel" is rather unstable, especially with respect to the French *romans* of the twelfth and thirteenth centuries. Their atmosphere is "contemporary," and they are not fantastical; the terminological boundary would be overstepped in both directions. We go back from *Don Quijote* to the twelfth-century French *roman* by way of a series of oppositions which are at the same time signs of continuity.[3] Literary history, as Shklovsky said, is the history of the successive murders of fathers, or attempts at reinstating uncles.

IV

Bakhtin identifies, in complete consistency with his theory, two currents in the ancient world. The first is that of Socratic dialogue, Menippean satire, and Lucianic dialogue; the second is that of the so-called Greek romance or Byzantine novel.[4] It is traditionally in this latter current, whose narrative substance is not historical but novelistic, that we recognize a preliminary version of what was to become the modern novel. Bakhtin, on the contrary, asserts that "the authentic spirit of the novel" should be sought in the first current, whose texts "anticipate the more essential historical aspects in the development of the novel in modern times" ("Epic and Novel" 22).

Bakhtin sees a somewhat similar situation in the vernacular literature of the Middle Ages. On the one hand, there is a great wealth of heteroglot experimentation, of stylizations and parodies in texts which are not (or are only in part) narrative texts, particularly in those which Bakhtin defines as "carnivalized." On the other hand, there are the narrative texts, in which one does not find this type of experimentation except by allusion. Bakhtin thus could not do other than to reaffirm the fundamental importance of the first type of phenomena (heteroglot and parodic texts) while merely pointing out early experiments in perspectivism in the "chivalric romance," particularly in Wolfram's *Parzival* ("Discourse" 377).

It is probably futile to debate the preeminence given to one element rather than the other, to polyphony rather than narrative. But it is not unfruitful to consider that the experimental and heteroglot texts constitute, outside the novel's development but also within it, a discontinuous, frequently interrupted series, while the narrative genre that has been called *roman* since the twelfth century develops, by means of its very transformations, uninterruptedly and coherently to the present day.

Bakhtin, in separating the history of polyphonic procedures from that of narrative invention, brings together in the category of polyphony phenomena with very different originls and functions. The polyphony identified by Bakhtin carries out two different programs: (1) separating the author's voice from those of the characters, distinguishing them by means of a proliferation of styles, and (2) representing the linguistic stratification of the society being described by emphasizing the registers, connotations, and allusions already established by collective usage, in particular by professional jargon, class variants, and so on. It is clear that the two programs manage to coincide when the characters oppose and conflict with their social milieu. However, there are writers who do not represent this conflict, especially in the Middle Ages.

In addition, polyphony serves to represent two different authorial attitudes vis-à-vis characters: (1) a participatory representation which can go so far as to become a temporary identification, and (2) a detached representation, at times also polemical, when the author portrays characters whose opinion he does not share; understanding it, he nonetheless condemns it. Because of the latter attitude, stylization and parody, with their attendant variations, are of great importance in Bakhtin's work. But this implicit polemic, which is generally linked to the social structure, is far from being exploited by all writers.

I have indicated by two parallel bifurcations the two programs which can be carried out under the rubric of polyphony and the two extreme attitudes which the writer can adopt vis-à-vis characters. These bifurcations reproduce the fundamental dichotomy which governs the history of the novel according to Bakhtin's model. For it is not only in the context of the ancient world that he perceives "two stylistic lines in the European novel," the first monoglot, the second heteroglot, the first abstract/idealizing, the second polyphonic in the social sense as well. He describes suggestively the two antithetical tendencies with a spatial metaphor: "Novels of the First Stylistic Line approach heteroglossia from above, it is as if they *descend* onto it. . . . Novels of the Second Line, on the contrary, approach heteroglossia from below: out of the heteroglot depths they rise to the highest spheres of literary language and overwhelm them" ("Discourse" 400). This dynamic way of linking the two lines offers historiographic possibilities as well—indeed, the identification and elaboration of these possibilities constitute an important part of this essay. Bakhtin, on the other hand, often gave his preference a legitimizing status and pronounced a negative judgment on the competing line.

As a rule, the medieval romance privileges the first solution in this dichotomy and in the others previously mentioned: that which is, so to speak, unmarked.[5] This is not only because of the limited dynamism of medieval society (experienced by its members as unshakably hierarchized even in its times of crisis) but also because of a different overall organization of genres and styles. While sermons, even in the vernacular, addressed the full range of classes and professions (I refer especially to the *états du monde*), there were specific literary genres (*fabliaux* or theater, privileged by its performative mode) which could evoke the lives and characters of the people, the bourgeoisie and the lower clergy. The courtly romance, "a self-portrayal of feudal knighthood with its mores and ideals" (Auerbach, ch. 6), considers the other social classes marginal and unimportant. Linguistic and social tension as well as the parodic tendency, no longer limited to "carnivalized" works, are to become evident and even decisive at the exact moment when the romance widens its field of interest to a larger social milieu and opens itself up to the disinherited, the pariahs, and, above all, that bourgeois class which is soon to be the herald of innovation.[6]

Heteroglot and parodic experimentation, very common in the Middle Ages, thus had little to do with the romance in its early stages;[7] we encounter it chiefly in the theater and in the *Roman de Renart*[8] as well as in Latin or bilingual Goliardic texts. This is not to say that the romance employs a crystallized literary language; on the contrary. As we shall see, it was above all the expansion of romance discourse to encompass the most widely varied social sectors that led, with no internal tension, to its appropriation of new areas of existence capable of interesting or showing themselves useful to courtly society.

V

What stands out in the courtly romance is a clear, conscious reduction of the radius of the sociosphere (as Lotman would say). The characters all stand in some relation to the courtly milieu, though sometimes a negative relation; those who appear only intermittently and indecisively are the representatives of other milieux.[9] If the mixing of styles and registers corresponds to social variegation, as Bakhtin thinks, we can understand why the medieval romance excluded it.[10]

The elements identified by Bakhtin can, then, be regrouped in a different way: on the one hand is the history of the narrative structure which we call the *roman;* on the other hand is the development of a perspectival perception of reality whose decisive establishment Bakhtin rightly locates in the Renaissance. If this narrative structure came into existence before perspectival techniques were grafted onto it, one cannot do otherwise than take this development into account and attempt a history of it.

This being said, even though the medieval romance does not involve true polyphony, it is nonetheless possible to discover in it what is, for Bakhtin, the primary precondition for polyphony: the author's ability to identify himself with or detach himself from the characters, to espouse their point of view or impose his own on them. In sum, it is a question of being able to see, behind the perspective of the various voices, the perspective of the overall vision. In this way Bakhtin's remarkable insights concerning the novel can be fruitfully exploited in the context of the medieval romance.

The author-character dialectic is probably what determines the narrative form of fiction, where obviously fictitious events become convincing because of their presentation by the author as he varies distances, modes (direct or indirect discourse, narration), and points of view (never a static perspective on the characters' movements). We must refine our perception so as to be aware of perspectivism in action,[11] even where linguistic and registral multiplicity is rare. In addition, we must note the possible emergence, through the course of history, of procedures which, harmonizing with perspectival effects, assist in their realization.

In this context, the medieval romance tried out for the first time procedures which were only to be perfected later, over the course of time. The most famous and widely studied of these, the monologue, was originally developed to portray the situation of one seized by love. The character concretizes the contradictory impulses of his soul in a spoken debate which simulates his duality.[12] We are already very near what will come to be called "point of view." And even if we cannot yet use this expression with the precise meaning it has acquired since Henry James and Wayne Booth, we can already see the characters as *Perspektiventräger,* to echo Nolting-Hauff.[13]

The signs of the distancing of author from character are even more interesting. I mention only in passing the extremely subtle use of the verbs *cuidier, penser,* and *veoir* whenever the imaginary, or at any rate mental, nature of the characters' perceptions is to be emphasized.[14] But our writers often play objective and subjective narrative against one another with great success,[15] sometimes using dreams and reveries (well before Freud),[16] at other times exploiting the device of two different characters perceiving the same event.[17] They often make skillful use of the true/false opposition,[18] as Ménard and Uitti have noted in *Cligés,* for example.[19] At other times they succeed in polarizing the discourse of the characters in such a way as to produce a simultaneous antidiscourse,[20] ironically stylized and addressed more to the reader than to the interlocutor, as in theatrical asides.[21]

The full import of certain key syntactic constructions (whose pres-

ence in the Old French literary corpus was first noted by Tobler and
by Lerch) has recently been revealed by discourse analysis. I refer to
studies such as those of Meiller, Stempel, and Lebensanft ("Adverbes," "Perspektivische") on the transitions from a direct to an indirect style and on direct discourse introduced by *que*. The interest
of these transitions lies in the imposition on the writer of the character's temporal or spatial perspectives, and even of the character's
affectivity (exclamations): the author takes the deixis and the psychological reactions on himself. One could speak of a "liberated" indirect style, as does Meiller, or of a "subjectivized" one, as does Stempel. There is thus evidence that the first *romanciers* were already
aware of narrative procedures later implemented with more sophis-
tication by modern novelists, as Rychner lucidly points out in his
study of *Lanval* and the *Chatelaine de Vergi,* where he shows the
way in which Marie de France foresaw the problems of free indirect
discourse and resolved them in a highly original manner.

VI

It is true that heteroglossia is quite rare in the courtly romance, although the romance effected a sort of generic phagocytosis, assimilating various traditional literary languages originally quite foreign
to it. This tendency was perceived by Bakhtin: "To realize its task of
stylistically organizing everyday language, it was of course necessary
for the chivalric romance in prose to incorporate into its own structure a multitude of diverse genres from everyday life, as well as
extra-literary ideological genres" ("Discourse" 385). However, he
immediately avers the "social disorientation and ideological rootless-
ness" of these romances without identifying them very precisely
("Discourse" 385). In fact, the insertion into verse or prose romances
of heterogeneous texts—letters or inscriptions, poems or lays—which
had often enjoyed an anterior independent circulation achieved several results at once, including heteroglot results.[22]

The intercalated texts, to begin with, increase the potential for ex-
pressiveness: they bring in echoes of new registers while preserving
the connection between registers and genres. Furthermore, the intercalated texts express particular affective states by means of a genre-
register-theme connection, whether a lovers' greeting integrated into
Flamenca[23] or lyric poems which the characters in *Guillaume de
Dole* find so relevant to their own situations that they sing them at
particular moments in the story.[24]

The intercalation of texts, in short, epitomizes the programmatic

intertextuality which is at the heart of the creative activity of medieval poets. Thus in *Flamenca,* the literary works (particularly the
romances) whose presence is consistently foregrounded over the
course of the narrative indicate the social as well as the cultural
milieux in which the story unfolds. Works of fiction cited in other
works of fiction create a realistic effect, but it is a reality allied to an
underlying fictionality—a kind of *trompe l'oeil,* not to say a *mise en
abîme* of literarity.

VII

The author-character dialectic, at least from the Middle Ages onward, determines the narrative forms of fiction. Bakhtin speaks of
the "appearance of the authorial image on the field of representation" ("Epic and Novel" 28). It is a matter of accentuating the probable while presenting the untrue, or of emphasizing the indexicality
of a subject matter which is false at the denotative level.[25] Fictional
narratives whose imaginary nature is often emphasized acquire the
aspect of truth by a subtle manipulation of distance and time, by a
variation of modes, by a shifting of point of view. There is never any
question of the chronicler's "objective" reporting, never any im-
passibility or immutability of perception on the narrator's part. As
Lukács has very cogently remarked: "The composition of the novel
is the paradoxical fusion of heterogeneous and discrete components
into an organic whole which is then abolished over and over again"
(84).

The relationships of author-text, author-message, and author-
reader are all part of this narrative organization. Examples of the
author-text relationship are such romances as *Le Bel Inconnu* or
Partenopeus de Blois, where the author declares himself ready to continue his work, or unhesitatingly embellishes it with new episodes,
as soon as his lady asks it of him (a similar phenomenon can be found
in *Jaufré,* vv. 2565–640). One could almost call this a forerunner, although in a wholly different modality, of the serial novel, with the
fictionality of the story very explicitly in the foreground.

The other two types of relationship are exemplified by the author/
sender in *Partenopeus, Le Bel Inconnu,* and *Joufroi de Poitiers.* The
principal narrative is interrupted several times by confidential asides
from the author to the reader, who is kept informed about the former's love affairs, his reflections and hopes, and the parallels between
what happens to him and what happens to his characters.[26] But it is
by no means rare, especially in Chrétien's works, for the author to

impart information concerning his handling of the narrative or to express reservations by means of "authorial internal monologues."[27] He may even appeal to the reader's experience for an accurate evaluation of the circumstances and invite the reader to counsel characters in difficulty. The author may, on the other hand, set limits to his own knowledge and emphasize the gaps in it.

It is clear that Bakhtin could not have taken the medieval romance into account, even if he had been better acquainted with it, for he concentrated his attention on the linguistic manifestations (polyphony) of phenomena which are primarily related to the manner in which an author works with his subject matter. This attitude seems all the more strange given that Bakhtin's *Dostoievsky* sets out precisely to reveal the polyphony underlying an otherwise uniform language (like Dostoievsky's), which is far removed from Tolstoi's heteroglossia.

VIII

I think I have sufficiently demonstated why it is important not to set in opposition the two parallel lines of the novel's development which Bakhtin formulated. Rather, we need to define *fabula* not only by an abstract statement of its content but also by its modes of communication and by its relationships with the communicative context. We can take as a starting point one of Bakhtin's own statements: "The novel . . . is determined by experience, knowledge and practice (the future)" ("Epic and Novel" 15). Even in the case of novels situated in the past, attention to what Bakhtin calls "the present, contemporary life as such, 'I myself' and 'my contemporaries,' 'my time'" remains essential ("Epic and Novel" 21).

It is informative to consider now a twentieth-century thinker of equal brilliance and equal indifference to the Middle Ages: György Lukács. Evincing striking analogies with Bakhtin, Lukács writes: "The inner form of the novel has been understood as the process of the problematic individual's journeying towards himself, the road from dull captivity within a merely present reality—a reality that is heterogeneous in itself and meaningless to the individual—towards clear self-recognition" (*Theory* 80). Lukács also emphasizes that the novel "seeks, by giving form, to uncover and construct the concealed totality of life" (*Theory* 60). Later he is more specific:

> If one is to represent the actual relationship of man with society and nature (that is, not only man's consciousness of these relationships, but

the being-in-itself which is at the heart of this consciousness), the only possible course is the representation of action. For only when he acts does man, through his social being, manage to express his true essence, the authentic form and content of his consciousness. ("Problemy" in *Ecrits* 144)

But what is the goal of this action? Bakhtin tells us: "The idea of testing the hero, of testing his discourse, may very well be the most fundamental organizing idea in the novel, one that radically distinguishes it from the epic" ("Discourse" 388).

The verifiable validity of the statements I have just quoted, even for the Middle Ages, only confirms a continuity in the novel's development which is exactly what Lukács and Bakhtin have called into question. It even allows us to characterize the novel vis-à-vis other genres once we have identified its own communicative characteristics. The novel's diegetic nature differentiates it from dramatic, mimetic forms and from lyric poetry, which can dispense with action and whose sole character is the "I." The reciprocal link between character and action (the former accomplishes the action, but the action in turn reacts upon him) establishes the split between the novel and other genres, where the characters, as well as the actions, are preexisting givens, linked, to be sure, but without an action-reaction relationship.

It is, moreover, the impingement of the character on the external world (society and nature) which necessitates the perspectival and polyphonic procedures of which we have spoken, for the writer cannot describe this impingement with detachment. No more for him than for his characters are society and nature givens. Rather, they are realities which can be penetrated by means of knowledge, with ups and downs and repeated attempts.[28] In identifying himself with and distancing himself from his characters through different points of view, the author not only participates in his heroes' quest, he goes on the same quest himself, along the paths of fabulation. As a contemporary writer has said: "In its self-awareness, fictional creation will reveal itself even as it reveals, will bring itself to produce its own reasons, will develop within itself those elements which can demonstrate how it is related to the rest of the real and in what ways it can be illuminating for it" (Butor 271; trans. Marianne Hirsch).

The dialectical relationships between author, subject matter, and characters in the novel are clearly defined by Bakhtin:

> The novelist is drawn toward everything that is not yet completed. He may turn up on the field of representation in any authorial pose, he

may depict real moments in his own life or make allusions to them, he may interfere in the conversations of his heroes, he may openly polemicize with his literary enemies and so forth. This is not merely a matter of the author's image appearing within his own field of representation—important here is the fact that the underlying, original formal author (the author of the authorial image) appears in a new relationship with the represented world." ("Epic and Novel" 27)

As we have already seen, Lukács understands better than Bakhtin that the best way to come into contact with reality, at least in the novel, is to confront it through action. On the other hand, Bakhtin has a deeper understanding of how the contact with reality that is openly carried out by the character is a part of the complex contact with reality effected by the writer through novelistic writing. It is also evident that Bakhtin, unlike Lukács, does not put character and reality in opposition; rather, he considers the reciprocal modifications produced by the one on the other in the context of a continual, limitless awareness—that of the author.

On this basis, it becomes easier to outline the history of the medieval romance, thus bypassing many questions of definition and of periodization. We must first realize that the twelfth and thirteenth centuries are a period of extraordinary eidogenetic activity. The romance acquires its individuality after having overlapped with narrative forms very close to it such as the *lais* (from those of Marie de France to Jean Renart)[29] and even the *fabliaux,* elements of which we see, for example, in *Flamenca* and *Joufroi.*[30] The romance, having once established itself as an autonomous genre, reveals a clear hegemonic tendency since it aspires to somehow encompass other genres, becoming, rather than a "guide" genre, a "total" genre. The late *chanson de geste* has a particularly marked tendency to converge with the romance, assimilating its development of amorous phenomenology and its receptiveness to the comic.[31] But the *chanson de geste*'s metric features and performative context continue to differentiate two genres[32] which will not completely fuse (except in the *cantari* and the Italian poems in octaves) until the *Orlando Furioso.*

In this perspective, the rather rapid establishment of the romance can be considered as the collective aspect of the experience of reality described by the romance itself; in less than a century, the authors of romances make a very thorough inventory of representable reality, from the *roman d'aventure* to the *roman courtisan,* from the *roman intimiste* to the *roman burlesque* or *comique,* from the *roman exotique* to the *roman picaresque* (including *Wistasse le Moine*). Those who have confined their discussion of the medieval romance solely to Chrétien, probably its greatest master, have given a restricted and unilateral image of it.

Following the rapid progress of this collective experience, we can tear down the signs posted here and there by various critics: "Here begins the authentic romance."[33] We can then confidently turn to historically proven facts,[34] passing from the *romans d'antiquité* (including the *Roman d'Alexandre*) and Wace to the romances of Tristan, those of Chrétien, and so forth. The fact that the *romans d'antiquité* are chiefly derived from Latin epic poems (to the degree that Virgil and Statius preserved the Homeric epic model) constitutes a real intermingling of the two genres of epic and romance, which have so often been forced into an abstract and anachronistic opposition because they first belonged to two widely separated, noncomparable literary systems.

One important aspect of the collective experience that the romances embody is an awareness of the reality of their own epoch, expressed with increasing boldness even in those medieval romances with seemingly remote Arthurian or Byzantine settings.[35] It is through descriptions of clothing and banquets, armor and accoutrements, and even, at times, handicrafts that medieval literature takes possession of the world and assimilates its specialized languages.[36] An early phase, encyclopedic so to speak, is constituted by the *romans classiques,* where the rudiments of the natural sciences are ingenuously expounded in a didactic form.[37]

Collective experience, it has been said, is only an extension of individual experience—that of the characters themselves.[38] This experience unfolds in relation to a reality which, in the beginning only, is limited to the Arthurian court: a qualifying ordeal initiates the hero into chivalric society, where his definitive integration is effected by a series of progressive ordeals (which can be read collectively as a single extended ordeal), functioning to purge him of his defects and faults.[39] The fact that the exalted personal identity thus achieved often coincides with a position in the feudal world is, of course, heavy with ideological implications, just as, conversely, the glorious deeds of the knight valorize and redeem the milieu in which he evolved.[40]

The great invention of the medieval romancers was to link love to glorious deeds so as to make love the direct cause and heroic personal identity and social position the indirect consequences.[41] The triangle hero-love-chivalry has a more widespread validity than the well-known and frequently encountered love triangle. The former is espe-

cially rich in possibilities when it is combined with the latter as in
the *Tristan,* where the socially static structure of hero–king (symbol
of chivalric society)–lady (object of love) simultaneously and strikingly embodies an erotic competition.

The link between love and chivalric exploits involves a true "constitutive model" for most medieval romances, and this model remains functional all the way to the modern novel[42] (although the
exploits are of another order, naturally). The author of the *Enéas*
thus took a decisive step when he conceived of portraying the love of
Enée and Lavinie on an Ovidian model[43] although, conditioned by
the structure of the *Aeneid,* he could not yet link this "Ovidian" love
to the primary narrative action, as the authors of the *Tristan* romances and Chrétien de Troyes were later to do with great acuity.

This constitutive model enables serial adventures to attain a meaningful unity in the face of the threatening centrifugal force of the
fantastic, largely Celtic or claimed as such. In addition, the action
often regains its coherence because of the two fixed points between
which it unfolds: the departure and the arrival. At the point of departure is the intention of following the hero's development, the
ideal of a *Bildungsroman* or an *Entwicklungsroman,* which from
Perceval, Jaufré, and *Le Bel Inconnu* develops perhaps all the way to
Wilhelm Meister and *Le Rouge et le noir.* At the point of arrival
is the result of the quest, which at times involves more tension than
fulfillment: it is no accident that the *Perceval* is unfinished. It was a
brilliant invention to make the quest into a transcendence of profane
love, to translate the hero-love-chivalry triangle into religious or mystical terms. The coherence between the *Bildungsroman* model and
the cognitive engagement of romance should also be emphasized;
the innocent, the *nice* is in an ideal position to describe, from his out-
sider's perspective, the particulars of a world which is not yet his but
soon will be.

Here, too, one of Bakhtin's theoretical constructs, the chronotope,
which he did not apply to the medieval romance because he lacked
documentation, is of great value.[44] It has often been remarked that
Chrétien's heroes leave the Arthurian circle to accomplish their chivalric exploits, making the court an ideal point of reference rather
than a place to remain (as if it were some terrestrial Jerusalem). It
has also been remarked that *Cligés* bridges the distance between two
symbolically marked locations, both legendary but for different reasons: Byzantium on the one hand and Arthur's court on the other.[45]
But all novels, not only medieval romances, involve taking possession

of the world, not simply of society. Cervantes understood this very well in his parody which is also a synthesis.

Through analysis of the chronotope, we can define a character not only on the basis of the relationships which he establishes with the outside world but also on the basis of the temporal line along which these relationships (and their history) are distributed.[46] (The slower temporal pace of the double declaration of love by Guilhem de Nivers and Flamenca, for example, corresponds to the painstaking precision of the chronological reference points in this romance.)

It will also be necessary to relate a semantic topochronology to the topochronology of narrative adventures, one that could synthesize the hero's decisive passages from one conceptual (thematic) situation to another, in short the phases of his *Entwicklung*. In the new combination of these two convergent topochronologies, the narrator's point of view has a revelatory function because it frequently effaces itself to better highlight the most significant phase shifts. I use "point of view" here both in the normal sense of the term and in Bakhtin's sense, that is, to indicate the critical tension between author and character. We can thus work toward an increasingly clear perception of the mental order subtending narrative meaning, which is the goal of our interpretive enterprise.[47]

Translated from the French by Elise Morse

Notes

[1] The first edition of *Problems of Dostoevsky's Poetics* was in 1929, while "Discourse in the Novel" was written in 1934–35 (published in 1972); *Roman vospitanija i ego znachenie v istorii realizma* (The Novel of Apprenticeship and Its Significance in the History of Realism) was written in 1936–38 (published in 1979; no English or French translation). "Forms of Time" was written in 1937–38 (published in 1974); *Iz predvstorii romannogo slova* was written in 1940 (published in 1965). Chapter 4 of *Dostoevsky's Poetics* contains a sketch of the history of the novel as genre. I do not know if this was already in the 1929 edition.

[2] Certain *chansons de geste* are also called *romans*, such as *Elie de Saint Gille, Aiol*, and *Fierabras*. But *Brut* and the *Roman de Troie* are self-defined as *romans* (Voelker; Marichal), and the term designates, among the works of Chrétien de Troyes, *Yvain* (v. 6805), *Lancelot* (vv. 2, 7101), and *Perceval* (v. 8). We must also take into account the wealth of terminology introduced to distinguish the content, form, and structure of the *roman*. Chrétien distinguishes between *livre* (Latin source, *auctoritas*), *conte* (the story found in the *roman* or in its source), and *estoire* (the story, but different from that of Chrétien); also *matiere* (subject or even source), *conjointure* (textual organization), *sens,* and *antancion* (the poet's creative plan). See Ollier.

[3] It should nonetheless be noted, as it was by Marichal (452), that there is a hiatus in the development of the French romance, though not in Spain and elsewhere, from the middle of the fifteenth to the middle of the sixteenth century; it resumes its evolution with the translation of the *Amadís* in 1573.

[4] One of the principal sources for this aspect of Bakhtin's analysis is of course Rohde, who is also used by a critic quite distant from Bakhtin, Frye. Hence, a series of resemblances: Frye contrasts the introverted and subjective "romance" with the extroverted and intellectual Menippean current, which leads to Rabelais, Swift, and Voltaire. This latter current, according to Frye, does not involve human beings so much as their spiritual attitudes.

[5] This statement is valid only quantitatively. See, for example, notes 36, 7, and 10. In thirteenth-century romances (such as *Ipomedon* and *Wistasse le Moine*) we encounter some noteworthy examples of linguistic parody.

[6] The definition of the novel as a "bourgeois epic" is Hegel's. The implications of this definition are pushed to their limits by Lukács ("Roman"), who considers that one cannot speak of the novel until after the establishment of the bourgeoisie and that the genre will no longer be possible after the decay of bourgeois ideology. I would maintain, on the contrary, that the link between novel and bourgeoisie is neither necessary nor sufficient in itself for the novel's existence. Rather, this link was established at a certain historical moment as the result of the sociolingustic factors discussed earlier and because the "management" of literature, at least since the Renaissance, has been assumed by the bourgeoisie.

[7] With some exceptions, such as the Latin-German bilingualism of the *Ruodlieb* (Dronke, *Poetic* 62).

[8] I choose two examples among many: the "Franglais," further enriched with Breton and Flemish elements, in a speech of Renart disguised as a minstrel (*Roman de Renart,* br. I, vv. 2351–466, 2511–28, and others); and the Franco-Italo-Latin juridical jargon which parodies the speech of a cardinal legate of Pavia (*Roman de Renart,* br. V, vv. 457–94).

[9] These are chiefly *vilains* and bourgeois. It would be excessive to impute the isolated episode of the Chastel de Pesme Aventure in *Yvain* to a conscious sociological awareness (that is, to see it as an early symptom of industrial exploitation and alienation).

[10] The rare instances involve language and styles "recognized" in the courtly milieu: for example, in *Flamenca,* the Latin of the mass (vv. 2470ff.), and various asemantic words, based perhaps on a musical practice: *turullutau* (v. 1053), *vasdoi vaidau* (v. 1054), and so on.

[11] The term *perspectivism* is employed by Spitzer, especially with regard to the paronomasia of the *Quijote,* which he saw as a manifestation of the "variegated phantasmagoria of human approaches to reality" (56). For the relations between narrative perspective and verisimilitude, see van Rossum-Guyon.

[12] There have been many studies of the Ovidian monologue (and its formal variations) in Old French romance, beginning with the *Enéas* (for example, in vv. 8134ff., 8279, 8348, 8676ff.). See, among others, Walker; Nolting-Hauff; Ménard, 742–46; and Uitti, *Story,* 161–62. It is important to note the extension of the monologue to other situations of confusion and psychological uncertainty, as in Archimbaut's jealousy (*Flamenca,* vv. 1157–70, 1269–311). See Nolting-Hauff 107, 115–16.

[13] We are already close to point-of-view technique in narrative situations where the reader learns of an unexpected change of affairs at the same time as a character and through the character's perceptions. For example: "A tant s'en torne [the subject is Guinglain] et voit Elie, / Et avec lui l'en vit aler, / Par mi l'uis les vit dont entrer: / Robert son escuier revoit / Et le nain, qui detriers venoit" (*Le Bel Inconnu*, vv. 3417–22). We are informed of the arrival of Elie, Robert, and the dwarf only because Guinglain sees them. An identical procedure occurs in vv. 3869–71.

[14] See Ménard 469–70.

[15] For instance, Lavinie, who sees herself through her mother's eyes (*Enéas*, vv. 8242ff.), or the perilous passage created by Guinglain's imagination, which transforms a moral obstacle into a physical one, starting from the simple *perce d'un esprevier* (*Le Bel Inconnu*, vv. 4551–78; note that the reader is implicated because the reality of the situation is only later communicated to him). See Uitti's insightful commentary (*Story* 211) on the blood drops on the snow episode in *Perceval*.

[16] For example, Dido who imagines kissing and making love to Enée, as Lavinie will also do (*Enéas*, vv. 1237–57, 8413); the dream-dialogue between Guilhem and Flamenca (*Flamenca*, vv. 2804ff.); Guinglain, who dreams of an amorous conversation with the Pucele as Blances Mains (*Le Bel Inconnu*, vv. 3695–704); the imaginary monologues and speeches of Jaufré and Brunissen (*Jaufré*, vv. 7387–486, 7595–626).

[17] In *Erec*, for example, "events in the romance are refracted through their effects upon each member of the couple" (Uitti, *Story* 222). In *Perceval*, the episode of the stolen kiss is recounted from the protagonist's perspective but later repeated in the words and from the viewpoint of the Orgueilleus de la Lande as well (vv. 3845–83).

[18] The function of the true/false opposition in the seventh day of the *Decameron* is analyzed by Segre, *Structures*, ch. 4.

[19] The emperor only dreams his night of love with Fénice but believes it to be real (*Cligés*, vv. 3309ff.). See Ménard 270–71.

[20] See the dialogue between Corras and Jouglet in *Guillaume de Dole*, vv. 819–28.

[21] The dialogue between the seneschal and Corras in *Guillaume de Dole* (vv. 3516–17, 3570–71, 4700–01) offers a perfect example of this.

[22] This phenomenon is particularly marked in the prose *Tristan* (see Lods, "Les parties," Maillard, and Baumgartner). The importance of the intercalated lyric pieces and *chansons de toile* in *Guillaume de Dole* and *Perceforest* has been widely noted.

[23] See Limentani 267–68. But the entire *Flamenca* is an apotheosis of "literature within literature," from Guillaume's use of the romance of *Blancaflor* as a psalter (v. 4477) to comparisons with characters and situations in other literary texts (Raimberge from *Audigier*, v. 1905; Isengrin, vv. 3687–90) and quotations of lyric pieces. In addition, the famous dialogue between Guilhem and Flamenca, with its bisyllabic responses spaced over a period of several weeks, forms, when the responses are assembled, an octosyllabic strophe very similar to one by Peire Rogier. See Limentani 275ff.

[24] Among the most characteristic cases are *Guillaume de Dole*, vv. 920–30, 3620–31, 3748–59, 4141–42, and 4594–97; in vv. 3196–97 an intercalated lyric poem is incorporated into the plot structure. It is interesting to note, as an

indication of generic interaction and even interaction between performative modes, the statement in *Guillaume de Dole,* v. 19: "l'en i chante et lit." On the prose *Tristan,* see Baumgartner. In *Perceforest* the intercalated *lais* sometimes function to summarize events previously narrated; see Lods, *Les pièces.*

[25] The varieties of the author-narrator configuration (analyzed in detail by Booth) have been studied in medieval texts by, for example, Grigsby, "Narrative Voices," and Uitti, "Narrative."

[26] This procedure has been described several times; see Fourrier, 428ff. and also Zumthor, *Essai* 343. Grigsby, "Narrator," has an extensive analysis; I consider inappropriate, however, the use of the term *narrator,* which involves the author-reader mediation of narrative content, to designate the author's appearance in the text as a character with his own story.

[27] In this connection see the analyses of Dembowski.

[28] A remark in Uitti, "Narrative" 165, is quite relevant in this context: "In *Yvain* narrator and protagonist grow together, in authentic *clergie* and *chevalerie.*" In general, I believe we must continue to consider the concept of irony as a sign of the "interior diversion of the normatively creative subject into a subjectivity as interiority, which opposes power complexes that are alien to it and which strives to imprint the contents of its longing upon the alien world, and a subjectivity which sees through the abstract and, therefore, limited nature of the mutually alien worlds of subject and object, understands these worlds by seeing their limitations as necessary conditions of their existence and, by thus seeing through them, allows the duality of the world to subsist. At the same time the creative subjectivity glimpses a unified world in the mutual relativity of elements essentially alien to one another, and gives form to this world" (Lukács, *Theory* 74–75). The novel would then achieve "a semblance of organic quality which is revealed again and again as illusory," in accord with a "skillfully ironic compositional tact" (Lukács, *Theory* 77).

[29] The potential for interaction between *lai* and *roman* can be illustrated by the fact that occasionally the narrative of a *lai* is transformed into a *roman* (as in *Eliduc* and *Ille et Galeron*), expanded to be sure (from 1184 verses to 6592 verses). See Wilmotte 194. Certain *lais,* such as the *Lai de l'ombre* or the *Lai d'Haveloc,* are on the other hand true *romans,* although somewhat abbreviated.

[30] Zumthor, "Chanson," rightly sees the *Chatelaine de Vergi* as an elaboration of *chanson* motifs, grafted onto a *fabliau* (85); he adds: "the lyric motifs supply the *san* for which the *fabliau* provides the *matiere*" (91). For *fabliau* elements in *Jofroi de Poitiers,* see Fay and Grigsby 14. It should also be emphasized (with Chênerie) that the *fabliau* protagonist is often a knight who, by his exploits, especially in tourneys, wins a lady who is most often already married. It is of course understood that the spirit and style are different.

[31] I refer to the *Charroi de Nimes* and the *Prise d'Orange.*

[32] See especially Köhler, "Quelques observations"; Jauss; Roncaglia, "L'Alexandre," and, on the technical aspects, Pollmann, "Von der *chanson.*" It should also be remembered that if the *chanson de geste* was sung in public, the *roman* on the other hand was intended for private reading, before a limited audience, or, simply, for silent reading.

[33] Gallais, for example, has romance begin with Chrétien de Troyes, excepting some prefigurations in the *Roman d'Alexandre,* that is, the central

position of individual destiny and the presence of the themes of voyage and adventure. But Köhler, *"Ideal"* 124–25, notes the continuity between Alexander and Arthur, who are both symbols of terrestrial harmony and the "reign of peace," while Frappier, "Remarques" 33, compares Alexander and Gauvain as types of the romance hero. Delbouille, for his part, considers *Apollonius de Tyr* (which survives only in fragmentary form) to be a protoromance; but at the same time he makes some very pertinent remarks concerning the "romanceness" of the *romans d'antiquité*. Raynaud de Lage starts instead with the *Roman de Thèbes*.

[34] See Faral 389–419, Marichal, and Frappier and Grimm, among others. It should be emphasized that the *translatio* of chivalry from Greece to Rome to France, which Chrétien celebrates in the prologue to *Cligés* on the model of the *translatio studii,* exactly follows the itinerary from the first *romans d'antiquité* to the *romans courtois*.

[35] One could in a sense invert the well-known hierarchy of truthfulness formulated by Jean Bodel in vv. 9–11 of the *Chanson des Saisnes* ("Li conte de Bretaigne, cil sont vain et plaisant, / et cil de Rome sage et de sens aprendant, / cil de France sont voir chascun jour aparant"): while the *chanson de geste* ("cil de France") offered a distorted, increasingly remote historical truth, the *roman* ("li conte de Bretaigne"), despite its fantastical settings, confronted the realities of its epoch. Compare the observations of Guiette 73–83 and Roncaglia, "Nascita," who stress, respectively, the *roman*'s symbolism and its search for values and meanings. Moreover, Bodel's lines correspond to a true topos: in *Brut,* vv. 1253–58, it is already said that the stories of Arthur were "ne tot mançonge ne tot voir, / ne tot folor ne tot savoir. / Tant ont li contëor conté / et li fablëor tant fablé / por lor contes anbeleter, / que tot ont fet fable sanbler"; in the *Vies des pères* (*ante* 1229) we read: "laissiez Cligés et Perceval, / qui les cuers perce et trait a val, / et les romanz de vanité" (qtd. in W. Foerster, *Cligés* [Halle: Niemeyer, 1884] xxii); and Rutebeuf affirms: "ge sai des romanz d'aventure, / de cels de la reonde table / qui sont a oïr delitable" (*Les deux Troveors ribauz,* Jubinal I, 334). Their contemporaries evidently viewed romance chiefly as escape literature, doubtless a limited judgment, but not an erroneous one. See also Voelker 516–17.

[36] I refer, among many possible examples, to the maritime terminology in *Brut* (vv. 2643–90), the medical terminology in *Cligés* (vv. 2971–87), and the gastronomical terminology in *Guillaume de Dole* (vv. 1239–47, 5449–58). On the presence of contemporary realities in Chrétien, see Fourrier 116.

[37] I am thinking of the scientific explanations in the form of miniature treatises in the "classical" romances. For example, in *Enéas:* "Le betumoi a tel nature" (v. 6498), "[abesto] tel nature a et tel costume" (v. 6516), "Li ditans est de tel vertu" (v. 9566); or the brief inserted treatises, such as the "de regimine principis" in *Thèbes,* vv. 1113–38. For geography, see the remarks of Fourrier 472ff. apropos of *Florimont*. For the sources of the "encyclopedia" in the *romans d'antiquité,* Faral 305–88 is still fundamental.

[38] It is for this reason, incidentally, that the Latin *Ruodlieb* has been identified as the first example of the medieval romance. See Dronke, "Ruodlieb," *Poetic.*

[39] In the context of an effective (if unilateral) sociological interpretation, Köhler, *Ideal* views the *aventure* as an attempt "to unite the interior and

exterior worlds," an attempt which can succeed on the condition that it remain an individual experience with the integration of the individual into society as its object (95).

[40] Köhler, "Quelques observations," *Ideal.*

[41] At the same time, the courtly love in our romances is very different from the *fin'amors* of the troubadours. This point has been made by Frappier, "Vues," and Pollmann, *Die Liebe,* chs. 4, 5, but it is important to reiterate it. In *fin'amors* the most significant moment is that of desire, of internal suffering; fulfillment is presented as infrequent and is, in any case, deferred. In the romances, on the other hand, love blazes up without warning and aspires to a consummation often achieved without delay. We should further note that *fin'amors* involves as a rule married women of high social status; the love of the romances involves as a rule single young women (albeit aristocratic) and does not exclude, but on the contrary often requires, a matrimonial outcome, which may coincide with the coming into possession of a fief. *Fin'amors* is autotelic and centripetal; the courtly love of the romances, essentially heterotelic and centrifugal, is one of several necessary components of chivalric perfection.

[42] Gauvain is the principal exception. This can be explained by his position at the court; see Nitze, Fierz-Monnier 81, and Kellermann, "Les types." Dinadan in the prose *Tristan* constitutes an "antimodel" (thus he reverses the basic principles, the love-chivalry relation). He is, as confirmation *ex negativo,* well accepted by his milieu; see Vinaver, ch. 8.

[43] See Faral 63–157; Wilmotte, ch. 5.

[44] I refer to Bakhtin, "Forms of Time." On the history and different meanings of the term *chronotope,* see Segre, "Cronòtopo."

[45] It is even possible to see in *Cligés* the beginning of a fusion between *matière antique* and *matière de Bretagne.* See Liborio 33–34.

[46] Several topological analyses of the *roman courtois* have been undertaken in the context of structural studies. I offer as examples, while emphasizing their different viewpoints, Kellermann, *Aufbaustil;* Woods; Dorfman; and Köhler, *Ideal,* ch. 7 as well as the final diagrams. Application of Lotman's topological models is found in Boklund, "Spatial," "Socio-sémiotique."

[47] I have elsewhere ("Punto") proposed this objective, as the ultimate goal of narratological analysis.

Works Cited

Auerbach, Erich. *Mimesis. Dargestellte Wirklichkeit in der abendländischen Literatur.* Bern: Francke, 1946.

Bakhtin, Mikhail. *The Dialogic Imagination: Four Essays.* Trans. Caryl Emerson and Michael Holquist. Ed. Michael Holquist. Austin: U of Texas P, 1981.

———. "Discourse in the Novel." Bakhtin, *Dialogic* 259–422. Orig. pub. as "Slovo v romane." *Voprosy literatury i estetiki.* Moskva: Izdatel'stvo "Chudozestvennaja literatura," 1975. French trans. in *Esthétique et théorie du roman.* Paris: Gallimard, 1978. 83–233.

———. "Epic and Novel." Bakhtin, *Dialogic* 3–40. Orig. pub. as "Epos i roman." *Voprosy literatury i estetiki.* Moskva: Izdatel'stvo "Chudozestvennaja literatura," 1975.

————. "Forms of Time and of the Chronotope in the Novel." Bakhtin, *Dialogic* 84–258. Orig. pub. as "Formy vremeni i chronotopa v romane." *Voprosy literatury i estetiki.* Moskva: Izdatel'stvo "Chudozestvennaja literatura," 1975. French trans. in *Esthétique et théorie du roman.* Paris: Gallimard, 1978. 235–398.

————. "From the Prehistory of Novelistic Discourse." Bakhtin, *Dialogic* 41–83. Orig. pub. as "Iz predvstorii romannogo slova." *Voprosy literatury i estetiki.* Moskva: Isdatel'stvo "Chudozestvennaja literatura," 1975.

————. *Problems of Dostoevsky's Poetics.* Trans. W. W. Rotsel. Ann Arbor, Mich.: Ardis, 1973. Orig. pub. as *Problemy poetiki Dostoevskogo.* 2nd ed. Moskva: Izdatel'stvo "Chudozestvennaja literatura," 1963.

————. *Rabelais and His World.* Trans. Hélène Iswolsky. Cambridge: MIT P, 1968. Orig. pub. as *Tvorcestvo Fransua Rable i narodnaja kul'tura srednevekov'ja i Renessansa.* Moskva: Izdatel'stvo "Chudozestvennaja literatura," 1965.

Baumgartner, Emmanuèle. "Sur les pièces lyriques du *Tristan en prose.*" *Etudes de langue et de littérature du Moyen Age offertes à F. Lecoy.* Paris: Champion, 1973. 19–25.

Blumenfeld-Kosinski, Renate. "Old French Narrative Genres: Towards the Definition of the *Roman Antique.*" *Romance Philology* 34 (1980): 143–59.

Boklund, Karin. "Socio-sémiotique du roman courtois." *Semiotica* 21. 3–4 (1977): 227–56.

————. "On the Spatial and Cultural Characteristics of Courtly Romance." *Semiotica* 20. 1–2 (1977): 1–37.

Booth, Wayne C. *The Rhetoric of Fiction.* Chicago: U of Chicago P, 1961.

Butor, Michael. *Répertoire I.* Paris: Minuit, 1962.

Calin, Françoise, and William Calin. "Medieval Fiction and New Novel: Some Polemical Remarks on the Subject of Narrative." Haidu, *Approaches* 235–50.

Chanson de geste und höfischer Roman. Heidelberger Kolloquium 30 (Jan. 1961). Heidelberg: Winter, 1963.

Chênerie, Marie-Luce. "*Ces curieux chevaliers* . . . Des fabliaux aux romans." *Romania* 97 (1976): 327–68.

Delbouille, Maurice. "*Apollonius de Tyr* et les débuts du roman français." *Mélanges offerts à Rita Lejeune.* Ed. F. Dethier. Gembloux: Duculot, 1969. 1171–204.

Dembowski, Peter F. "Monologue, Author's Monologue and Related Problems in the Romances of Chrétien de Troyes." Haidu, *Approaches* 102–14.

Dorfman, Eugene. *The Nareme in the Medieval Romance Epic.* Toronto: U of Toronto P, 1969.

Dronke, Peter. *Poetic Individuality in the Middle Ages.* Oxford: Clarendon, 1970.

————. "*Ruodlieb:* Les premières traces du roman courtois." *Cahiers de civilisation médiévale* 12 (1969): 365–82.

Faral, Edmond. *Recherches sur les sources latines des contes et romans courtois du Moyen Age.* Paris: Champion, 1913.

Fay, Percival, and John L. Grigsby, eds. *Joufroi de Poitiers.* Genève: Droz, 1972.

Fierz-Monnier, Antoinette. *Initiation und Wandlung. Zur Geschichte des altfranzösischen Romans im zwölften Jahrhundert.* Bern: Francke, 1951.

Fourrier, Anthime. *Le courant réaliste dans le roman courtois en France au Moyen Age*. Vol. 1. Paris: Nizet, 1960.

Frappier, Jean. "Remarques sur la peinture de la vie et des héros antiques dans la littérature française du XIIe et du XIIIe siècle." *L'humanisme médiéval dans les littératures romanes du XIIe au XIVe siècle*. Ed. Anthime Fourrier. Paris: Klincksieck, 1964. 13–51.

———. "Vues sur les conceptions courtoises dans les littératures d'oc et d'oïl au XIIe siècle." *Cahiers de civilisation médiévale* 2 (1959): 135–56.

Frappier, Jean, and Reinhold R. Grimm, eds. *Le roman jusqu'à la fin du XIIIe siècle*. Grundriss der romanischen Literaturen des Mittelalters 4.1. Heidelberg: Winter, 1978.

Frye, Northrop. *Anatomy of Criticism*. Princeton: Princeton UP, 1957.

Gallais, Pierre. "De la naissance du roman. A propos d'un article récent." *Cahiers de civilisation médiévale* 14 (1971): 69–75.

Grigsby, John L. "The Narrator in *Partonopeu de Blois, Le Bel Inconnu,* and *Joufroi de Poitiers.*" *Romance Philology* 21 (1968): 536–43.

———. "Narrative Voices in Chrétien de Troyes: A Prolegomenon to Dissection." *Romance Philology* 32 (1979): 261–73.

Guiette, Robert. *Forme et senefiance*. Genève: Droz, 1978.

Haidu, Peter. *Aesthetic Distance in Chrétien de Troyes: Irony and Comedy in* Cligés *and* Perceval. Genève: Droz, 1968.

———, ed. *Approaches to Medieval Romance*. Yale French Studies 51. New Haven: Yale UP, 1974.

Jauss, Hans-Robert. "Chanson de geste et roman courtois." *Chanson de geste und höfischer Roman*. Studia Romanica 4. Heidelberg: Winter, 1963. 61–77.

Kellermann, Wilhelm. *Aufbaustil und Weltbild Chrestiens von Troyes im Percevalroman*. Zeitschrift für romanische Philologie, Suppl. 88. Halle: Niemeyer, 1936.

———. "Les types psychologiques de l'amour dans les romans de Chrétien de Troyes." *Marche Romane* 20.4 (1970): 1–9.

Köhler, Erich. *Ideal und Wirklichkeit in der höfischenepik*. 2nd ed. Tübingen: Niemeyer, 1970. French trans. *L'Aventure chevaleresque: Idéal et réalité dans le roman courtois*. Paris: Gallimard, 1974.

———. "Quelques observations historico-sociologiques sur les rapports entre la chanson de geste et le roman courtois." *Chanson de geste und höfischer Roman*. Heidelberg: Studia Romanica, 1963. 4: 21–30.

Lebensanft, Franz. "Adverbes de temps, style indirect et 'point de vue' dans la *Queste del Saint Graal.*" *Travaux de linguistique et de littérature* 19 (1981): 53–61.

———. "Perspektivische Rededarstellung (Erlebte Rede) in Texten des französischen und spanischen Mittelalters." *Zeitschrift für romanische Philologie* 97.1/2 (1981): 65–85.

Lejeune-Dehousse, Rita. *L'oeuvre de Jean Renart. Contribution à l'étude du genre romanesque au Moyen Age*. Paris-Liège: Droz, 1935.

Lerch, Eugen. *Historische Französische Syntax*. 3 vols. Leipzig: Reisland, 1925–34.

Liborio, Mariantonia. "'Qui petit semme petit quelt.' L'itinerario poetico di Chrétien de Troyes." *Studi e ricerche di letteratura e linguistica francese*. Napoli: Istituto Universitario Orientale, 1980. 1: 9–70.

Limentani, Alberto. *L'eccezione narrativa. La Provenza medievale e l'arte del racconto.* Torino: Einaudi, 1977.

Lods, Jeanne. *Les pièces lyriques du* Roman de Perceforest. Genève-Lille: Droz, 1953.

Lods, Jeanne. "Les parties lyriques du *Tristan en prose.*" *Bulletin bibliographique de la Société Internationale Arthurienne* 7 (1955): 73–78.

Lukács, György. "Problemy teorii romana." *Literaturnyi kritik* 2 (1935): 214–49. Fr. trans. in *Ecrits de Moscou.* Ed. Claude Prevost. Paris: Ed. Sociales, 1974.

————. "Roman kak burzuaznaja epopeja." *Literaturnaja enciklopedija* 9 (1935): 795–831. Fr. trans. in *Ecrits de Moscou.* Ed. Claude Prevost. Paris: Ed. Sociales, 1974.

————. *The Theory of the Novel.* Trans. Anna Bostock. Cambridge: MIT P, 1971. Orig. pub. as *Die Theorie des Romans.* Berlin: Cassirer, 1920. French trans. Genève: Gonthier, 1963.

Maillard, Jean. "Lais avec notation dans le *Tristan en prose.*" *Mélanges offerts à Rita Lejeune.* Gembloux: Duculot, 1969. 1347–64.

Marichal, Robert. "Naissance du roman." *Entretiens sur la Renaissance du 12e siècle.* Ed. M. de Gandillac and E. Jeauneau. Paris-La Haye: Mouton, 1968. 449–92.

Meiller, A. "Le problème du 'style direct introduit par *que*' en ancien français." *Revue de Linguistique Romane* 30.119–20 (1966): 353–73.

Ménard, Philippe. *Le rire et le sourire das le roman courtois en France au Moyen Age (1150–1250).* Genève: Droz, 1969.

Nitze, W. A. "The Character of Gauvain in the Romances of Chrétien de Troyes." *Modern Philology* 50 (1952–53): 219–25.

Nolting-Hauff, Ilse. *Die Stellung der Liebeskasuistik im höfischen Roman.* Heidelberg: Winter, 1959.

Ollier, Marie Louise. "The Author in the Text: The Prologues of Chrétien de Troyes." Haidu, *Approaches* 26 41.

Pollmann, Leo. *Die Liebe in der hochmittelalterlichen Literatur Frankreichs.* Frankfurt am Main: Klostermann, 1966.

————. "Von der *chanson de geste* zum höfischen Roman in Frankreich." *Germanisch-Romanische Monatsschrift* 47 (1966): 1–14.

Pouillon, Jean. *Temps et roman.* Paris: Gallimard, 1946.

Raynaud de Lage, Guy. "Le premier roman." *Orbis mediaevalis. Mélanges . . . R. Bezzola.* Ed. Georges Günter, Marc-René Jung, Kurt Ringger. Berne: Francke, 1978. 323–27.

Rohde, Erwin. *Der Griechische Roman und Seine Vorläufer.* 2nd ed. Leipzig: Breitkopf und Härtel, 1900.

Roncaglia, Aurelio. "L'*Alexandre* d'Albéric et la séparation entre chanson de geste et roman." *Chanson de geste und höfischer Roman.* Studia Romanica 4. Heidelberg: Winter, 1963. 37–52.

————. "Nascita e sviluppo della narrativa cavalleresca nella Francia medievale." *Convegno internazionale Ludovico Ariosto.* Roma: Accademia dei Lincei, 1975. 229–50.

Rychner, Jean. "La présence et le point de vue du narrateur dans les deux récits courts: le *Lai de Lanval* et la *Chatelaine de Vergi.*" *Vox Romanica* 39 (1980): 86–103.

Scholes, Robert. *Approaches to the Novel.* New York: Chandler, 1961.

Segre, Cesare. "Cronòtopo." *Logos Semantikos. Studia linguistica in honorem E. Coseriu.* Vol. 1. Madrid: Gredos, 1981. 157–64.

———. "Punto di vista e plurivocità nell'analisi narratologica." *Atti del Convegno Internazionale "Letterature classiche e narratologia."* Perugia: Istituto di Filologia latina, 1981. 51–65.

———. *Structures and Time.* Chicago: U Chicago P, 1979.

Spitzer, Leo. "Perspectivism in *Don Quijote." Linguistics and Literary History: Essays in Stylistics.* Princeton: Princeton UP, 1948. 42–85.

Stempel, Wolf-Dieter. "Perspektivische Rede in der französischen Literatur des Mittelalters." *Interpretation und Vergleich. Festschrift für W. Pabst.* Berlin: Schmidt Verlag, 1972. 310–30.

Tobler, Adolf. *Vermischte Beiträge zur französischen Grammatik.* 5 vols. Leipzig: Itirzel, 1886–99.

Uitti, Karl D. "Narrative and Commentary: Chrétien's Devious Narrator in *Yvain." Romance Philology* 33 (1979): 160–67.

———. *Story, Myth, and Celebration in Old French Narrative Poetry.* Princeton: Princeton UP, 1973.

van Rossum-Guyon, Françoise. *Critique du roman. Essai sur "La modification" de Michel Butor.* Paris: Gallimard, 1970.

Vinaver, Eugène. *A la recherche d'une poétique médiévale.* Paris: Nizet, 1970.

Voelker, P. "Die Bedeutungsentwicklung des Wortes Roman." *Zeitschrift für romanische Philologie* 10 (1886): 485–525.

Vossler, Karl. "Der Roman bei den Romanen." 1927. *Aus der romanischen Welt.* Karlsruhe: Stahlberg Verlag, 1948. 107–25.

Walker, E. *Der Monolog im höfischen Epos. Stil- und literatur-geschichtliche Untersuchungen.* Stuttgart: Kohlhammer, 1928.

Wilmotte, Maurice. *Origines du roman en France. L'évolution du sentiment romanesque jusqu'en 1240.* Académie Royale de Langue et de Littérature Française de Belgique, Mémoires 15. Liège: Vaillant, 1941.

Woods, William S. "The Plot Structure in Four Romances of Chrétien de Troyes." *Studies in Philology* 50 (1953): 1–15.

Zumthor, Paul. "De la chanson au récit: *La chastelaine de Vergi." Vox Romanica* 27.1 (1968): 77–95.

———. *Essai de poétique médiévale.* Paris: Seuil, 1972.

———. "Le roman courtois: Essai de définition." *Etudes littéraires* 4.1 (1971): 75–90.

———. "Roman et histoire. Aux sources d'un univers narratif." *Langue, texte, énigme.* Paris: Seuil, 1975. 237–48.

AMOROUS IMITATION
Bakhtin, Augustine, and *Le Roman d'Enéas*

Stephen G. Nichols

I. Dialogism and Love

Love and lyric tend to be synonymous when we consider the representation of love in the late eleventh and early twelfth centuries. We have been taught to regard the early troubadours, from Guillaume IX to Bernart de Ventadorn, as the founders of the imitation of love in poetry. And this is so even when we consider the love narrative rather than the love lyric.

Gaston Paris was one of the first to point to the troubadours as the main source of technique and themes for the early romance narrative, but W. P. Ker, in his influential *Epic and Romance,* first published in 1896 but still available in paperback until a few years ago, formulated the connection with what seems to be enduring authority:

> It is impossible to separate the spirit of French romance from the spirit of Provençal lyric poetry. The romance represents in a narrative form the ideas and spirit which took shape as lyric poetry in the South; the romances are directly dependent upon the poetry of the South for their principal motives. The courtesy of the Provençal poetry, with its idealism and pedantry, its psychological formalism, its rhetoric of antithesis and conceits, is to be found again in the narrative poetry of France in the twelfth century. (345)

Such assumptions—still prevalent in our teaching and some of our writing today—ignore both early medieval and modern distinctions between the discourse of love in the lyric and in narrative. By focusing simply on thematics, one ignores the fundamental generic differences between lyric and romance, differences arising, as Mikhail Bakhtin has shown, from the relationship between the speaker and his discourse.

Both the image and the intentionality of lyric discourse differ radically from those of romance. If the former seeks to represent a highly focused image of the language of an intense emotional state—discrete, unresolved, and unprolonged—the latter seeks to portray "the totality of all the languages and consciousness of language" associated with love as narrative (Bakhtin 366). Lyric may represent love as celebration, but romance necessarily focuses on contradictory and antagonistic images of love and desire, self and other. More specifically, the expansiveness of romance permits a conjoining of languages which yields a very different image of discourse from that available to lyric.

This is so in part, Bakhtin argues, because of the representational relationship of the speaking subject to the poetic word as trope or symbol. Although capable of richly diverse forms of expression,

> these types of relationships between various meanings do not and cannot go beyond the boundaries of the relationship between a word and its object, or the boundaries of various aspects in the object. The entire event is played out between the word and its object; all of the play of the poetic symbol is in that space. . . . The polysemy of the poetic symbol presupposes the unity of a voice with which it is identical, *and it presupposes that such a voice is completely alone within its own discourse*. As soon as another's voice, another's accent, the possibility of another's point of view breaks through this play of the symbol, the poetic plane is destroyed and the symbol is translated into the plane of [narrative]. (Bakhtin 328; emphasis mine)

This suggests that lyric deals essentially with love as an object of poetic expression. Lyric discourse focuses on the whole status of the poetic voice with respect to the language and symbolism of love. Although lyric does recognize love as problematic for the speaker, it concentrates almost exclusively on its ontological rather than social or metaphysical aspects.

Lyric seeks to establish an identity, to claim the right of access to the amorous state, implicitly perceived as just beyond the speaker's horizon. Like Guillaume de Lorris's lover, circling outside the Garden of Delight, or Fabrice at the Battle of Waterloo, the lyric lover speculates on the indeterminacy and mystery shrouding the desired condition or at least access to it.

Love poetry ultimately affirms itself as a language of metamorphoses where the speaker hypostatizes himself, in the manner of such classical Ovidian figures as Actaeon or Daphne, into the symbolic state where word and object mediate each other endlessly without fear of intervention from the outside world. Only by such a transformation can the lover attain the solipsistic condition which assures unique possession of the loved object.

This is why the specter of interruption—literally the intrusion of another's voice, another's word—haunts the love lyric. The Provençal *alba,* from this perspective, embodies the fragile paradox of lyric discourse. Situated in the liminal moment between possession and loss, it is the eruption of another's voice (the cry of the watchman) announcing the intrusion of alterity (the day, the husband, the world) that signals the rupture of the privileged relation between word and object and hence the end of (the) lyric.

Ovid's tale of Pygmalion, rather than Shaw's play, stands as the model for lyric monologism, where the artist-lover does all the making and the speaking. Once animated, the bride retains both the anonymity and the taciturnity of her previous status as artistic object: "Shee felt the kisse, and blusht therat; and lifting fearfully / Hir eye-lidds up, hir Lover and the Light at once did spye" (*Metamorphoses* 10.319–20).

Romance poses just the reverse question. It takes the same asymmetry between the subjective emotional state whose fragile ecology lyric tries to isolate and protect but opens it up to the social context. Rather than placing the closed circuit of word and object between speaking subject and world, romance asks how love mediates between them.

In terms of the problematic of the *alba,* romance might be said to pick up the story of the night of love at daybreak and ask what happens when the sun comes up and the *jaloux* (the jealous husband) demands to know where and how his wife has spent the night. Indeed, in a famous scene in Chrétien de Troyes's *Lancelot, ou le Chevalier de la Charrete,* one finds precisely such a situation: the account of a passionate night of love between Lancelot and Guenevere followed the next day by a kind of inquisition by a jealous rival.

In posing such questions, romance ironizes love; that is, it subjects love to interpretations other than those flattering constructions placed on it by the bemused lover in his solitary lyric reverie. It opens love up to the intrusion of other viewpoints while still focusing on the central perspective. In romance, however, this central perspective has been expanded to include the voice of the beloved who, no longer content, like Pygmalion's bride, simply to "feel the kisse and blush therat" and still less to equate "the Light and her Lover" without question, now seeks, like Shaw's Eliza Doolittle, to speak in her own voice and to ask her own questions.

The voice of the beloved may be the first intimation of alterity intruding into the monologism of the lover. Within most romance, the tuning of the voices of lover and beloved remains a central preoccupation. At the center of the emotional world of love, where unity implies unison—at least in lyric—the irony of contradiction or mixed motive hovers when the beloved poses awkward questions. And medieval romance seems to abound in ladies who refuse to take their lovers at face value—or, worse still, who do take them at their word and, inconveniently, expect them to keep it.

After the ladies come the onlookers. In the manner of a Greek chorus, romance includes a collectivity—sometimes socially differentiated into nobles and peasants, as in the *Roman de Tristan*—who watch and pose questions of their own regarding the behavior of the lovers. Not infrequently, both lover and mistress must justify their behavior before the collectivity. More interestingly, the presence of the onlookers forces the lovers to call their love by another name, to make a metaphor of their true relationship, thereby creating a dual existence—an inner world within the social context of public life—and a corresponding double narrative.

The double narrative highlights the status of romance as an essentially dialectical genre which, like the socratic dialogue or its paleo-Christian avatar the autobiographical *confessio,* seek to mediate the asymmetry between immanence and transcendence in the individual's experience of the world. The claims of sensory versus rational knowing have been debated since Plato, but with Christianity they assumed a special urgency, as Augustine made clear.

To privilege the emotional over the rational was to reverse the process that would, according to the dictates of Christian Neoplatonism, lead from the worldly to the spiritual domain, in short, from immanence to transcendence. In this progression, it mattered very much not only what or who one loved but how one loved. A radical form of amorous skepticism, of questioning—as Perceval discovered to his cost—became *de rigueur.*

Double-voicedness, to use Bakhtin's term, introduced not only a narrative predicated on questioning in the romance but also multiple points of view. The issue is not ambiguity but irony, which calls into question the very possibility of erecting a unified philosophical system within the romance narrative. The dialectical indeterminacy of romance made it by nature a genre subversive of the privileged discourse requisite for unity in the totalizing systems favored by medieval society and therefore a natural choice for authors like Chrétien de Troyes or Jean de Meun who sought to question received opinion. At the same time, we can see why romance would then be a natural target for the hostility of reformers like Saint Bernard or Dante.

The tension between the dual narratives does not simply raise questions about the true nature of events, it continually underlines the uncertainty of the answers and the danger inherent in wrong answers. For the onlookers, the questions may be relatively straightforward, even trivial: Do Lancelot and Guenevere, or Tristan and Iseut, engage in adulterous activity? Does Erec's attachment to Enide really constitute a form of dereliction (*recréantise*)? Every romance poses some such question to motivate the intervention of the onlookers.

For the reader, alerted to the broader issues by the narrator, the questions assume true philosophical proportions. We are meant to see the issue in terms of a hermeneutics of love predicated, as in all issues of interpretation, on a process of blindness and insight. And, as Paul Armstrong recently observed, the hermeneutic approach inevitably underlines the dialogic nature of interpretation:

> Every interpretive approach reveals something only by disguising something else that a competing method with different assumptions might disclose. Every hermeneutic standpoint has its own dialectic of blindness and insight—a ratio of disguise and disclosure that stems from its presuppositions. To accept a method of interpretation is to enter into a wager—to gamble, namely, that the insight its assumptions make possible will offset the risk of blindness. (343)

With this in mind, we can understand why in answering the question of how love guides the individual toward the path of transcendence, or whether it can, medieval romance did not resort to pluralism and attempt to postulate multiple answers, all more or less acceptable. Instead, it faced up to the conflict of interpretations occasioned by the religious and political intolerance toward philosophical pluralism within the context of twelfth-century Europe.

This means that we find at least two viewpoints in romance narrative predicated on two different and opposing answers to the problem of love as an agent of transcendence. These two perspectives correspond roughly to the dichotomy between the head and the heart, rationality and desire, schematized in the well-known medieval genre of the debate poem. Both rationality and desire recognize that love is the sensory experience par excellence by which the *cogito* may mediate between the worlds of rationality and sensuality. Each postulates desire as the central factor of the mediation. But they differ radically in the scope each is willing to allow to the language of desire.

The first sees desire as inherently chaotic, threatening, by a radical assertion of individual will, to destroy the harmony of the microcosmic order so carefully constructed by Christian Neoplatonism. Rationality had to control and contain manifestations of desire to ensure that humans would move upward in the hierarchy that led from the material world to the plane of transcendence from which emanated the essences or true forms. Love narrative, in this view, should be didactic, a demonstration of how the *cogito* dominated the world of sensory experience.

The second perspective made the case for a freer approach to sensuality by arguing that knowledge through love could be gained in several stages. From this viewpoint, amorous adventure simply constituted the worldly counterpart to spiritual love and could, in fact, help humans recognize and know spiritual ecstasy. Our interest focuses less on the existence of the two viewpoints, however, than on the consequences of their resultant dialogism for our understanding of the transformation of romance from at least a potentially didactic genre, in its early stages, to a pseudo- or even an anti-didactic genre.

II. The Augustinian Paradigm

The first extensive recognition of the problems desire would pose for the postclassical love narrative occurs not in the early troubadours but in books 1–4 of Saint Augustine's *Confessions,* where Augustine examines the Dido and Aeneas episode of Virgil's *Aeneid*. As a student of legal rhetoric, Augustine not unnaturally focuses on the discourse of the work and its effect on the reader. He objects less to the representation of desire per se than to the mimetic strategies used by Virgil and other classical authors:

> See how he arouses himself to lust, as if by heavenly instruction, as he says
>
> > "Ah, what a God!
> > He shakes the highest heavens with his thunder!

> Shall I, poor mortal man, not do the same?
> I've done it, and with my heart. I'm glad."

In no way, in no way whatsoever, are these words used here learned more easily because of this filthy scene, but because of these words that vile deed is more boldly perpetrated. I do not condemn the words, which are as it were choice and precious vessels, but that wine of error which through them was proffered to us by drunken teachers. (Augustine 1.16.26)

Augustine demonstrates that the linguistic structure of Book 4 of the *Aeneid* could arouse and encourage the emotional identification of the naive reader with the pitiful figure of Dido. The homology between the linguistic structure of the text and the structures of desire of the reader was too exact, thereby occasioning in the reader an emotional sympathy with Dido rather than an intellectual understanding of the reasons for her fall.

He punningly equates the wanderings and uncertainties of his own situation in early youth with those of Aeneas (*Aeneae . . . errores*), giving as an example the greater pity he felt for Dido's plight than for his own spiritual health:

> I was required to learn by heart I know not how many of Aeneas's wanderings, although forgetful of my own, and to weep over Dido's death, because she killed herself for love, when all the while amid such things, dying to you, O God my life, I most wretchedly bore myself about with dry eyes.
>
> Who can be more wretched than the wretched one who takes no pity on himself, who weeps over Dido's death, which she brought to pass by love for Aeneas, and who does not weep over his own death, brought to pass by not loving you. . . . I wept over the dead Dido "who sought her end by the sword" . . . if I had been forbidden to read those tales, I would have grieved because I could not read what would have caused me to grieve. (1.13.20–21)

Some years ago, John O'Meara pointed to the extraordinary influence of the *Aeneid* on Augustine's writing in the *Confessions*. O'Meara concerned himself with the way in which Augustine wrote the *Aeneid* into his own work as an important subtext. In passages like the one just quoted, however, we see less the influence of an important classical work than a significant rewriting, a transformation of its rhetorical strategies for philosophical purposes.

In the *Confessions,* Augustine sets his own language apart from that of Virgil. The latter, Augustine takes pains to show us throughout the first book, is the shared language of the community, the language taught in the schools and even inculcated by the schoolmasters using the threat of corporal punishment: "A task was assigned to me that disturbed my mind, either by reasons of the praise or disgrace to be awarded or for fear of flogging. I was to speak Juno's words, as she expresses both anger and sorrow because she could not 'turn back the Trojan king from going to Italy'" (1.17.27).

Augustine uses the incident to make a point that Bakhtin also insists on: that mimetic participation takes place through the language of a text; the images conveyed by the work depend on the language spoken by the characters or, in the case of the young Augustine, by the boy declaiming Juno's speech. The languages within a narrative may be marked by ideological differences from the society at large—as in Augustine's case—or even from one another, as Augustine differentiates his language from that of Virgil or Cicero within the *Confessions*. A strong narrator will control the disparate languages so as to leave no doubt about the authoritative discourse.

Bakhtin makes much the same observation:

> Characteristic for the novel as a genre is not the image of a man in his own right, but a man who is precisely the *image of a language*. But in order that language become an artistic image, it must become speech from speaking lips, conjoined with the image of a speaking person.
>
> If the subject making the novel specifically a novel is defined as a speaking person and his discourse, striving for social significance and a wider general application as one distinctive language in a heteroglot world—then the central problem for a stylistics of the novel may be formulated as the problem of *artistically representing language, the problem of representing the image of a language*. (336).

Augustine responded to the need for a strong narrative voice to control the multiple languages woven into his text. He did so in a manner that also permitted the narrative to control the irreconcilable differences between the language of desire, symbolized by Dido—or by the young Augustine's own passion for reading about her ("et si prohiberer ea legere, dolorem")—and the rhetoric of moral example. The most obvious device used to accomplish this purpose is his shift from Virgil's third-person narrator to the pervasive first-person voice of the *Confessions*. The shift doubly distinguishes him from Virgil. Augustine presents events in which he himself participated at an earlier phase of his life while still maintaining the ironic distance of a dispassionate observer via the voice of the older narrator/commentator.

The metacommentary of the older Augustine ironizes the *errores Aeneae*—as well as those of the young Augustine himself—in a way that allows the reader little occasion to participate in them emotionally. He represents the wanderings not as events whose distance from us has been foreshortened by brilliant narration but rather as morally marked examples (*errores*): not as youthful trips but as adolescent trippings up. Each anecdote contains a vignette of the young Augustine framed by a moral commentary on the part of his censorious senior.

In this manner, the narrator of the *Confessions* fulfills the role of Mercury, the *deus ex machina,* in the *Aeneid,* who resolves the opposing languages of duty and desire by recalling Aeneas to the path of destiny. At the same time, the narrator's metacommentary establishes a textual dialectic; it is a continuous narrative voice rather than an abrupt manifestation of authorial control, as in the case of Mercury's descent to Carthage. The substitution symbolizes a major difference between Virgil's work and Augustine's.

Criticizing Virgil for his distance from the events he recounted, Augustine argued the necessity for more direct control by the writer of his discourse. He argued and demonstrated that the asymmetry between the discourse of desire and that of ideology—theological and political—could be overcome by a carefully controlled conjuncture of the subtexts with the principal discourse.

In the *Confessions* this meant a rewriting of the *Aeneid* by substituting a first-person narrative voice for Virgil's third person; by recounting real rather than imagined history; and by subordinating classical subtexts like Cicero, Virgil, and Horace to Christian architexts like Saint Paul and the Desert Fathers.

In short, Augustine attempted to counter the dialogism of the language of desire by implementing a process of what we might call "narrative indirection." For Augustine, the representation of the carnivalesque realm of desire could not be ignored, but it could be repressed, carefully bounded and covered by a narrative *cogito* fully cognizant of the difference between empirical reality and fantasy, between intellectual control and emotional abandonment such as that represented for character and reader alike in the Dido episode. What was the fate of Augustine's initiative? Was it successful in containing dialogism in romance?

III. Saint Alexis and Narrative Indirection

Bakhtin called attention to the heterogeneity of language consciousness in the chivalric romance which drew its materials from such widely disparate sources as Celtic mythology, Christian legend and literature, and ancient texts. Bakhtin emphasized the "manifold degrees of mutual inter-orientation with alien discourse, alien intention" as the principal "activities shaping the literary consciousness that created the chivalric romance" (377).

While these elements played an undeniable role, as Bakhtin claims, I would like to focus on the representation of love—more specifically on the attempt to censor or deflect the representation of love—in romance. But I would place the beginnings of the trends Bakhtin associated with the courtly romance somewhat earlier than he did.

In my book *Romanesque Signs,* I have shown that one of the earliest vernacular texts, the eleventh-century Franco-Provençal *Passion* of Clermont-Ferrand, employs an intense, if sublimated, language of emotivity in representing the maternal love of Mary for Christ. But it is above all in another text of the period, *La Vie de Saint Alexis,* that we find a fully elaborated narrative that utilizes the Augustinian paradigm of narrative indirection in an attempt to deflect the dialogism of amorous discourse.

The young Roman nobleman, Alexis, becomes a speaker and agent for the first time in the narrative at the moment when, on his wedding night, he faces the fact and act of physical love. At this juncture, the text stands poised for a rather explicit portrayal of the nuptial rite:

> When the day waned and it was night,
> The father said: "Son, now go lie
> with your wife, as God in heaven ordains."
> The child did not wish to anger his father;
> He went into the bedchamber with his wife. (51–55)

The new bride lies on the bed, receptive, or at least resigned; Alexis enters the room, stands erect beside the bed, and suddenly speaks for the first time. But just at the moment when the tradition of love representation seems about to commit itself uncompromisingly to an unrepressed portrayal of desire, a deflection occurs:

> When he sees the bed, looks at the Virgin,
> Then he remembers his heavenly lord,
> Whom he holds dearer than any earthly possessions.
> "Oh! God," said he, "How strongly sin oppresses me!
> If I don't flee now, I fear I may lose you." (56–60)

For our purposes, it matters less that Alexis's subsequent speech renounces love and exhorts the bride to preserve her chastity than that in showing us the potential action (the gratification of desire) and the actualized speech, the poem postulates two conflicting texts, two opposing languages. It also places immense metaphysical weight on the choice between them.

Alexis recognizes that to take on the role of lover urged by his father would constitute a line of demarcation between a spiritual life of worldly renunciation on the one hand and, on the other, a commitment to the physical relationship with the woman and a courtly career as a Roman noble that his role as husband and lover would entail. Moreover, his speech indicates that the choice lies between repression and desire and that language mediates both courses.

Alexis's renunciation goes beyond the repression of temptation. It is not a mere "Vade retro, Satanus," but a use of language, the discourse of repression, to suppress a dangerous identity, as Augustine suppresses the Virgilian narrator in his rewriting of the *Aeneid*. Alexis renounces a primary identity and persona to assume the guise of anonymity, to transform himself into an emblematic being devoted to works which bring not personal reward but honor to a Virgin other than the one who tempts him on the nuptial bed. The emblematic value of his new life, and the mark of its success, is conferred on him in the next section of the story by the icon, the *imago,* of the distant woman he has so faithfully served. When the image of the Virgin in the church miraculously speaks and confers on him the generic title "Saintly Man," we recognize a courtly topos. Just as Guenevere will be the first person to name Lancelot in the *Chevalier de la Charrette* or Isolde alone will recognize Tristan in his disguises, so the Virgin alone can recognize the anonymous hero, Alexis, and bestow on him the emblematic title of "saint homme."

The text utilizes a monologic discourse both in the highly stylized narrative and in the few passages of direct discourse, such as Alexis's speech to his bride. These might serve as a model for the text as a whole in which the narrator as speaking subject or occasionally his surrogate—Alexis or the icon of the Virgin—addresses a passive audience such as the bride or the reader.

The text limits the opportunities for dialogism by providing an image of artistic language in which the intellect acts as the guide and censor of the senses. That first scene in the bedchamber, for example, portrays two reciprocal actions: the double set of seeing with the eyes—the windows of desire—and with the intellect, the instrument of reflection and repression. Alexis's discourse stresses, albeit crudely, the opposing scenarios invoked by seeing and intellection. In rereading the passage, we realize that this confrontation of sight and thought engenders the Old French version, the work as we have it. For, unlike the Latin text that preceded it, the Old French *Vie* graphically depicts the two paths open to Alexis at the moment he faces the recumbent woman, thereby stressing the gesture of renunciation as a refusal to enact the script set in motion by the father.

The Latin work does not suggest the swerving of the narrative produced by the explicit confrontation of desire and repression. On the contrary, it narrates the scene as a smooth transition devoid of tension:

> Ut autem intrauit, coepit nobilissimus juuenis et in Christo sapientissimus instruere sponsam suam et plura ei sacramenta dissere.

[When he went in [to the chamber], this most noble and wise youth began to instruct his wife and reveal to her the many sacraments.]

The Old French text forces our attention on the opposition of sensual and intellectual perception as Alexis sees the two objects of physical desire—the metonymic bed and the synecdochic woman— then calls to mind the heavenly father:

> Cum veit le lit, esguardet la pucella: Dunc remembret de sun seinor celeste. (57–58)

The turning inward to memory of the spiritual text literally shuts out the competing physical act of vision.

But what is the fate of desire here? Alexis does not conquer desire; he deflects it from the physically present object to the mental image. But this displacement from the physically present object, the bride, to the absent, spiritual concept of the Father requires an explanation, a narrative, and thus initiates the Old French text, a quite different one from its predecessors. What appears relatively simple and straightforward in earlier texts no becomes opaque and ambivalent precisely because the language at a crucial moment registers the consciousness of choice and raises the possibility of hesitation, even though the textual intentionality clearly seeks to deny the possibility of choice and to warn against hesitation.

What we witness in the *Alexis* may be called a hermeneutics of desire: a language of indirection which inscribes a suppressed text within the work, a censored narrative whose traces we find intersecting the principal story at regular intervals. This language of indirection relies on allegorical discourse to create a specular counterpart to the dominant language of the work. The principal discourse and its double, read together, generate not clarity—the intention of the main tale—but enigma.

The enigma underlines the hierarchical structure of narrators and readers bequeathed to the love narrative by the Augustinian paradigm. The dangerous waters of desire may be navigated only by clerkly narrators and readers. And so the love narrative typically inscribes hermeneutic paradigms—maps of reading and misreading—in the text. Thus the *Alexis* incorporates a specular image of the monologic narrative in the form of the autobiographical *chartre,* or letter, which Alexis writes just before his death to explain to his family, with whom he has lived anonymous and unrecognized for seventeen years, who and what he is. Like the *Vie* as a whole, this text cannot be correctly interpreted by the uninitiated (the family and the reader) without the intercession of an authoritative witness: the pope himself. All these symbols of text production and reception convey the message of the dangers inherent in any departure from monologism: meaning requires reflection; the text contains multiple layers and hidden meanings that lead astray those who rely only on sight uninformed by the inward vision of intellection. But these same signs also attest to the elaborate defenses erected against the encroachment of dialogism: the text as other.

IV. *Le Roman d'Enéas:* The Discourse of Deflection

In his last and still influential book, *Literary Language and Its Public in Late Antiquity and the Latin Middle Ages,* Erich Auerbach inadvertently offers an illustration of how the association of love and lyric with which we began distorts the perception of romance—the love narrative—of otherwise sophisticated readers of medieval literature. Auerbach, too, views love almost purely as thematics rather than a combination of discourse and theme.

This perspective leads Auerbach to play down the importance of the *Enéas* in the development of twelfth-century love narrative, even though he devoted a full chapter to the work. Instead, he locates the "important" milestones of the genre elsewhere: in the works of Marie de France, *La chastelaine de Vergi,* and Chrétien de Troyes, where

> a serious and high-minded narrative art is in the making, [whose] central theme is love: the fires of passion, love unrequited, or the perils of lovers. And soon the sensual aspect of love will be transcended. The utterly unclassical notion of the beloved as sovereign commander over her lover's thoughts and destinies originated in Provençal love poetry; it makes its first appearance in epic [*sic*] in Chrétien's Lancelot fragment; and through the prose *Lancelot,* which made a deep impression

on Dante (*Inf.* 5 and *Par.* 16.13ff), this lofty, humble, adulterous love becomes a European ideal. In the Italian *stil nuovo* the beloved becomes an incarnation of the divine; love is represented as the appanage of the noble heart, a way to virtue and knowledge; indeed the terminology and even the reality of its torments and transports come to be associated with the ecstasy of *unio passionalis*. (219–20)

What Auerbach ascribes to the *stil nuovo* begins, as we have seen, much earlier, with Augustine's attempt to co-opt the discourse of desire. Had he not been so partisan to the theory of lyric origins of the love narrative, he might have seen that the *Enéas* already implements the concept of *"unio passionalis"* using the principle of responsive mimesis we find in Augustine.

Morrison points out that responsive mimesis placed the burden of symbolizing activity on the reception of the images by the reader or beholder (ch. 1–3). All artistic activity should engage the faculty of "reason, which Aristotle considered the essential characteristic of man and his most intimate likeness to God" (17). In the *Confessions,* Augustine constructed the narrative in such a way as to actually show the dialogue between emotion and reason by which humans could make reason dominant in the mental processes they employed in art and, subsequently, in life. Not by accident do the *Confessions* move with the precision of mathematical symbolism from the narrator's birth to conversion in an autobiography that is also a story of progressive perfection of a whole being. Then, from Books 10 to 13, we find a kind of abstract recapitulation, a replay of the scenario but in terms of the dynamics of the mind.

This autobiography of the mind takes us behind the scenes, as it were, to show us the mental processes involved in the physical conversion story we followed in books 1–9. If in those books we experienced the conversion language, or "metanoia," in action, the last four show us the mechanics of the discourse of metanoia, "the image of the language itself." As we might expect, it is an image dominated by the rational faculties, but where emotion plays the important, if subordinate, role of capturing and focusing the attention of the intellect:

> Doubtless, that heaven of heaven which you made in the beginning is some kind of intellectual creature. Although in no manner coeternal with you, the Trinity, it is yet a partaker of your eternity, and because of its most sweet and happy contemplation of you, it firmly checks its own mutability. Without any lapse from its first creation, it has clung fast to you and is thus set beyond all the turns and changes of time. (12.9.9)

In his recent article "The Conscience of Narrative," Cyrus Hamlin calls this progression from the exterior, material world to the inner life of the mind a "theology of narrative" (218). He shows it to be crucial to the internalization of experience—the mind's consciousness of itself—that constitutes the strategy of correction by which Augustine hoped to demonstrate how art and literaure could be "powerful devices of moral insruction" (Morrison 17).

In this sense, Augustine subscribed to the Aristotelian concept of corrective mimesis whereby "reason dominated the scheme in which the arts replicated the order of life, moving from less to more perfect forms, even as logic itself reproduced 'the circular process of coming-to-be in nature'" (Morrison 19). The great strength of the *Confessions* sprang from its success in combining the account of personal spiritual progress based on the subordination of emotional love by *ratio* with a simultaneous process of narrative history and metacommentary. This made the text as much a discovery of motivations and hidden meanings as it was a history—in short, as much a hermeneutics of the language of the mind as an account of historical events.

Narrative as a hermeneutic of experience is crucial to the *Roman d'Enéas,* although, as Auerbach's comments demonstrate, this aspect of the work has been downplayed, when it has been recognized at all. The *Enéas* builds on Augustine's model to make romance a hermeneutics of love. Although, like the *Alexis,* it faces the fact and act of love, Enéas, unlike the ascetic Alexis, cannot resort to flight as a means of resolving the contradictions of *ratio* and *passio.* In consequence, this text had to find a means of imposing a monologic censorship on the incipient dialogism of romance. Augustine's "rewriting" of the *Aeneid,* for much the same purpose, provided the key by which the anonymous twelfth-century poet "translated" the Latin work—in the medieval rather than the modern sense of *translatio.*

In the first place, the Augustinian preoccupation with love replaced the Virgilian emphasis on history. In a narrative where metanoia, in the sense of "conversion" or "repentance," motivates the text, history in the Virgilian sense (at least as Virgil was read in postclassical and medieval times) of collective imperial achievement proved unsatisfactory. It diffused the focus on the individual hero's story, his halting progress on the path of transcendence. Above all, it forced the narrative to admit all the diffuse voices of the collective cultural enterprise, to cast the hero against the canvas of Roman history.

Metanoiac narrative requires a more intimate approach. It needs to narrow the focus to highlight the process by which the minds of the central characters respond to the inchoate stimuli of the world, gradually sorting and ordering them into a coherent worldview: that of the conversionary perspective. For this purpose, love provides the ideal substitute for history. One of the most intimate and subjective of emotions, it is both of the mind and capable of going beyond the mind of the individual toward a transcendent union. Above all, it stresses a discourse based on the mind-as-consciousness.

Space constraints do not permit a consideration of the larger patterns of Augustinian intertextuality in the *Enéas:* such questions as the metanoiac trajectory of Enéas himself, modeled more closely on the younger and the mature Augustine of the *Confessions* than on Virgil's hero, or the *Roman*'s curious reticence regarding *poiesis,* poetic self-consciousness, even to the point of omitting to mention Virgil's name or the skill of the translator in adapting the work. The emphasis of the title, *Enéas,* reflected textually at key moments such as the peroration (beginning on l. 10,032) where we find repetitions of Enéas's name, also points to the shift from the Virgilian emphasis on Roman imperial achievement to the more Augustinian notion of the making, the conversion of a perfected rational human, an individual, rather than an eponymous icon for a collective history.

To see just how neatly the rhetoric of metanoia inscribes a monologic discourse in the work, we need only look at two devices, one conceptual, the other stylistic. Both enable the *Enéas* poet to thematize the Augustinian conventions of responsive mimesis in a way that not only transforms the focus of the Virgilian narrative but also illustrates how the limited horizon of individual love and personal experience was meant, in a monologic narrative, to link individual fate to collective destiny via spirituality and salvation history, the transcendent correlates of love and experience. Both devices are thus hermeneutic, stressing "reading" and interpretation of life.

The first of these devices emphasizes the dynamic involvement of the mind, or *motus animi,* that occurs in response to an external stimulus. It illustrates how, in metanoiac narrative, subject/object interaction begins with emotional confrontation whose purpose is to problematize the external object in terms of the subject's own peace of mind. The process abolishes the distance between the subject and object, interiorizing—within the mind of the speaking subject—a relationship that might otherwise remain "unattached" and capable of articulation in another's voice.

The second device, stichomythic dialogue, arises as a natural consequence of the speaking subject's attempt to deal with the troublesome objects that have come to consciousness. Emotional interaction between subject and object leads characters to interrogate themselves in an extended monologue or to question others. The device occurs in Virgil, where Dido's *furor*—as well as the pathetic hopelessness of her situation—becomes apparent to the reader through self-questioning monologue.

The *Enéas*-poet makes much more extensive use of the Virgilian device: first in the Dido episode, then with Lavinia and her mother, and finally in a long "night of love" in which Enéas, like Jacob wrestling with the angel, comes to terms with his passion for Lavinia. The difference between self-interrogation (Enéas's case) and a true interrogatory dialogue (Dido and Anna or Lavinia and her mother) is not innocent, as we shall see, because reliance on another's wisdom suggests a lack of self-knowledge, acceptable in a supporting character but not in the main hero.

We must remember that the Old French *roman* casts Enéas's story more in terms of a psychomachia than of a *historia*: Enéas progresses from being the "coward of Troy" to the "wolf of Italy," from the libertine of Carthage to the rational lover/husband of Italy. This change in emphasis from a collective historical imperative to a quasi-biographical case history of an individual's sentimental or spiritual development—his awakening to the pluridimensionality of self—is the major difference between epic and romance bequeathed to the medieval tradition by Augustine and transmitted through the *Roman d'Enéas*.

Self-questioning monologue in response to an external stimulus favors the rhetoric of metanoia. It allows the single-voiced discourse to structure the event-as-interpretation around a dominant world-view while simultaneously focusing on the mental processes by which the intellect comes to grips with, and subdues, inchoate emotion. The monologic process also facilitates the structuring of narrative around a single set of universal principles of "right" and "wrong." As we shall see, Lavinia and Enéas fall in love with each other, but the text structures the *prise de conscience* of love and their outward manifestation of it very differently for each character, although the same interrogatory rhetoric appears in both cases. Lavinia confronts the issues primarily from an emotional standpoint, without mastering the rhetoric of metanoia Enéas brings to the debate.

The reader never doubts that Enéas confronts the issues with the same trials and triumphs he brings to his military campaigns, and for the same reason (the text repeatedly makes the equation between success in the strategies of love and of combat that becomes a commonplace in the chivalric romance). Of the two characters, Enéas dominates, while Lavinia plays the subordinate role because of Enéas's greater success in subsuming emotion to intellect.

Yet without emotion, there would be no love. Lavinia's inability to dominate her feelings leads her to declare her love, thereby initiating the train of events that leads to their romance and makes the point of this work. Emotion thus constitutes the motivation that transforms generic life experience to generic literary discourse. By means of the monologue which represents gender difference as gender-motivated discourse, the text demonstrates the doctrinal concept that males and females differ in their strengths and weaknesses in love. The difference and the roles it leads the characters to play are hypostatized into a genre, the medieval debate between the head and the heart. Lavinia, a corrected version of Dido, takes the role of the heart and Enéas takes that of the head in this perennially popular medieval genre. In this way, the text incorporates the characters and their different viewpoints into the totalizing dialectic of a union that made difference a question of hierarchy and authority. Reader expectation that in the debate between the head and the heart, the head usually won led medieval readers of romance to anticipate the appropriateness of Enéas's conduct, no matter how unrealistic the thematic suppression of desire may appear to modern readers.

Difference between male and female could not be dealt with realistically, but it could be schematized so as to incorporate and thus neutralize desire within the order of things. By assigning to the two partners the opposing themes of emotion and intellect—not as absolutes but as dominant gender traits—that will be ultimately reconciled by the submission of Lavinia to Enéas, the romance avoids the threat of double-voicedness: the lovers express similar concepts in different ways. And that, after all, was how the rhetoric of metanoia was supposed to control the expression of desire in romance. Let us look briefly at several key passages of the *Enéas* to discover just how the poetics of metanoia function.

The moment when Lavinia falls in love with Enéas appears as a transcendent experience in which her intentionality of the world undergoes transformation. The result of a combined sensory, emotional, and intellectual perception, Lavinia's experience changes her from a simple narrative agent into a character in her own right. The scene thus forms an excellent example of responsive mimesis, an intratextual icon of the kind of reaction the twelfth-century reader might usefully have imitated.

Cast almost as a "reading lesson," Lavinia's affective perception of Enéas stresses the theme of mental response to external stimuli. It shows how the rhetoric of metanoia represents love as a "conversion response," awakening the intellectual powers of the subject to the question of the intentional standpoint of the self vis-à-vis the external world. Lavinia's sudden perception of the Trojan hero constitutes an "invention" in the medieval, lyrico-religious sense of the term:

> Lavine fu an la tor sus,
> d'une fenestre garda jus,
> vit Eneam qui fu desoz,
> forment l'a esgardé sor toz.
> Molt li sanbla et bel et gent,
> bien a oï comfaitemant
> lo loënt tuit par la cité
> et de proëce et de bialté;
> *bien lo nota an son corage*
>
> . . .
>
> Quant voit que eschiver n'en puet,
> Vers Eneam a atorné
> *tot sun corage et son pansé:*
> . . .
>
> Tote ert sole la damoiselle,
> l'uis de la chanbre ala fermer,
> revient a la fenestre ester
> . . .
>
> d'iluec esgarde lo vasal.
> (8047–55; 8062–64; 8068–70; 8072)

[From a window high above on the tower, Lavinia looked down, saw Enéas below, and stared hard at him above all others. He seemed to her very handsome and courtly; she had heard everyone in the city praise him as such and for his prowess and beauty. *She registered all this carefully in her heart and mind* [corage, "the seat of her inner life"]. . . . When she sees that she can't escape it [love], *she turns all her thoughts and inner self toward Enéas* . . . The maiden was all alone; she went to close the door of her room, comes back to stand by the window . . . from where she can look at the nobleman. Emphasis mine.]

Although conventions still remained in flux around the mid-twelfth century, Lavinia's experience here departs from the normative representation of the act of falling in love. Unlike the convention where Cupid's arrow wounds the lover at the moment of the initial visual contact, Lavinia's initial sight of Enéas *and* the psychic response it triggers precede her wounding by Love's dart.

The act of seeing, stressed throughout the passage quoted above— *garda, vit, forment l'a esgardé sor toz, voit, esgarde*—actively underscores the projection of the external scene on the retina of Lavinia's mind. And this physical imprinting of the scene on her mind occasions a physical reorientation of her whole being toward the object of her intense regard.

This physical attraction translates into gestural terms a corresponding psychic tropism. The image is that of the iron needle turning toward the lodestone—a bit of popular science not unknown to the period—or, to use an astronomical analogy also current at the time, the attraction of a lunar satellite to the source of its light. The passage establishes Lavinia's orientation to Enéas as inevitable; subsequent narrative has only to demonstrate the rational grounds for this natural tropism.

The force of responsive mimesis in this passage derives precisely from the conclusive manner by which the passage demonstrates how textual discourse imitates and rationalizes nature. It illustrates the Neoplatonic principle then current that art (here in the form of discourse) translates into second nature the givens of inchoate experience. Art ultimately improves on nature by its ability to organize experience into rational categories (Wetherbee, ch. 1, 3; Morrison, ch. 7; Jauss).

As Lavinia looks at Enéas, looks again, then goes to shut the door so she can be alone, uninterrupted, and finally returns to the window to look again, all the while undergoing an inner transformation, we cannot help but see an intertextual exploitation of a famous conversion text. In book 8, chapter 6, of the *Confessions,* exactly at the midpoint and six chapters before the famous conversion scene in the garden, Augustine recounts Ponticianus's story of the Roman official's conversion, a transcendent moment occasioned by a fortuitous glance, followed by the reading of a few paragraphs of a *Life of Saint Anthony.*

This archetypal image of metanoia explictly links the external regard to the mental transformation that occurs. Metanoia connotes at once the double movement of repentance, a turning away from a previous life, and conversion: turning with or toward a new intentionality of the world. Thus the repeated movement of looking out and turning in is crucial to the *motus animi* of metanoia:

> He spoke these words, and in anguish during this birth of a new life, he turned his eyes again upon those pages. He read on and was changed

within himself, where your eye could see. His mind was stripped of this world, as soon became apparent. For as he read, and turned about on the waves of his heart, he raged at himself for a while, but then discerned better things and determined on them. (Augustine 8.6.15)

The description of the metamorphosis here serves as an icon or even a model of the intellectual process by which raw emotion motivates yet remains subordinate to intellectual understanding. The metaphor of the storm at sea conveys the sense of emotional turmoil that figuratively casts the narrator up on the shore of a new land and a new life: *volvit fluctus cordis sui* ("thrown about on the waves of his heart"). Undeniably vivid, the image appeals at once to the senses and to the mind, thereby illustrating how metanoiac discourse dominates and circumscribes emotion.

Relying on a web of intertextual signification, conversion passages such as the preceding generally incorporate some marker pointing to a controlling matrix of texts that will permit it to be seen as like them and interpreted accordingly. Here the reference to the storm-tossed heart on a wild sea of emotion first recalls the literal storm of *Aeneid* 1 that throws Aeneas on the shores of a new life and then the figurative avatar of that storm in *Confessions* 1. The latter context, as we saw, is a responsive re-presentation of the former, a *prise de conscience* that launches Augustine's conversionary rewriting of the *Aeneid*.

Such transcendent moments must leave their mark on the text: there has to be some form of mimetic response demonstrating the effectiveness as well as the "sincerity" of the narrator's conversion. In the Ponticianus anecdote, Augustine himself verifies the official's responsive reading of the *Life of Saint Anthony* by representing the kind of subjective response the reader ideally should undergo:

Ponticianus told us this story, and as he spoke, you, O Lord, turned me back upon myself [*retorquebas me ad me ipsum*]. You took me from behind my own back, where I had placed myself because I did not wish to look upon myself. You stood me face to face with myself. (Augustine 8.7.16)

Metanoia ironizes the old self, forcing the reader to view himself from a new vantage point, symbolized by the physical reorientation of the speaker (*retorquebas me . . .*). Augustine seems to suggest here that the text does not simply function as a passive reflector for the reader but actually "reads" the reader in the sense of forcing a subjective identification of reader and mimetic subject in the same way that Augustine identifies with the official.

When Augustine the narrator intervenes to perform the correct response to Ponticianus's anecdote, he does more than simply demonstrate for his reader its authoritative interpretation. He also furnishes a language of response, a conversion discourse which is itself a metanoiac reading of Ponticianus's anecdote. With consummate skill, Augustine uses the single voice of conversionary rhetoric to bridge the gap between self and other in a manner that avoids dissonance. He preempts the possibility of contradictory interpretations (within the confessional context of the time) by asserting that only such a physical and spiritual reorientation can lead one to the path of perfection.

Metanoia, we see, requires a turning away from the world of dissonance, the world of heteroglossia. At the same time, it motivates a turning with or toward the self, perceived now as a vehicle for a potential new life. But simultaneously, metanoia offers a new way of looking out at a world just as complex as before, but now unified by an intentional focal point that transforms a once objective, indifferent scene into a subjectively valorized one. The beginning of the process is the turning inward—*mutabatur intus*—in response to an external stimulus such as religious texts, as in the case of the Roman official or Augustine, or another person, as in the case of Lavinia.

For might we not say that Lavinia's situation when she suddenly sees Enéas conforms with uncanny fidelity to the Augustinian model of metanoia? We even find an Old French equivalent for the Latin phrase *mutabatur intus:* "Bien lo nota an son corage" (8055). We also find an elaborate physical set of gestures indicative of Lavinia's reoriented intentionality of the world. Enéas serves not only as external stimulus but also as the focal point that forces her to "turn herself towards herself" ("retorquebat se ad se ipsam"), to paraphrase Augustine's formula.

Lavinia ultimately does not attain the same level of spiritual self-knowledge as Augustine's narrator, that role being reserved for Enéas. She does undergo a long period of self-examination and instruction, looking first, as did the young Augustine, in the conventional places—in her case, she interrogates her mother in a long, stichomythic dialogue. Her mother represents the outmoded teaching that has to be surpassed (familiar to us from *Confessions* 1). Enéas becomes the embodiment of the new doctrine, but ultimately Lavinia shows herself to have grasped the major tenet of Augustine's teaching when she concludes that in matters of conversion—and in the *Enéas,* love constitutes a kind of conversion—a third party can

never provide the self-knowledge that comes from introspection—
mutabatur intus:

> n'an pooie pas tant savoir
> par nul autre come par moi;
> molt an sui sage, bien i voi;
> Amors a escole m'a mise,
> an po d'ore m'a molt aprise. (8180–84)

[I could not learn nearly so much about love from anyone else as I
can from myself. I am very knowledgeable in it; I see clearly. Love
sent me to school and taught me a great deal very quickly.]

Lavinia has indeed learned much, not least of all to speak the language of love, a codified discourse controlled by the narrator and en-
suring, as Augustine understood, that all the principal characters
would literally "speak the same language." The long monologue
(vv. 8900–9118) by which Enéas arrives at his own perfected model
of the conversionary discourse thus necessarily involves the same linguistic register. Indeed, this passage demonstrates perhaps even more
specifically than Lavinia's speeches the adaptation of the rhetoric of
metanoia to romance as genre and experience. In spite of its structural importance, however, Enéas's monologue does not reflect the
"potential drama" of the *Roman.*

A critical moment in the development of twelfth-century romance
occurs when Lavinia first sees Enéas and feels herself constrained by
a sudden change in her psychic and physical being. In its present
form, the scene does not explicitly treat the drama that could have
attended her discovery of love-as-difference nor the intrusion of a
voice of her own speaking against and across the as-yet-unlearned
discourse of love. But the components for such a drama do exist; and,
while quickly deflected, sufficient traces of them remain for us to see
that the text simultaneously recognized Lavinia's potential for difference and undertook to neutralize it.

When Lavinia asks her mother, "Tell me, what is love?" (7889–90)
and her mother responds: "You will never learn it by words" (7895),
we find ourselves in the presence of a symbolic confrontation between love and discourse where desire and repression struggle to
mark the boundaries between didacticism and dialogism in romance.

Desire flourishes in a climate of unreflective action, while discourse, especially the self-questioning kind encouraged by the rhetoric of metanoia, inhibits the free expression of desire. In Lavinia's
sentimental education, passion and discourse contend for control of

the narrative. Thus the opposition between "amors" and "parolle" implicitly recurs in the mother's diagnosis of Lavinia's halting description of her malaise: "In faith, you love him *par amour*" (8530). Lavinia herself betrays a marked sense of the risk attendant on conflating love and discourse when she hesitates to pronounce the name of her lover, that is, to transform Enéas's name from a private love-totem to a common language of communication:

> —Il a non E . . ."
> puis sospira, se redist: "ne . . . ,"
> d'iluec a piece noma: "as . . . ,"
> tot en tranblant lo dist en bas.
> La raïne se porpensa
> et les sillebes asanbla.
> "Tu me diz 'E' puis 'ne' et 'as';
> ces letres sonent 'Eneas.' " (8553–60)

[He is named E . . ." Then she sighed and added, "ne . . . ," then after a while, "as . . ." She spoke it softly, all trembling. The queen thought and assembled the syllables. "You tell me 'E,' then 'ne,' and 'as'; these letters spell 'Enéas.' "]

At the most simple level, Lavinia simply fears her mother's reaction to the name of the hated rival to her candidate for Lavinia's hand, Turnus. More profoundly, however, transposing Enéas's name from the register of mute love-totem to the realm of communal discourse opens both the name and her love to interpretation and debate. Lavinia's reluctance proves justified, as the queen quickly replaces the revered name with substitute epithets, such as "traitor" and "sodomite," that do not simply ironize it but call into question Enéas's status as lover.

Within the larger theme of the work, the mother's language parodies the conversionary rhetoric of self-discovery, but it also underscores the incompatibility of desire and discourse in the Augustinian paradigm. The one exception to this rule appears to be the privileged vehicle of direct written communication between the lovers. Driven by her desire, Lavinia writes a letter to Enéas in which she reveals "tot mon estre, tot mon corage" ("all my being and my inner self") (8771). She wraps the letter around an arrow which she has an archer shoot at Enéas. In so doing, she breaks the military truce established between the Latins and the Trojans, but she also breaks another kind of truce by declaring love.

The letter episode features all the panache of romanesque description at its most intriguing: we see the writing of the letter; the novel "air mail" delivery; the alarm and anger of the Trojan troops when the arrow falls at the feet of their leader; Enéas's chagrin at the Latin perfidy that gives way before our eyes to a more complex set of emotions as he reads the letter. Only subsequently do we realize that there is a glaring omission: the text of the letter—with its language of passion—appears nowhere in this crucial episode. We hear every syllable of the monologues in which Lavinia masters the language of love, but we are not permitted to read a single word of the letter written and sent so aggressively *before* she has been sent to the "school of love." Since this whole section originates with the twelfth-century romancer—nothing remotely like it exists in the Virgilian original—we have to believe that it tells us something significant about textual intentionality.

Like the *Vie de Saint Alexis,* the *Roman d'Enéas* pointedly depicts the onset of love, then quickly deflects it. Although it may convey traces of Lavinia's difference, the romance resists doing more; it steadfastly suppresses her potential double-voicedness. In consequence, the true drama of Lavinia lies not in what she actually says but in what she does. Those long monologues where Lavinia learns to suppress her own voice in favor of the "official" language of love, when read attentively, yield a fascinating web of traces of differences and double-voicedness that the narrative strives consistently to purge.

The battle between desire and intellect disputed in those nocturnal debates between head and heart must be traced back to Augustine's *Confessions* rather than directly to Virgil, as we saw. But in the adaptation of the rhetoric of metanoia to romance, the concept of confession itself, as an agent of repression, turned out to be at risk. Lavinia "confesses" to her mother and to herself, revealing the inner state of her mind and heart and even managing to reconcile them in the approved Augustinian manner, or so it appears. Yet underlying this manifest text lies a suppressed one: Lavinia's letter. The romance surrounds this missile-text with a curiously ambiguous set of markers. Written secretly in a tower, wrapped around an arrow, and shot from the tower at Enéas, it is openly perceived as an aggressive, truce-breaking act and artifact.

Markedly visible in the narrative, the letter nevertheless remains a mystery to us. We know that it contains an intimate confession of love, perhaps even of desire—which is the way the modern translator renders the Old French "corage" in the passage. We understand perfectly well why the letter, or its contents, have been "purloined" by the programmatic intentionality of the work. Lavinia's language in the letter could hardly have accorded with the conversionary rhetoric she strives so hard to master elsewhere. The independent voice of difference would certainly have been felt in that letter, initiating a polyphonic narrative at odds with the Augustinian paradigm the text otherwise manages to adapt so brilliantly to the romance form.

Lavinia's purloined letter tells us something about the proclivities of romance. Even in the most closely monitored texts, subversive elements tend to push the discourse toward dialogism. For all the success of the *Enéas*-poet in transcoding Augustine's conversionary rhetoric into a confessional doctrine of human love, he still could not entirely control the markers of desire. The suppressed text of the letter arouses our curiosity and draws attention to a lacuna, a gap in our experience of the narrative. It also marks an aporia in the sequential logic of the romance. We cannot forget that this missing text occasions the long "night of love" in which Enéas wrestles with the demons of desire, solely as a result of having read Lavinia's amorous confession. In the final analysis, the *Roman d'Enéas* clearly could not do without the letter, but the conspiracy of silence with which it shrouds Lavinia's actual words suggests that the romance could hardly do *with* it, either.

Thus, at the core of even the most didactic of romances, we find a "confession" that threatens to slide over toward the category of "True Confession," with all the overtones of soft-core eroticism the term connotes. Lavinia may learn the language of metanoia, but we cannot help but wonder which of her voices is the truly confessional one.

Works Cited

Armstrong, Paul B. "The Conflict of Interpretations and the Limits of Pluralism." *PMLA* 98 (1983): 341–52.

Auerbach, Erich. *Literary Language and Its Public in Late Latin Antiquity and in the Middle Ages.* Trans. Ralph Manheim. Bollingen Series 74. Princeton: Princeton UP, 1965. Orig. pub. as *Literatursprache und Publikum in der Spätantike und im Mittelalter.* Bern: A. Francke A. G. Verlag, 1958. Chapter 3, "Camilla, or the Rebirth of the Sublime," deals specifically with *Le Roman d'Enéas.*

Augustine. *The Confessions of Saint Augustine.* Trans. John K. Ryan. New York: Doubleday, 1960.

Bakhtin, Mikhail Mikailovich. *The Dialogic Imagination: Four Essays.* Trans. Caryl Emerson and Michael Holquist. Ed. Michael Holquist. Austin: U of Texas P, 1981.

Bloch, R. Howard. *Etymologies and Genealogies: A Literary Anthropology of the Middle Ages*. Chicago: U of Chicago P, 1983.

Crosland, Jesse. "Enéas and the *Aeneid*." *Modern Language Review* 29 (1934): 282–90.

Hamlin, Cyrus. "The Conscience of Narrative: Toward a Hermeneutic of Transcendence." *New Literary History* 13 (1982): 205–30.

Jauss, Hans Robert. "Poeisis." *Critical Inquiry* 8 (1982): 591–608.

Ker, W. P. *Epic and Romance: Essays on Medieval Literature*. 1908. New York: Dover, 1957.

Morrison, Karl F. *The Mimetic Tradition of Reform in the West*. Princeton: Princeton UP, 1982.

Nichols, Stephen G., Jr. *Romanesque Signs: Early Medieval Narrative and Iconography*. New Haven: Yale UP, 1983.

Nims, John Frederick, ed. Introduction and Notes. *Ovid's Metamorphoses: The Arthur Golding Translation, 1567*. New York: Macmillan, 1965.

O'Meara, John. "Augustine the Artist and the *Aeneid*." *Mélanges offerts à Mlle. Christine Mohrmann*. Utrecht/Antwerp: Spectrum Editeurs, 1963. 252–61.

Stock, Brian. *The Implications of Literacy*. Princeton: Princeton UP, 1983.

Wetherbee, Winthrop. *Platonism and Poetry in the Twelfth Century: The Literary Influence of the School of Chartres*. Princeton: Princeton UP, 1972.

William of Saint Thierry. *The Nature and Dignity of Love*. Trans. Thomas X. Davis. Cistercian Fathers Series 30. Kalamazoo, Mich.: Cistercian, 1981.

ROMANCE AND THE VANITY
OF CHRÉTIEN DE TROYES

Douglas Kelly

Karl Kerényi wrote more than a decade ago that Greco-Roman romance offered simple entertainment and excitement spiced with religious stimulation and hope—in short, a cheap and easy means to expand one's life. This, he asserts, is the function of romance.[1] In other words, romance offers a superficial kind of excitement, founded on emotional but inarticulate religious experience. Does this generalization hold for Chrétien's romances? The question is of some importance, given common modern views of romance as distinguished from the novel, views which may insist on its variety, but hardly its serious meaning. Consider Webster's definitions: "A species of tale, orig. in meter in the Romance dialects, afterward diffused in verse or prose, such as the tales of the court of Arthur; hence, any fictitious and wonderful tale; now, esp., a sort of novel, whose interest lies esp. in adventure, surprising incident, etc.; also, the class of literature including fiction of this type" (1959 Collegiate edition). These evaluations are consistent with descriptions of narrative in Cicero and the pseudo-Ciceronian *Ad Herennium*. From the *Ad Herennium* we may cite the "narrative based on the persons" (as distinguished from narrative that is a mere exposition of facts or events), which "should present a lively style and diverse traits of character, such as austerity and gentleness, hope and fear, distrust and desire, hypocrisy and compassion, and the vicissitudes of life, such as reversal of fortune, unexpected disaster, sudden joy, and a happy outcome."[2] A definition hardly inconsistent with Webster's! This kind of narrative, which the *Ad Herennium* says should be confined to classroom exercises, passed into pupils' instruction in the medieval schools where authors such as Chrétien de Troyes learned to write and where the influence of treatises like the *Ad Herennium* was thorough and lasting.

Did Chrétien's contemporaries perceive his romances as their Roman predecessors and as modern critics and lexicographers have described romance? There is evidence that they did. Jehan Bodel, for one, in a well-known passage, describes the matter of Britain (*matière de Bretagne*) as pleasing but vain.[3] Others, mostly hagiographers, castigate Chrétien, if not by name, at least through the names he made famous—Cligés and Perceval, for instance, who appear in "romanz de vanité,"[4] which are full of lies, deter from good conduct, and darken the light of the soul. They incite to sin and idle thoughts. But the thirteenth century offers not only occasional attacks like these. The Lancelot-Grail cycle and Jean de Meun's *Roman de la Rose* undermine Chrétien's vision of Lancelot and Guenevere, of the Grail and the Round Table, more surely and effectively than Chrétien himself is frequently said to have done with the Tristan legend and the kind of love it illustrates. His critics seem to argue that Chrétien and many of his contemporaries—Marie de France and the anonymous *Partonopeu de Blois* are singled out for special mention[5]—are models of composition, wonderfully enthralling because of their marvelous adventures and exquisite prosody. And all the worse for them, as they entice their public to sin, to fascination with the vanities of this world.

How should we view these statements regarding the vanity of Chrétien's romances and those of his peers? What, indeed, does vanity have to do with romance?

After the mists of Celtic source study rose from Chrétien's romances and left them—*orfèvrerie*—glistering bright and fair in their French splendor, a tendency arose to elucidate systematically these writings, much as one might explicate a fable by La Fontaine, working toward the moral. La Fontaine's fables often do append a moral, but one which abuts the fable proper, as the various *chastoiements* given to Perceval seem to stand in stark contrast to the marvelous and entertaining tale of the grail which they gloss or, at least, to which they provide a frame of reference. Perceval hardly understands them. What relation may we perceive between the grail adventures and the rules delivered pell-mell to Perceval by his mother,

Gornemant de Goorz, and the hermit? Marvelous *matière* and chi-valric *san,* or *roman de vanité,* romance as Kerényi described it with its easy spirituality and pseudo moralizing? "Set aside Cligés and Perceval," advises the *Vies des pères,* "works which slay and undo the heart, and the romances on vain subjects" (vv. 34–35).

The anonymous *Evangile de l'enfance,* a thirteenth-century life of Christ, refers as well to the secular lies professed by Arthurian ro-mance: "romances . . . about the lies of this world and of the great Round Table."[6] The unknown author of the *Vies des pères* tells what such lies and vanity consist of: "Strength, beauty, chivalry, comfort and domination, and everything visible" (vv. 47–49). It does indeed sound like the *san* of a Chrétien romance, hardly unaccept-able to a Gornemant de Goorz. This puts the onus not on the unreal, the marvelous or dreamlike quality of romance, which even Chré-tien's critics admit is charming, but rather on the ideals it upholds—the this-worldly faith of the aristocracy—"which will all pass away" (*Vies,* v. 49), just as Ecclesiastes insists that all vanity will pass away and as Jean de Meun announces for the Garden of Deduit as well.

But what do romancers themselves say about Chrétien? Jean Renart, who wrote shortly after him, helps us define our problem even better while revealing some of the conflicts raised by romance in contemporary minds less rigorous than our hagiographers'—no one reading Jean Renart will, I think, see in him a Christian apolo-gist or moralist; his characters are even more openly sensual and pleasure-loving than Chrétien's. Jean Renart is supposed to have in-vented the so-called realistic romance to correct the excessively mar-velous, and hence incredible, image of the world drawn in Chrétien and other Arthurian romances. In the *Escoufle* prologue, Jean at-tacks those who abandon truth for lies which are inadmissible in the royal or aristocratic court.[7] And yet, as Michel Zink has recently demonstrated, the realism of Jean Renart is, in its own way, as in-credible as Chrétien's,[8] although perhaps more like Hollywood. How can one consider Jean Renart a critic of Arthurian romance when he constantly likens his protagonists to Gauvain, Arthur, Perceval, Tris-tan, Iseut, and Guenevere? When a lady of wondrous beauty arrives at the emperor's court in *Guillaume de Dole,* the astonished onlook-ers are reminded of similar appearances at Arthur's court.[9] And Jean Renart himself seems at least as preoccupied with the legend of Tristan and Iseut as Chrétien de Troyes was.[10] The truth of the realist Jean Renart is as much a blend of *chevalerie* and *clergie* as it is in Chrétien, and Renart evinces the same concern for the extraordinary and for love as a source of worth. His realism is an extraordinary realism and thus marvelous, his truth is discovered in the same world Chrétien represents in Broceliande—far removed from that drawn in vernacular hagiography.

This aristocratic truth and idealization is what the *Vies des pères,* the *Evangile de l'enfance,* and other works saw as a danger to the soul and an enticement to sin. Their condemnation is as adamant as that of other strictly clerical critics who recall the sinful attraction of Arthurian stories,[11] where *chevalerie* and *clergie* unite in *bele conjointure*—a civilization founded on a perversion of *clergie* and thus a lie which darkens the heart and soul. Chrétien's truth is secular, and as such necessarily vain in the eyes of those who are not of his persuasion and who turn their minds to heavenly things—such as the elect knights in the *Queste del saint graal.*

Chrétien does not, it would appear, believe his inventions to be idle and useless. The knight could demonstrate that all was not necessarily vain. About 1136-37—the same time that Geoffrey of Monmouth produced his *Historia regum Britanniae* and began the Arthurian vogue in Europe—Alberic de Pisançon wrote his *Alexandre* to show that, *pace* Solomon, all is not vanity, and he used Alexander the Great as evidence for his argument.[12] Shortly thereafter, Geoffrey Gaimar encouraged the inclusion of more aristocratic pastimes in chronicles,[13] and Wace made Gauvain uphold *uisdive* and other "idle" or peacetime activities rather than constant warfare.[14] The scribe of B. N. française 1450 even inserted Chrétien's first five romances in the *Brut* as an apt illustration of laudable Arthurian activities.

To return to Jehan Bodel: Does he perceive the same vanity in Chrétien—or at least in the *matière de Bretagne*—as the anonymous author of the *Vies des pères* seems to? Karl Uitti has noted that Bodel's *Saisnes* "claims to serve truth."[15] But its "truth" lies in the realm of chivalry, love, and jousts and tourneys (*Saisnes,* v. 26)— that is, in the very domain where Chrétien and Jean Renart, Geoffrey of Monmouth and Geoffrey Gaimar, found theirs. *Chevalerie* for Bodel embraces love and prowess as surely as it does for Chrétien in *Erec* and *Yvain.* Where, then, is the vanity? The vanity is in relying on an unsubstantial matter—one that is a figment of the imagination and is not drawn from the history of France and Rome. French matter in particular glorifies "Charles and his France," which in effect glorifies Philippe Auguste and his France, for the crown of France ought to be second to none: "The crown of France

ought to stand out so prominently that all other kings must be subservient to it" (*Saisnes,* vv. 13–14).[16]

But does Bodel really differ in this from Chrétien? *Chevalerie* and
clergie come from Greece and Rome to France, not to Arthur's or
anybody else's Britain except insofar as that Britain is subject to
France—and God grant that they remain in France, he exclaims in
the *Cligés* prologue.[17] Arthur, in Chrétien's scheme of things, has no
historic role, and his crown is the stuff of dreams. This is precisely
how critics of romance consider the genre—the stuff of empty
dreams.

But what was there in *chevalerie* and *clergie* that could disturb
Chrétien's contemporaries? Was not the *translatio* topic a venerable
theme in twelfth- and thirteenth-century France? Certainly civilization was conducive to peace, and Gauvain's own words in Wace suggest that peace had something to offer that war alone did not. *Chevalerie* and *clergie* were thus instrumental in the pacification of the
nobility, which heretofore, following the prevailing ethos of the
chansons de geste, gave prominence to *chevalerie* as the ability to fight
well for a given cause that was embodied in a principal figure:
Roland, Guillaume, Raoul, or Bernier. *Clergie* was left to monks
praying in dark monasteries. In twelfth-century romance, the knight
is still prominent, but the notion of *chevalerie* has taken on qualities
other than that of riding a horse and using a sword and lance with
deadly skill; the knights of the Round Table epitomize a courtly,
civilizing, even pacifying role. King, Church, and lower classes are
to be maintained by the knight, whose distinction extends into the
realms of courtesy, counsel, love, and even direct mystical communion with God. These new qualities assumed a place alongside other
values traditionally handed down according to the principle of *translatio.* That, in any case, is what Chrétien's romances proclaim explicitly and implicitly. The aristocracy now represents a tradition
parallel to but still largely distinct from that of Christianity. And romance was to represent that tradition after Chrétien de Troyes.
"Now I shall begin the tale that shall remain ever memorable, as
long as Christianity will endure—of this Chrétien has made boast!"[18]
Chrétien's boast links the fate of romance to that of Christianity.
But it also establishes a clear line of demarcation between the two
traditions. For Christianity does not rest on *chevalerie* and *clergie,*
let alone on their combination, but on revealed truth which chivalry
and learning may defend and uphold but which they may not tam-
per with. And here is where the novelty of Chrétien's formulation,

even its semirevolutionary character, becomes apparent behind the surface humor which plays on the names of author and religion. *Clergie* is being separated from its traditional service to the Church and is being made to serve the secular ends of *chevalerie,* a principle based on the idealization of the *chevalier*—the knight—not on the established Church or even the established secular order which would place royalty before vassals and knights errant. Recent historical scholarship has identified the social and psychological problems that arose in the twelfth century with the emerging prominence and the ennobling of *cavaliers.*[19] Jean Flori's studies in particular have demonstrated that Chrétien stood in the vanguard of those who raised *chevalerie* to an ideal and incorporated it into the careers of his knights, from Erec to Perceval.[20] In doing so, he also served the interests of those who were distinguishing sharply between the lower classes—the *vilains* and the *communes*—and the knights, who, united in a new nobility idealized in the Round Table, upheld their own values and customs together. Knights lingered at or went to Arthur's court rather than remaining at home to assume their birthrights.[21]

Arthur's court was founded on adventure and celebration, on quest and tournament. Quest established unique excellence, tournament demonstrated prowess, worth, even lovableness. Geoffrey of Monmouth knew that much, and he used tournaments as scenes to inspire love, just as love itself inspired prowess in tournaments.[22] Love, a *bele conjointure* with its marvels and morals, superseded prowess and became at the same time, at least in the romances, the focus of all activities and adventures. And this is true from Marie de France to Chrétien and from Jean Renart to Jehan Bodel.

What is love in romance?

First and foremost, it is sexual gratification for privileged people. Hue de Rotelande announces that his two heroes, Ipomedon and La Fiere, had been such faithful virgins that when, after trials and adventures, they finally are married and in bed together, "Il se entrefoutent tute jur"—they did it all day long.[23] Of course, they were very much in love. But is their comportment in any way different from that of Lancelot and Guenevere or of Erec and Enide before and after their quest? "The hunted stag panting with thirst does not desire the fountain so much, nor the sparrowhawk come to the call so willingly when he hungers, than they hastened until finally being locked in embrace. That night they made up for everything in proportion to the length of the delay" (*Erec,* vv. 2027–34; cf. vv. 5200–11). Isn't Chrétien describing the same love as Hue de Rotelande? As Jean de Meun has Reason remind us, if we call *coilles reliques* and *reliques coilles* . . . (*Rose,* vv. 7076–85).

This is the love Chrétien builds *chevalerie* and *clergie* on and of which, in *Yvain,* he laments the decline before retreating into British or Breton castles and forests and Round Table romances to escape contemporary villains and villainy. His courtly love springs from the very fount which, as Montaigne puts it, quickens "an insatiable thirst of enjoying a greedily desired object." How many romances represent it otherwise? This state of affairs brings us back to love as healthy sex and, indeed, to Kerényi's notion of simple narrative designed to please easily and to satisfy a certain public. It certainly helps explain Chrétien's popularity and the critics' carping at his *romans de vanité.* In fact, this is the import of all thirteenth-century criticism of romance, not only in passages like those cited but also in works like the *Queste,* Jean de Meun's *Rose,* or even in later attempts to make love platonic, such as Machaut's or Christine de Pizan's. These authors fault the idealization of an aristocracy founded on a representation of love which is little more than straightforward sex first long desired and then deliberately, even exhaustingly, enjoyed.

But Chrétien himself suggests a corrective which many scholars have taken seriously. Gauvain, the spokesman for *uisdive* in the *Brut,* favors tournaments as an alternative to love in *Yvain*—or, at least, he argues for its moderating influence on uxoriousness. "Let's you and I go tourneying, so that no one may call you jealous. You should not spend your time day dreaming, but rather frequent tournaments, learn to do battle and to joust vigorously, whatever may be the cost to you!"[24] But throughout the twelfth century and, notably, at the Lateran Council of 1179 (near the time *Yvain* was written), tournaments were condemned and banned.[25] Those slain in tournaments were denied burial in holy ground, and participants were refused absolution if they had not made restitution for what they had gained. Yet, if this were so, what knight would ever be saved? asked William Marshall on his deathbed in 1229.[26] Certainly neither Yvain nor Gauvain, for whom pride and rapine, as the Church called the vices of tourneying, were real goals. For if neither is in need of ransom or plunder as such (but remember Gauvain's veiled warning, "Whatever may be the cost to you!"), they do seek renown, or *pris* (vv. 2501, 2685). And Yvain is a *larron* in Laudine's eyes for making off with her heart (vv. 2726–47). In the realm of love, this reduces Yvain to the level of the robber barons Erec defeated in his quest. Yvain in fact goes mad, alone in the woods where he lives like an animal—or a robber baron—by rapine! Is it any wonder that Erec never participates in a tournament after his marriage? There is a fundamental difference between his view and that of his men, just as there will be between Yvain and Gauvain by the end of the *Chevalier au lion*—which, seemingly paradoxically, brings both *Erec* and *Yvain* closer together in the final resolution of their respective romances: each returns to love and his wife.

This, then, is the vanity of romance: the representation of ideals and activities of which all would readily perceive the vanity, the nefarious darkening of the soul that follows from the vain goings-on of this world, the *trufles* and *fanfelues* of the Garden of Deduit excoriated by Genius in the *Roman de la Rose,* a garden where all is subject to corruption and dissolution (*Rose,* vv. 20319–38). Jean Renart realistically evokes the average tourneyor whose lot is not a very happy one: "Worthy men seek renown with great travail, going from country to country. But what do you expect? It can't be otherwise."[27] This view would certainly corroborate Robertson's contention that Chrétien sought, through *conjointure,* to uncover the folly and vanity of human pursuits alien to those traditionally established by the Church.[28] The Church condemned the practice of tournaments, and Chrétien showed their effects to be as foolish as those of courtly love. Robertson also argues that *Cligés* in particular describes the vain pursuit of earthly fame,[29] and any discerning reader or hearer would have understood as much. He indeed wrote *romans de vanité*—romances about vanity.

This promising line of argument will not stand against the judgment made of Chrétien by medieval critics. By the expression *roman de vanité,* the *Vies des pères* meant romance that extols vanities of no redeeming moral value. *Cligés* is a *roman de vanité* because it corrupts the heart, and truth is not to be found in it. The only *Cligés* such an accusation could fit in the twelfth and thirteenth centuries was Chrétien's.[30] We are brought back to a distinction between the traditional clerical view and the chivalric view of vanity. We have already observed that even as early as the time of Geoffrey of Monmouth's *Historia regum Britanniae,* which first related performance in tournaments to love, Alberic de Pisançon objected to the traditional ecclesiastical view of Alexander's vanity, expressing rather the wish that antiquity—in the event, the life of Alexander—might teach us that not all is vanity. His proud desire evinces the same confidence Chrétien does in the *Erec* prologue. That confidence is both a source of hope in the permanence of what his romances profess and a foreshadowing of the deception following on the discovery of the abyss separating ideal and reality. We first encounter such a separation in *Yvain* in the opening discussion of the difference between the Arthurian past, nonexistent in the *Cligés* prologue, and the French and European present, where *courtoisie,* that product of *chevalerie* and *clergie,* has given way to villainy. Romance became, toward the end of Chrétien's career, an escape into castles in Brittany and the marvels of Broceliande before it surrendered to the downgrading of Arthur in the *Perceval*.[31] Perceval himself, having learned of his failure at the Grail Castle, goes off for five years and more of adventures which are not worthy of being related[32] and in which—like Chrétien heretofore?—he forgets God and remembers only Arthur, to whom he dispatches the fifty knights he defeats during his wanderings.[33] Perceval's quest opens to the curious blend of love and simple mysticism found not only in the *Perceval* continuations but also in the Gauvain branch of the *Conte du graal* itself. The *conjointure* seems to unravel as sensual love and mystic vision pop up haphazardly, in no apparent contradiction—like crusading ideals and adulterous love in Bodel's *Saisnes*.[34]

If a coherent significance can be adduced from such romance, we will have discovered what Chrétien's romances have to offer, and the discovery can be applied to and attested by those that follow him. And given the demonstrable prominence of Chrétien's *oeuvre* in the twelfth and early thirteenth centuries and in modern scholarship, we may hope to be able to say something about romance as Chrétien invented it and passed it on to those who imitated as well as criticized his achievement.

Chrétien's romances have three levels of significance, all recognized by the author himself, by medieval commentators, and by modern critics: the marvelous, the narrative, and the topical. The arrangement of marvelous adventures into a coherent narrative is the very achievement of *conjointure*. But Chrétien himself emphasizes as much, if not more so, the significance of his narrative—what meaning it may have for his contemporaries, what profit the latter may derive from what he represents in the romances. This is explicit in the ears and heart topic invoked by Calogrenant at the outset of his report, a topic rehearsed by many others after Chrétien for their own chivalric romances.[35]

What are we to make of such protestations of meaning? Do they refer to the superficial ersatz-learning described by Kerényi in Greco-Roman romance? Chrétien's marvels do indeed offer an exciting, absorbing display of fascinating and, if not always supernatural, at least extraordinary images: from the Grail and the love of Lancelot and Guenevere through the quest in pursuit of various goals to the varied and variegated adventures that startle us and the protagonists on those quests—all of which Chrétien designates as in some way marvelous. These marvelous adventures are just as remarkable for Chrétien's apparent unwillingness to resolve them entirely into discrete, thoroughly explicable experiences. The walls of Mabonagrain's garden, the flaming lance in the *Charrette,* the rationale of the magic fountain in Broceliande—even Lancelot and Guenevere's night in Gorre—are wonders so great that, as Chrétien puts it for the last adventure, they should not be related.[36] Elsewhere, he never even bothers to suggest that an explanation would be appropriate. Wonders transpire and, in the presence of a knight, become adventures whose significance depends on the knight, not on the marvel. The tendency, already noted by others, of prose romance to explain the adventures thoroughly, causally, psychologically, morally, or mystically, or to leave open the possibility of explanation, or to explain why, regarding the mysteries of the Grail, an explanation in human language is impossible—this tendency is nowhere apparent in Chrétien. Perhaps more than any other romancer of his time, he achieved a beautiful balance between mystery and significance, in *conjointures* that raise partiality to an artistic ideal, such that *Erec,* for example, in contrast to its original *conte d'aventure,* may be said to be neither *depecié* nor *corrompu* (*Erec,* vv. 19–22)—that is, a text neither dismembered nor corrupt in the technical sense.[37] It is a *bele,* a *plaisante conjointure,* as Jehan Bodel seems to imply in his reference to the *matière de Bretagne.* And, no doubt like other Arthurian stories, it was profoundly moving to those who wept over it and yet felt in their heart of hearts, on reflection, that their souls were threatened by such beauty.

There is a critical problem here that can be usefully illustrated by comparison with Alain de Lille's criticism of Gautier de Châtillon and Joseph of Exeter (or, in any case, the two authors referred to under the names Ennius and Maevius, whom most scholars identify with these two medieval poets). Alain faults their meaningless baubles—they contain "mirlifiques" and "oberliques," but no "bagues plus autentiques," to use Charles d'Orléans's language. "The painting's face seemed distracted," Alain exclaims, "and to be begging a better form, but neither the glitter of gems, day-bright in splendour, nor the gleam of silver nor gold with its more attractive sheen can serve as a defense for the full-blown crime represented in the painting or keep it from growing dull and pale amidst its gold."[38] This criticism, which likens such works—paintings or epic poems—to dreams and madness, rings with the language of the hagiographers who fault Arthurian romance. The splendid cup given Alexandre in *Cligés* (vv. 1521–28), which for many epitomizes Chrétien's art, grows pale for lack of substance. What these authors lack is what makes a work substantial. We can only speculate on what that is in any given instance; in any case, it is less important for my purposes than the obvious fact that the splendid inventions of both the epic poets and Chrétien appear as products of a consummate art but offer nothing which Alain and the hagiographers considered of redeeming moral value.

The criticism directed at Chrétien and romance in general stems, with the sole exception of Jehan Bodel, from those who write hagiography or works of moral didacticism or from those who feel that romance incites to sin or to a misconception of what is important in the world and for the soul. They reflect, then, that discrepancy between the ecclesiastical and aristocratic orders which Georges Duby has shown to find its first expression in Benoît de Sainte-Maure's *Chronique des ducs de Normandie,*[39] a difference in view which divided Henry II and Thomas à Becket during the very time Chrétien was writing and which Guernes de Pont-Saint-Maxence enunciates so remarkably in his life of Thomas. Duby notes a singular disinterest in ecclesiastical and religious concerns in aristocratic literature, including Andreas Capellanus;[40] one might add the saintly hermits of certain romances who retain many aristocratic features and predilections, even in some of the most austere circumstances.[41] This disinterest has often been remarked on in twelfth-century romance and in Chrétien himself, with the possible exception of the *Conte du graal.* We perceive here two conflicting hierarchies which are not assimilable into a single order.

The one exception among the critics, Jehan Bodel, distinguishes in the *Saisnes* prologue not on the basis of the moral and romance ideals of chivalry, love, and sport but on political, or, more properly, dynastic preeminence: the crown of France comes before all others, even Arthur's. Such "self-evident" assertions are expressed on the topical level of significance in the *Saisnes,*[42] the validity or credibility of which may require argument for those who would disagree—for example, British kings—but not for those who are like-minded and go to romance for the pleasure of seeing what they believe illustrated in splendid narrative and description. In the *Saisnes,* what is French is first and foremost, whether in the person of Charlemagne or of Philippe-Auguste; what is British may be pleasant to read, but the claims of an Arthur and, presumably, a John Lackland are empty, vain, without substance.

Romance insists on the right kind of audience from its beginnings. As early as the *Roman de Thèbes,* only knights and clerics were admitted to it;[43] Chrétien—like Jehan Bodel and the twelfth-century vernacular historians—excludes the ignoble, rejecting as unworthy the tales of jongleurs, even when they speak of the nobility and whatever the historical kernel may be to what they relate: their art and mind are unworthy of serious consideration. Chrétien sees *chevalerie* and *clergie* united in a common, complementary effort in the appropriation and establishment of an aristocratic civilization. The *sans* of Marie de Champagne descries significance, or *san,* in the *matière* she gives to Chrétien so that he may use his own *sans* to fashion the *Chevalier de la charrette.* In the initial *Yvain* digression, the narrator seeks in vain those of a mind to love well and finally retreats to the world of romance to find them. In that dreamlike world, Calogrenant tells us—anticipating many romancers—to lend both ears and heart in order to understand his tale of adventure. All insist on a distinct *sans,* which many descriptions of romance knights and ladies present as an aristocratic quality, superior to the *engin* and the *diversité* of the villainous. Those possessed of such *sans* may hear, understand, and believe—here too one believes in order to understand, that is, to understand love and knighthood. Chrétien's romances, like Bodel's *Saisnes,* were written for true believers, especially those in the aristocracy represented by knights and clerics who saw arms and love as their proper activities, as sources of worth, and as means to realize their inborn aristocratic potentiality. Take away love and prowess based on chivalry and one begins to perceive the doubts of a Dinadan, who sought *tout le sens du monde* and failed to find, to invent it.[44] Romance needs easy truths, no matter how profoundly the marvelous narrative may present them; note that even Kerényi is not arguing that romance lacks profundity for all its ease of comprehension; the Jungian bent to his analysis in treating specific romances shows that he took such writing very seriously. He perceives that romance meets a need that is felt by those who want confirmation of their world as they believe and want it to exist. For those who do not see the world the way romance represents it, romance narrative becomes vanity, a farce or a sin. And the very medium of romance can be turned to demonstrate its vanity, as occurred in the thirteenth-century French prose adaptations of Chrétien. Just as pagan romance could be moving even for Christians, and therefore they restored it to respectability by Christianizing the *matière,* so Chrétien underwent a similar metamorphosis in the Vulgate prose cycle. Vanity could indeed seem to be that superficial quality apparent in the works of the ancients. Authorial *sans,* to use Marie de France's argument, could penetrate that surface to uncover the truth that gave meaning to the marvels.[45] Nonetheless, here as elsewhere, the truth is in the eye of the beholder. Remove that truth and only the marvel remains, as in science fiction. Is that residuum vanity?

For Chrétien's knights it was.

When Calogrenant asked the Giant Herdsman whether he knew of any marvels or adventures, the latter replied that he didn't know anything about adventures as such, but that he could direct the knight to a good marvel (*Yvain,* vv. 364–73). Calogrenant proceeded to seek out that marvelous adventure—being a knight, not a villein, he could recognize the link between the two because knights have adventures, and villeins do not. But Calogrenant's adventure alone at the Magic Fountain does not make that link apparent to his Arthurian or his French audiences. For Calogrenant fails to achieve the adventure, and it and its awful defender remain mysterious and threatening to knights and what they seek to achieve. If Calogrenant saw more in Broceliande than Wace did, what he saw did not for all that make any sense. It became meaningful only through Yvain's adventure, which was achieved as the realization of a love that establishes Arthurian civilization in the realm of antichivalric forces. That civilization, with its intense interest in love and arms, would have been perfectly credible and desirable to a twelfth-century knight, just as Charlemagne's superiority over Arthur would have been self-evident in the court of Philippe-Auguste. The distancing this imposes on a modern audience, which may not find either truth to be particularly self-evident, is a real problem in the appreciation of romance today—a body of works written without concern for genre as such, but with obvious medieval values no longer credible. *Genus* as a term did, of course, exist; but this kind of genre was a word for class, and class was integral to a social order about which, as Duby has shown, there could be deep differences of opinion and of faith. The problematic vanity of romance is an issue of historical criticism, an idiosyncratic feature of romance which makes it a distinct class of writings. For to exclude the *san* of medieval romance as no longer significant in critical discussion is to reduce Chrétien's romances to the marvelous *contes d'aventure* he sought to lift them out of and thus to effect an amputation no less grave than that effected by the moralizations of Ovid on their Latin text. We are then left with either the ignorant incomprehension shown by the Giant Herdsman or the "rigorism" Erich Köhler identified in Chrétien's critics. In the last analysis, as a hypothesis for discussion of Chrétien's romances, we must postulate that only knights and clerics can understand them.

Yet perhaps here we have as well the beginning of a resolution to the historical problem of the vanity of romance. Early romance identified itself in terms of a new social order—the union of *chevalerie* and *clergie* in the marvelous adventure. This is still true in the romances that criticize Chrétien by reinterpreting *chevalerie* and *clergie* in the light of a different hierarchy of values. Insofar as we can still take the "implied author" to be the "historical author," we can perceive romance as the endless attempt to achieve a given society's vision of order and truth, a truth which, as Chrétien's own romances make explicit, is ultimately a *misterium*—a union of mystery and significance which confounds the very words that would express it. His romances teach that, to escape vanity, we must believe in what they profess. But to know what that is, we must go beyond the ears to the heart of the matter, to that realm where Lancelot and Guenevere meet in the night and remain unseen by Kay, where the names of God may be heard but not pronounced, where knights pass through unseen walls to confront voluptuous women and violent headhunters, or where magic fountains rain down destruction—a realm the author points to through marvels and adventures; the realm of love and tournaments in which *chevalerie* and *clergie* unite to promote *courtoisie* and *bonté*. The glory and the vanity of Chrétien's romances lie in such marvelous narrative where recognizable figures perform in an admirable way.

Notes

[1] Karl Kerényi, *Der antike Roman: Einführung und Textauswahl* (Darmstadt: Wissenschaftliche Buchgesellschaft, 1971) 65.

[2] *Ad Herennium,* ed. Harry Caplan (Cambridge: Harvard UP; London: Heinemann, 1968) 23, 25; cf. 24–25, note e. Cicero, *De inventione,* ed. Eduard Stroebel (Leipzig: Teubner, 1915), 1.19.27.

[3] Jehan Bodel, *Saxenlied,* ed. F. Menzel and E. Stengel, Ausgaben und

Abhandlungen aus dem Gebiete der romanischen Philologie 99–100 (Marburg: Elwert, 1906–09), v. 9.

[4] *Vies des pères,* ed. Paul Meyer, *Histoire littéraire de la France* 33 (1906): 293 (v. 35). For a good general discussion of this problem, see Rüdiger Schnell, "Grenzen literarischer Freiheit im Mittelalter: 1. Höfischer Roman und Minnerede," *Archiv für das Studium der neueren Sprachen und Literaturen* 218 (1981): 241–70.

[5] Denis Piramus, *La Vie de saint Edmund le rei, ed.* Hilding Kjellman, Göteborgs kungl. Vetenskaps-och Vitterhets-samhälles Handlingar, fol. 5, ser. A, vol. 4.3 (Göteborg: Elander, 1935), v. 25–56.

[6] Cited from Ulrich Mölk, *Französische Literarästhetik des 12. und 13. Jahrhunderts,* Sammlung romanischer Übungstexte 54 (Tübingen: Niemeyer, 1969), sec. 76, vv. 15–16. Also see Paul Meyer, "Légendes hagiographiques en français," *Histoire littéraire de la France* 33 (1906): 331, *Piramus,* vv. 1–24, 59–70.

[7] *Escoufle,* ed. Franklin Sweetser, *Textes littéraires français* (Geneva: Droz, 1974), vv. 10–25.

[8] Michel Zink, *Roman rose et rose rouge: Le Roman de la Rose ou de Guillaume de Dole de Jean Renart* (Paris: Nizet, 1979) 17–44. Cf. Michel Zink, "Une Mutation de la conscience littéraire: le langage romanesque à travers des exemples français du XIIe siècle," *Cahiers de civilisation médiévale* 24 (1981): 23–26.

[9] Jean Renart, *Le Roman de la Rose ou de Guillaume de Dole,* ed. Félix Lecoy, CFMA (Paris: Champion, 1965–70), v. 4681. Cf. Zink, *Roman* 32.

[10] See Daniel Poirion, "Fonction de l'imaginaire dans l'*Eracle,*" *Mélanges de langue et de littérature françaises du Moyen Age et de la Renaissance offerts à Charles Foulton* (Rennes: Institut Français de l'Université de Haute-Bretagne, 1980) 1: 287–93.

[11] Edmond Faral, *Les Jongleurs en France au moyen âge* (Paris: Champion, 1910) 171–76, 287 (l. 77). Cf. Michel Zink, *La Prédication en langue romane avant 1300,* Nouvelle Bibliothèque du moyen âge 4 (Paris: Champion, 1976) 9, 365–88.

[12] Alfred Foulet, ed. *The Medieval French "Roman d'Alexandre,"* Elliott Monographs 38 (1949; New York: Kraus, 1965) 37–38 (vv. 1–26).

[13] Geoffrey Gaimar, *L'Estoire des Engleis,* ed. Alexander Bell, Anglo-Norman Texts 14–16 (Oxford: Blackwell, 1960), vv. 6495–512. See Maria Luisa Meneghetti, " 'L'Estoire des Engleis' di Geffrei Gaimar fra cronaca genealogica e romanzo cortese," *Medioevo romanzo* 2 (1975): 232–46.

[14] Wace, *Le Roman de Brut,* ed. Ivor Arnold, SATF, 2 vols. (Paris: SATF, 1938–40), vv. 10765–72.

[15] Karl D. Uitti, *Story, Myth, and Celebration in Old French Narrative Poetry, 1050–1200* (Princeton: Princeton UP, 1973) 242.

[16] Also see Kelly, "Rhetoric in French Literature: Topical Invention in Medieval French Literature," *Medieval Eloquence: Studies in the Theory and Practice of Medieval Rhetoric,* ed. James J. Murphy (Berkeley: U of California P, 1978) 237–39.

[17] Chrétien de Troyes, *Cligés,* ed. Alexandre Micha, CFMA (Paris: Champion, 1957), vv. 25–42.

[18] Chrétien de Troyes, *Erec et Enide,* ed. Mario Roques, CFMA (Paris: Champion, 1966), vv. 23–26.

[19] Erich Köhler, *Ideal und Wirklichkeit in der höfischen Epik: Studien zur Form der frühen Artus- und Graldichtung,* 2nd ed., Beihefte zur Zeitschrift für romanische Philologie 97 (Tübingen: Niemeyer, 1970); Erich Köhler, "Il Sistema sociologico del romanzo francese medievale," *Medioevo romanzo* 3 (1976): 321–44; and Erich Köhler, "Literatursoziologische Perspektiven," *Le Roman jusqu'à la fin du XIIIᵉ siècle, Grundriss der romanischen Literaturen des Mittelalters* 4.1 (Heidelberg: Winter, 1978) 82–103.

[20] See especially Jean Flori, "Pour une histoire de la chevalerie: l'adoubement dans les romans de Chrétien de Troyes," *Romania* 100 (1979): 21–53. See as well Georges Duby, *Les Trois Ordres ou l'imaginaire du féodalisme* (Paris: Gallimard, 1978) 352–70.

[21] Cf. Köhler, *Ideal* 5–36, and Marie-Luce Chênerie, *"Ces curieux chevaliers tournoyeurs* . . . des fablaiux aux romans," *Romania* 97 (1976): 327–68.

[22] Geoffrey of Monmouth, *Historia regum Brittaniae,* ed. Edmond Faral, *La Légende arthurienne: études et documents,* 3 vols. (Paris: Champion, 1929) 3: 246. But the love was not always courtly! See Chênerie 347–50.

[23] Hue de Rotelande, *Ipomedon,* ed. A. J. Holden, Bibliothèque française et romane 17 (Paris: Klincksieck, 1979), v. 10516.

[24] Chrétien de Troyes, *Le Chevalier au lion* (*Yvain*), ed. Mario Roques, CFMA (Paris: Champion, 1971), vv. 2503–08.

[25] See in general Sidney Painter, *French Chivalry: Chivalric Ideas and Practices in Mediaeval France* (Ithaca: Cornell UP, 1940) 155–56; Chênerie 330–31, 347. One may compare this material with the aristocratic attitudes toward marriage and sexual freedom indicated at both ends of the social spectrum by Georges Duby, *Medieval Marriage: Two Models from Twelfth-Century France,* trans. Elborg Forster, Johns Hopkins Symposia in Comparative History 11 (Baltimore: Johns Hopkins UP, 1978), and Emmanuel Le Roy Ladurie, *Montaillou, village occitan de 1294 à 1324* (Paris: Gallimard, 1975) 230–33. Although the evidence is rare and scattered, it is useful in our present context.

[26] Painter 89–90; Chênerie 331.

[27] Jean Renart, *Le Roman de la Rose ou de Guillaume de Dole,* ed. Félix Lecoy, CFMA (Paris: Champion, 1962), vv. 2938–40. Cf. Zink, *Roman* 18–22; Chênerie 341–47.

[28] D. W. Robertson, Jr., "Some Medieval Literary Terminology, with Special Reference to Chrétien de Troyes," *Studies in Philology* 48 (1951): 669–92; and D. W. Robertson, Jr., *A Preface to Chaucer: Studies in Medieval Perspectives* (Princeton: Princeton UP, 1962).

[29] D. W. Robertson, Jr., "The Idea of Fame in Chrétien's *Cligés,*" *Studies in Philology* 69 (1972): 414–33.

[30] The *Cligés* exemplum in the *Marques de Rome* branch of the *Sept Sages de Rome* prose cycle stigmatizes the sin of Cligés and Fénice; the author of the *Vies* probably could not have read the Middle High German adaptation of Chrétien's romance, which, as the surviving fragment indicates, is very close to the original; see Albert Bachmann, "Bruchstücke eines mhd. Cliges," *Zeitschrift für deutsches Alterthum und deutsche Litteratur* 32, n.s. 20 (1888): 123–28.

[31] See Rupert T. Pickens, *The Welsh Knight: Paradoxicality in Chrétien's "Conte del Graal,"* French Forum Monographs 6 (Lexington, Ky.: French Forum, 1977). For the representation of Arthur after Chrétien, see Beate Schmolke-Hasselmann, *Der arthurische Versroman von Chrestien bis Froissart: zur Geschichte einer Gattung,* Beihefte zur Zeitschrift für romanische Philologie 177 (Tübingen: Niemeyer, 1980).

[32] Chrétien de Troyes, *Le Conte du graal (Perceval)*, ed. Félix Lecoy, 2 vols., CFMA (Paris: Champion, 1973–75), vv. 6016–29.

[33] *Conte du graal,* v. 6025. Perceval's quest for adventure is therefore not unlike Calogrenant's: the vain quest of adventures and marvels that will please and satisfy Arthur's court. Most manuscripts report sixty victories; see Alfons Hilka, ed., *Der Perceval-roman* (Halle: Niemeyer, 1932), v. 6233, and variants.

[34] See Charles Foulon, *L'Oeuvre de Jehan Bodel,* Travaux de la Faculté des Lettres et Sciences Humaines de Rennes, ser. 1.2 (Paris: PUF, 1958), esp. 454–57, 484–88, 511–13, 539–46, 557–83.

[35] See Ruth H. Cline, "Heart and Eyes," *Romance Philology* 25 (1971–72): 263–97; Gerald J. Brault, "Chrétien de Troyes' *Lancelot:* The Eye and the Heart," *Bulletin bibliographique de la Société Internationale Arthurienne* 24 (1972): 142–53.

[36] Chrétien de Troyes, *Le Chevalier de la charrete,* ed. Mario Roques, CFMA (Paris: Champion, 1970), vv. 4674–84.

[37] On partiality, see Sandra N. Ihle, *Malory's Grail Quest: Invention and Adaptation in Medieval Prose Romance* (Madison: U of Wisconsin P, 1982) 8–26.

[38] Alain de Lille, *Anticlaudianus,* trans. James J. Sheridan (Toronto: Pontifical Institute of Mediaeval Studies, 1973) 51.

[39] Duby, *Trois Ordres* 327–37.

[40] Duby, *Trois Ordres* 404–13.

[41] See Angus J. Kennedy's important articles "The Hermit's Role in French Arthurian Romance (c. 1170–1530)," *Romania* 95 (1974): 54–83, and "The Portrayal of the Hermit Saint in French Arthurian Romance: The Remoulding of a Stock-Character," *An Arthurian Tapestry: Essays in Memory of Lewis Thorpe,* ed. Kenneth Varty (Glasgow: French Department, U of Glasgow, 1981) 69–82.

[42] Kelly, "Rhetoric" 237–39.

[43] *Roman de Thèbes,* ed. Guy Raynaud de Lage, 2 vols., CFMA (Paris: Champion, 1968–71), vv. 13–20. See Erich Köhler, "Zur Selbstauffassung des höfischen Dichters," *Trobadorlyrik und höfischer Roman: Aufsätze zur französischen und provenzalischen Literatur des Mittelalters,* Neue Beiträge zur Literaturwissenschaft 15 (Berlin: Rütten & Loening, 1962) 9–10.

[44] Eugène Vinaver, *A la recherche d'une poétique médiévale* (Paris: Nizet, 1970) 163–77.

[45] Alfred Foulet and K. D. Uitti, "The Prologue to the *Lais* of Marie de France: A Reconsideration," *Romance Philology* 35 (1981–82): 242–49.

LA CHEVALERIE CELESTIEL
Spiritual Transformations of Secular Romance in *La Queste del Saint Graal*

Nancy Freeman-Regalado

On the eve of Pentecost when the companions of the Round Table were all assembled at Camelot, at the hour of none when the office was sung and the tables were being set up, a maiden of great beauty came riding into the hall.[1]

These lines could open any sequence in Arthurian romance, but they are those of the Vulgate version of *La Queste del Saint Graal* (c. 1225–30), which has been read far more often as a doctrinal treatise or as a religious work than as a romance. The generic elements of Arthurian romance in the *Queste*—motifs, characters, plot structure—have been little studied, since the Arthurian elements have often been dismissed as an ill-fitting romance garb or seen as an allegorical husk to be discarded after interpretation.[2] But as focus on the *Queste* has begun to shift to this work's place in the great thirteenth-century romance cycles and to the chivalric ethos it is now judged to glorify,[3] full understanding of the *Queste* requires that we reclaim it as romance, that we establish its Arthurian paternity. We must study the function of the Arthurian elements in the *Queste* to understand the play between the generic motifs and discursive modes of romance and those of religious or didactic texts and the relationship within the *Queste* between the narrative events of Arthurian romance and the religious thematic commentary.[4] Such inquiry will finally lead us to assess the place of the spiritual transformation of Arthurian motifs within the romance genre itself and to inquire into the meaning of the spiritual elements in the *Queste.*

The fictional account of authorship in the *Queste*'s epilogue gives us clues to locate it within thirteenth-century literary practice and confirms that the text is indeed to be read in terms of both romance and religion:

> When they had dined King Arthur summoned his clerks who were keeping a record of all the adventures undergone by the knights of his household. When Bors had related to them the adventures of the Holy Grail as witnessed by himself, they were written down and the record kept in the library at Salisbury, whence Master Walter Map extracted them in order to make his book of the Holy Grail for love of his lord King Henry, who had the story translated from Latin into French. And with that the tale falls silent and has no more to say about the Adventures of the Holy Grail. (Matarasso, *Quest* 284; Pauphilet, *Queste* 279)

The epilogue draws together the two worlds of the *Queste* as Bohort returns from the spiritual palace of Sarras to tell his tale to Arthur at Camelot. It joins, too, in the fictional attribution of the *Queste* to Walter Map as author and King Henry as patron, the worlds of its author and its readers. These are clerks and knights; a clerical author offers his book to a courtly patron.[5] But the epilogue unites also the two discursive modes of the *Queste:* the terms of the Arthurian fiction whose adventures are a tale to be told and those of a learned tradition whose signs are those of the written book, the library and Latin. Where the Arthurian fiction is represented throughout the *Queste* as a spoken tale, *li contes dist* ("the story relates"), the learned and religious commentaries in the discursive modes of the learned tradition are represented throughout as truth and introduced by formulas such as *il est voirs que* ("It is true that . . .").

Neither set of terms in the epilogue can be dismissed, and neither can be taken alone. Together they place the *Queste* squarely within the thirteenth-century taste for works combining Latin and vernacular, religious, and secular narrative motifs and thematic commentary. Works like the *Queste* that articulate a thematic significance quite unlike their narrative matter are as much a part of what Zumthor has defined as the thirteenth-century poetics of contrast[6] as are the romances with lyric insertions, the *jeux-partis,* the *descorts,* the pastourelles and debate poems opposing knights and shepherdesses, clerics and knights, the secular or erotic parodies of Latin prayers and moralized bestiaries, and even the *fatrasie* and the *sotte chanson* where the absurd and the obscene disrupt the motifs of the courtly *chanson*. Such effects of contrast signal a high degree of awareness of generic motifs and discursive patterns; they suggest also that the thirteenth-century authors saw typical generic patterns as highly porous structures. The presiding genius of recombination in thirteenth-century literature might well be the magical figure from *Huon de Bordeaux* (c. 1220), Auberon, son of Julius Caesar and Morgan le Fay. In it we find an art of polyphony which, as in the motet, creates expressive works built on formal combinations and contrasts of elements defined both generically and discursively. These combinations can best be perceived, however, only if we keep the whole of a text like the *Queste* before our eyes. In the form and art of these works of textual polyphony, no voice must be stilled or go unheard.

The *Queste* constantly draws upon the fictional material of Arthurian romance, upon the experience of its readers, to establish its own unique structure and significance. The *Queste* recalls the romances we know by representing their motifs and values as both recollected and transformed. It thus uses, reinforces, and undermines the reader's expectation of what will be found in a story that begins "On the eve of Pentecost," when yet another damsel arrives to say that all has changed in the story, both to invoke and deny the values of chivalric adventure, recalled not as fiction but as reputation. There has been "change" (*muemenz*) in Lancelot's name:

> "Alas, Lancelot, this day has seen a sad change in your circumstance."
> "I pray you, tell me how."
> "In faith," she said, "you shall hear it in front of the whole court. Yesterday morning you were the best knight in the world; those who spoke of you as Lancelot, the paragon of chivalry, said but the truth, for so you were. But were anyone to call you that now, he would be a liar, for there is a better than you, as is clearly proved by this sword which you dared not set your hand to. *This is the change in your name and title* which I have brought to your mind lest you continue to think yourself the foremost of your peers." (Matarasso, *Quest* 41–42; Pauphilet, *Queste* 12–13)

The damsel's words at first seem to us, as to Arthur and the queen, to be a misunderstanding, a misinterpretation to be corrected by the story to come: How could Lancelot not be the best knight in the world? It is, of course, an established pattern in Arthurian romance that Lancelot, the knight in the infamous cart, be both humiliated

and admired. But to the end, the *Queste* will cast upon Lancelot the
heaviest burden of carrying both recollection of the typical motifs
and values of the Arthurian romance and the weight of the new
significance they bear in the *Queste*. Lancelot's confessions, his re-
grets, remind the reader of what he once knew, of the romances he
has read and of what he must now understand. Lancelot weeps "as
bitterly as if he had seen the object of his dearest love lying dead before him" (Matarasso, *Quest* 145). The object of his grief, *la riens el
monde que il plus amast* (Pauphilet, *Queste* 128), is expressed in
terms that had always, in earlier romances, described Guenevere. But
here we do not know if Lancelot weeps for her or for his innocence,
for what he must give up or for what he has already lost.

If we seem to perceive the changes the *Queste* makes in the familiar generic structures of Arthurian romance as changes in "meaning," it is because the shifts in narrative motifs are explicitly portrayed as depending on shifts in moral evaluation and because we
are accustomed in some sense to equating such moral evaluation with
the "meaning" of a work. The transformations themselves are further thematized by their presentation of characters who lack moral
understanding and who are puzzled by the events of the story in
which they appear. Gauvain, for example, is painted as a "heinous
sinner" (Matarasso, *Quest* 174; Pauphilet, *Queste* 161) and is baffled
because nothing at all happens on his Grail quest: "Sir Gawain pursued his wanderings from Whitsun to St. Magdalene's day without
coming across an adventure that merited recounting; he found it
most surprising, having expected the Quest of the Holy Grail to fur-
nish a prompter crop of strange and arduous adventures than any
other emprise" (Matarasso, *Quest* 162; Pauphilet, *Queste* 247).
When an adventure does finally come, it is a mistake in terms of the
old Arthurian story, a "misadventure" (Matarasso, *Quest* 268; Pauphilet, *Queste* 154), for Gauvain inadvertently kills Yvain, his dear
companion of the Round Table. The devil himself recalls the typical
motifs of Arthurian romance when he poses as just the sort of disinherited damsel Perceval and his fellow knights are sworn to help
(Matarasso, *Quest* 127; Pauphilet, *Queste* 108). When Lancelot's terrible blows land, for the first time in vain, on white-clad adversaries
who do not seem to feel them, it is because he has joined the wrong
side, that of *li chevalier terrien,* the sinful black knights of this
world, not that of *li chevalier celestial,* the "knights of heaven"
(Matarasso, *Quest* 159; Pauphilet, *Queste* 143–44). To the end, Lancelot misconstrues the narrative grammar of the *Queste* story and is

represented as unable to grasp fully the new meanings which have altered the sequence and outcome of narrative events. For the medieval reader familiar with the stylized gestures of Arthurian romance, as we are, Lancelot's hand lifting his sword against the two lions guarding the gates of Corbenic makes the "right" gesture. When a flaming hand strikes down his sword, our understanding of the generic adventure is also abruptly shifted and redefined. For prowess in the *Queste* consists not in courageous gestures alone but also in understanding meaning and seeing revelation. A hermit instructs Gauvain (and the reader) in these new adventures: "Do not imagine moreover that the adventures now afoot consist in the murder of men or the slaying of knights; they are of a spiritual order, higher in every way and much more worth" (Matarasso, *Quest* 174; Pauphilet, *Queste* 161). Transformations of romance motifs in the *Queste,* then, are tied to a shift from representation of a secular world of combat and prowess, in which the worst offense is *recréantise,* want of valor, to that of a spiritual world in which *mescreance* (225), want of faith, is opposed to chivalric prowess. By thus both describing and interrupting the familiar élan of the knight charging into combat, the author recalls Arthurian motifs and instructs his readers to revise their generic expectations as well as instructing both characters and readers in new sequences of narrative syntax where knights abandon their horses, refuse to fight, and worry about bloodshed.

The moral and religious interpretation conferred upon the Arthurian romance elements gradually bring the generic chivalric motifs to a halt in the *Queste*. Nothing happens to some heroes; Lancelot at Corbenic is told to go home because there is no more story for him. "Sir Knight, you can leave off the hair-shirt now, for your quest is ended; there is no use your striving any longer to seek the Holy Grail; for you should know that you will not see more of it than you have seen" (Matarasso, *Quest* 256; Pauphilet, *Queste* 259). From the first, the Grail quest was foreseen in elegiac terms as an ending not only of the Grail adventures but also of the Round Table. Arthur laments: "No Christian king ever had so many good knights or men of rank and wisdom at his table as I have had this day, nor will again when these are gone, nor shall I ever see them reunited round my table as before; it is this that hurts me the most" (Matarasso, *Quest* 45; Pauphilet, *Queste* 17). Formulas abridging years' worth of adventure for Galaad appear toward the end of the *Queste,* marking the surcease of secular chivalry. Yet to the very end of the *Queste* the chivalric romance motifs appear and reassert their vigor; they are rejustified by the spiritual elements of the *Queste,* as when Galaad, Perceval, and Bohort massacre the infamous sons of Count Ernol (Matarasso, *Quest* 239–42; Pauphilet, *Queste* 230–33).

These changes in representation of the chivalric elements of secular romance are complemented by amplification of narrative motifs that portray the early history of the Grail, of Joseph of Arimathea and his son Josephus, and of the evangelization of Britain. These narrative materials are also "Arthurian" in the sense that they are elaborated within the texts of chivalric romance. Yet they retain the aspect of a foreign matter within the *Queste;* their concerns for political clashes between pagan and Christian in the mid-East or for baptism of infidels in Logres are not those of either Gauvain or Galaad; the rag-tag band of evangelizers led by Josephus is profoundly different both in appearance and in actions from the proud knights who sit at the Round Table. While elaborating a moral reappraisal of secular chivalry, then, the *Queste* alters the outcome of typical romance plot events, develops the "Eastern" story line of the early Grail history, and reshapes the overall narrative from a structure where the narrative movement is carried forward to resolution by successive feats of valor to a structure that progresses through renunciation of dynamic acts of chivalry toward a final state of religious contemplation.

Moral and religious redefinition of the Arthurian narrative motifs are carried implicitly by shifts in narrative action but are elaborated explicitly in extended passages of thematic commentary in the *Queste*. Although such thematic commentary has seemed one of the most striking generic innovations of the *Queste,* Eugène Vinaver has shown that from the first, vernacular romance joined "matter and meaning," narrative and thematic commentary.[7] The Arthurian mold thus provided the *Queste* author with models for insertion of interpretation, for passing from a mode of fictional narrative to one of thematic commentary.

Of the several modes of thematic commentary used by Chrétien de Troyes in his twelfth-century romances, only one or two, greatly expanded, survive fully in the thirteenth-century prose romance. Most striking in the Vulgate cycle is the reduction of the interior monologue and the virtual disappearance of allegorical personification, forms which carried much thematic commentary in twelfth-century romance. In the *Queste,* as in the other *Lancelot* proper texts, emotions, thoughts, and spiritual reflection are most often expressed in authorial description or in dialogue. The occasional brief soliloquies seem quite foreshortened compared with the lengthy passages of *ratiocinatio* in Chrétien or in Thomas's *Tristan*. Despite the intensely prayerful, reflective attitudes of characters in the *Queste,* they are seldom represented as thinking to themselves, more often expressing their thoughts in dialogue with other knights, in confession, or in spiritual consultation with hermits, recluses, and *preudons* dressed like monks or priests.

Greatly expanded in the *Queste,* as in the other Vulgate cycle romances, are the elucidations, passages of thematic commentary which explain narrative events. While explanations in twelfth-century romance, like those of Perceval's cousin and the Loathly Damsel after Perceval's visit to the Fisher King in Chrétien's *Conte du graal,* are often as enigmatic as events, elucidations in thirteenth-century prose romances tend to be strongly rationalizing. Thus, in the prose *Lancelot,* the strange custom of keeping prisoners in Gorre is explained as a repopulation policy of King Bademagu.[8] However, except for the *Queste,* thematic commentary and explanations in both the twelfth-century *roman* and the thirteenth-century prose *Lancelot* remain closely tied to the chivalric themes of the narrative plot. They provide information about lineage and political connections; they anticipate or fill out narrative events; they emphasize ideals of a piece with a purely secular chivalry, respectful of love, friendship, prowess, and the Church as an institution. In contrast, while the *Queste* provides thematic commentary in the same position as in the typical Arthurian romance—that is, in dialogue or after a combat, a puzzling encounter, or a dream—it consistently substitutes for secular ethical commentary a religious explanation whose content is often quite different from the narrative it explains. Hence our impression of a new "meaning." Thus in the prose *Lancelot* the combined *force de clergie* of the nine wise men who explain Galehaut's prophetic dream find only biographical and political meaning in it,[9] whereas in the *Queste* the nearest hermit finds all the themes of Christian eschatology in Lancelot's dream.

Moreover, the studies by Pauphilet and by Savage have shown that religious interpretation in the *Queste,* while fitting into a locus provided for commentary within the typical structure of secular romance, is formulated in terms that owe little to romance and much to Latin traditions of religious and moral exegesis of Scripture and the classical authors as well as to the didactic tradition of sermons and exempla. Arthurian romance texts do not, for example, contain numerous citations from the Bible nor relate Gospel parables within passages of thematic commentary as does the *Queste*. Finally, the means used in the *Queste* to link thematic commentary to narrative event also owe much to formal procedures and patterns of religious exegesis or moral reinterpretation of texts from pagan antiquity.

We may, for the sake of convenience, group these procedures of interpretation under the notions of *fabula* and *figura,* using them in a general nontechnical sense to describe modes of passing from narrative to thematic commentary.[10] *Fabula* is that mode of suggesting or initiating thematic commentary whose content is quite unlike that of the literal narrative. *Figura* establishes analogies between juxtaposed narratives so that thematic commentary may be derived. Both *fabula* and *figura* cause an effect of textual doubling in which second meanings oppose or extend the literal sense of the primary text.

The notion of *fabula* corresponds to both a creative and an interpretive process, to a theory of writing and of reading. *Fabula* as writing was understood in the twelfth and thirteenth centuries to mean elaborating a fiction that would serve to veil philosophy and cosmology from the ignorant and unworthy while it would provide a pleasing, teasing garment to entertain and indoctrinate the wise. If we were to agree with Pauphilet that the *Queste* author employed the Arthurian motifs as such a fictional garment, using their empty forms for systematic exposition of Cistercian doctrine, we would also have to state that this would be an exceptional proceeding in thirteenth-century literature. The principal examples of vernacular *fabulae* in thirteenth-century France, that is, texts that explicitly clothe didactic themes in fictional garb, are found not in Arthurian romance but in the abundant production of personification allegory for religious and moral exposition, as in Raoul de Houdenc's *Songe d'Enfer* (1215–25) and Huon de Meri's *Tournoiement d'Antechrist* (1235), as well as for topics of courtly didacticism, as in the *Ailes de Prouesse* by Raoul and Guillaume de Lorris's *Roman de la Rose,* all works contemporary with the *Queste*. But the *Queste* itself contains virtually no personification allegory and makes only the most sparing use of the etymologizing and numerological bric-a-brac that mark the typical *fabula* of personification allegory. On the other hand, the *Queste* has much in common with the contemporary pious tale, in its thematic emphasis on tearful confession and penitence. But the thirteenth-century pious tales seldom use the usual motifs of Arthurian romance. Moreover, while the *Queste* has a strong exemplary cast, it does not explicitly attempt to enter the reader's world with the authority of didactic exhortation as does the pious tale *Le*

Dit du buef, which concludes: "You who have heard this goodly tale retold should contemplate yourselves and your sins in the mirror of this example and go to confession."[11] The *demonstrances* and *sene-fiances* of the *Queste* are explicitly destined to remain within the story and are portrayed as *exempla* only for the characters.

The *Queste,* however, provides us with many examples of *fabula* as reading, as an allegorical interpretation of narrative which attributes a moral or religious second meaning to events, characters, or objects represented in a fictional mode.[12] A monk explains the defeat of the inexperienced knight Melias through such allegorical interpretation:

> "After leaving the abbey where you were made a knight you first encountered on your road the sign of the true Cross: the sign in which a knight should place his greatest trust. Nor was this all. There was an inscription as well, which indicated the two roads open to you, one leading to the left, the other to the right. For the right-hand road you must read [*devez vos entendre*] the way of Jesus Christ, the way of compassion. . . . In the left-hand road you perceive [*devez vos entendre*] the way of sinners. . . . Reason played you false [*einsi fus tu deceuz par entendement*] for the words referred to a spiritual order whilst you, seeing only the temporal [*tu entendoies de la seculer*] were filled with pride and fell headlong into mortal sin." (Matarasso, *Quest* 71; Pauphilet, *Queste* 45)

The knight's choice of the right road is a well-known romance motif; here, as elsewhere, the *Queste* shifts such motifs from a moral to a religious plane, both intensifying and further defining the ethical atmosphere of Arthurian fiction. But the repetition of the key word of *fabula—entendre—*sets into the *Queste* a passage of exegetical allegorical discourse quite unlike the thematic commentary of romance, although familiar enough to us from allegorized didactic texts such as bestiaries.

Several modern critics have felt that this sort of allegorical religious interpretation of vernacular narrative was a commonplace reading in the thirteenth century, *chose courante* in Todorov's phrase, for an age of faith.[13] But a closer look at thirteenth-century vernacular literature will help us to sense better the unique place of the *Queste* and to amend the allegorizing tilt of some modern criticism of medieval French literature. It is indeed unusual to find the familiar gestures and encounters of Logres subjected to reinterpretation through religious allegory. The most significant parallel to the *Queste* is the contemporary *Perlesvaus,* whose proper names give it a profoundly

moral feeling (*Chatel Mortel, Chastiax del Enqueste*), further defined by declarations asserting that the combats within the *Perlesvaus*
signify the struggle between the Old Law and the New Law of
Christianity and by a cast of characters that includes a large number
of devils. But the processes of commentary are unlike those of the
Queste, for the *Perlesvaus* contains just two passages offering allegorical interpretation of only fourteen of its hundreds of knightly encounters: that vouchsafed Gawain at the Castle of Inquiry and that
given Perceval by the Hermit King (brs. 6, 9). Moreover, where interpretations in the *Queste* are anticipated and coherently integrated
into the subsequent story, those in the *Perlesvaus* seem to play on
surprise and unexpected reversal of meaning; these interpretations
do not alter the story motifs, which remain imperturbably chivalric
throughout.[14]

Philip Rollinson reminds us that medieval readers were "accustomed to reserve their interpretive ingeniousness for certain established texts of the past, mainly the Bible but possibly including Virgil
and other classical texts, where the assumed concealment could be
sophisticated."[15] Indeed, there is no evidence to support the view that
in the twelfth and thirteenth centuries readers usually elaborated religious allegorical exegetic readings of vernacular texts. The notion
of *fabula* and its related terms *fable, entendre, integument,* and
gloser continues in the vernacular works of the twelfth and thirteenth
centuries, as in the Latin tradition, to define the process of "saving"
the canonical texts of pagan antiquity and ancient mythological lore
through moral or rationalizing allegory and the labor of patristic
elaboration of moral, tropological, and analogical readings of Scripture.

It is significant of the distance separating the learned Latin tradition of *fabula* and *integumentum* from vernacular literary practice
in the twelfth century that Bernard Sylvester's systematic allegorical
commentary on the *Aeneid* should be contemporary with the French
Enéas, which adapts Virgil to a secular chivalric mode without adding any moral or religious allegorical commentary. Ovidian works
such as the *Narcisus* are translated in the twelfth century as caution-
ary tales about the power of love; no gloss furnishes religious second
meanings. From Marie de France to Jean Bodel and Jean de Meun,
well-known passages confirm that allegorical integuments are the
secret of philosophy, the domain of schools and of specialized learning, and that their object is the Latin *auctores,* the *matière de Rome,*
"sage et de sens aprendant."[16]

Vernacular texts of the twelfth and thirteenth centuries that include explicit moral or religious allegorical interpretations are not only usually imitated from classical models. They are works which already were normally written with commentary within the Latin tradition itself: the Aesopic fables, the bestiaries, the exempla collections, the *Gesta romanorum.* Secular and religious genres which were not moralized in the Latin tradition—saints' lives, chronicles, adventure romances—are not explicitly allegorized in the vernacular either. Texts whose literary development occurs largely in the vernacular— epics, *lais,* drama, and lyric poetry—may contain religious themes but seldom include passages of religious or moral commentary which oppose the literal sense of the rest of the text.

Only a few works from didactic genres undertake to outfit secular literary texts with religious allegory. One of these is the famous Latin sermon by Stephen Langton, Archbishop of Canterbury, who moralized the lyric poem "Main se leva Bele Aalis."[17] Another is the "Moralité sur ces six vers," the song of Enmelot, forbidden by her mother to dance in the meadow with young squires. In the rhymed *moralité,* the meadow represents worldly riches and power, Enmelot the vanity of the flesh, her mother the soul, and the dancing *bachelers* the seven deadly sins.[18] But the Arthurian matter is unwieldy in length; it does not lend itself readily to such formal and moral manipulations. Moreover, the Arthurian story of the *Queste* is not merely cited to be allegorized; it is composed by the very author of the spiritual thematic commentary. Furthermore, Matarasso's careful study demonstrates how infrequently one might find an author equally versed in both Arthurian romance and Cistercian observance and patristic exegesis.[19] Setting religious allegorical interpretations into an Arthurian adventure would seem to have been, then, an exceptional undertaking in thirteenth-century literary practice.

The relationship between spiritual gloss and narrative text in the *Queste* is also unlike that of fable and moral. In Latin and French moralized works, allegorical exegesis does not disrupt or transform the primary text: Virgil and Aesop are not rewritten to conform to the moral commentary; Bele Aalis is not represented as hearing the sermon and mending her ways. In these texts allegorizing remains entirely separate and distinct from the passage commented. In the *Queste,* on the other hand, the moral penetrates into the story, altering typical romance plot motifs. The commentators are themselves part of the Arthurian story line, offering lodging, meals, and transportation with their sermons. The characters hear and heed the religious gloss; their actions are transformed when they understand the interpretations. Understanding of hidden meanings in the *Queste* is not portrayed as the exclusive domain of the author or the reader but is opened gradually, *mostré apertement,* to characters embedded in the literal plot. Narrative linearity and forward movement owe more to the revelation of spiritual significance than to action in the plot. Allegorizing thus feeds into the narrative structure of romance, altering its course.

Figura, that is, figural or analogical narrative, like *fabula* transforms the shape and meaning of Arthurian motifs in the *Queste.* The *Queste* attributes to interpreters (or to written *briefs* discovered by the characters) analogical narratives from Scripture, biblical legend, and the recently elaborated versions of the early Grail history. The *Queste* author thus frees his work from the constraints of Arthurian geography and time; his characters are not all living simultaneously in the land of Logres. Narrative elements penetrate into the thematic commentary, just as the commentary invades the narrative. Stories thus proliferate in the thematic commentary as well as in the narrative; the author moves his narrative freely both forward and far backward in time through superimposed layers of dream visions, typology, and prophecy.[20]

The key words in the *Queste* governing the processes of *figura* which establish significant relations between narrative segments are *semblance* and *remembrance.* The Arthurian, biblical, prophetic, and legendary narrative motifs are not merely interlaced sequentially; in the words of the *Queste, ils s'entreacordent* (Pauphilet, *Queste* 39); they harmonize to create rich, elaborate patterns of significant analogy. Many pages of citation would be needed to tie in all the textual parallels in the *Queste* to Hector's dream:

> Hector, meanwhile, his mode of life unaltered, wandered aimlessly hither and yon till he came to a great man's house where a splendid wedding feast was in progress. He stood outside the gate shouting: "Open up!" And the lord came out and said to him:
> "Sir Knight, this is not the house you are looking for: for no one enters here so proudly mounted as yourself." (Matarasso, *Quest* 165; Pauphilet, *Queste* 150)

The dream recalls a parable told earlier to Lancelot in his second confession; it is renarrated in the future tense with a moral allegory of pride in anticipation both of Lancelot's hunger to partake of the Grail communion at Corbenic and of the final sorrowful moment when Hector is refused entry to the castle of the Rich Fisher where his brother Lancelot is seated at the table served by the Grail. But one would have to cite the whole *Queste* and all the works the *Queste* cites analogically to trace the more intricate patterns of inexhaustible reference in the *Queste:* the eschatological parable of the wedding feast (Matt. 22:2); Perceval's aunt's story of the three tables, which recalls the manna that fed the Israelites, the miracle of loaves and fishes, the table of the Last Supper, the Grail table of Joseph of Arimathea and Josephus, and finally the Round Table, which signifies also "the roundness of the earth, the concentric spheres of the planets and of the elements in the firmament; and in these heavenly spheres we see the stars and many things besides; whence it follows that the Round Table is a true epitome of the universe" (Matarasso, *Quest* 99; Pauphilet, *Queste* 76).

Figural narratives thus enable the *Queste* author to thicken his plot with narrative motifs unlike those of the chivalric Arthurian tradition and to develop the eschatological motifs expanded in the story line of the early Grail history. Moreover these figural narratives seem as freely variable as the motifs of chivalric matter. *Queste* studies have emphasized its doctrinal and scriptural sources, but to a significant degree the *Queste* escapes the constraints of orthodoxy. At times the author does maintain Christian orthodoxy in the traditional hierarchy of exegesis expressed by John of Salisbury: "Any particular thing has inherent in it as many meanings of other objects as it has likenesses to them, on condition that the more important is never the sign of the less important thing."[21] A *preudhons* thus both predicates Galaad's likeness to the Redeemer and emphasizes that Christ surpasses Galaad in sublimity:

> "Today the similitude is renewed whereby the Father sent His Son to earth for the deliverance of His people. For just as folly and error fled at His advent and truth stood revealed, even so has Our Lord chosen you from among all other knights to ride abroad through many lands to put an end to the hazards that afflict them and make their meaning and their causes plain. This is why your coming must be compared to the coming of Jesus Christ, in semblance only, not in sublimity [*de semblance ne mie de hautece*]." (Matarasso, *Quest* 64; Pauphilet, *Queste* 38)

In other passages, however, the Christian hierarchy of signification is abandoned. The *Queste* is filled with typological narratives from the Christian tradition which are made to prefigure the very events of the Arthurian story itself. The Arthurian romance thus acquires spiritual meaning not only by being interpreted in religious terms but also by being transformed into the endpoint, the final *signifié,* of figural typology. Galaad is thus portrayed as the final virgin in the lineage of Solomon, the Virgin Mary, and Joseph of Arimathea in the *Queste*'s "Legend of the Tree of Life." In the "Legend" the hierarchy of Christian values is emphatically overturned; for when Solomon is represented thinking of his lineage, he is led

> to study every sign accorded him, whether waking or in dream, in the hope of coming at the truth about the ending of his line. He sought so diligently that the Holy Ghost revealed to him the coming of the glorious Virgin, and a voice told him in part what was to be. When Solomon learned of this, he asked whether this maid was to mark the end of his lineage.
>
> "No," said the voice, "a man, himself a virgin, shall be the last: one who shall pass in valour Josiah, thy step-brother, by as much as that Virgin shall surpass thy wife." (Matarasso, *Quest* 230–31; Pauphilet, *Queste* 221)

We must not gloss over such an astonishing disparity between religious orthodoxy and the *Queste*'s representation of Christian history and doctrine that has embarrassed religiously oriented *Queste* critics from Pauphilet to Matarasso.[22] Savage's 1973 dissertation on the *Queste* at last enables us to begin to account more fully not only for the religious elements in the *Queste* but also for the divergence between these and Christian orthodoxy. Savage argues convincingly that "the 'Christian' substance of this romance, which has persuaded critics of its doctrinal intent, is really no more than a fictional system of beliefs chosen as the most appropriate medium for the glorification of Galaad, . . . for a fictional representation of an ideal existence."[23] The Christian religious motifs would not, therefore, have theological value or didactic intent but would be pressed into service to represent a fictional world of spiritual revelation. The words of "truth," repeated in the *Queste,* are therefore not so much to be taken literally as to be read as markers indicating fictional representation of spiritual motifs. The abundant citations and reminiscences of Scripture documented by Matarasso would also serve to identify the fictional motifs of "religion." Spiritual elements in the *Queste* would thus be as distinct from medieval religious beliefs and practices as is the motif of Arthurian romance from the historical customs of feudal society and as are the erotic motifs of troubadour and *trouvère* lyric from what we know of love and marriage in the twelfth and thirteenth centuries.

Without attempting to follow all the implications of such a distinction between religious doctrine and fictional representation of religion, we may at least undertake here to evaluate some of the narrative functions of the "truth" represented in the *Queste*. The notion of "truth" is foregrounded in both the thematic commentary and in the figural narratives of the *Queste* by the often-repeated introductory formula *voirs fu* ("It was true that") and by representation of characters impelled to seek interpretation. Thus Perceval says of his dream, "I shall never rest content until I know the meaning of it" (*devant que je en sache la verité*) (Matarasso, *Quest* 121; Pauphilet, *Queste* 101). Truth is, of course, a concern present in the Arthurian narratives preceding the *Queste*. But in twelfth-century texts like Chrétien's *Chevalier de la charrette,* the terms of "truth" (*verité, voirement*) serve to emphasize the completeness or accuracy of hyperbolic comparison or the description of a fantastic object. Of Guenevere's hair, Chrétien says: "But what was this hair like? If I tell you the truth about it, you will think I am a mad teller of lies."[24] *Verité* may also mean the explanation of obscure narrative events, as when Perceval in the *Conte du graal* undertakes to discover the "truth" (*la veritez provee*) of whom the Grail serves and why the lance bleeds. In the thirteenth-century *Lancelot* proper, the expression "Or dit li contes," not *voirs fu,* is used as a narrative link. "Truth" in the *Lancelot* proper emphasizes opinion in passages of direct discourse, as when Arthur denounces Lancelot before the body of the Lady of Escalot: "In truth, lady, verily you may well say that he for whom you have died is the worst knight in the world and the most valiant."[25] Although in both twelfth- and thirteenth-century Arthurian narrative, the notion of a truth to be discovered gives a powerful narrative impulse to romance texts, only in the *Queste* does "truth" consistently frame separate planes of thematic commentary and analogical narratives different in motif, meaning, and chronological definition from the chivalric Arthurian plane.[26]

The *Queste* author is freed of the constraints of orthodoxy because he writes in a fictional mode, and the "truth" enables him to link his figural narratives to the Arthurian material not only by analogy and *semblance* but also by an improbably fantastic material continuity, freely forwarding objects and characters from one epoch to another. The Arthurian romances had already established a pattern of adventures recurring within a single text or reused from one romance to another. Galaad's cooling of the boiling spring which Lancelot had been powerless to quench is an example of such recurrence (Matarasso, *Quest* 270; Pauphilet, *Queste* 263; Sommer 5: 243–48). But the

Queste author expands both thematically and chronologically the generic patterns of recurrence. The Grail is but one object surviving from the past of the figural narratives into the present of the Arthurian *Queste* story. Galaad's shield bears a red cross painted in the very blood of a nosebleed of Josephus (Pauphilet, *Queste* 34); this same shield was carried by the pagan king Evelac (baptized Mordrain in A.D. 75) against his enemy Tholomer: "ce est icel escu meimes que je vos conte" (Pauphilet, *Queste* 34). The same Mordrain miraculously survives, blinded and paralyzed by his vision of the Grail from the time of Josephus until he is delivered by the redeeming Galaad, like Simeon in the Gospel of Luke (2:38–40); Josephus himself reappears to serve the mass at the last Grail vision. The *Queste* author thus expands both chronologically and thematically the habit of typical linking episodes between the various romances. The figural narratives mingle into the Arthurian adventures just as did the allegorical thematic commentary, thereby creating themes of prophecy unanticipated by the Old Testament and questions of figural typology unknown to patristic exegesis of Scripture. Isaiah does not attempt to communicate with Jesus in the Bible, but Solomon in the *Queste* is represented as puzzling over how to get a message through the ages to Galaad: "He bethought himself how he could make known to the last of his line how Solomon, who had lived so long before him, had had foreknowledge of his coming" (Matarasso, *Quest* 231; Pauphilet, *Queste* 221).

The narrative motifs combined from the religious and Arthurian genres and the passages of spiritual thematic commentary are not then merely layered together in distinct slabs. Rather, the various motifs and commentaries flow together among the planes of adventure, recollection, dream, gloss, and prophecy. But because both the Arthurian and the religious material retain a distinctive generic stamp, the reader can always recognize them, see the play of contrast and combination at work, enjoy the mingling of the iconography of Arthurian *merveilleux* with that of Christian revelation. The spiritual transformation of Arthurian motifs that began with the *muemenz,* the change of Lancelot's name, yields finally a remarkable narrative art of *muance,* of transmutation, in which narrative motifs are freely transformed and combined to reveal new levels of narrative event and spiritual meaning.

On the simplest level of *muance* a single image may be both amplified and transformed within the allegorical gloss. In the commentary on Gauvain's dream, the single term *lande,* the moor into which the bulls representing knights of the Round Table stray from hayrack and meadow (Pauphilet, *Queste* 149), becomes "the moor, the wasteland, taking the way which is barren of flowers and fruit, even the path of hell, the way in which all things are laid to waste and nothing salutary can survive" (Matarasso, *Quest* 171; Pauphilet, *Queste* 157). This five-part restatement changes the *lande* from a woodland place to a wasteland path, interprets it as Hell, and in a final image expresses both the literal and moral senses of the moor. Far greater complexity in the poetic *muance* of shifting images is achieved when the images themselves are first transformed within a single passage, then doubled and tripled through analogy to other changing images within the thematic commentary.[27] In Lancelot's dream, the significant image of the last man in the line of seven kings and two knights becomes first a lion and then a winged lion, who rises and grows until his wings cover the earth to soar over all chivalry before vanishing in the opening sky (Matarasso, *Quest* 148; Pauphilet, *Queste* 131). Within the elucidation, a hermit sets these images in a figural analogy to the image of a rushing torrent, murky at its source but infinitely sweet and clear at its end, the last of the nine rivers in Mordrain's prophetic dream. The hermit's final interpretation repeats and resolves the images of lion and river into a statement of Galaad's lineage and messianic role within the world of Logres.

Although the poetry of *muance* freely commingles the iconographic and temporal planes of the *Queste,* its movement is never random: the series of images progresses always toward moral, genealogical, or spiritual revelation. The vision of the White Stag, itself an Arthurian motif, escorted by four winged lions, an ancient legendary symbol, changes into the symbols of the evangelists who bear the enthroned Stag through an unbroken window, condensing the mysteries of the Incarnation, Passion, and Resurrection.[28] The *preudons* who served the mass speaks to the knights:

> "For to you has Our Lord revealed His secrets and His hidden mysteries, in part indeed today, for in changing the Hart into a heavenly being, in no way mortal, He showed the transmutation that He underwent upon the Cross, cloaked there in the mortal garment of this human flesh, dying, He conquered death, and recovered for us eternal life. This is most aptly figured by the Hart. For just as the Hart rejuvenates itself by shedding part of its hide and coat, so did Our Lord return from death to life when He cast off his mortal hide, which was the human flesh He took in the Blessed Virgin's womb." (Matarasso, *Quest* 244; Pauphilet, *Queste* 236)

Metamorphosis is here attributed to the highest spiritual motif, that of the Lord's transmutation upon the cross (*la muance qu'il fist en la Croiz*) (Matarasso, *Quest* 244; Pauphilet, *Queste* 235–36).

Little in the *Lancelot* proper can be compared to such poetry of *muance*. Transformations within the *Lancelot* proper are attributed to magic and do not initiate beautiful sequences of metamorphosing motifs. The messenger of the Lady of the Lake saves Lionel and Bohort from Claudas de la Terre Déserte by magically giving them the appearance of two greyhounds, but this disguise hides no further mysteries or transformations. The power of enchantment surrounds the *Val sans retour* with walls of air, but within we find only an ordinary *locus amoenus* with chess and dancing to pass the time.[29] Nowhere else do we find the *Queste*'s unique art of *muance,* of dreamlike, melting metamorphoses of images that fill the text with splendid iconographic tableaux. Moreover, these always tend to express with great economy and force ineffable mysteries, "what tongue could not relate nor heart conceive" encompassing the ultimate beginning of valor and the final end of prowess, "the source of valour undismayed, the spring-head of endeavor" (*la començaille des granz hardemenz et l'achoison des proeces*) (Matarasso, *Quest* 283; Pauphilet, *Queste* 278).

Even these final words of spiritual vision, however, are still cast in the language of chivalry. All the transformations of Arthurian motifs through the modes of *fabula* and *figura* have not lifted the *Queste* out of the orbit of the romance genre. Those who have elaborated powerful doctrinal readings of the *Queste* have been reluctant to leave it in the embrace of the prose *Lancelot,* in part because of the vexed question of authorship but also because the *Queste* seems far removed from the thirteenth-century prose romance both in significance and in greatness.[30] But manuscript associations provide precious evidence for the medieval generic definition of the *Queste:* only four of the forty-three extant manuscripts copy the Vulgate *Queste* independently of other sections of the *Lancelot* proper. Authors and compilers confirm their reading of the *Queste* not as a doctrinal treatise or as a didactic work but as a secular romance, as a "chapter in the story of Logres,"[31] by locking the *Queste* into the Vulgate cycle manuscripts and by incorporating it into larger romance compilations like the prose *Tristan*. Enhanced by the brilliant new character from the *Queste,* Galaad, the magnetic motif of the Grail quest continued to attract the scattered pieces of the *matière de Bretagne* into symmetrical patterns by giving it a narrative and ethical center of coherence. In the post-Vulgate *Queste*,[32] Galaad becomes the redeeming figure around whom the principal Arthurian themes of the weapons, the wounds, the wasteland, and the Grail finally coalesce into one coherent whole. While the *Queste*'s innovations in Arthurian motifs survive and prosper, however, later prose romances do not continue to expand the learned allegorical glosses and figural narratives from Scripture. The serious, spiritual significance of the Grail motifs remains, but the typologies and allegories of the thematic commentaries seem to have appeared to later redactors as handsome but not essential accessories; these interpretive elements are sloughed off to make way for expansion of adventure motifs.

Yet it is the opening of Arthurian romance to broad spiritual dimensions which may be said to have preserved the generic motifs of chivalric adventure to this day. Of all the medieval romance types, the Arthurian has remained most intact and alive in the creative imagination, in popular fiction as in the work of learned poets. From Malory, Spenser, and Tennyson to T. H. White and *Camelot,* the Grail still feeds romance.

But why should spiritual transformation ensure survival of the motifs of a secular romance? By developing within the Arthurian genre a system of powerful images, motifs, and characters able to represent and express spiritual experience, by imposing on the random adventures of knights errant the teleology of a quest, the *Queste* forever gave to romance the weight of seriousness. Such spiritual gravity within romance is represented by the final images of book, author, library, and Latin in the *Queste*'s epilogue. In like manner, religious terminology confers lofty seriousness on expression of human love in the contemporary courtly *chanson,* just as it did in Chrétien's *Charrette,* where Lancelot kneels to worship Guenevere, "holding her more dear than the relic of any saint."[33] Through its spiritual seriousness the *Queste* made Arthurian romance seem important as well as amusing, worth telling again and again. But in return, secular romance gave lasting life and its weight of tender warmth and compelling story to spiritual matters. Galaad holds the reader because he is embodied as a figure of romance, because he is the son of Lancelot.

But the *Queste*'s spiritual transformations of Arthurian romance also ensured the survival of the genre by conferring on its motifs a mythological dimension. Myth, in this sense, is a story that reveals within its singular events paradigmatic truths about human existence.[34] The great enduring myths of the *Queste* are, for our culture, irrevocably bound to the Arthurian motifs that express them: Lancelot, whose name, like Tristan's, is inseparable from the myth of endless desire; Galaad and the quest, the defining image for us of the myth of human aspiration to perfection and knowledge of spiritual secrets. When, like Dante, we wish to represent endless desire, we turn once more the pages of *Lancelot* as did Francesca and Paolo in Canto 5 of the *Inferno*. The truth of these myths is inseparable from the stories that express them.

Eros and gnosis, desire and knowledge of revelation: these are, in turn, inextricably related in the *Queste* by the kinship bond between Lancelot and Galaad. Kinship both joins and distinguishes between father and son, desire and revelation. Kinship enables us to perceive the relation between desire and revelation; it posits that relation as necessary, inborn. The *Queste* establishes the extraordinary importance of this kinship bond through a variation on the romance motif of delayed identification.[35] Although Galaad's paternity is declared from the first, Lancelot is only gradually acknowledged as Galaad's father, at first through the grandiose dreams and tales that tie revelation of lineage to the messianic mission of Galaad and finally through the tender reconciliation of father and son. Projecting adventure onto a legendary scale, the *Queste* made Arthurian romance the story by which we still represent endless desire and spiritual revelation. When we wish to tell these myths again, we turn always to the motifs of Arthurian romance, acknowledging the story's power to bring them into being, just as Galaad finally greeted and embraced his father, Lancelot, at the end of the *Queste,* saying:

> "Truly, Sir, . . . I wish you welcome too. Upon God's name I have desired to see and be with you beyond all men alive. And it is only natural that I should, for in you is my beginning" [*car vos estes commencement de moi*]. (Matarasso, *Quest* 257–58; Pauphilet, *Queste* 250)[36]

Notes

[1] Albert Pauphilet, ed., *La Queste del Saint Graal* (Paris: Champion, 1949) 1; P. M. Matarasso, trans., *The Quest of the Holy Grail* (New York: Penguin, 1969) 31.

[2] An updated bibliography of critical studies on the *Queste* appears in Emmanuèle Baumgartner, *L'Arbre et le pain: Essai sur* la Queste del Saint Graal (Paris: CDU and SEDES, 1981) 155–63. Religious questions have dominated *Queste* studies from the initial work of Albert Pauphilet, *Etudes sur* la Queste del Saint Graal *attribuée à Gautier Map* (Paris: Champion, 1921), and E. Gil-

son, "La mystique de la grâce dans la *Queste del Saint Graal*," *Romania* 51 (1925): 321–47, to F. W. Locke's study of the scriptural bases of the artistic unity of the *Queste* in *The Quest for the Holy Grail* (Stanford, Calif.: Stanford UP, 1960) and to Charlotte Morse, *The Pattern of Judgment in the* Queste *and* Cleanness (Columbia: U of Missouri P, 1978). Most recently see the exhaustive evaluation of the *Queste*'s debt to Scripture in P. M. Matarasso's *The Redemption of Chivalry* (Genève: Droz, 1979).

[3] Frappier's definition of the chivalric character of the *Queste* supports the reading of the *Queste* as a secular romance, suited to the courtly ethos of its thirteenth-century public. See Jean Frappier, "Le Graal et la Chevalerie," *Autour du Graal* (Geneva: Droz, 1977) 89–128, rpt. from *Romania* 75 (1954): 165–210. See also Erich Köhler, *L'Aventure chevaleresque: Idéal et réalité dans le roman courtois,* trans. E. Kaufholz (Paris: Gallimard, 1974) 110 n9, 258–68; Baumgartner 147–54; and Grace Armstrong Savage, "Narrative Techniques in the *Queste del Saint Graal,* diss., Princeton U, 1973, 366–68.

[4] Current work now offers new perspectives for evaluation of the *Queste* within the prose romance cycles. See E. Jane Burns, "Feigned Allegory: Intertextuality in the *Queste del Saint Graal,*" *Kentucky Romance Quarterly* 29 (1982): 347–63, and Savage. Helen Hennessy undertook preliminary evaluation of romance elements in the *Queste* from a Spenserian perspective like that of her Harvard teacher, Rosemond Tuve, emphasizing the incongruity between "two relatively inflexible elements, the legend of the Holy Grail and the events of the Bible." See Helen Hennessy, "The Uniting of Romance and Allegory in *La Queste del Saint Graal,*" *Boston University Studies in English* 4 (1960): 189–201, as well as Rosemond Tuve, *Allegorical Imagery: Some Medieval Books and Their Posterity* (Princeton UP, 1966) 335–436.

[5] On the questions of attribution and authorship raised by this passage, see Baumgartner 22–31 and Matarasso, *Redemption* 205–41.

[6] Paul Zumthor, *Langue et technique poétiques à l'époque romane (XIe–XIIIe siècles)* (Paris: Klincksieck, 1963) 172–78. See also Charles Méla, "Romans et merveilles: l'art des mélanges," *Précis de littérature française du Moyen Age,* ed. Daniel Poirion (Paris: PUF, 1983) 216–18.

[7] Eugène Vinaver, *The Rise of Romance* (New York: Oxford UP, 1971) 23.

[8] Alexandre Micha, ed., Lancelot: *Roman en prose du XIIIe siècle,* 9 vols. (Paris: Droz, 1978–83) 1: 84–85. Ferdinand Lot points out the euhemeristic, rationalizing spirit of the prose *Lancelot* in his *Etude sur* le Lancelot en prose (Paris: Champion, 1918) 273.

[9] Micha 3: 12–22. Religious allegorical interpretation in the *Lancelot* proper seems to occur exclusively in the context of didactic instruction. The Lady of the Lake thus offers an allegorical meaning for a knight's armor in her exhortation to the young Lancelot as he undertakes chivalric adventure (Micha 7: 250–53); a priest interprets Arthur's dream of the lion in the water allegorically as part of a moral lesson in princely conduct. See H. O. Sommer, ed., *The Vulgate Version of the Arthurian Romances,* 8 vols. (Washington, D.C.: Carnegie Institution, 1908–13) 3: 220.

[10] For the classical and medieval sense of *fabula,* see Peter Dronke, *Fabula: Explorations into the Uses of Myth in Medieval Platonism* (Leiden: Brill, 1974); James A. Coulter, *The Literary Microcosm: Theories of Interpretation of the Later Neoplatonists* (Leiden: Brill, 1976); Philip Rollinson, *Classical*

Theories of Allegory and Christian Culture (Pittsburgh: Duquesne UP, 1981); F. J. E. Raby, *"Nuda Natura* and Twelfth-Century Cosmology," *Speculum* 43 (1968): 72–77. For *figura,* see Erich Auerbach, "Figura," *Scenes from the Drama of European Literature,* trans. Ralph Manheim (New York: Meridien, 1959) 11–76. For the exegetic tradition within medieval theology, see Henri de Lubac, *Exégèse médiévale,* 4 vols. (Paris: Aubin, 1961).

[11] A. Jubinal, ed. *Nouveau Recueil de contes,* 2 vols. (Paris: Panier, 1839–42) 2: 72.

[12] On allegory in the *Queste,* see Burns; Tuve 418–36; and Douglas Kelly, *"Translatio Studii:* Translation, Adaptation, and Allegory in Medieval French Literature," *Philological Quarterly* 57 (1978): 287–310. Tzvetan Todorov, "Les Genres du récit," *Les Genres du discours* (Paris: Seuil, 1978) 68–74, uses the *Queste* to distinguish between a *récit mythologique,* whose narrative structures and transformations are focused on events, and *récit gnoséologique* or *épistémique,* whose narrative transformations are those of interpretation.

[13] Tzvetan Todorov, "La Quête du récit," *Poétique de la prose* (Paris: Seuil, 1971) 129–50.

[14] See Tuve 426–27 and Thomas E. Kelly, *Le Haut Livre du Graal: Perlesvaus, A Structural Study* (Genève: Droz, 1974) 99–102.

[15] Rollinson 83. Judicious views of allegorical readings of romance have been expressed by Jean Misrahi, "Symbolism and Allegory in Arthurian Romance," *Romance Philology* 17 (1963–64): 555–67; by Robert Guiette in his studies reprinted in *Forme et "senefiance,"* ed. J. Dufournet, M. De Grève, and H. Braet (Genève: Droz, 1978); by Morton W. Bloomfield, "Symbolism in Mediaeval Literature," *Modern Philology* 56 (1968): 73–81; and by Daniel Poirion, "De l' 'Enéide' à l' 'Enéas': Mythologie et moralisation," *Cahiers de civilisation médiévale* 19 (1976): 213–29.

[16] Marie de France, *Lais,* ed. J. Lods (Paris: Champion, 1959), prologue, vv. 11–24; Jean de Meun, *Le Roman de la Rose,* ed. Félix Lecoy (Paris: Champion, 1968) 1: 218–19, at the end of *Raison*'s discourse to *l'Amant,* vv. 7123–27; Jean Bodel, *Saisnes,* 2 vols., ed. F. Menzel and E. Stengel (Marburg: Elwert, 1906–09), prologue, vv. 9–10.

[17] See Michel Zink, *La prédication en langue romane avant 1300* (Paris: Champion, 1976) 147–48.

[18] Jubinal 2: 297.

[19] Matarasso, *Redemption* 205–41.

[20] Among the excellent studies of analogical narratives within the *Queste,* see Savage; Burns 354–61; and Todorov, "Quête." For analogies with Scripture, see Matarasso, *Redemption* 168–71.

[21] *Policraticus* 2.16, *Frivolities of Courtiers and Footprints of Philosophers,* trans. Joseph B. Pike (Minneapolis: U of Minnesota P, 1938) 81.

[22] See Pauphilet, *Etude* 145, and Matarasso, *Redemption* 91–95. Hennessy (192) points out other theological incongruities such as Gauvain's being reproached for killing the seven deadly sins (Pauphilet, *Queste* 54).

[23] Savage 458–59.

[24] Chrétien de Troyes, *Chevalier de la charrette,* vv. 1479–81, *Arthurian Romances,* trans. W. W. Comfort (London: Dent, 1914) 239.

[25] *La Mort le roi Artu,* ed. J. Frappier (Genève: Droz; Paris: Minard, 1964) 90.

[26] Burns 355. See Baumgartner 83–95. Gérard Moignet's study of the moods

and tenses of verbs in the narratives represented as dreams concludes that the *Queste*'s author portrays dreams with the same degree of fictional reality as its principal narrative line of chivalric adventures. "La grammaire des songes dans la Queste del Saint Graal," *Langue Française* 40, *Grammaires du texte médiéval* (1978): 113–19. The value of "truth" is enhanced by the prose form of the *Queste;* see D. Poirion, "Romans en vers et romans en prose," *Grundriss der romanischen literaturen des mittelalters* (Heidelberg: Winter, 1978) 4: 74–81.

[27] See Burns (356–58) for an analysis of the metamorphosis of the six variants of the temptation motif using the lion and serpent first encountered and then dreamed by Perceval in the *Queste.*

[28] The relationship between the *Queste* and vernacular sermons, pious tales, and exempla is amply studied by Pauphilet, *Etudes,* and Savage. Bright images of the Incarnation are the common coin of pious tales about the Host; see Caesarius of Heisterbach, *Dialogue on Miracles,* 2 vols., trans. H. von E. Scott and C. C. Swinton Bland (London: Routledge, 1929), bk. 9, "Of the Sacrament of the Body and Blood of Christ"), 2: 103–69.

[29] Micha 7: 119–22; 1: 276–79.

[30] Pauphilet, *Etudes* 120, 173; see also Matarasso, *Redemption* 179, 205.

[31] Studies of the *Queste* within the Vulgate *Lancelot* cycle include Lot 77; Alexandre Micha, "L'Esprit du *Lancelot-Graal,*" *De la Chanson de Geste au roman* (Genève: Droz, 1976); Baumgartner 11–12, 143–44.

[32] See Fanni Bogdanow, *The Romance of the Grail: A Study of the Structure and Genesis of a Thirteenth-Century Arthurian Prose Romance* (Manchester, Eng.: Manchester UP, 1966) 203.

[33] Chrétien, *Charrette,* vv. 4652–53, Comfort 329. See Leo Spitzer's critique of religious readings of troubador lyric, "L'Amour lointain de Jaufré Rudel et le sens de la poésie des troubadours," *Etudes de style* (Paris: Gallimard, 1970) 81–133.

[34] On the gravity of myth in story, see C. S. Lewis, "On Myth," *An Experiment in Criticism* (Cambridge: Cambridge UP, 1969) 40–49.

[35] See Grace Armstrong Savage, "Father and Son in the *Queste del Saint Graal,*" *Romance Philology* 31 (1977–78): 1–16. For configurations of eschatology in medieval romance, see Donald Maddox, "The Awakening: A Key Motif in Chrétien's Romances," *The Sower and His Seed: Essays on Chrétien de Troyes,* ed. Rupert T. Pickens (Lexington, Ky.: French Forum, 1982) 31–51.

[36] With warmest thanks to the participants in the 1982 Dartmouth Colloquium, to Mathilda Bruckner, Antonio Regalado, Kathryn Talarico, E. B. Vitz, Nathan Horwitz, and Bradley Berke for their readiness to discuss the *Queste,* and to E. Jane Burns and Grace Armstrong Savage, who generously shared their ongoing work with me.

JEAN de MEUN
AND THE LIMITS OF ROMANCE
Genius as Rewriter of Guillaume de Lorris

Kevin Brownlee

The success of the *Romance of the Rose* among medieval readers was extraordinary. Close to three hundred manuscripts are still extant, dating from a period of nearly three hundred years.[1] Yet this success seems to have resulted from a rather exceptional form of literary "collaboration": the ostensibly uncompleted 4,000-line poem of Guillaume de Lorris (dating from the late 1220s) was continued and ultimately "finished" forty years after Guillaume's death by a second poet, Jean de Meun, whose continuation amounted to more than 17,000 lines. As Pierre-Yves Badel has recently demonstrated, the immediate and enduring success of the *Rose* was definitively linked to the appearance of the conjoined text as conceived and realized by Jean.[2] Jean's work constituted and was perceived by contemporary readers as a kind of vernacular, poetic *summa*.[3] As such, it thematized the very poetic and rhetorical processes that had generated it. In this context, the status of Guillaume de Lorris in the conjoined *Rose* of Jean de Meun assumes a particular importance. Guillaume's poem is simultaneously an independent literary entity and an integral part of a larger literary entity, which "contains" it.

Jean de Meun's *Rose* explicitly treats the issue of the poetics of continuation, that is, the status of Guillaume de Lorris, on two separate and highly significant occasions: the speech of Amors near the midpoint of the conjoined *Rose* and the speech of Genius near the work's end. These two loci involve the most explicit instances of generic self-consciousness manifested in Jean's continuation: in each case the limits of the romance genre (as well as the limits of this particular romance) are clearly at issue.

This study considers in detail the way in which Jean de Meun's character Genius explicitly undertakes a corrective rewriting of the *Romance of the Rose* of Guillaume de Lorris that had served as the generative kernel for Jean's own text. In this context, the generic self-consciousness of Jean's poetic enterprise is examined, with special attention given to his programmatic expansion and transformation of the romance genre.

Before considering Genius as a rewriter of Guillaume de Lorris, it is first necessary to focus briefly on two key structural aspects of Jean de Meun's poem: (1) the narrator-protagonist configuration and (2) the diegetic speech situation. The latter element is of particular importance in Jean's *Rose,* where direct discourse assumes such major proportions. Indeed, the entire work is structured by means of a series of long speeches by personification characters whose identities are coterminous with their discourse.

The narrator-protagonist configuration that is explicitly established in Jean's *Rose* takes as its necessary point of departure the first-person configuration initiated by Guillaume de Lorris in his prologue. This, as Uitti has observed, involves a *je*-protagonist who "is the twenty-year-old lyric lover (later to be identified as Amant)." Guillaume's *je*-narrator "though 'the same person' is the twenty-five-year-old romance-type clerk" (Uitti, *Clerc* 212).[4] This initial Guillaumian first-person narrator-protagonist configuration (itself a striking generic innovation in terms of the Old French courtly romance tradition) is simultaneously continued and expanded by Jean de Meun in the course of Amors's speech to his troops near the mid-point of the conjoined *Rose* text (vv. 10495–678). Here, Guillaume is explicitly named as Amant, the lover-protagonist: Amors asks that he be helped qua lover in his quest to win the Rose:

Si vous cri merci jointes paumes
Que cist las doulereus Guillaumes,
Qui si bien s'est vers mei portez,
Seit secouruz e confortez.
    (vv. 10657–60)[5]

[And I beg you with joined palms that this poor wretched Guillaume who has borne himself so well toward me, may be helped and comforted.]

Amors then goes on to name Jean de Meun (as yet "unborn" in the fiction of the text) as the poet-narrator who is to finish the romance: Amors asks that Jean be helped to *"write* more easily" ("Qu'il *escrive* plus de legier,*" v. 10664; emphasis added). Because he is continuing Guillaume, however, Jean employs *je* to refer both to the lover-protagonist and to the poet-narrator. While transforming it radically, then, "Jean retains Guillaume's first-person device: narrator and protagonist ostensibly stay one and the same."[6]

It is of the utmost importance to recognize that this textual articulation of Guillaume's transformed and reduced status qua protagonist coincides with and motivates a radical change in the diegetic speech situation of Jean's *Rose:* Amant ceases to be the privileged internal addressee.

The long speeches of Raison (vv. 4229–7228) and Ami (vv. 7237–10002) are addressed directly and exclusively to Amant, as are the shorter discourse of Richesse (vv. 10071–10267) and the first speech of Amors (vv. 10319–10438). Indeed, each of these four discourses is, to a greater or lesser degree, a dialogue in which Amant actively participates.

The shift occurs as Amors turns from Amant to address the assembled body of his troops and makes the very speech that redefines Amant's status as lover-protagonist in terms of Jean de Meun's larger poetic enterprise. When "Guillaume de Lorriz" (v. 10526) is named for the first time in the entire work, a significant transformation from the second to the third person is effected: Guillaume/Amant will no longer function as the diegetic "target" of the long discourses that together make up most of the remainder of Jean's *Rose.* Faux Semblant's speech (vv. 10952–12010) is addressed to (indeed is a dialogue with) Amors before an assembled audience which simply includes Amant, who thus functions as witness to rather than participant in the primary diegetic speech situation. The long speech of La Vieille (vv. 12555–14679) is addressed to Bel Acueil, and the now-absent Amant is reduced to an indirect witness to their dialogue:

> Si con cil puis me raconta
> Qui tout retenu le conte a
>
> . . .
>
> Ce me fiançait e jurait,
> Autrement ne m'asseürait.
> > (vv. 12993–94, 12999–13000)

[Thus Bel Aceuil, who remembered the whole story, told me after-ward. . . . He so guaranteed to me by oath; he assured me in no other way.]

With the appearance of Nature, an even more radical change in the diegetic speech situation is effected. Amant the *je*-protagonist is sup-pressed entirely as witness figure, and Nature's Confession (vv. 16729–19405) is addressed exclusively to Genius and recounted by the *je*-narrator, who adopts an omniscient authorial stance. It is this first-person voice which abruptly shifts the narrative setting from the Garden of the Rose to "Nature's Forge" (vv. 15891ff.). It is this same first-person voice which "introduces" the personification character by means of a self-consciously (and playfully) literary discussion of Na-ture's struggle against death, of Art as a necessarily imperfect imita-tion of Nature, and of the transformative power of the "true art" ("art veritable," v. 16084) of Alchemy. This introduction ends with a particularly elaborate deployment of the "unutterability topos" with regard to the impossibility of an adequate verbal description of Nature's beauty, explicitly addressed to an extra-diegetic reading public:

Bien la vous vousisse descrire,
Mais mes sens n'i pourrait soufire.
. . . se je poïsse,
Volentiers au meins l'entendisse;
Veire escrite la vous eüsse,
Se je poïsse e je seüsse.
          (vv. 16165–66; 16211–14)[7]

[I would willingly describe her to you, but my sense is not equal to it . . . I would at least have tried if I had been able; indeed, I would have described her to you in writing if I could have and had known how.]

By this stage, the enunciating *je* of the poet-narrator has become, as it were, detached from the temporarily suppressed *je* of the lover-protagonist. This altered narrator-protagonist configuration (in which the je-narrator has been implicitly "expanded" to the point where it "contains" its subject matter) is foregrounded by the couplet which introduces Nature's actual Confession: "sa confession, / . . . je vous ci aport escrite / Mot a mot, si come el l'a dite" (vv. 16726–28) [I bring her confession to you here in writing, word for word, just as she said it]. The conclusion of Nature's Confession directly motivates the speech of Genius that is the primary subject of the present study as well as the last long discourse by a personification character in the poem. This speech (vv. 19505–20667) ostensibly relocates the narrative in the Garden of the Rose and ostensibly reintroduces the *je*-protagonist as direct witness to the discourse. Nature, remaining in her Forge, sends Genius to deliver a message of crucial importance to the assembled troops of Venus and Amors.

Significantly, however, the third-person plural pronoun is used exclusively to designate Genius's diegetic addressees both before and after his speech. On his arrival before the army or the barons ("l'ost," "li baron"; vv. 19444, 19495), Genius "Si come il dut touz *les* salue;/ E l'achaison de sa venue, / Senz riens metre en oubli, *leur* conte" (vv. 19465–67; emphasis added) [greeted *them* all as he was supposed to and, forgetting nothing, told *them* the reason for his coming]. Immediately after the conclusion of his discourse we find "Genius ainsinc *leur* preesche, / E *les* resbaudist e soulace" (vv. 20668–69; emphasis added) [Genius preached to *them* thus, delighting and comforting *them*]. The precise status of Guillaume/Amant, the lover-protagonist (as well as his spatiotemporal location in the narrative), thus appears to be somewhat problematic. He is not, apparently, included among the intended addressees of Genius (there is no use of the first-person plural). He seems, however, to be present. Yet this presence is established in a most indirect, even ambiguous, manner. The first-person singular is used to refer to the protagonist—but only in a subordinate clause which functions to identify an absent secondary character in terms of past narrative events:

> . . . Faus Semblant . . .
> Partiz s'en iert plus que le pas
> De lors que La Vieille fu prise
> Qui *m*'ouvri l'uis de la pourprise
> E tant *m*'ot fait avant aler
> Qu'a Bel Acueil *me* lut paler.
> (vv. 19445–50; emphasis added)[8]

[Faux Semblant . . . had left in a hurry as soon as La Vieille was captured, the one who opened the door of the enclosure for *me* and helped *me* to advance to the point where *I* was allowed to speak to Bel Acueil.]

In contrast to this attenuated presence of the *je*-protagonist, the *je*-narrator appears to speak with the same strengthened authority and the same expanded perspective established in the Nature sequence, with regard both to his subject matter and to his extra-diegetic audience:

> *Je* ne vous quier ja faire conte
> De la grant joie qu'il li firent
> Quant ces nouveles entendirent;
> Ainz *vueil ma* parole abregier
> Pour voz oreilles alegier.
>   (vv. 19468–72; emphasis added)

[*I* shall not try to make a story out of the great joy they showed when they heard the news; instead, *I* want to shorten *my* account and lighten your ears.]

Having situated Genius's discourse with regard to its diegetic speech situation and to the narrator-protagonist configuration of Jean's *Rose,* let us consider that discourse itself. Genius's speech contains two major components.[9] On the one hand, a particular behavioral code is presented as an absolute and universal imperative for human life on earth. This is the so-called Gospel of Procreation—for Genius repeatedly claims, on the basis of the authority vested in him by Nature, that man's foremost obligation is to engage in sexual activity to perpetuate the species.

The second component of Genius's speech involves an elaborate description of the eternal punishments and rewards that await those who shirk and those who fulfill the imperatives of the Gospel of Procreation. Failure to procreate during one's earthly existence (whether through homosexuality, sterile "courtly love," or virginity/chastity) leads to Hell and damnation in the afterlife. Conversely, successful procreative activity on earth will be rewarded by an eternity in Paradise—authentic, Christian salvation, described in elaborate and symbolically unambiguous detail.

The relationship between the two components of Genius's speech has preoccupied nearly all modern critics to one degree or another.[10] How can there be a direct causal link between a purely "natural" (even prelapsarian),[11] procreative virtue exercised in a postlapsarian world and a fully "spiritual," Christian reward in Paradise? Is there not a fundamental contradiction here?

While the limited aims of this study preclude a fuller treatment of these important matters, we can nevertheless make certain general observations in this context. First, the behavioral code advocated by Genius certainly involves the most radical displacement of the courtly behavioral code articulated in Guillaume de Lorris's *Rose.* (It is of course true that the discourse of every major personification character in Jean's *Rose* involves a deformation or displacement of Guillaume's code of courtliness. Genius, I suggest, represents the extreme.) Second, both components of Genius's speech involve an equally radical displacement of Guillaume de Lorris's courtly linguistic code, his courtly discourse. The poetic diction employed (even embodied) by Genius is of two very different registers: that of procreative sexual activity and that of Christian spirituality. While both represent linguistic—and experiential—realms necessarily excluded from Guillaume de Lorris's courtly world and thus implicitly invite comparison with Guillaume's model, it is in the context of Genius's spiritual register that this comparison becomes explicit.

Having metaphorically identified the Paradise that awaits those who follow Nature's laws as the "parc dou champ joli" (v. 19935) [park of the lovely field], Genius shifts (about two-thirds of the way through his speech) from description to comparison:

> Car, qui dou bel jardin carré,
> Clos au petit guichet barré,
> Ou cil amanz vit la querole
> Ou Deduiz o ses genz querole,
> A ce beau parc que je devise,
> Tant par est beaus a grant devise,
> Faire voudrait comparaison,
> Il ferait trop grant mespreison
> S'il ne la fait tel ou semblable
> Come il ferait de veir a fable.
>   (vv. 20279–88)

[If anyone wanted to draw a comparison between the lovely square garden, closed with the little barred wicket, where this lover saw the carol where Deduit dances with his people, and this fair park that I am describing, as wondrously fair as one could wish it, he would make a very great mistake if he did not draw the comparison as one would between truth and a fable.]

This passage introduces the extended and highly explicit critical treatment of Guillaume de Lorris's Garden that occupies roughly the final third of Genius's discourse (vv. 20279–626). In addition, this introductory passage establishes the terms of Genius's critical comparison. Several important points are at issue. First, Genius is rewriting, "correcting," Guillaume de Lorris's *text:* The Garden of Deduit is treated from the outset as *écriture,* written object. Genius begins—in a pattern that will be repeated throughout the entire sequence—with a deformed textual citation of Guillaume de Lorris that duplicates the latter's rhyme words. Genius's "Car qui dou bel jardin *carré* / Clos au petit guichet *barré*" (vv. 20279–80; emphasis added) [If anyone wanted to draw a comparison between the lovely square garden, closed with the little barred wicket] echoes Guillaume de Lorris's "Hauz fu li murs e toz *carrez* / Si en estoit clos e *barrez*" (vv. 467–68; emphasis added) [The wall was high and quite square; (a garden) was enclosed and shut off by it]. Second, the status of Guillaume de Lorris throughout Genius's extended comparison is that of a poet-narrator (even when he is treated as lover). Thus, as we shall see in detail later, Guillaume/Amant is always referred to by Genius in the third person—he is never addressed directly. He is an object of discourse and thus his presence qua character amounts to a kind of personification of his poetic text, of his *Romance of the Rose*. This becomes apparent in the second couplet of Genius's comparison where, once again, a specific Guillaumian subtext is evoked, but with a crucial transformation of rhyme words. Genius's "Ou cil amanz vit la querole / Ou Deduiz o ses genz querole" (vv. 20281–82) [where this lover saw the carol where Deduit dances with his people] recalls Guillaume de Lorris's "Ceste gent don je vos parole / S'estoient pris a la querole" (vv. 727–28) [These people of whom I tell you were formed into a carol]. The first-person voice in the subtext is that of Guillaume the poet-narrator addressing his extra-diegetic audience in the present time of writing. Genius's double transformation (into the third person and into the preterite) highlights Guillaume's status (even qua *amanz*) as poet, as producer of *écriture* in Genius's comparison. Further, this transformation involves an implicit substitution: Genius as enunciating subject (*je devise*) replaces the suppressed Guillaume de Lorris (*je vos parole*). But the act of enunciation in the case of Genius (the character) thus appears to be implicitly equated with the production of a written poetic text. The initial terms of the comparison thus oppose Guillaume de Lorris as poet with Genius, as an implicit poet figure.

That the very foundations of Guillaume de Lorris's poetics are at issue becomes evident with the opposition of the categories *veir* and *fable*. A reversal is thus effected with regard to the opening of Guillaume de Lorris's prologue, where the equivalent primary functional opposition is between *songe* and *mensonge:* a key rhyme-word pair, with *mensonge* linked to *fable* and *songe* thus being, paradoxically, invested with a "truth component."

Let us turn now to a global consideration of Genius's comparative criticism of the Garden of Guillaume de Lorris, which uses a three-part rhetorical strategy. First, Genius rewrites (that is, summarizes by abbreviated and transformed textual citation) various elements of Guillaume de Lorris's text. Second, these elements are treated "negatively": they are explicitly denigrated, judged inadequate according to a standard external to Guillaume de Lorris's poetic world. Third, selected elements of Guillaume de Lorris's text (from the Garden of Deduit) are "corrected" in a "positive mode": Genius elaborates a corresponding series of superior features from his *beau parc*.

After an initial hierarchical contrast—the superiority of the round to the square shape—Genius explicitly establishes the techniques of citation and *abbreviatio* that he will use throughout his treatment of Guillaume de Lorris, stressing once again the latter's status as poet and that of his text as *écriture:*

> Palons des choses qu'il vit lores
> E par dedenz e par defores
> E par briés moz nous en passon
> Pour ce que trop ne nous lasson.
>   (vv. 20299–302)

[Let us now speak of the things that he saw at that time both inside and outside, and in order not to tire ourselves, we will pass over them in a few words.]

Genius then treats the section of Guillaume de Lorris's text that begins with the Dreamer's first sight of the *vergier* and ends with his discovery and description of the Fountain of Love (vv. 129–1614), up to but not including the moment when Amors *directly* enters the narrative to transform the Dreamer into the Lover. While the narrative order of Guillaume de Lorris's text is generally followed, Genius's own procedure involves a careful rhetorical strategy: an exaggerated *abbreviatio* of Guillaume de Lorris's text up to the discovery of the Fountain.

Genius begins his comparison with an abbreviated summary of the outside of Guillaume de Lorris's Garden, in which the presence of the latter as (implicit) producer of written discourse is foregrounded: "Il vit dis laide imagetes / Hors dou jardin, ce dit pourtraites" (vv. 20303–04) [He saw ten ugly little images painted, he said, outside the garden]. Not only have Guillaume de Lorris's *ymages* been reduced to *imagetes,* but his 337-line description (vv. 129–466) has been reduced to a single couplet. Genius then corrects Guillaume de

Lorris's text "positively" with a description of the "superior" exterior of his *beau parc:* the entire created universe—Hell, Earth (that is, the four elements), and the Heavenly Spheres (vv. 20305–34).

The rest of Genius's comparison is devoted to the interiors of the two enclosures (vv. 20335–626, 291 lines): "Or au jardin nous en ralons / E des choses dedenz palons" (vv. 20335–36) [Now let us go back to the Garden and speak of the things inside]. He begins, once again, with a programmatically abbreviated summary passage (of eleven lines, vv. 20337–48). It is important to note that the rhetorical organization of Genius's proleptic summary (even the summary as such) is derived from a subtext in which Guillaume de Lorris speaks explicitly qua poet-narrator:

> Dès orc, si con je savrai,
> Vos conterai coment j'ovrai:
> Primes de quoi Deduiz servoit,
> E quel compaignie il avoit,
> Senz longue fable vos vueil dire;
> E dou vergier trestot a tire
> La façon vos redirai puis
> Tot ensemble dire ne puis,
> Mais tot vos conterai en ordre
> Que nus n'i sache que remordre.
> (vv. 691–700)

[From now on, I shall recount to you, as well as I can, how I went to work. First, I want to tell you, without any long story, about what Deduit served and about his companions; and then, I will tell you in a full and orderly way about the appearance of the garden. I cannot speak of everything together, but I will recount it all to you in such order that no one will have any criticism to make.]

Two points must be noted here. First, the configuration *je/vous,* repeated four times, is clearly that of narrator/reader. Second, Guillaume de Lorris is claiming immunity to criticism on the grounds of his rhetorico-poetic expertise. This passage of proleptic summary introduces a sequence of 723 lines (vv. 701–1424) in Guillaume's *Rose.*

Let us now consider in detail Genius's strategy of rewriting and abbreviating Guillaume in this context. It should be mentioned at the outset that the *je* of Guillaume the narrator is systematically transformed by Genius into a series of third-person avatars. It is also worth noting that Genius does not, in fact, criticize Guillaume's rhetorico-poetic organizational principle but rather makes use of it himself.

Genius's proleptic summary may be broken down into the following three parts. First, "Il vit, ce dit, seur l'erbe fresche / Deduit qui demenait sa tresche, / E ses genz o lui querolanz / Seur les flouretes bien olanz" (vv. 20337–40) [He said that he saw Deduit leading his farandole on the fresh grass, and his people with him, caroling on the sweet-smelling flowers].

Genius's four lines involve an *abbreviatio* of a 572-line passage in Guillaume (vv. 712–1284) as well as a total suppression of Guillaume's elaborate introduction of the God of Love. Further, Genius's utilization of a set of Guillaume's rhyme words again foregrounds the process of textual citation as such and thus the fact that Genius treats Guillaume as text, as *écriture*.[12]

Genius continues his proleptic summary with a second four-line passage that drastically abbreviates lines 1285–1424 of Guillaume's text:

> E vit, ce dit, li damoiseaus
> Erbres, arbres, bestes, oiseaus
> E ruisselez e fonteneles
> Bruire e fremir par les graveles
>   (vv. 20341–44)

[And the young squire also said that he saw plants, trees, animals, birds, brooks and springs babbling and singing over the gravel.]

The careful correspondence between the two texts again emphasizes Genius's treatment of Guillaume as *écriture* as well as the programmatic suppression of the God of Love. Genius concludes his proleptic summary with a radical new departure:

> E la fontaine souz le pin
> E se vante que puis Pepin
> Ne fu teus pins; et la fontaine
> Restait de trop grant beauté pleine.
>   (vv. 20345–48)

[And the fountain under the pine; and he boasts that since the time of Pepin there was not such a pine, and that the fountain was also filled with very great beauty.]

For the first time the proportions of Genius's rewriting have changed dramatically: his four-line summary now restates only ten lines of Guillaume de Lorris (vv. 1425–34, including the rhyme words *pin/*

Pepin from Guillaume's vv. 1427–28). This change in proportion indicates that Genius has arrived at what is to him the single most important element of Guillaume's text: the Fountain and the Pine. The transformation of the *je* of Guillaume-narrator into the third-person *li damoiseaus* (v. 20341) is also highly significant. The most important of the three uses of this word in all of Guillaume de Lorris is to identify Narcissus in the verse that introduces his story: "Narcisus fu uns damoisiaus" (v. 1439)[13] [Narcissus was a young man].

Genius next employs his "negative mode" to criticize everything he has presented (in summary form) as being inside Guillaume de Lorris's garden as inferior by virtue of being mortal. Most explicitly, the *queroles* (v. 20355) "seen"/described by Guillaume de Lorris are perishable. But of course, all of the "choses . . . encloses" (vv. 20357–58)[14] [things enclosed] in Guillaume de Lorris's Garden are subject to death. It is at this point that Genius shifts to his "positive critical mode": "Mais or palons des beles choses / Qui sont en ce bel parc encloses" (vv. 20369–70) [But now let us talk of the beautiful things that are enclosed in this lovely park]. Genius's programmatic strategy of displacing Guillaume de Lorris qua poet is again foregrounded on the textual level by the conspicuous use of the rhyme pair "choses/encloses." In the brief "general"[15] corrective *remaniement* of Guillaume de Lorris's Garden that follows, certain key elements are re-presented—now marked, as it were, for immortality. Of special importance in this context are Genius's eternal *queroleur* (v. 20381) and, most particularly, Genius's *fontaine* (v. 20387) of eternal life.

The mention of this fountain triggers the final instance in which Genius summarily rewrites a specific sequence of Guillaume de Lorris's text. This entire passage, however (vv. 20405–60)[16] involves a new and more systematic deployment of Genius's "negative critical mode." After each descriptive feature of Guillaume de Lorris's fountain has been rewritten by Genius, an explicit, negative judgmental intervention follows.

What emerges is, on the one hand, a programmatic and self-conscious deformation of Guillaume de Lorris's experience at the fountain qua protagonist. The fundamental opposition between Amant and Narcissus that is operative in Guillaume de Lorris's text at this point[17] is collapsed by Genius in such a way as to present Guillaume qua protagonist as an implicit Narcissus figure. This suggested transformation had already been initiated by Genius's earlier identification of Guillaume (qua poet-narrator) as *li damoiseaus* (v. 20341).

On the other hand, the three key descriptive features of Guillaume de Lorris's fountain are systematically undermined in Genius's selective and "corrective" rewriting: (1) the fountain's sources of water, (2) its brightness and transparency, and (3) its two crystals and their powers. (In the last two of these cases the fountain's status as mirror—and thus the question of narcissism—is very much at issue.)

Once again, Guillaume de Lorris's *text* is cited, reworked and deformed, with a series of important rhyme-word pairs serving as a particularly visible sign of this process.

The remainder—and single largest part (vv. 20461–596, 135 lines)—of Genius's comparison involves the most elaborate instance of his "positive critical mode": the superior fountain of the *beau parc* is elaborately described in terms of Trinitarian and Christological imagery. The import of Genius's utilization of this clearly Christian poetic register has been cogently analyzed by Daniel Poirion, Pierre-Yves Badel, and Nathaniel Smith.[18] For the purposes of the present study, the single most important aspect of Genius's critical comparison is that it treats Guillaume de Lorris as poet-narrator, as producer of poetic discourse, and that it treats this discourse as written object, as *écriture*.

The full import of this becomes evident only when one considers that Genius's own discourse is presented as *écriture* as it is being produced, the only time this occurs in the entire *Rose*. That Genius is presented as reading from a written text is repeatedly made clear. First, Nature requests Genius to transcribe, to write down, her words —to announce before Amors's troops "Cet pardon e cete sentence / Que je vueil que ci seit *escrite*" (vv. 19404–405; emphasis added) [the pardon and the judgment that I wish to be *written* here]. The ensuing act of transcription is explicitly noted: "Lors *escrit* cil, e cele dite" (v. 19406; emphasis added) [Then he *wrote* it at her dictation].

Genius's entire speech to Amors's troops is framed by reference to his act of reading from a written document. As soon as he explains "l'achaison de sa venue" (v. 19466) [the reason for his coming] to the assembled troops, they are seized by an intense desire "D'oïr cele sentence *lire*" (v. 19483; emphasis added) [to hear his judgment *read*]. Before his discourse begins, Genius mounts a large platform ". . . *pour lire meauz la letre,* / Selonc les faiz devant contez" (vv. 19492–93; emphasis added) [*the better to read the text* according to the things told about before]. As soon as his diegetic audience is seated, Genius begins by unfolding *"sa chartre"* (v. 19497; emphasis added) [*his document*].

After the conclusion of Genius's discourse, its diegetic status as *écriture* is again foregrounded. Amors is described as spreading "la nouvele . . . *de la chartre leüe*" (vv. 20680, 20679; emphasis added)[19] [the news that was *read from the document*]. Finally, the reaction of Amors's barons is described as taking place after "Genius ot *tout leü*" (v. 20683; emphasis added) [Genius had *read everything*].

Further, Genius himself refers repeatedly to his discourse as *écriture*—as he is in the very process of articulating it. These references are, indeed, strategically situated. When, at the close of his extended *comparison,* Genius calls upon his diegetic addressees to judge between Guillaume de Lorris's Garden and his own *beau parc,* it is on the basis of ". . . les erremenz / Que *leüz* vous ai ça darriere" (vv. 20612–13; emphasis added) [the evidence that I have *read out* to you above]. Finally, as he is about to sum up his entire discourse—and, most especially, his rendition of Nature's commandments[20]—Genius proleptically justifies this peroration by announcing that "leçon a briés moz *leüe* / Plus est de legier retenue" (vv. 20633–34; emphasis added) [a lesson *read out* in few words is more easily remembered].

The full implications of this repeated self-presentation of Genius's discourse as *écriture* begin to emerge only when we consider that Genius also treats Nature's Confession as *écriture*. Further, this is done in a way which explicitly raises the issue of the generic status of Jean de Meun's entire poem as well as the question of the limits of romance.

As Genius is exhorting his diegetic audience to avoid the vices that Nature had enumerated and condemned in her earlier Confession to him, he decides not to bother naming them explicitly himself:

> Ces vices conter vous voudraie,
> Mais d'outrage m'entremetraie.
> Assez briement les vous expose
> Le jolis *Romanz de la rose;*
> S'il vous plaist la les regardez,
> Pour ce que d'aus meauz vous gardez.
>   (vv. 19879–84)

[I would tell these vices to you, but to do so would be an excessive undertaking. The lovely *Romance of the Rose* explains them to you quite briefly; please look at them there so that you may guard against them better.]

This is the *only time in all of Jean de Meun's poem that Guillaume de Lorris's full title reappears*. Moreover, it is applied by Genius to a section of Jean de Meun's poem (most precisely vv. 19225–34)[21] that is most emphatically not derived from Guillaume de Lorris. The primary (and highly visible) subtext for Nature's Confession in Jean de Meun is the *De Planctu Naturae* of Alain de Lille. Indeed, with the introduction of Nature into Jean de Meun's poem, we seem to have passed beyond the limits of the *Romance* as conceived by Guillaume de Lorris, or, in other words, beyond the limits of Guillaume de Lorris's text (qua romance) as model for Jean de Meun's continuation/*amplificatio*.[22]

Significantly, the only other time in the entire conjoined *Rose* text in which the generic term *romance* is used onomastically, as part of the work's title, is in the prologue, where Guillaume de Lorris, speaking as poet-narrator, says:

> E se nus nule demande
> Coment je vueil qui li romanz
> Soit apelez que je comenz,
> Ce est li *Romanz de la Rose,*
> Ou l'Art d'Amors est toute enclose.
> (vv. 34–38)

[And if anyone asks what I wish the romance to be called which I begin here, it is the *Romance of the Rose,* in which the whole art of love is contained.]

Genius's use of the title *Romance of the Rose* is thus itself a citation of Guillaume de Lorris—in a context where the act of citation works simultaneously to transform, to deform, and to continue. In the extended comparison between the *Jardin de Deduit* and the *Beau Parc,* Genius, by means of a complex program of textual citation and deformation, has reintroduced Guillaume de Lorris's *Rose* back into Jean de Meun's larger poetic enterprise at a point where it seemed that Guillaume de Lorris's poetic system of courtly diction and behavior as well as his narrative model were no longer operative. By means of his extended "comparison" with certain aspects of Guillaume de Lorris's text—presented as poetic text, as *écriture*—Genius remotivates Guillaume de Lorris in terms of the conjoined encyclopedic text—the poetic *summa* of Jean de Meun which thus *contains* both Guillaume de Lorris and Genius as two extreme examples, two *cas limites* with regard to the possibilities open to poetic discourse. Neither the courtly poetic mode of Guillaume de Lorris nor the modified vernacular Chartrian poetics of Genius can be considered definitive in the context of the larger *containing* poetic structure that is Jean de Meun's text viewed as a whole.

In this sense, it is the *comparison,* the confrontation, of Guillaume de Lorris and Genius that is significant, that works to produce meaning within the larger containing structure of Jean de Meun's poetic *summa.* Genius the character (in Jean de Meun's text) becomes a poet figure. But, at the same time, Genius's rewriting of Guillaume de Lorris works to transform the latter (a "real" poet, with a privileged extratextual existence in terms of the entire *Rose* enterprise) into a "character," also "contained" by Jean de Meun's poetic *summa.*

The opposition between the "extreme" poetic systems represented by Genius and Guillaume de Lorris functions, in Genius's speech, to generate a continuing *poetic* dialectic that transcends both of the participating terms as such. This kind of dialectic production of meaning in which—ultimately—only the extra-diegetic, the extratextual reader can function as privileged addressee is thus, as it were, thematized, rendered explicit qua process in Genius's rewriting of Guillaume de Lorris. This is of course particularly fitting since Genius is the last of Jean de Meun's major personification characters, and, by this point in Jean's *Rose,* Guillaume de Lorris qua poet has retrospectively become (at least in one sense) the first of these personifications of different systems of poetic discourse. No single one is "adequate," but their dialectical interaction—resulting from the very structure of Jean's *Rose*—produces the "meaning" of the text: a "meaning" which can only be seen as coterminous with the reading process.

Nancy Freeman-Regalado[23] has very astutely analyzed how, on the structural level, Jean's *Rose* programmatically both opposes and contains contrary or extreme positions, embodied in the various personification characters. Jean himself, as Freeman-Regalado notes, implicitly instructs his reader in this regard:

> Ainsinc va des contraires choses:
> Les unes sont des autres gloses;
> E qui l'une en veaut defenir,
> De l'autre li deit souvenir,
> Ou ja, par nule entencion,
> N'i metra diffincion;
> Car qui des deus n'a quenoissance
> Ja n'i quenoistra diference,
> Senz quei ne peut venir en place
> Diffinicion que l'en face.
>   (vv. 21573–82)

[Thus things go by contraries; one is the gloss of the other. If one wants to define one of the pair, he must remember the other, or he will never, by any intention, assign a definition to it; he who has no

understanding of the two will never understand the difference between them, and without this difference no definition that one may
make can come to anything.]

Genius's rewriting of Guillaume de Lorris is the most explicit exemplification of this dialectical production of meaning situated in—
indeed, synonymous with—the reading process.

   In this way Genius provides the final and most explicit instance
of Jean de Meun's expansion of the generic limits of romance. Here,
as always in Jean de Meun, Guillaume de Lorris is the *point de
départ*. For in Guillaume de Lorris the generic term "romance" is
used almost exclusively by the first-person voice of the poet-narrator.[24]
In Jean de Muen, by contrast, this key generic term is used only by
characters: by Amors near the midpoint of the conjoined *Rose* text
and by Genius near its end. Amors not only names the two poets of
the conjoined *Rose,* he also establishes the limits of their respective
parts of the work. In each case Amors uses the generic term
"romanz" to designate the "collaborative" literary enterprise, and in
each case the limits are established by means of direct textual citation.
Guillaume de Lorris is to

> Deit il comencier *le romant*
> Ou seront mis tuit mi comant,
> E jusque la le fournira
> Ou il a Bel Acueil dira,
> Qui lanquist ore en la prison
> Par douleur e par mesprison:
> "Mout sui durement esmaiez
> Que entroublié ne m'aiez,
> Si en ai deul e desconfort,
> Jamais n'iert riens qui me confort
> Se je pers vostre bienveillance,
> Car je n'ai mais ailleurs fiance"
>   (vv. 10549–60; emphasis added)

[begin the *romance* in which all my commandments will be set
down, and he will finish it up to the point where he will say to Bel
Acueil, who now languishes, unjustly and in sorrow, in the prison:
"I am terribly afraid that you may have forgotten me, and I am in
sorrow and pain. If I lose your good will, there will never be any
comfort for me, since I have no confidence elsewhere."]

The last six lines of Amors's speech here duplicate precisely the last
six lines of Guillaume de Lorris's poem (vv. 4053–58).[25] Jean de
Meun, on the other hand,

>. . . avra le *romanz* si chier
>Qu'il le voudra tout parfenir . . .
>Car, quant Guillaumes cessera,
>Johans le continuera,
>Emprès sa mort, que je ne mente,
>Anz trespassez plus de quarante,
>E dira pour la mescheance,
>Par peeur de desesperance
>Qu'il n'ait de Bel Acueil perdue
>La bienveillance avant eüe:
>"E si l'ai je perdue, espeir,
>A po que ne m'en desespeir"
>   (vv. 10584–85; 10587–96; emphasis added)

[will be so fond of the *romance* that he will want to finish it right to the end . . . For when Guillaume shall cease, more than forty years after his death . . . Jean will continue it, and because of Bel Acueil's misfortune, and through the despairing fear that he may have lost the good will that Bel Acueil had shown him before, he will say: "And perhaps I have lost it. At least I do not despair of it."]

The final two lines of Amors's speech here duplicate precisely the couplet that opens Jean de Meun's continuation of the *Rose* (vv. 4059–60). The limits of this romance, of the *Romance of the Rose,* are thus explicitly established by a process of textual autocitation, a process that is thereby not only thematized but incorporated into the very "plot" of the romance whose "limits" it serves to define.[26]

Similarly, in Genius's rewriting of Guillaume de Lorris, a process of textual autocitation (this time programmatically distorted) establishes the limits of the romance as genre. If Guillaume de Lorris is, as it were, reintegrated into Jean's poetic *summa* by means of Genius's rewriting, a new kind of generic category (one which at once articulates and surpasses the limits of romance) is being created. This involves, on the part of Jean de Meun, a self-conscious continuation, incorporation, and *dépassement* of the generic system of *courtly* "romanz" as exemplified by Guillaume de Lorris. At the same time Jean's *Rose* creates a new kind of (greatly expanded) vernacular poetic discourse: in Uitti's words, "an open-ended, marvelously ambiguous, and yet *total* discourse."[27]

Jean's expansion of the limits of romance into a new vernacular generic entity—self-consciously opposed to the Latin *Speculum*[28] and intentionally *unnamed* by the first-person voice of Jean qua poet-narrator—opened the way for—indeed, necessitated—the extraordinary series of generic innovations that characterized late medieval French literature.[29]

Notes

[1] See Pierre-Yves Badel's important study *Le* Roman de la Rose *au XIVe siècle: Etude de la réception de l'oeuvre* (Genève: Droz, 1980) 55–62. Badel notes that this figure is "tout à fait exceptionnel pour un ouvrage en langue vulgaire" (55).

[2] See Badel 55–56 and esp. 62: "La continuation de Jean de Meun a donné un élan décisif à la diffusion du *Roman de la Rose.* Dès lors . . . cette oeuvre a été tout au long du XIVe siècle lue et appréciée comme un tout. Mieux: c'est l'ensemble qui a été porté au crédit de Jean de Meun."

[3] For the status of Jean's conjoined *Rose* text as a poetic *summa,* see Karl D. Uitti, "From *Clerc* to *Poète:* The Relevance of the *Romance of the Rose* to Machaut's World," *Machaut's World: Science and Art in the Fourteenth Century,* Annals of the New York Academy of Sciences 314 (New York: New York Academy of Sciences, Oct. 1978) 210.

[4] See also Karl D. Uitti, "Foi littéraire et création poétique: Le problème des genres littéraires en ancien français," *XIV Congresso Internationale di Linguistica e Filologia Romanza: Atti I,* ed. Alberto Várvaro (Napoli: Macchiaroli, 1978) 171–73.

[5] This and all subsequent quotations from the *Rose* are taken from Ernest Langlois, ed., *Le Roman de la Rose* by Guillaume de Lorris and Jean de Meun, 5 vols. (Paris: Firmin Didot, 1914–24). Translations are from Charles Dahlberg, *The Romance of the Rose* (Princeton: Princeton UP, 1971), with selective emendations.

[6] Uitti, *"Clerc"* 214. See also Uitti, "Foi" 173–75.

[7] At the same time, this passage is a playfully ironic response to its subtext, Alain de Lille's *De Planctu Naturae,* where the elaborate description of Nature takes up the entire first prose section as well as the second metrum. See Nikolaus K. Häring, "Alan of Lille, *De Planctu Naturae,*" *Studi Medievali* 19.2 (1978): 808–20. Jean's subsequent "avowal" of a failed attempt in this regard (vv. 16215–32) differentiates him still further from his Chartrian model in the eyes of his own reading public. Cf. Langlois 4: 300.

[8] This reference is to an episode that took place almost five thousand lines earlier, vv. 14706ff.

[9] The articulation of these two components is not rigorously sequential but involves, rather, a pattern of interpretation.

[10] See esp. Winthrop Wetherbee, "The Literal and the Allegorical: Jean de Meun and the *De Planctu Naturae,*" *Mediaeval Studies* 33 (1971): 264–91; Badel 29–54. See also Gérard Paré, *Les Idées et les lettres aux XIIIe siècle: Le* Roman de la Rose (Montréal: Bibliothèque de Philosophie, 1947) 279–97; Alan M. F. Gunn, *The Mirror of Love: A Reinterpretation of* The Romance of the Rose (Lubbock: Texas Tech P, 1952) 205–75; Wetherbee, *Poetry and Platonism in the Twelfth Century* (Princeton: Princeton UP, 1972) 255–66; Daniel Poirion, *Le* Roman de la Rose (Paris: Hatier, 1973) 186–99; Jane Chance Nitzsche, *The Genius Figure in Antiquity and the Middle Ages* (New

York: Columbia UP, 1975) 116–25; Nathaniel Smith, "In Search of the Ideal Landscape: From *Locus Amoenus* to *Parc du Champ Joli* in the *Roman de la Rose*," *Viator* 11 (1980): 225–43.

[11] The significance of the divine imperative of Genesis 1:28 ("Crescite et multiplicamini") for Genius's Gospel has been discussed by Gunn 213–15. See also Badel 29–32.

[12] Cf. Guillaume's vv. 743–46: Lors veïssiez querole aler / E genz mignotement baler / E faire mainte bele *tresche* / E maint bel tor sor l'erbe *fresche* (emphasis added).

[13] Genius's use of the rhyme-word pair *damoisiaus/oisiaus* in vv. 20341–42 duplicates Guillaume's practice in the two other instances where the word *damoisiaus* appears in his text: Deduit is described as a "juenes damoisiaus" wearing "un samit portrait a oisiaus" (vv. 819–20); the Fountain of Love is portrayed as the locus where Cupid sets his traps to capture "Damoiseles e damoisiaus, / Qu'Amors ne viaut autres oisiaus" (vv. 1593–94).

[14] Cf. in addition the crucial lines from Guillaume de Lorris's prologue: "Ce est li *Romanz de la Rose*, / Ou l'Art d'Amors est toute enclose" (vv. 37–38). It is interesting to note that the word *enclose* appears five other times in the rhyme position in Guillaume de Lorris: twice in the pair *chose/enclose* (vv. 1567–68, 2887–88)—this being the rhyme pair twice duplicated by Genius—and three times in the pair *enclose/rose* (vv. 3365–66, 3777–78, and 3997–98, where the order is reversed, in a return to the initial sequence: ". . . la rose, / Qui est entre les murs enclose").

[15] Genius is explicit on this point: "Je vous en di generaument / Car taire m'en vueil erraument" (vv. 20371–72).

[16] This passage of 55 lines in Genius's speech treats a sequence of 189 lines (vv. 1425–1614) in Guillaume de Lorris. It should be stressed, however, that Genius programmatically suppresses the ensuing passage in Guillaume (vv. 1615–80), in which the Dreamer, looking into the mirror of the Fountain, sees the rosebushes and is thus moved to go and seek out the Rose.

[17] For this opposition see Michelle A. Freeman, "Problems in Romance Composition: Ovid, Chrétien de Troyes and the *Romance of the Rose*," *Romance Philology* 30 (1976–77): 158–68.

[18] See Poirion 194–98; Badel 29–32, 46–54; and Smith 238–43.

[19] The use of the same word (*chartre*) for Genius's document both immediately before and immediately after the text of his discourse emphasizes its function as frame.

[20] There is a suggestive parallel here with Amant's rendition of Amors's commandments near the midpoint of the conjoined *Rose* text (vv. 10403–12). These ten lines radically abbreviate the elaborate original version of Amors's commandments in Guillaume de Lorris (vv. 2077–264).

[21] Langlois remarks on the "surprising" use of this title to refer to a passage in Nature's Confession, "à quelques centaines de vers seulement en arrière." At the same time, Genius's reference is of course an *abbreviatio* of Nature's commandments. This is emphasized by the fact that Genius's figure ("vint e sis," v. 19870) reduces the number of commandments that Nature had actually given—twenty-seven. Langlois 5: 102.

[22] If we except Faux Semblant (a "special case"), La Vieille is the last character that may be viewed as generated out of an element in Guillaume's kernel

text by means of Jean's exploitation of *amplificatio*. For the status of Faux Semblant see Jean Batany, *Approches du* Roman de la Rose (Paris: Bordas, 1973) 97–110.

[23] Nancy Freeman-Regalado, " 'Des Contraires choses': La Fonction poétique de la citation et des *exempla* dans le *Roman de la Rose* de Jean de Meun," *Littérature* 41 (1981): 62–81.

[24] In vv. 35, 2060, and 2062 the poet-narrator uses the term to refer to the *Roman de la Rose* itself. In v. 1599 he uses it to contrast his own treatment of the Fountain of Love with earlier (and inferior) literary treatments of the same subject: "Don plusor ont en maint endroit / Parlé en romanz e en livre." The single instance of a character employing the term occurs when Amors (echoing the words of the poet-narrator in v. 1599) remarks to Amant that the sorrows of love cannot adequately be recounted "en romanz ne en livre" (v. 2607).

[25] Cf. Amors's earlier use of the term *romanz* (v. 10399) in the first part of his speech in the midpoint sequence—the one addressed directly and exclusively to Amant.

[26] It is interesting to note that Amors's speech also establishes the final limit of Jean's *Rose* by means of a "proleptic" textual autocitation. Amors predicts that Jean will continue the romance: "Jusqu'a tant qu'il avra coillie / Seur la branche vert e foillie / La trés bele rose vermeille / E qu'il seit jourz e qu'il s'esveille" (vv. 10599–602). In the poem's final two couplets, this passage is recalled in such a way as to authenticate the ending as ending: "Par grant jolieté coilli / La fleur dou bel rosier foilli. / Ainsinc oi la rose vermeille. / Atant fu jourz, e je m'esveille" (vv. 21777–80). Cf. Langlois 3: 304.

[27] Uitti, *"Clerc"* 215.

[28] This is done not by the poet-narrator but by the character Amors, who "renames" the work *Le Mirouer aus Amoureus* (v. 10651). See Kevin Brownlee, "Reflections in the *Miroër aus Amoreus:* The Inscribed Reader in Jean de Meun's *Roman de la Rose,*" *Mimesis: From Mirror to Method, Augustine to Descartes,* ed. John D. Lyons and Stephen G. Nichols, Jr. (Hanover, N.H.: University P of New England, 1982) 60–70.

[29] The development of the *dit* as a new (and new kind of) generic category is particularly important in this regard. See Jacqueline Cerquiglini's groundbreaking article "Le clerc et l'écriture: le *Voir Dit* de Guillaume de Machaut et la définition du *dit,*" *Literatur in der Gesellschaft des Spätmittelalters,* ed. Hans Ulrich Gumbrecht (Heidelberg: Winter, 1980) 151–68.

RENEWAL AND UNDERMINING
OF OLD FRENCH ROMANCE
Jehan de Saintré

Karl D. Uitti

The five centuries or so leading from the Old French *Life of Saint Alexis* to the completion of the prose narratives of Rabelais—the span of medieval vernacular literature in France—may justifiably be seen as one of the most extraordinary laboratories of literary experimentation in recorded history. Nowhere is this "experimental" character more pronounced than in the area of romance narrative. Even though we limit our concern to France (and, for the time being, set aside the pan-European implications of this production), the romance traditions of renewal and creativity remain staggering, with each century "inventing" anew, always however, I believe, within the framework of an ideal and constant "restoration."

I propose here to discuss a text of narrative fiction—a prose text dating from the middle of the fifteenth century (probably 1456)—that, to judge from the bibliographies, has often been spoken and written about but that, curiously, has not been nearly so much read as one might have thought. (Indeed, despite the efforts of the late Charles A. Knudson and Jean Misrahi, the work still stands in need of a proper edition.) I refer to *Jehan de Saintré,* until recently known to most readers as *Le Petit Jehan de Saintré,* by Antoine de la Sale, composed when its author was in his late sixties.[1]

Jehan de Saintré has done a superb job of defying attempts by critics to classify it generically. An older generation of scholars proved to be fascinated by what they considered to be the work's "realism"—its meticulous attention to observed detail and to the technical vocabulary of fourteenth- and fifteenth-century chivalry as well as to court life.[2] Others have detected "bourgeois"—anticourtly—elements in the work; for them, Antoine de la Sale professes much skepticism about chivalric values.[3] (No phenomenon, it seems, has appeared with greater regularity for the convenience of literary historians than the "rise of the bourgeoisie.") Still other scholars, while expressing boredom at the work's lavish and lengthy descriptions of coats-of-arms, of tourneys, and of jousting, nevertheless praise Antoine de la Sale's delicate and acute sense of psychology. His depiction of the central love affair between his young protagonist, Jehan de Saintré, and the slightly older lady who takes an interest in him is, in their view, worthy of the great French tradition of the "psychological novel," a kind of antecedent, one suspects, of the *Princesse de Clèves*.[4] All these views hold, then, in one way or another, that there is something essentially true to life in *Jehan de Saintré* and, consequently, one concludes, something not characteristically "medieval." With Antoine de la Sale we are on our way to the Renaissance and, via Mme de Lafayette, to the "realist" novel of the nineteenth century.

Perhaps in part because *Jehan de Saintré* was placed on the program of a French university examination during the mid-1960s,[5] it was unable to escape the attention of recent theorists of literature or of semioticians. Julia Kristeva's 1967 thesis, supervised by the late Lucien Goldmann and Roland Barthes, was devoted *in extenso* to this work.[6] Shot through with an appalling ignorance of Old French literature,[7] Kristeva's dissertation focuses, quite naturally, on the "otherness" of *Jehan de Saintré*. *Saintré* is "unlike" Arthurian romance; indeed, it is "disjunctive" in regard to older romance in general and it is therefore symptomatic of a crisis of both language and conscience;[8] it is France's first "novel."[9] (Much pseudo algebra and many diagrams and neologisms are pressed into the service of Kristeva's transforms, but, in essence, she is content to refurbish the image of "modernity" offered of Antoine de la Sale by the scholars alluded to above.)[10]

Of course, both Kristeva and her historicist predecessors are "correct": Antoine de la Sale displays great interest in what in France is called *les intermittences du coeur,* and he does so in a fashion that announces future novelists and dramatists. He explores with acumen the area of displacement between the appearances and realities of

chivalry—of chivalric codes and practices and disjunction. The
Saintré is, indeed, "other" with respect to narrative texts preceding it.
All these things are true. But are they not equally true, say, of
Chrétien de Troyes in regard to the earlier romances of Antiquity
and Wace? Or of Guillaume de Lorris with respect to Chrétien,[11]
and of Jean de Meun to Guillaume? Of Froissart to Machaut? Indeed, as we shall observe in due course, a case may be made supporting the contention that Antoine de la Sale rewrites Froissart in a
fashion quite analogous to that great chronicler's replication-in-transformation of the tradition issued from the *Romance of the Rose*.[12]
The error of Kristeva and earlier scholars resides, I believe, in their
failure to take sufficient stock of the very medieval celebration and
practice of *restoration,* which governs French romance narrative
throughout its history and which, as such, is thematized in the
Saintré. *Jehan de Saintré* is a self-consciously *historical* narrative,
treating events that are presented as having happened a century before its own composition. It *restores* these events, and in restoring
them, it recodifies them. Thus, in a very real sense, *Jehan de Saintré*
resembles its great contemporary text, the *Grand Testament* of François Villon. What, then, has been perceived by some scholars as its
"modernity" in fact is its extraordinary fidelity to quintessentially
medieval poetic procedures. And, of course, these very procedures are
utilized by Antoine de la Sale—as they had been by Chrétien, by
Froissart, and by others—to gain a purchase on and to articulate a
sense of the "real" or of the "historical."

Summary of the plot of *Jehan de Saintré* would be helpful, I think,
at this juncture, as well as some reference to the historical context
which this romance elaborates for itself.

As its brief prologue indicates, the text purports to speak of
a dame, or lady, who, because she is referred to by the Queen as *Belle
Cousine* (she is related to royalty), is known only as the *Dame des
Belles Cousines*. No name or surname, we learn, will be given for
her, and for very good reason.[13] The text also will speak of *the* most
valiant knight, *le sire de Saintré: a* lady and *the* knight, a hint, perhaps, that "ladyness" is to be personified in Madame des Belles
Cousines, whereas the youthful Jehan (his surname is not revealed
until a third of the way into the book) will come to epitomize
knightliness. A lady (that is, a category) will become a person; the
boy (that is, a person, albeit as yet unformed) will become, so to
speak, a category.

This story is designed to be the first of three tales. The second deals with the loyal love and pitiable end of Lord Floridan and Lady Elvyde and consists in a translation from Latin into French, which does not identify its characters except as it moves from episode to episode; the third story, so the author (who does not identify himself) informs us, is an adaptation of part of the "chronicles of Flanders." The entire work is dedicated to Antoine de la Sale's former pupil Lord John of Anjou, Duke of Calabria and Lorraine (a fact not without piquancy as one reads, in the *Saintré,* of Madame's pedagogical efforts on behalf of Jehan). *Jehan de Saintré* thus forms part of a larger, tripartite work, although the second and third texts apparently are very short. Interestingly, however, *Jehan de Saintré* is presented as preceding a very classical romance-type love story and a rather more "historically" conceived—or chronicle-like—narrative. *Translatio*—both translation and adaptation—is also at issue.

The action of *Jehan de Saintré* is situated during the reign of "good" King John II of France, eldest son of Philip of Valois. In many respects, this was one of the blackest periods of French history. After acceding to the throne in 1350, John led the flower of French chivalry at the battle of Poitiers in September 1356, where it met a crushing defeat at the hands of the English. (The disaster was all the more humiliating in that it was largely the doing of "ignoble" English and Welsh crossbowmen, a detail not without relevance to the *Saintré*.) John himself was taken prisoner to England and was not released until an enormous ransom had been paid. His was a reign marked by military debacle, peasant uprisings, a seditious nobility, and plague.

The sad events of King John's reign had been amply described by earlier vernacular chroniclers, but usually, and especially in the case of Froissart, these disasters were depicted within an overriding context of praise for the chivalric ethos; Froissart never ascribes blame to the institutions of chivalry. Meanwhile, these events are never alluded to in *Jehan de Saintré*. Yet they stand out in the text if only by their very absence. Antoine de la Sale appears to work systematic distortions into his material. Thus, the King and his Queen—identified at the start of the work as "Bonne de Bouesme" (Bohemia)—are shown as presiding, respectively, over brilliant courts to which knights and noble ladies from all over Europe pay homage. Now Bonne of Luxemburg had indeed been John's first wife, but only while he was heir to the throne; she died of the plague in 1349, and he succeeded his father in 1350. She never became Queen of France. Moreover, unlike the "Bonne" of the *Saintré* the real Bonne was hardly thought of by her contemporaries as a paragon of ladylike virtue; on the contrary, it was notoriously rumored at the time that her son, the future Regent and King Charles V the Wise, had not been fathered by John II. Quite simply, Antoine de la Sale reverses, or inverts, what must have been known by his readers to be "historical" fact or, rather, perhaps he seemingly presents, in ironic fashion, as historical reality the idealistic ideology which, as they (and we) read, for example, in Froissart, the French chivalry and such allies as John of Luxemburg, the blind King of Bohemia (and real-life father of Bonne), affected to champion. In short, King John and his court—the world of the *Saintré*—is deliberately and outrageously romanticized by Antoine de la Sale so as to underscore the "straighter" kind of romanticizations found in Froissart. (Chrétien de Troyes some three centuries earlier had used analogous procedures in *Cligés* to pinpoint the essential romanceness of the *Tristan* story as recounted, for example, by Béroul.)

Some of my preceding analysis has been suggested by critics who, while praising Antoine de la Sale's "realism" in depicting concrete details, deplore what they consider his inconceivable distortion of courtly insufficiency. If, however, one takes stock of the intrinsically romance nature of King John's court—of its distorted state, precisely— matters become clearer. For John, like Arthur or Mark, is a romance king: namely, he is at the center of things but not himself particularly active. (Meanwhile, curiously, the real-life Bonne resembled more accurately the Guenevere, or Iseut, of romance tradition than Antoine's idealized Queen.) Feats of prowess and of love—the two courtly and romance activities *par excellence*—are the province of the knights and, to a very important extent, of the ladies affiliated with the court. In the Arthurian world, for example, it is not Arthur but Lancelot, Perceval, Yvain, Gauvain, Lunete, and Guenevere who, by their deeds, supply the action that brings luster or disgrace to the Round Table. Antoine de la Sale has shunted the factuality of precise but selectively chosen (and therefore distorted) historical coordinates into the frame of the self-referential, ostensibly unhistorical or antihistorical romance narrative text. In this way King John and his court are deliberately rendered potentially ambiguous, even though they are historically "real." (Mme de Lafayette, as I suggested above, employs a similar procedure in the *Princesse de Clèves,* where she shifts the action of her novel to a period dating, like that of *Jehan de Saintré,* about a century earlier than that of the work's composition and reception.) In this way the kind of prose narrative epitomized by Froissart's *Chronicles* is further undermined by Antoine de la Sale. Froissart writes about and, for complex reasons, tends to idealize contemporary events, whereas *Jehan de Saintré* pointedly exploits an unmistakable *recul historique*—a historical detachment underpinned by a very specific distinction between the then of the story and the now of its writing. And, to be sure, the historical events intervening in France toward the close of the years between, roughly, 1350 and 1450—the Agincourt disaster, Joan of Arc, the end of the Hundred Years War—were obviously on the minds of both Antoine de la Sale and his readers. Perhaps, in a sense, the defeat at Poitiers and other earlier debacles simply no longer mattered to them too much; or, at the least, they were sufficiently remote so as to lend themselves by their absence in the *Saintré* text to Antoine de la Sale's subtle and ironic poetic manipulation.

But—and this, to my knowledge, has not yet been noticed by critics and scholars—*Jehan de Saintré,* in quintessentially romance fashion, inverts another of Froissart's narratives, the lengthy, "archaizing" (that is, pseudohistorical) verse romance entitled *Méliador*. Composed in traditional romance octosyllabic rhyming couplets, *Méliador* tells the story of the youth of the Arthurian court—of brilliant tourneys, of love, and of crusades in "pagan" Ireland, set in a time before the (hi)stories recounted by Chrétien de Troyes and his successors. This, then, as Peter F. Dembowski has demonstrated,[14] is the story of Arthurian prehistory, when the ideal rules of the Arthurian game were being "invented." Meanwhile, the Irish Crusade, narrated by Froissart as a brilliant feat of arms performed by the united chivalry of a unified Christian Europe, is, according to Dembowski's entirely convincing analysis, a transposition into romance terms of the frequent but sporadic participation of numerous—especially young—Christian knights and knights aspirant in the ongoing eastern European struggles against genuine Lithuanian pagans during the fourteenth century. Such participation was construed by these youths as both chivalric adventure and Christian duty. Froissart's *Méliador,* composed, I repeat, in verse at about the time he was abandoning his earlier courtly love poetry style for the writing of the prose *Chronicles,* can thus be read as a putting to good use of romance narrative procedures in what can be understood as at once the denunciation of the fratricidal wars between French and English—that is, Christian—chivalry and the idealization of a potentially pan-Christian, and proper, military effort. (The 1360s and beyond were also a period of great Turkish menace on the eastern frontiers of Christendom.) *Jehan de Saintré,* as we demonstrate later in greater detail, is largely a response to *Méliador.* One of the salient characteristics of medieval French romance, a characteristic directly related to the principle of restoration, is that each romance text by definition responds to a previous romance text or even to the body of earlier romance texts in general. *Jehan de Saintré* is no exception. Its inversion of Froissart constitutes part of its strength as a participant in the romance corpus, or "book." And that strength lies at the root of its genuine efficacy as a historically oriented venture. In other words, while seeming to be a historical narrative—a kind of memoir-biography located in a recognizable past—*Jehan de Saintré* is in actuality a romance; and the very ambiguity of its status proves to be the source of its authenticity as an example of historiographical commentary. Meanwhile, I believe that *Jehan de Saintré* underscores what Antoine de la Sale considers to be the fundamental romance-ness—the nonhistoriographical character—of the type of idealized historiography one finds in Froissart's *Chronicles,* in their merely apparent or ostensible contemporary witness and recording.

With this much posited, let us now return to the plot of the narrative. I am convinced that the events of this plot and their order (or "conjoining") will take on surprising relevance as we place them within the romance and historical framework I have just briefly sketched—within the context, that is, of romance restoration. Froissart's "restoration" of the young Arthurian world in *Méliador* elicits Antoine de la Sale's "restoration-inversion" of both *Méliador* and the *Chronicles.*

We are first introduced to a young page, in his fourteenth year, at King John's court; we learn that he is called Jehan. (Antoine de la Sale himself began his career at age fourteen as a page, and we might remember Froissart's obsession with the sequence of his own "ages" in texts such as *Le Joli Buisson de Jeunesse.*) He is handsome, well liked, and judged by all to be full of promise. Meanwhile, at the court of Queen Bonne, John's consort, we find the young widow known as Madame des Belles Cousines. A lengthy digression on the virtuous and honorable state of widowhood ensues. The narrator, curiously, is simultaneously unidentified and referred to, in paragraph rubrics, as *L'ACTEUR* (actor, author); the narrative "I," or ego, is present but downplayed through the use of circumlocutions. The reader or audience is frequently addressed as "vous." (The story alludes continually to "real people"; in addition to King John and Queen Bonne, characters like Boucicaut and the Sire de Craon—

whose real-life flourishing sometimes postdated the times of King John but who share, with the King, their presence in Froissart's *Chronicles*—rub elbows with totally fictitious personages. In addition, functions attributed to various characters often possess not only general but also specific historical accuracy, a kind of historical allusiveness. Thus, as lady-in-waiting to the Queen, Madame des Belles Cousines occupies a position very similar to that of the historical Christine de Pizan at the turn of the century—a celebrated and virtuous widow if ever there was one!) Like the widows of ancient Rome (and, by implication, like Christine de Pizan, who praised widows), Madame is a model of proper conduct and reputation, refusing to remarry or to engage in courtly dalliances. However, she displays an interest in young Jehan, whose naiveté and great promise —like Aeneas's, his future lies before him—prompts her to take him under her wing. With absolute secrecy—an attribute, incidentally, of the practice of *fin'amors*—she initiates him in the ways of courtly behavior, providing him with money to purchase suitable clothing and advancing his cause at court. She becomes his *éminence grise,* his means to social and professional advancement. She also takes charge of his moral and religious education, described with an extraordinary wealth of detail. Not only very gifted but also learned, Madame prepares a reading list for "young" (*petit*) Jehan—a veritable syllabus: Roman writers, "ancient poets," Saint Augustine. (Again one is uncannily reminded of the learned Christine de Pizan whose moral fervor in defense of women as she participated in the Quarrel of the *Romance of the Rose* against the defenders of the rather misogynistic Jean de Meun and, especially, as she drew the portraits of virtuous women in her *Livre de la Cité des Dames* [1405][15] is replicated by the apparently equally authoritative courtly Madame des Belles Cousines. The Madame of the first two-thirds of the *Saintré* could easily have been the subject of one of Christine's biographical sketches. It is as though the fame of Christine de Pizan were being put to use in a fiction, only later, as we shall see, to be brutally undermined.) An amusing detail deserves mention. When Madame desires to meet with Jehan, she signals him at supper by cleaning her teeth fastidiously (and somehow sensually) with a silver toothpick. This remains her sign to him throughout the book and symbolizes concretely their secret pact.

A deep and loving affection develops between Madame and her young protégé; no hint is given of a *liaison dangereuse*. Jehan is devoted to her in all respects, and she loves him. Their intimacy is great, involving much hugging and kissing, though the completeness of their union is never precisely spelled out. Certainly, they come to spend many hours together, in each other's arms, at night. It would seem, however, that Madame does not accord the *surplus* to her young friend, that their love remains short of full physical consummation. (The reader thinks of such ambiguous romance couples as Perceval and Blanchefleur in Chrétien's *Conte du Graal.*)

In short, as matters turn out, Jehan de Saintré is Madame's creature: the signs of which he is made up—his code, how we are to "read" him—are entirely of her doing. He is, in effect, a systematic response to her. And, by the same token, her existence is, as far as we know it, completely a function of her *oeuvre,* of her playing the Pygmalion to his Galatea. He, as Galatea, creates—imprisons—her in her role as Pygmalion. They are both what the romance-type logic of their relationship causes them to become. Admirable as it may be in so many important respects—like the ladies' portraits in Christine's *Cité?*—this relationship, in its formality, presents traits of sterility and, especially, of circularity. What, one asks, will all this lead to? The issue of what I have called elsewhere romance *dépassement*[16]— of a kind of leap onto a higher plane (sometimes through sin or other types of lack of virtue) that romances typically effect (either "positively" or "negatively")—raises itself, but no answer is immediately forthcoming. That particular romance "slot" is glaringly empty here.

The first third of the *Saintré* ends with the by now fully programmed Jehan ready to prove himself in tourneys both abroad—the first takes place at the court of Aragon—and at home. Jehan consistently wins these highly stylized encounters, gaining glory for himself and also for the prestige of French chivalry; he turns into the pure Froissardian hero. All Europe is the theater of Jehan's exploits: west and east, north and south—Poland, Italy, Spain, and England. The lavishly descriptive pages devoted to recounting Jehan's feats of prowess in these many tourneys resemble nothing so much as the chronicle of a brilliant and elegant, as well as costly, social season. Jehan is *primus inter pares* within a body of chivalry comprising both young and older knights. Meanwhile, the tender love affair between Jehan and the educated, well-dressed, and beautiful Madame— the chaste and unattainable widow—continues, as before, in secret; no one suspects the existence of their relationship. Jehan accedes, moreover, to a high position at court, well thought of by "good" King John. The program—one of purely formalized romance ritual—

works itself out as flawlessly as the clockwork that fascinated Froissart in *L'Horloge amoureuse*. Tourney follows upon tourney, prize upon prize. During these expensive pageants (as in *Méliador*) nobody is seriously wounded, let alone killed; the entire second third of *Jehan de Saintré* is as devoid of bloodshed as, one is sure, the love affair between Jehan and Madame is empty of consummation. All this perfection—this romance stylization carried to an extreme in what is purveyed as a "real-life" situation—is, finally, a kind of gamesmanship, a lifeless play of rules.

But at this point, once again, Antoine de la Sale, with considerable genius, responds to Froissart's *Méliador*. Just as Froissart's youthful Arthurian chivalry encounters *dépassement* in its "crusade" against the "pagan" Irish—a transposition of Froissart's belief that the knights of his own time would do better to join forces with the Teutonic knights in the east against real infidels rather than continue their bloody and wasteful internecine warfare in the west—so Antoine de la Sale, more resolutely and directly "historical" (and in prose!), recounts *in his fiction* the fictitious story of how, under Jehan de Saintré's leadership, knights and reigning nobility from all over Europe (the list of these noblemen alone takes up over twenty pages!) undertake a "trip to Prussia" to engage and defeat the "Saracens" there. This enterprise simultaneously closes the second third of the *Saintré* and opens the final part. The Christian forces win a resounding victory, but at the cost, this time, of much bloodshed and death. Jehan at their head, they return home, covered with glory, to the immense relief and joy of King John, Queen Bonne, the court, and, naturally, Madame des Belles Cousines. (Incidentally, it is before the great battle in Prussia that Jehan finally receives the "order of knighthood" at the hands of none other than the "King of Bohemia"; henceforth he will be known as "le seigneur de Saintré." This is clearly a reference to the universally admired, blind John of Luxemburg, the real King of Bohemia, who lost his life at Crécy in 1346. Froissart's romance/chronicle world is explicitly engaged on numerous levels.)

Of course, in reality no Jehan de Saintré or splendid army of the sort described by Antoine de la Sale ever set foot in Prussia; the real-life "trips to Prussia" usually were undertaken by small groups of mainly young knights under the general supervision of the Teutonic Order, not under the command of western leaders. Though purportedly historical, the episode is in fact as fictional as the Arthurian crusade in Ireland, and surely it was perceived as such by Antoine's readers. The episode constitutes yet another example of Antoine de la Sale's upending of Froissart by romanticizing—fictionalizing—a supposedly historical, or at least verisimilitudinous, event. Antoine de la Sale shows up Froissart by doing just the opposite of what he had done in *Méliador*.

It is when Jehan de Saintré returns to the court that, from the point of view of traditional romance programming, the text goes haywire. Within the framework of "normal" romance expectations, the triumphant hero (as in *Méliador,* for instance) should return to court, get the lady, inherit a kingdom, and live contentedly forever after. But, as we noted earlier, the very perfection—the exaggerated perfection—of Antoine's romance structure up to the Prussian battle imparts a definite bloodlessness, a sterility, a sort of closed, merry-go-round quality to his narrative—or rather, I venture to say, to the narrative's referentiality (especially to what it seemingly refers to). On the one hand, in that it is a romance text, the *Saintré* by definition refers to itself, to an inner system of dynamics. On the other hand, the dynamics are simply not very dynamic. The Prussian victory can legitimately be construed (outwardly) as a form of chivalric *dépassement:* the programming to which Jehan has been subjected— his "education"—has enabled him, quite literally, to earn his spurs and even, by his exemplarity, to earn respect for the chivalry he is called upon to incarnate. But this *dépassement* is undermined by the very fact of Antoine de la Sale's turning the Prussian victory into fiction. An all-too-real fourteenth-century political and military problem has, like the Waterloo of Stendhal's *Chartreuse de Parme,* been incorporated into a recognizable fiction, not, as in Froissart, transposed or transformed into an Irish "crusade." The problem—the *chanson de geste*-like ideal of the "trip to Prussia"—has been trivialized or made into pure legend. Meanwhile, Saintré and Madame are stymied in their love. There is simply nowhere that their love can go; the author can invent nothing more to say about it. The very romancelike "Roman widow" motif—what Antoine de la Sale might very well have borrowed from Christine de Pizan—whose prevalence we noted at the start of the *Saintré* provides a possible key to the problem. Likened to the virtuous *Roman* widows of yore, Madame is now, in effect, required by Antoine de la Sale's text to play out the role of the *Carthaginian* widow Dido. Her Dido-ness—or perhaps the Dido-ness of her role in the *Saintré*—undermines the ostensibly "Roman" virtuousness of her character, as this character is revealed to us. There can be no question of marriage between

Jehan and Madame, or so it would seem; yet Madame is neither a Guenevere nor an Iseut. Jehan de Saintré is in a bind: he cannot leave Madame as Aeneas abandoned Dido, for in the name of what genuine mission could he do so? Nor, really, can he continue with honor to be her creature. He is now ostensibly a mature man—a thirty-year-old who, like the Villon of the *Testament,* ought already to have "drunk all his shames"—but he is deprived by the romance format of any place to go. His "de-generation" is at issue here. And, as we shall see, Madame will have the occasion to assume the sinfulness—in romance, courtly terms, at least—of Dido's lustfulness.

Nevertheless, the problem of Jehan's destiny remains on two counts: (1) in romances the hero's destiny must be resolved, and (2) the text specifically purports to tell the story of Jehan's life (that is, it offers itself as his biography). Thus, in effect, the world of the *Saintré* falls apart for lack of glue to hold it together. Everything, at least up to this point, has been too perfect. No overwhelming passion as in the case of Lancelot and Guenevere, no ironic celebration of clerkly artistry as in *Cligés,* no black (and fascinating) sin as in *Tristan,* no quest as in *Perceval* or in the *Rose.* Just the possibility—and the romance impossibility—of a return to business as usual. But can either Madame or the Seigneur de Saintré accept it, no matter how much each would presumably wish to do so?

The answer to that question is, of course, no, and the consequences of that answer are momentous, both for the text of the *Saintré* and for romance textuality in general.

For no reason, except perhaps boredom—a reversal of the truly heroic destiny (one is reminded of the "folly" of Don Quijote, of Cligés's departure for Arthur's court, and indeed of the importance to that romance of "boring" descriptions of tourneys)—for once, *on his own,* Jehan decides to assemble a little troop of knights and to go off with them on a set of tourneys. He asks leave of no one. Like Chrétien's Yvain, he presents those to whom he owes allegiance— the King and Madame—with a *fait accompli,* replying to the King's displeasure by saying that he has given his word to his companions and it would be dishonorable of him to go back on his word. The King reluctantly allows Jehan to depart, remarking just the same that it is high time he hang up his spurs, stop behaving like an adolescent, and, presumably, take up some serious office at court. Madame is disconsolate and angry; she feels betrayed. She is definitely shunted into the role of Dido, but, as we shall see, with a difference. Her demise, like Dido's, results from passion and impotence, but instead of being a physical death it is, perhaps even more poignantly, a moral one: it is most intriguing that she will be forced either against her will or by the revelation, at long last, of her deepest will and nature (her true character)—the matter is profoundly ambivalent—to forsake her lineage as a Roman widow and, concomitantly, to complete the (maybe) too one-sided picture of virtuous womanhood given by Christine de Pizan in her *Cité des Dames*.[17]

Jehan and his party leave the court in order to play out their childish games. Through a series of ruses and feigning of physical illness (to account for her misery)—she still refuses to acknowledge her passion for Saintré—Madame obtains permission from the Queen to repair for some time to her own lands. She promises solemnly to return when she is feeling better. En route with her retainers (who are presented as a society of gullible and rather superficial ladies), she reaches the confines of her domains—an abbey church where she and her companions obtain the hospitality of the abbot. Quite taken with Madame, the abbot—a lubricious, clever *fabliau*-type character—plies her with rich food and drink. In most uncourtly fashion— indeed, burning with desire—she succumbs to his advances and, in very short order, becomes his most willing partner in lust, to the point of forgetting or no longer caring about her duties at court. She does not answer letters addressed to her by the Queen; her love for Saintré disappears. Her cynicism is complete. She eagerly commits all seven deadly sins—sloth, anger, lust, gluttony, and pride foremost among them. She has come to incarnate the fickleness and animality of womanhood denounced by so many medieval clerics. Nevertheless, we can never forget that all these developments were in fact provoked by Saintré's most inconsiderate, and yet inevitable, decision to leave her and the court.

On his return to court, Saintré learns of Madame's "illness." He requests permission to visit her. He dines with her and the abbot, but is tricked into a wrestling match with his powerfully built rival (who speaks words of scorn concerning "knights and squires"). Saintré is vanquished in this ignoble struggle: his chivalric training is of no use in this base form of combat. He resembles the French knights at Crécy and Poitiers, decimated by churlish crossbowmen from remote England and Wales. Madame openly sides with her new lover. Humiliated and disgusted, Saintré is forced to seek revenge and, also by trickery, lures Madame and the abbot to a dinner in his quarters where he cajoles the abbot to arm himself. Outfitted as a knight, the abbot is obliged to accept combat with Saintré. This time, of course, Saintré wins, and, avenging himself, he pierces the abbot's cheeks and tongue with his dagger, telling him nevermore to speak ill of knights. He then addresses Madame, accusing her of disloyalty and removing the blue belt-cloth—symbol of loyalty—that she was wearing. The break between them is complete and irreparable.

Madame finally returns to court. In her presence Saintré tells the Queen and her ladies of the faithlessness of a lady to her knightly lover without, at first, revealing names. He asks the court—an improvised *cour d'amour* of the sort one frequently finds, for example, in the poetry of Machaut or of Alain Chartier[18]—to pronounce on the lady's guilt. After it has vehemently done so, he displays the blue belt-cloth. The secret of Madame and Saintré's love is at last disclosed, as is the fact of her treachery. She is disgraced. May all ladies heed her sad example! The story ends. The *ACTEUR* intervenes to say that Saintré lived a long life of chivalric service, even once taking on twenty-two renegade Christians at the Sultan's court in Cairo and defeating them; but, he adds, to tell further of such things would take too much time. When Saintré finally died, the grave diggers, preparing his last resting place, discovered—in true romance style— a little coffer containing a note that read: "Here will rest the body of the most valiant knight of France, and more—of the entire world!"[19] A brief epilogue closes the text. Everything appears, simply, to peter out. To all intents and purposes Saintré's "life" had ended with his denunciation of Madame; the rest is not worth talking about.

Part 3 of *Jehan de Saintré,* with its introduction of the base-born abbot—a stock character in many Old French *fabliaux*—and with its almost stereotypically clerkly vindictiveness about female inconstancy, jars with everything that precedes it, although it depends as entirely on previous romance structures as do parts 1 and 2. Not nearly so much to blame as Jehan makes her out to be, Madame des Belles Cousines becomes a sort of spurned fairy-figure; Jehan himself is an Yvain who never really grows up; the artificiality and decay of King John's court—like that of Arthur in the later *Lancelot-Grail* texts—after having been hinted at in Antoine de la Sale's distortion of the realities of that court, finally become patent (it literally ceases to exist). The celebration of jubilant youthfulness one finds in Froissart's *Méliador* is replaced by Antoine's analysis of the potential, built-in debility of any mythic principle. Also, very significantly, part 3 takes on an extraordinary dramatic—that is, theatrical—tonality and form: act 1, Jehan's departure for the tourneys; act 2, the departure and fall of Madame; act 3, Jehan's first encounter with Madame and the abbot; act 4, Jehan's vengeance on the abbot; act 5, the court scene and Madame's disgrace. Even the epilogue is like that of a play. Staging seems to be called for. Reinforced by the presence of the *ACTEUR,* this theatrical progression constitutes a kind of present-tense resolution of, or commentary on, the narrative historicity (situated in the past) of parts 1 and 2 of the *Saintré*—a restoration and a conveying of the meaning of the two initial sections.[20] And what is being dramatized, I believe, is an attitude that pervades the work of Antoine de la Sale (we find it also in his *Tannhaüser*-like *Paradis de la reine Sybille*), namely, that of nostalgia for and yet recognition of the impossibility of what the Basel-born philologist Johann Jacob Bachofen labeled *Mutterrecht:* the notion of Woman—Mother, Lover, and Teacher—as lawgiver and repository of authentic order (the Roman widow motif developed at the start of the text).[21] Forbidden by the very structure of *Jehan de Saintré* to become her protégé's wife—and thereby to combine, so to speak, in "real life" these three attributes of Woman—Madame's doom was sealed. Parts 1 and 2 of the *Saintré* recount in historical form the deployment of the *Mutterrecht,* or Eternal Feminine, principle—a past-centered narrative located in a time when, ironically, war, not love, prevailed in France; part 3, in theatrical fashion, plays out its present-centered destruction. The lady of medieval romance, or so Antoine de la Sale (along with Christine de Pizan) seems to be telling us, has (unrightfully?) lost her power, and with this loss—which, in fact, Antoine sadly commemorates, I think—a certain kind of chivalry also must cease to exist or be seen to have existed merely in the imagination of romancers. Ironies abound in Antoine's restoration of this fund of romance imagination. It is nevertheless because of his romance form that he can both share in and express the nostalgia of, for example, Villon, whose refrains "Mais où sont les neiges d'antan?" and "Mais où est le preux Charlemagne?" come directly to mind. Not only does Antoine de la Sale depict and judge the twilight of a certain order—he pulls no punches in indicting Jehan's empty chivalric estheticism—he also deplores this passing of the "best and the bravest," the fact that, like Jehan himself in his later years, they no longer have a story worth telling. What is to replace the forms of the past, as well as their content? he seems to be inquiring. With Antoine de la Sale, I believe, the romance quest commences to be the active search for the earthly—the real—El Dorado (America?) and, perhaps above all, for Dulcinea. Antoine's extreme nominalism leads him (and the romance genre as a whole) to experiment with a new realism—with the imparting of romance names to (otherwise irreal?) places and people. Meanwhile, this new transformation of the real by romance will feed itself back into romance narrative too, restoring it, as Antoine de la Sale had done, by renovating and conjoining anew the very ideas of writing and adventure.

Notes

[1] Until the mid-1920s the standard edition of the text was that of J.-M. Guichard (1843) and its derivatives. MS *F,* Paris Bibliothèque Nationale nouv. acq. fr. 10057, served as the base for P. Champion and F. Desonay, eds., *Le Petit Jehan de Saintré* (Paris: Ed. du Trianon, 1926), with reproductions of miniatures from other manuscripts. All references in this essay are to C. Knudson and J. Misrahi, *Jehan de Saintré,* 2nd ed., Textes Littéraires Français (Genève: Droz, 1967), which, unfortunately, by its thin introductory material and too brief glossary is not as useful as it might otherwise be. This edition offers a modified version of the text of Vatican Reg. Lat. 896. As the editors admit, they were working against the clock to "Faire paraître dans le plus bref délai possible une édition moderne de ce texte capital" (vii) and promised "une seconde édition amplifiée," which never appeared.

[2] See A. Coville, *Le Petit Jehan de Saintré: recherches complémentaires* (Paris: Droz, 1937); F. Desonay, "Le Petit Jehan de Saintré," *Revue du Seizième Siècle* 14 (1927) 1–48, 213–280; and the sections "Armures, Costume, Joutes, Tournois, etc." and "Blason" in Knudson and Misrahi xxv–xxviii.

[3] See, for example, the short but rich appreciation of the *Saintré* by L. Foulet, *"Le Petit Jehan de Saintré,"* Histoire de la littérature française, 2 vols., ed. J. Bedier and P. Hazard (Paris: Larousse, n.d.): "Et ce qui est vaincu avec Jean de Saintré, on n'en saurait douter, c'est l'idéal qu'il représente, c'est la chevalerie elle-même" (1: 108).

[4] "En revanche, les chapitres du début . . . sont d'une délicatesse charmante. L'éducation du page est traitée d'une main légère à souhait. On a comparé ces espiègleries et ces jolis sermons aux entretiens de la Comtesse et de Chérubin dans le *Mariage de Figaro,* mais le petit Saintré est plus naïf, plus naturel et plus sympathique que Chérubin, et 'ma dame', avec tout son latin, autrement vivante que la Comtesse. . . . Antoine de la Sale a écrit le premier roman où apparaisse, indistinct encore et peu flatté, l'esprit moderne" (Foulet 1: 108). See also J. M. Ferrier, *Forerunners of the French Novel: An Essay on the Development of the Nouvelle in the Later Middle Ages* (Manchester, Eng.: Manchester UP, 1954).

[5] Knudson and Misrahi vii.

[6] Julia Kristeva, *Le Texte du roman: Approche sémiologique d'une structure discursive transformationelle,* Approaches to Semiotics 6, ed. T. A. Sebeok (The Hague: Mouton, 1970). The published work is marred by countless misprints.

[7] Kristeva's study of the *roman* never mentions Chrétien de Troyes; a potted survey of French literature "au temps d'Antoine de la Sale" informs

us that by his time "l'Italie . . . a déjà accompli son renouvellement," that French poetry is not in too bad a state, but that *la prose balbutie encore.*" Froissart (a *balbutieur?*) is not named, nor are other prose chronicles or, for that matter, the Lancelot-Grail cycle. Consequently, we learn, *Jehan de Saintré* "est d'une originalité inattendue" (20). Statements of this ilk "justify" Kristeva's decision "de tenter de saisir les lois de l'élaboration du roman dans le texte d'Antoine de la Sale." Her *tabula rasa* allows her axiomatically to affirm (or to deny) anything she chooses (for example, "le règne de la LITTERATURE est le règne de la VALEUR MARCHANDE" [53]; "la dévalorisation explicite dont la femme sera l'objet à partir du XIVe siècle dans la littérature bourgeoise [les fabliaux]" [61]; "Le type d'écriture qui s'installera à partir de la Renaissance sera une parole consciente d'avoir pour référent une autre parole" [105]).

[8] The "disjunctiveness" of the novel (*roman*) in regard to older literary productions resides, however, in the "non-disjunctive function of the novelistic [*romanesque*] utterance" which "opposes" such utterances to "la disjonction exclusive du symbole et témoigne de l'effort de la pensée occidentale pour accéder à la dialectique" (189–90). The novel, in other words, symbolizes nothing: "le discours romanesque tourne dans la clôture de la non-disjonction en se donnant une infinité transformationnelle signifiante cernée par l'immobilité (l'équivalence) des 'signifiés'" (189). Nevertheless, the development of the novel itself "symbolizes" an important step in what Kristeva construes to be Western civilization's efforts to free itself from Platonism and Christianity; it betokens progress, at times depicted by her as quite linear (190). She hedges her bet, however: "Si le roman a détruit le mythe de l'épopée, on parle de nos jours d'un retour du roman au mythe [here she presses into service Thomas Mann's *Doctor Faustus*]. Ce retour dont l'importance est capitale pour notre civilisation, n'entre pas dans le cadre de notre recherche; signalons-le pourtant, *puisqu'il dessine le trajet complet de cette transformation que le discours occidental accomplit pour revenir à son idéologème initial*" (15; emphasis added to point out what must be the reactionary side to Western discourse, its Vico-like *corsi* and *ricorsi*).

[9] Ignorance perhaps also underlies the following two statements: "'Jehan de Saintré' est le premier roman français écrit en prose" and, nine lines later, "Les historiens de la littérature française attirent fort peu l'attention sur Antoine de la Sale et 'Jehan de Saintré' qui est peut-être le premier écrit en prose qui puisse porter le nom de roman *si nous considérons comme roman le texte qui relève de l'idéologème ambigu du signe*" (22–23; emphasis added). Hedging again: words say anything and, once again, are forgotten; problems—"romance," "novel"—are swept under the rug; enormously important blocks of text are simply not mentioned; what of prose (versus verse) narrative? And so on. For an interesting study of the ambiguity of sign-readings (and, by extension, of their equally ambiguous *idéologèmes*), so important to twelfth-century romance, see Michelle A. Freeman, "Transpositions structurelles et intertextualité: le *Cligés* de Chrétien," *Littérature* 41 (Feb. 1981): 50–61. Freeman focuses on a key text of the period, which, as we shall observe, set up a framework of the problematics within which Antoine de la Sale very deliberately worked.

[10] Kristeva 190–92. What Antoine de la Sale (and the novel) accomplished

is credited by Kristeva with permitting "la formation de la sémiologie comme science des MODELES (signifiants) applicables à des signifiés." We are indeed deep in the country referred to, disrespectfully, by Descartes as a *pays de roman*.

[11] A single example suffices to illustrate this point, though the question of Guillaume's relationship to Chrétien deserves full and detailed study. Calogrenant's tale-within-a-tale (Chrétien de Troyes, *Yvain*, ed. Mario Roques, CFMA [Paris: Champion, 1971], vv. 142–580) uncannily foreshadows Guillaume de Lorris's *Roman de la Rose:* (1) its "classic" clerkliness (for example, a well-delineated prologue; a midpoint—locus of identity—at which words defining the adventure, or matter, of the text are also to be read as referring to the composition of the text); (2) in both instances, the narrator, adopting a clerkly stance, tells of a chivalric adventure that befell him some years earlier—an unsuccessful adventure in each case; (3) the Magic Fountain in *Yvain* bears a striking similarity to the Perilous Fountain of Guillaume; (4) the prologues to both texts employ the *songe/mençonge* rhyme (with Guillaume inverting Calogrenant in his evaluation of the truth of dreams), and so on. The analogies are too powerful to be ignored, especially when one remembers that at the time Guillaume was writing (1220–25), vernacular romancers were making systematic efforts to restore to favor a romance textuality accused by many as mendacious or frivolous.

[12] See Karl D. Uitti, "From *Clerc* to *Poète:* The Relevance of the *Romance of the Rose* to Machaut's World"; Kevin Brownlee, "The Poetic Œuvre of Guillaume de Machaut: The Identity of Discourse and the Discourse of Identity"; M. A. Freeman, "Froissart's *Le Joli Buisson de Jonece:* A Farewell to Poetry?" in *Machaut's World: Science and Art in the Fourteenth Century,* ed. M. P. Cosman and B. Chandler, Annals of the New York Academy of Sciences 314 (New York: New York Academy of Sciences, 1978) 209–47.

[13] "avoit une assez josne dame vesve qui des Belles Cousines estoit, mais de son nom et seignorie l'istoire s'en tait, a cause de ce que aprés pourrez veoir" (Knudson and Misrahi 2–3).

[14] See Peter F. Dembowski, "Considérations sur Meliador," *Etudes de philologie et d'histoire littéraire offertes à Jules Horrent* (Tournai: GEDIT, 1980) 121–31, and especially his monograph on Froissart's *Méliador, Jean Froissart and His* Méliador: *Context, Craft, Sense,* Edward C. Armstrong Monographs on Medieval Literature 2 (Lexington, Ky.: French Forum, 1983). See also Beate Schmolke-Hasselmann, *Der arturische Versroman von Chrestien bis Froissart: zur Geschichte einer Gattung,* Beihefte zur Zeitschrift für romanische Philologie 177 (Tübingen: Niemeyer, 1980).

[15] Christine de Pizan's work, virtually unavailable in a reliable version of the French original, is now accessible in a splendid and accurate English-language translation done by E. Jeffrey Richards: *The Book of the City of Ladies* (New York: Persea, 1982), including a foreword by Marina Warner and an excellent scholarly introduction by Richards. The *Cité des Dames* in part derives from and both responds to and expands on Boccaccio's *De claris mulieribus*. Richards rightly stresses Christine's effort as an attempt *to restore* to women the values rightfully associated with them:

> In *The Book of the City of Ladies* [whose title alludes directly to Augustine's *City of God*] Christine expands her defense of women to the past and

future so that she can expose the utter falseness of "masculine myths" once and for all. Christine sought a more perfect *realization* of the ideals transmitted by the tradition which she had inherited, which she had cultivated, and which she hoped to transform. (xxix)

Both the form and the *matière* of Christine correspond to romance procedures.

[16] See Karl D. Uitti, *Story, Myth, and Celebration in Old French Narrative Poetry, 1050–1200* (Princeton: Princeton UP, 1973) 217–31.

[17] Christine de Pizan refers several times to Dido in the *Cité des Dames*, and devotes two chapters to her: "Here Reason speaks of the prudence and attentiveness of Queen Dido" and "Concerning Dido, queen of Carthage, on the subject of constant love in women." (Dido obsessed Old French romancers from the very beginning; her story is told in the mid-twelfth-century *Roman d'Enéas*, and she, so to speak, constitutes the subtext for several of the heroines of Marie de France as well as for the Laudine of Chrétien's *Yvain*, for example.) Christine presents Dido with great sympathy as essentially a victim of male inconstancy and perversion. However, her first portrayal of Dido—as resourceful and prudent queen—in every respect corresponds to the Madame des Belles Cousines of parts 1 and 2 of the *Saintré*. The following is Reason's (that is, Christine's) summary:

> Because of her prudent government, they changed her name [from Elissa] and called her Dido, which is the equivalent of saying *virago* in Latin, which means "the woman who has the strength and force of a man." Thus she lived for a long time in glory and would have lived so the rest of her life if Fortune had not been unfavorable to her, but Fortune, often envious of the prosperous, mixed too harsh a brew for her in the end, just as I will tell you afterward, at the right time and place. (Richards 95)

From having been what I have called the Roman widow, Dido/Elissa is, like Madame, transformed by Fortune into the Dido of romance tradition, the new (and not entirely accurate) symbol of womanly animality and fickleness; in both instances the role of Fortune is assumed by men (Aeneas in the first case, Jehan/abbot in the second). The active and strong Dido/Elissa of Christine (pt. 1, ch. 46) (again analogous to Madame in Antoine de la Sale, pts. 1 and 2) turns into the passive, victimized Dido/Madame des Belles Cousines of, respectively, Christine (pt. 2, ch. 55) and Antoine part 3. Assuming, as I believe we must, that Christine's *Cité* acts as an important subtext for the *Saintré*, Madame, though disgraced at court (but, really, what *kind* of court is at issue here!), remains exemplary as victim; the blame is not all hers. One more point deserves mention. Christine stresses Dido's generosity toward Aeneas. Dido gives Aeneas shelter, clothes, money, and the like; he has nothing. Is that not precisely the behavior of Madame toward Jehan in part 1 of the *Saintré* (a behavior, incidentally, described as "curious" by L. Foulet, *op. cit.*)? Does not the moral "afterlife" of Christine's Dido live on, or adhere to, Antoine's Madame?

[18] For example, Machaut's *Le Jugement du roy de Navarre* and *Le Jugement du roy de Bohême,* or the controversy surrounding Chartier's *La Belle Dame sans merci.*

[19] *"Cy reposera le corps du plus vaillant chevalier de France, et plus, que pour lors sera"* (Knudson and Misrahi 308). This trivializes a scene like that

of Chrétien's Lancelot discovering his future tomb and its portentous writing (*Le Chevalier de la Charrette,* ed. Mario Roques, CFMA [Paris: Champion, 1970], (vv. 1856ff.).

[20] On this complex issue of restoration and completion, see the interpretation of Marie de France's general prologue, vv. 15–16 ("K'i peüssent gloser la lettre / E de lur sen le surplus mettre") in Alfred Foulet and K. D. Uitti, "The Prologue to the *Lais* of Marie de France: A Reconsideration," *Romance Philology* 35.1 (August 1981): 242–49.

[21] See *Myth, Religion, and Mother Right: Selected Writings of J. J. Bachofen,* trans. Ralph Manheim, Preface by George Boas, Introduction by Joseph Campbell, Bollingen Series 84 (Princeton: Princeton UP, 1967).

RABELAIS, ROMANCES,
READING, RIGHTING NAMES

Edward Morris

Some people say romance is a "genre." What does that mean? As entities go, is a genre a thing out in the world somewhere, or is it a construct, a shape we make up to tell the fiction of the history of literature as we see fit? Why is it that we can't name it with a plain English word, but must have recourse to an imported one nobody can pronounce? Questions like those are a bother, and it would be gratifying just to be able to say, "Well, there was romance, and it was a genre, and then Rabelais came along and transformed it." Something like that may have been what the American scholar Nemours H. Clement had in mind in 1926 when he published a monograph entitled *The Influence of the Arthurian Romances on the Five Books of Rabelais*. Clement's thesis, stated categorically at the outset, is that Rabelais's enigmatic work is best understood as "a burlesque imitation of the French medieval romances, but particularly of the romances of the Round Table" (150). He observes that some eighty-five prose adaptations of medieval epics and old stories of adventure had been printed in France by 1553, the year of Rabelais's death; on the evidence of *Pantagruel* and *Gargantua* it is reasonable to suppose that Rabelais knew at least twenty-five of them. Like any attentive reader, Clement must have noticed how high good storytelling ranks in Rabelais's list of worthwhile activities and how often and how gladly Rabelais works the heroes and titles of medieval tales into one turn of his book or another. But even with that evidence, "restoring order in [the] apparent chaos" of Rabelais's writings, to use Clement's expression (147), is no easy task. Some scholars, he says, have mistakenly argued that Rabelais was chiefly inspired not by the stories of Arthur and his knights but by prose versions of the epic poems, "the so-called Romances of Chivalry" (149); they are misled, in part, by faulty terminology. For such texts, he asserts, "a better name would be Gest Romances, and under this name they are listed [in this book]" (152); for Clement, a right taxonomy—of romances, in this case—and right nomenclature are of the essence of scientific history. Some good terms are ready at hand, the legacy of the seven hundred years or so during which writers have been trying to find their way in the territories of modern fiction, for example, to quote Clement, "Arthurian romances in general, of which the *Great Prose Lancelot* is a representative specimen" (151). Yet other names, like "Gest Romances" or "Grail-quest romances," remain to be coined if we are to make clear distinctions.

Curiously, the first occurrence of the word *romance* in Clement's book falls in a byway of his argument, as part of the somewhat puzzling technical term "popular romances" (148). Aren't fine manners, spiritual elevation, and the knightly code the soul of what we mean by "romance," and a court amidst faery woods its necessary setting? Or shall we decide to use the word as the first generation of Old French writers themselves used *roman,* just meaning a text written in some Romance vernacular, as distinct from its Latin model if it has one? In that case, don't we risk giving up any possible distinction between romance and literature itself? Does that matter?

At all events, Clement's first specimen of a popular romance is the book Rabelais vaunted above all others in the prologue to *Pantagruel.* *Pantagruel* was printed in Lyons sometime in 1532; earlier that same year, in the same place, the popular romance in question had appeared, published anonymously and entitled, as one might translate, *The Great and Inestimable Chronicles of the Great and Enormous Giant Gargantua, Containing His Genealogy, the Greatness and Strength of His Body; Also the Marvelous Deeds He Did for King Arthur, as You Will See Hereinafter.* For all the claims of that title, it wasn't a very long book, only sixteen smallish leaves of Gothic type; but Rabelais contended that, brief or not, it could help knights while away their time with damsels, cure toothache, and ease the pain of poor devils being sweated with quicksilver ointment for the pox. In the *Great Chronicles* the genealogy of Gargantua isn't long to tell; with the help of some magic hammers and an anvil the size of a tower, the enchanter Merlin fabricated Gargantua's father Grandgousier from the skeleton of a whale and a vial of blood collected, after a tourney, from Lancelot's wounds. Gargantua's paternal blood line goes back to Lancelot and stops there. Rabelais makes Pantagruel's genealogy a lot longer and a lot more entertaining; he takes Gargantua to be Pantagruel's father and Grandgousier his grandfather, but, for whatever reason, he omits Lancelot's name from the list of fifty-eight ancestors in generations before that and puts in Galehaut's instead. Sooner or later, any writer of romances is bound to run out of episodes or get tired. When the author of the *Great Chronicles* decided to call a halt, he thought of a simple, effective device, one that Rabelais was to find suited to his own, more complicated purposes. "And then," says the last sentence of the book, "[Gargantua] was carried to fairyland by Morgan le Fay and so was Mélusine, along with several other people who are still there at present."

For his part, Nemours H. Clement, like many serious scholars, is not so fond of the *Great Chronicles* as Rabelais seems to have been; such books appear to him naive, insipid, and pointless. For that matter, he's not too comfortable with *Pantagruel* itself, and he is much relieved that in 1534 Rabelais brought out his book of the father, *Gargantua*. "Of the five books," says Clement with assurance, "[*Gargantua*] is the best; it has fewer tiresome passages; its interest is better sustained; it excels the others in construction and style; it is the most philosophical; it avoids the exaggerations that disfigure the *Pantagruel*. In fine, the *Gargantua* is far less popular than the *Pantagruel*" (165). It appears that "popular romances," then, must all along have been a learned name made up to cover an embarrassment, the intermittent dismay of a dignified man more at home with philosophy than with stories as such, especially plebeian, goofy, or exaggerated ones. But if Nemours H. Clement doesn't care for silly stories, can we trust him on stories in general? Isn't there some silliness in the very nature of stories, some unseemly frivolity? If we aim to ask about the presence of romance in Rabelais, we will do well to ask on Rabelais's own terms, to focus on the most relevant Rabelaisian textual loci.

In this context, let us look again at *Pantagruel*. Where have all the old knights gone? What has become of Lancelot of the Lake? What of names themselves, their shifting and exchange and concealment? How does the code of chivalry fare? The art and act of reading?

Some answers are provided by the sixteenth chapter of the first

printing of *Pantagruel* (1532). One of the first names we hear there
is the name of Morgan le Fay, that sister of King Arthur who furnishes salves where they are needed and carries wearied champions
to rest in the Blessed Isles. Soon after, we come upon the trace of
Lancelot himself, clearly discernible through the flimsy disguise of
the name Marotus de Lac, Marot of the Lake. And next—just as in
Chrétien's romance *Yvain* Laudine had sent her messenger Lunete to
accuse the forgetful Yvain of being "disloyal, a traitor, a liar, a
mocker" (vv. 2721–22)—Pantagruel will receive an enigmatic message from a lady, taxing him with abandonment, and calling him (of
all people) the least loyal of knights. If we are to find the shadow
of romance falling across *Pantagruel* anywhere, it will probably be
in this place.

I have no reason to assume that you have reread *Pantagruel* in the
last few days, so I shall sketch out for you the bare narrative linea-
ments of Rabelais's chapter, as well as its place in the tale told by the
whole book. The title of the sixteenth chapter of *Pantagruel* (I should
say, incidentally, that the original compositor slipped up and mis-
numbered it "XV") is "How Pantagruel left Paris, hearing news that
the Dipsodes were invading the land of the Amaurots. And the reason why leagues are so small in France. And the expounding of a
word written in a ring." Syntactically, that is a rich and complicated
title. At first glance it looks like a sequence of four equivalent terms,
presumably events: a departure, an invasion, a reason (or cause), an
exposition. But is receiving news of the invasion an event distinct
from the invasion, a fifth event? Is a cause an event? Is the "expounding" an occurrence we can locate somewhere in the past or an
explanation offered, as it were, outside of time and thus not really a
happening at all? What do we mean by "an event"? In any case the
title connects the motifs of words inscribed in closed forms, and the
interpretation of such words, and the measuring of the earth, and
the transgression of boundaries marked off by measuring the earth. If
interpretation means inquiring into the limitation of writing and the
limitation of the world, we should begin ours by asking where this
chapter lies within the whole graphic space of *Pantagruel*.

The original *Pantagruel* tells its story in twenty-four chapters of
widely varying length: the longest, presenting a seemingly inter-
minable lawsuit all argued in double-talk, runs to some nineteen
crowded pages of Gothic type, while the chapter which tells of Gargantua's joy at the birth of his son and his grief at his wife's death in
childbirth is only about one-seventh as long. Still, however prolix or

laconic any one may be, the individual numbered chapters, like leagues in France, are the basic units which measure the book's cadences. The chapter informing us that Pantagruel left Paris is the sixteenth of twenty-four, completing the second third of the text. Is two-thirds of the text the same as two-thirds of the story? To know that, of course, we would have to have some ideal or generalized model for what we mean by "the whole story."

On the basis of his reading of many texts, along with some observations made by Gaston Paris, N. H. Clement provides a simple and sensible model of "the typical biographical romance," which he sees as the prototype of *Pantagruel* (180). In Clement's view, such stories fall into four discriminate parts (omitting the prologue): the ancestry of the hero (along with his birth); his youth and education; his exploits; and his marriage. The segment conspicuously missing from *Pantagruel* is the story of the hero's marriage; it is mentioned in the last chapter, where the storyteller informs us that what we have just read is only a beginning and writes out a checklist of the unfinished business to come, including six well-delineated major episodes (Pantagruel's marriage among them) and a thousand others that aren't specified. In fact, we shall learn late in Rabelais's third book (printed twelve years hence) that the question of Pantagruel's marriage will have to be put off until later, until the moment it has been decided whether his friend Panurge should get married or not; and since Rabelais's last surely authentic book, the *Quart Livre* (completed in 1552, a year before his death), presents only the first stages of an extended quest after the truth about Panurge's putative marriage, the matter of the hero's taking a wife is postponed for eternity. Marriage figures in the world of romance, but not in Pantagruel's. We should therefore be looking for three parts, not four.

The twenty-four chapters of *Pantagruel* do fall neatly into three distinct sequences of eight, and with no trouble at all one can locate the stories they tell on the map of Clement's generalized scheme. The first four chapters set forth Pantagruel's ancestry, the miracles attaching to his birth, and his early childhood. The next four make a start on youth and education—a tour of nine French universities, an encounter with a student, a visit to a library, and, finally, an epistle from Dad about what education should be—and that makes eight. This first third of the book thus ends on a letter—a text supposed not to have been written by Rabelais but by one of the characters within his story—and on the momentous signature "From Utopia, this seventeenth day of the month of March, Your father, Gargantua."

Such an ending may inspire further thoughts on how to read the book. In the first place, as we make this quick survey of *Pantagruel* as a written place, we would do well at the same time to ask which fictional people within it are themselves writing, and what they write. It is already apparent that in some, if not all, cases, words written by the characters may make up a portion of the words composing *Pantagruel*. Some of the characters, then, are Rabelais's imaginary collaborators in the factification of his book; he must feel especially close to them. Thus already in the third chapter we read a very polished decasyllabic octave that Gargantua, clearly a man or giant who knows the ways of letters, had composed as an epitaph for his wife. Now, as the first part of the book comes to a close, he writes out in lofty Ciceronian what will quite simply be his last words before he disappears from the story. In the second place, we may well think that fatherhood and the relay of generations—the very conceptual framework into which Gargantua sets the question of learning and studying in his letter—bears on the way the book is divided. And, finally, if we introduce lines of type as a different unit of measure (using Saulnier's edition as a tool for making approximations), we can appreciate that in this first third of his book Rabelais, despite what we might be tempted to think, has been efficiently going about his business and making impressive headway in his journey into the unwritten story ahead. As he finishes chapter 8 he has used up only about 900 lines—something like a fourth or a fifth of the not quite 4,200 lines of the whole text. Part 1 of *Pantagruel,* to call it that, turns out to be composed of a sequence of quick little chapters of about 100 lines each or even less, symmetrically flanked by two longer chapters, 1 and 8, which come out near the average length of the twenty-four chapters of the book: about 175 lines. That doesn't mean that the reader can go as fast as Rabelais does; the catalogue of St. Victor's library, for instance, isn't even fifty lines long, and by now, as successive annotated critical editions will attest, it has taken us some 450 years to begin to learn how to decipher it. What it does show is that the writer himself is really making tracks.

In the ninth chapter Pantagruel meets Panurge, "whom he loved his whole life," and a new cycle of eight is begun. We could look on this section as continuing what Clement calls the hero's education, since Pantagruel does in fact learn many things from Panurge (among them that native wit is more to be trusted than book learning), but it is also a second birth, since the hero's personality is rounded out: shrewd, mocking, base Panurge is like the other side of noble Pantagruel, the side he doesn't too much like to think about, and they are henceforth inseparable. Six of these eight chapters put Panurge in the foreground, but by the use of a romance convention which Vinaver very aptly calls "the poetry of interlace," the second of them presents Pantagruel's first exploit (passing a wise judgment on that dreadful lawsuit) and the last, chapter 16, focuses anew on Pantagruel, to tell of that climactic moment at which he must decide to leave off learning, put youth and France behind him, and go home to take his father's place.

Having made such a fast start at the outset of his book, in this second section Rabelais pretends not to be a purposeful swift tortoise after all, but a forgetful, dawdling hare. There aren't any short chapters at all; four are of "average" length, three others are well in excess of that, and one is a great monster of 500 lines. Part 2 is some 2,100 lines long, more than half the length of the whole book; by the time he reaches the end of it Rabelais is at least two or three chapters in arrears, so to speak. In his delight at writing down whatever comes into his head about Panurge, he appears just to dally and delay, without a care for getting on with the story of Pantagruel. And then, with no advance warning at all, he zaps us with the shocking news that the father has been kidnapped: all gone! And the kid is on his own. Of course: he wasn't napping all along; we were.

In part 2, two imaginary writers stand out. The first, as we might expect, is Panurge himself. We learn that he has composed (Rabelais's term) a fine big book about codpieces, with illustrations; but as it's not yet printed, we are not given it to see. Panurge must be counted in any list of authors whose works, or some of whose works, for all practical purposes have disappeared. What we do see in print, though, is a rondeau Panurge composed as a step in his campaign against the Parisian lady. It turns out he is a master verse writer, one who can swerve without notice from the tone of courtly manners to the aggressive and obscene: an author who reminds us, curiously enough, of Rabelais.

The other writer who makes a difference here—and that seems hardly a strong enough way to put the matter—is of all things a woman, or more precisely a lady. We do not know her name, but she is the author of the second of the two important letters which, recalling Pantagruel to his duty, mark the endings of parts 1 and 2 of the book. (We might note in passing that as Pantagruel spells out those two epistles, he is not only the hero of the book but also the most conspicuous reader in it—should we say of it?) Like Gargantua and Panurge, the lady who writes to Pantagruel is skilled in verse; she addresses her letter with a perfect twelve-syllable line. In other respects she is a strange writer indeed, one who manages the resources of the alphabet and other signs in a very idiosyncratic way. When she writes Pantagruel's name, she uses capital letters but leaves out all the vowels, and the name stands there, curiously disfigured and thus highlighted, like a bizarre allographic signature echoing the "Gargantua" of chapter 8 and bringing youth and education to an end. That enigmatic end, written by an invisible woman with no name, can only leave the reader all agape.

Speaking of headway, I should be trying to make some myself. The last eight chapters of *Pantagruel* compose the section N. H. Clement has categorized as the exploits of the hero. Like the first eight chapters, they divide into two sequences of four. The first sequence recounts the engaging of hostilities and the Pantagruelian victory over the invading Dipsodian army; the second, Pantagruel's largely peaceful investment of Dipsodia itself and his installation as the new and better monarch of that land. We thus finally reach the fulfillment promised pages ago, in the title of the book, by the designation "Pantagruel, King of the Dipsodes." It is near the beginning of this third part, too, that Pantagruel joins the company of authors. His first exploit is not martial but literary. Calling for metaphors on Fabius, Scipio, and the game of chess, invoking the knightly ideal, he composes a poem of stunning formal intricacy which serves to commemorate the battle his companions had won as he himself stood to one side. A little further on, in the twentieth chapter, he will achieve a spectacular and decisive victory in single combat; already now he is a poet.

Part 3 is another short, fast-moving section, scarcely longer than part 1, and it proposes a rhythmic model we had not seen before: a smooth sequence of chapters having just about the "normal" length of 175 lines, an order of classical proportion. That order is occasionally broken by a very short chapter reminiscent of the brief units of part 1 (a hundred lines or less). There are three such chapters. The shortest of all is the last; having recounted Pantagruel's great sickness and his cure, it goes on to announce adventures for years, and books, to come, but it rattles them off at a dizzying speed, and before we know it *Pantagruel* is all over, in a blip.

The title of the sixteenth chapter, then, announces four events, more or less: Pantagruel's departure, the invasion of Amaurotia, the origin of little leagues, and the interpretation of a written word. It forgets to tell us about the two others the chapter will relate: a world-circling voyage and a council of war. To call these happenings events, of course, is to enter willingly into the fiction itself as though it were a world given in advance, like France in 1532, or Utopia whenever it was; and that will be our pleasure, as we read along dreaming. At other moments, we will be brought up short—by a word we can't make out, perhaps, or an episode that pits our most archaic thoughts one against the other. The flow stops, we call a halt to being Pantagruel and snap back to being ourselves. Then we see it hadn't been a world at all, but only a stream of words.

At such moments we note that the text, too, starts and stops; it is a set of segments, or even fragments. Those segments aren't typographically marked out for us; sixteenth-century books were very sparing in the use of paragraph breaks, and the divisions introduced by modern editors are capricious and wholly untrustworthy. But we all have some feeling for the way a story begins and ends, and just on that intuitive basis (for the sake of convenience, not rigorous truth) we can divide the sixteenth chapter of *Pantagruel* into five narrations of unequal length, each quite complete in itself: five small verbal systems. Next we can consider each one apart and in turn, as a way of shielding ourselves a bit from the driving energy of Rabelais's tale. That should allow us to observe with detachment the proportion between the written, printed space occupied by each segment or the time it would take to read it aloud on the one hand and, on the other, the likely duration of each imaginary event and the space it would take up in a world not too much unlike ours, if that world were measured with reasonable accuracy. That proportioning of verbal measures (in a book) to temporal and geographical measurements (on earth, or in a world of fantasy) is the question suggested to us by Rabelais's complex chapter title; in this section of my essay I hope to bring it more clearly into focus.

The first part of the sixteenth chapter is only nine lines long in Saulnier's edition, about one-twentieth the length of the chapter itself. It is hard to say how long the events it reports might have taken, but as you will see, succession, acceleration, delay, and the play of the old days against the new days are of the essence of the story. Since this segment is so short and so rich, I will translate it instead of summarizing it. "A little while later" ("peu de temps après"): those are the first words of the text, and before we go on, it may be worth pausing over this preeminence given to temporal matters. Along with numerous notations of mere sequences like "then," "thereupon," and words and phrases like "diligence," "wasting time," "being urgent," the chapter counts a dozen and a half adverbial expressions noting points in time, or lengths of time, or quickness, or timelessness: "formerly," "at present," "once a day," "in so little time," "immediately," "never." And so on. A few of those phrases mention chronological units such as "for a week," "an hour later," "in a few days," "for all of today." Time is never out of mind, but the durations of the tale, its hastening and infrequent slackening of pace, are for the most part left loose. Just as our imagination starts to float and hover with them, it turns out a clock is running somewhere, and we are snubbed up to the workaday world.

"A little while later," then, "Pantagruel heard news that his father Gargantua had been translated to the land of the fairies by Morgan, as in the old times Enoch and Elijah had been; and simultaneously that, the report of his translation having been heard, the Dipsodes had gone beyond their limits and had laid waste a great territory of Utopia, and at present were holding the great city of the Amaurots at siege. So he left Paris without saying goodbye to anyone, for the matter called for diligence, and came to Rouen." Since the beginning of a story is ordinarily the whole story in germ, it appears that the chapter will be the unwinding of more threads about the eclipse of fathers, trespassing boundaries—or, if you will, exceeding them— omitting speech, and traveling fast, among other things. The chapter opens on two moments of audition (Pantagruel heard, and the Dipsodes had heard); at its end we shall hear the words of Pantagruel and his friends.

The instant of translation also occurs twice, once for Pantagruel, once for the Dipsodes, so that even as Pantagruel hastens from Paris to Rouen the story seems to be doubling back to the same point, not making any headway at all. You may remember that the *Great Chronicles* didn't say that Gargantua was translated to fairyland, but only that he was carried there. "Translation" is a favorite word of Rabelais's for what he does as a writer. At the beginning of his next book, about Gargantua, he tells about Pantagruel's genealogy being found, dug up by accident, in a manuscript written "not on paper, not on wax, but on elm-bark," so worn with age that you could scarcely make out three letters in a row. "I was called in," says the narrator, "and with lots of pairs of spectacles, practicing the art by which invisible writing can be read, as Aristotle teaches, I translated it, as you can see (*Gargantua* 24; ch. 1). Invisible writing, obscure letters in a row, and optical troubles generally will come up soon enough, in the chapter we are considering. For the moment, we should just be aware that the removal of the father and the transport of meaning from one idiom to another are denoted by the same word.

The translation of Gargantua is said to be just like the translations of Enoch and Elijah. "Enoch" and "Elijah" are the two most usual names for people transported from earth to heaven without passing through death, so Rabelais didn't have to make them up or search very hard for them. His simile advises us that Gargantua is probably not deceased but just gone. The story of Enoch, in Genesis 5, is short and stirring, but not, in its narrative lines, very straightforward. It occurs in a list of generations. Near the beginning we are told "And Enoch walked with God," and then at the end, as the King James version has it, "And Enoch walked with God, and he was not." (The meaning is not that Enoch used to walk with God, or that he was walking, but that on just one occasion he did so: the Vulgate translates "ambulavit.") Like the story of Pantagruel making haste to Rouen, the tale of Enoch is a tale of walking, and like the story of the translation of Gargantua, it doubles back to its starting point. Both stories are stories of false starts. Unlike Gargantua, who as far as we're concerned engendered only Pantagruel, Enoch begat sons and daughters. His whole life was 365 years, a long year measured not in days but in years. Where the King James says bleakly that "he was not," the Vulgate is more guarded: "non apparuit" ("he didn't appear"). Other translators report that "he disappeared." Enoch was a walker and a father and then some; you could compare him to an invisible letter, or a disappearing letter.

The story of Elijah, in 2 Kings, is also a story of disappearance. Elisha the disciple had a feeling that Yahve was going to suck the prophet Elijah up off the earth in a twister. That made Elisha nervous. When Elijah said to him, in effect, "You stay here. I'm only going as far as Bethel, no farther," Elisha refused to leave his side. (You see that this is also a story about traveling, and how far one might travel. The King James gives Elijah's words as "Tarry here," thus introducing the motif of delay.) Then Elijah said, "I'm only going as far as Jericho," and, again, "I'm only going to the river Jordan": both times Elisha stuck to his heels. Later Elisha asked Elijah to leave him, as an inheritance, a double share of his spirit. Elijah said that was a difficult request to honor, but that if Elisha could see him as he was ravished away, then Elisha would indeed inherit a double portion of spirit. Just then a fiery chariot came down and pulled Elijah up into the twister. Elisha cried, "My father! My father!" and added something about the chariot. Then he couldn't see Elijah any more. But as it turned out, he did get a double share of spirit.

Earlier in *Pantagruel,* almost the same story about legacy and inheritance appears, but told from the other point of view, the father's. In his memorable letter, Gargantua writes to say that he is sure Pantagruel will live on after him as his "visible image" on earth; he is concerned, though, lest only the lesser part of himself, which is the body, live on, while the better part, the soul, might turn "degenerate and bastardized." It is understandable that the legitimate father should fret lest the son not live up to the paternal spirit. We can also imagine the burden the father's demand for perfection would impose on the son; he might just want to go away somewhere else or wish that his father would go away somewhere else. In the story of Elisha and Elijah we see things mostly from the son's viewpoint; sharing all his anxiety, we can easily feel how he shouldn't want any space at all to open between the father and himself.

In the second segment of Rabelais's chapter, Pantagruel undertakes to close the space between himself and the father, or at least the fatherland. This second section is some thirty lines long, three times as extended as the first. Things seem to be swelling. It's mainly about traveling to Rouen (which is a little strange since we thought we had already arrived in Rouen, or at least Pantagruel had, and thereafter to Honfleur). I don't know how long it took to go from Paris to Rouen at the time—the distance is about 125 kilometers, or not quite thirty French leagues—but it must have been a matter of days, not seconds or weeks or years. On the way to Rouen Pantagruel noticed that the leagues in France were excessively small in comparison to those of other countries. So he asked his friend Panurge the cause and reason. We hadn't known Panurge was along, but now we do. Panurge, in answer, told a story that Marot of the Lake, the monk, *Marotus du Lac, monachus,* sets down in the *Chronicles of the Kings of Canarre.*

I think we should tarry a moment, to ask what's happening. "Marot of the Lake, the monk" mixes Lancelot with some Marot or other. Some scholars think Rabelais got the idea for the name from seeing Lancelot Island (in the Canaries) next to Marocellus Island, in old pilot books; both islands were apparently named for one Lancelot Maloesel, or Lancialotto Marocello. Other scholars remain very skeptical but have no better guesses to offer. Certainly maps and islands seem appropriate enough in this chapter. Marot, though, is a good French name, a well-known one. Here, it could refer to Jean Marot, a chronicler and court poet who wrote two celebrated long poems with titles beginning *Voyage de*. More likely it refers to his son Clément; another dubiety bears on fathers and sons. Clément Marot was also a poet, a friend and contemporary of Rabelais. Here, too, he is a writer: not a poet, but a court chronicler, which is what Rabelais pretends to be as he tells the story of Pantagruel. Marot was not a monk, but Rabelais was. Rabelais and Clément Marot were kindred spirits, touched by the same enthusiasms for a new Christianity and a new literature. Beyond that, to be honest, I have no idea why Rabelais should have elected Marot to be the imaginary author of a page or two in *Pantagruel,* and I'd like to ask your leave to think about the question for a few more years. It might even have to do with the fact that Marot was not Clément Marot's father's real name, but an alias. The family name was actually Maretz or Desmaretz, which means "marsh"; hence, perhaps, the joke about being from the lake. Rabelais didn't put his real name on the title page of *Pantagruel,* either. He scrambled the letters of "Françoys Rabelais" and came up with the Arabo-Greco-French-sounding pseudonym "Alcofrybas Nasier," Al-Kofrybas Nosey. You'll notice that we're accumulating authors as we go. We already have Alcofrybas Nasier and François Rabelais lurking behind him and Thomas More who made up the story of Utopia in the first place, and the writer of the *Great and Inestimable Chronicles* and the writers of Genesis (if any) and of the second book of Kings, and now Marot of the Lake. Identities are fusing and wavering. It's becoming less and less clear who's in charge here.

The story told by Marotus and retold by Panurge goes like this: In the old days, countries weren't yet distinct—that's Panurge's word—by leagues, miles, or parasangs. (Thomas More, by the way, is also the author of the name Amaurots, which means "indistinct people.") So King Pharamond distinguished them. In Paris he convoked a hundred lusty fellows and a hundred beautiful wenches from Picardy. He fed them well for a week and gave them lots of money and sent them off in couples toward the frontiers of the realm and told them to put down a merestone every time they made love, and that would be a league. At the start the lads were fresh and rested, and they stallioned their wenches just down the road every little bit; and that's why leagues are so short in France. But after they'd gone a long way they were bushed, and there was no more oil in the lamp—oil in the lamp is a usual figure in Rabelais, as in ancient authors, for energy of writers—so they didn't horse so often and were satisfied with one lousy time a day—that is, the men were. And that's why leagues are so big in Britanny and other faraway countries.

Marotus's tale does not at first seem like one you'd hear in a romance. Yet in its own way, it goes over the same ground as Chrétien's story about the salve in *Yvain* (vv. 2942–3003): the unmeasurable ground itself. Both stories are about squandering and desire, or, if you will, sexuality and prodigality. Marotus's story sounds like a very old one that somebody thought up amid an economy of scarcity and hoarding. It begins when a liberal fairyland king unexpectedly gives you everything your heart could possibly desire—plenty of food and coddling and women and money—just as Chrétien's story starts from Morgan le Fay's free gift of a salve to cure madness. (The "you," the recipient, is made collective—a hundred lusty fellows—so that irrelevant questions of competition and private property won't arise. That might not happen in a romance.) Then the king says, "I have only one order to give. Will you please go for a walk and measure my country for me, and be sure to take lots of pleasure in sex, all you can." It sounds like a great deal—the greatest.

We'll never know how Marotus went about telling this story, but in retelling it Panurge does a fine job. Such stories depend for their effect on an appeal to the authority of ancient truth (a very old book, in this case) and deadpan solemnity in the telling. Also on foisting off without comment an assumption that stands the waking world on its head—isn't that how everybody measures leagues? One meaning of the story is "Hey it's fun walking along like this. It's as much fun as playing sex," and of course Panurge's reason for telling it is to make walking the road from Paris to Rouen faster and easier. That works very well: as the story stands printed in *Pantagruel,* it wouldn't take more than five mniutes to recite, yet as it ends Pantagruel and Panurge have already completed their three-day trudge without Pantagruel's even noticing: "leaving Rouen," says the text, not bothering to mention that they'd got there, "they arrived at Honfleur"—sixty or seventy more kilometers in the trice of one word, "arrivérent." Panurge played that kindly trick on Pantagruel. By embedding the story of the hundred lusty fellows traveling in the story of Pantagruel traveling, Rabelais has played it on us.

This is supposed to be an essay about reading. Listening to a story told out of an old book is closely analogous to reading, and I should try to describe the effect Marotus's fable has on its intended audience, Pantagruel, beyond the simple pleasure of listening while walking. One can easily imagine that the story mixes up Pantagruel's feelings, his feelings about kingship, for instance. Pharamond was that legendary grandson of Priam who already by the eighth century had been invented and intercalated in the list of actual, historical Merovingian kings to make a connection to Trojan royalty and thus provide greater legitimacy to the realm. Rabelais not only writes Pharamond with *ph*—that's not unheard of, though Latin writers most often use *f*—but also "Phées" for "fairies," a completely wild spelling. Linking the two words thus, perhaps he is inviting us to think of Greek *phaino* ("to appear"), and thus of disappearances. At a few removes, the realm of Pharamond is the France of François I, in which François Rabelais benefits from having protectors in high places: the king's sister, to name one. What must Pantagruel feel about a monarch who casually gives away the secret that the order and measure of his realm are founded on the merry copulations of the common people? Then, too, those copulations aren't just merry, they're exhausting; they waste the vital substance. Pantagruel is an adolescent giant on the road to becoming a writer and a king and a father; beneath his seemly modesty and self-effacement he needs the thought that his power is unlimited. If you tell him a story about no more oil in the lamp, he will doubt and worry. It seems reasonable to suppose that that's why he reacts to Panurge's story as he does. He doesn't laugh, he doesn't weep or fly into a rage; with serene dignity and grace he "willingly consents" to agree that the story contains a large measure of truth. The surface of courtesy goes unruffled by anger or giddy delight.

Perhaps I should also say another word or two about my contention that in Marotus's fable, making headway is a figure for writing or for telling stories. The oil in the lamp, or no longer in the lamp, is a clue. The coincidence of Panurge's recital with the walk to Rouen is another. But beyond that, there is a curious inverse relationship between sexual expenditure and narrative power. At first Panurge's voice is very faint, and we almost think we're listening to indirect discourse: it is Marotus's story, and Panurge just retells it, "disant que" ("saying that"). Then the conjunctions of subordination fall away, and we hear somebody saying straight out: "King Pharamond took a hundred fellows . . . he had them well treated . . . he called them together," and so on. For their part, the fellows perform only one action rendered by a finite verb in the perfect tense: they "joyeusement partirent" ("went off joyously"), just as, a few lines back, Pantagruel "partit de Paris" ("left Paris"), and then their troubles begin. Thereafter, as they weaken and run dry, they are depicted in various states, but never in action: they are the grammatical subject of imperfect verbs only: "they were already as worn out as poor devils, they didn't use to horse so often, they were content with one time a day." In that sense, the tale isn't a well-formed story at all; instead of ending with a decisive action, it simply peters out as the fellows slow down and dwindle away. But as they decline, Panurge begins to rise and emerge, and we hear him offering comments on his own: "and that's why leagues in France are so small," and so on. As he concludes the story, his presence is not only audible but commanding: "others give other reasons, but that one seems the best to me." Using the pronoun to let us know that he is present in the words spoken, he decides what makes sense or doesn't. It is as though Panurge, standing aside while the sexual horseplay goes on, were drawing up into his own acts of narration all the energy spilled and wasted by the fellows. (We may be reminded of Ronsard or Mallarmé: the plot of their poems, too, often seems to show them gathering verbal strength by sexual abstention.) Maybe that's why the original writer of the story Panurge tells aloud should be a *monachus,* a monk having sworn vows of chastity even if he doesn't necessarily observe them.

A last word about Marotus's fable: the women may be treated like objects, but the joke is on the men.

So they came to Honfleur, Pantagruel and Panurge. The name of the city is an old Saxon one, "Huno's flood" or "Huno's estuary": it appears late in the twelfth century, as "Honneflo" (Longnon; Dauzat, *s.v.* "Honfleur"). Rabelais spells it *Hommefleur* (nobody else does, as far as I can discover) and uses it, indeed, to mark the flowering of his man. Getting to Honfleur at last, we learn for the first time that we've been traveling with a company not of two but of five. Pantagruel, it turns out, has four companions with names like the virtues he aspires to in himself. For the first time anywhere in the book Rabelais puts all the names together and spells them off like an incantation: "Pantagruel, Panurge, Epistemon, Eusthénes et Carpalim," Thirsty, Crafty, Knower, Strongman, and Speedy. They all put to sea. Thus ends *Pantagruel,* chapter 16, segment 2.

The third section fills eighty lines. The events it places in the foreground could easily transpire in about two hours. It is not only the longest narration in the chapter (and, up to now, the most leisurely and circumstantial) but also far and away the most startling, the most baffling and instructive. It is a story of writing and reading, the story we've been aiming at all this time.

The section breaks up into two parts, which I shall consider separately.

The first begins by annulling some progress we had made, yanking Pantagruel and his men back onto land, after they'd put to sea. Now they're waiting for a propitious wind and caulking their ship. Navigation is a figure for writing, especially writing epics; it is so usual in Rabelais and everywhere else that I don't think we need pause to gather examples. Waiting for the wind, the *spiritus,* is what writers do between times, before they embark. Caulking ship is a sexual image in Rabelais (he uses it, for instance, in the third chapter of *Gargantua*), and if you think about the relation of chisel to oakum to groove it isn't hard to see why. In the fourth book of the *Aeneid* (which is about to come into play in Rabelais's chapter), when Dido saw Aeneas's men smearing their hulls with pitch and watching the winds, she knew that the sexual gift she had made of herself, thinking of it as a marriage, was about to be betrayed. In Virgil's text and Rabelais's, this is a moment of gravid latency and pressing expectation. If messages come through, we shouldn't be surprised. In Aeneas's case, one of them comes from his late father Anchises via Mercury, who appears in a dream to shame Aeneas and goad him to move on: "Madman, can't you hear the propitious breathing of the zephyrs? . . . No more delay! . . . Always a woman is a variable, mutable thing!" (*Aen.* 4.562, 569–70; translation mine).

In Honfleur Pantagruel, for his part, received a message from a lady in Paris. Only now, once we're safely away from Paris, do we learn that Pantagruel had had anything to do with ladies there. Alcofrybas the narrator had forgotten to tell us, at the time; his unconscious may have had its reasons. This is a lady whom Pantagruel "avoit entretenu bonne espace de temps." Sixteenth-century usage won't allow us to decide for sure whether that means they had simply kept company for a good space of time or shared a sexual commerce. The latter idea is a little uncomfortable because of the discrepancy of size between a young giant and a lady of ordinary stature. Perhaps that discomfort is one reason the narrator hadn't wanted to face up to telling about their romance.

The message took the form of a letter, "unes lettres," as the text puts it in a stylish Latinism. In Latin the plural *litterae* is one common way of saying "an epistle," but then Latin doesn't use articles, and in French the bizarre plural singular "unes" confronts us with the dichotomy between the many written letters or characters and the single missive or utterance. This letter had an inscription on the outside: "Au plus aymé des belles, et moins loyal des preux. PNTGRL."

The first element of that inscription is a deft and elegant twelve-syllable verse with what is technically known as an "epic caesura," an unelided mute *e* at the end of the first hemistich. It breaks the easy, chatty, meandering prose of the story by the obtrusion of its perfect crystalline form. One might translate it "To the most beloved of the fair, and the least loyal of the brave"; "preux" is a special term for valorous knights. In their syntax and rhythm the two halves of the line are so exactly parallel that the second is like a repetition of the first: this is another false start or back-to-square-one piece of writing. The line uses grammar as a tool for wit: each half is a superlative, a dative of address made up of five words; identical constructions ("des" plus a plural noun) are used to convey two completely different syntactical functions (in the first case an ablative of agent, in the second a genitive of appurtenance); the ellipse of "au" ("to the") in the second hemistich softens and loosens the tight fit of the two halves, giving the lines more grace and zip. Whoever wrote this knew what she was doing. She may well have been a reader of *Yvain,* where the hero received a message calling him disloyal, "desleal" (v. 2722); perhaps also of the *Aeneid,* where to his face Dido calls Aeneas "perfide," a faith-breaker (*Aen.* 4.305). The second element of her inscription is of course Pantagruel's name, all in capital letters, written as though it were Hebrew, with the vowels left out. It stands there on the outside of the letter, and on Rabelais's page, like a bunch of strange unsignifying marks. Probably in this case too the lady knew what she was doing. But we should postpone finding out about that until we've finished this first part of the story.

When Pantagruel had read the inscription, even before he opened the letter, he was "bien esbahy," so dumbfounded he could only gape. (As we said earlier, Pantagruel is usually cool civility itself, hardly the type to stand around with his mouth open. Later, Rabelais will coin "Pantagruelism" as a synonym for equanimity. It must be that in this place some large chunk of an unconscious, untold story is cropping out.) He asked the messenger the lady's name: a move to protect his own, as it were, and to parry the threat by localizing it, finding out what quarter it was coming from. How can it be that Pantagruel didn't know the lady's name? Had there been many such ladies? Was he too dumbfounded to remember? Had there never been such a lady at all? In any case, we are not given the messenger's answer; we never learn whether he spoke the name or not. Pantagruel opened the letter(s). Inside he found nothing, or at least nothing written, only a gold ring with a diamond. (In romances, rings stand for faith committed; thus, for example, after Yvain had broken his promise, Lunete took Laudine's ring away from him.) So he called on his friend Panurge. Panurge was quite unfazed. He said confidently that certainly the sheet of paper was written on (here the medium of the message becomes concrete and material) but with such subtlety that you couldn't see any writing. And that's the first part of the third section of the story.

The section we have just walked through is thirteen lines long. Its Emphasis on Writing (to borrow the title of a program at Cornell) is so clear that there's really no need to belabor the point: we have only to take it at face value, as it ticks off writing epics, writing verses, writing words or letters, visibly or invisibly. But we might have another look at those omitted vowels. Here's the view of modern linguistics: "Any sequence is built of syllables; they are the fundamental divisions of any sequence. . . . Vowels function in languages as the only or at least as the most usual carriers of the syllabic nuclei, whereas the margins of syllables are occupied chiefly or solely by consonants" (Jakobson and Waugh 85). In other words, in any string of signifying sounds, vowels are the indispensable little nuts or kernels, nuclei; consonants are the husks or dividers, occurring at the margins. No speech without vowels, then, can be nutritive, nor indeed exist at all. For our story of boundaries, where people are stretched to their limit or go off to find the limit, the word "margins" seems pertinent; we are trying to find the divisions Rabelais hid within his text, so as to inspect its nuclei one by one. In Honfleur, at the margin of France and the sea, Pantagruel waits for the wind that will move his carrier, his ship; what comes to him first is an echo of his own name without vowels, hence without syllables.

At Rabelais's time, the science of language took its metaphors not from chemistry or molecular biology, but naturally enough from theology, whether Christian or ancient Greek. In his *Champ Fleury* Geofroy Tory gives instructions for writing the letters of the alphabet, or rather constructing them by geometry, so as to make them formally perfect. The word he uses for vowels, the usual one at the time, is "vocales" ("voice-letters"). He declares that the five Latin vowels, with the Greek ypsilon and the *h* of rough breathing ("aspiration") make up a sequence of seven letters which stand for the four cardinal virtues plus the three graces (Tory, f. xxviii). (In modern French, by the way, "rough breathing" is "esprit rude," literally "rough spirit.") In the French of that century *voix* ("voice") is one of the words for "word"; in a famous sentence, Montaigne writes "le nom, c'est une voix" ("the name is a voice, a word") (*Essais* 2.16). *Voix* can also mean "utterance" or even "cry," since to emit a cry one must make the vocal cords go. Huguet's dictionary records many examples of a proverbial locution "n'avoir [or n'ouir] ny vent ny voix," literally "not to have [or to hear] wind nor voice"; the usual meaning is to have no news of something or somebody, but sometimes the last word is spelled as the homonym "voye" ("way, road") and sometimes the meaning is "to go looking for something and not find it" (Huguet, *s.v.* "vent"). By itself, that phrase gives rise to a reading of the sixteenth chapter of Pantagruel: Pantagruel hears news that he will no more get wind of his father nor hear his father's voice; if he goes looking for him, he won't find him. He stands at a place on his way, waiting for a breath of wind, a *spiritus*. He gets a word or voice, a "voix": it is his own name with the voice-letters left out, his own name without virtues or grace, a voice without voice.

In the second part of the third section of chapter 16, Panurge used twelve highly technical methods for decoding and found nothing at all. (In the description of Panurge's efforts, the language becomes formalized. Each new sentence begins "Puis" ("and then"). The words "inscription," "writing," "written," and "write" occur twenty times.) He said to Pantagruel, "I don't know what to say or do. I've used the methods set down in writing by Messer Francesco di Nianto [Francis Nothing] and others, but I see nothing." They looked at the ring; the diamond was fake, "un diamant faux." Inside the ring were inscribed the words "Lamah Hazabtani." They asked Epistémon what that meant. He said it was a Hebrew name—"un nom hebraïcque"—meaning "Why hast thou forsaken me?" Then Panurge understood; the message was "Pray tell, false lover ("dy, amant faulx"), why hast thou forsaken me?" In Matthew's gospel, Christ's last words begin *Eli, Eli* ("Lord, Lord"), and the scoffers say, in effect "Listen to him, he's calling on Elijah." Elie is also the French name for Elijah; it has appeared at the beginning of the chapter but dropped out here. Pantagruel remembered that he had not said goodbye to the lady and was very sad. He wanted to go back to Paris to make peace with her, but Epistémon put him in memory of Aeneas leaving Dido and said he should put aside all such thoughts and hasten to the city of his birth, which was in danger.

In the fourth section of the chapter Pantagruel and his friends go halfway round the world in just thirteen lines, using the route of

Vasco da Gama; it had taken Vasco ten months. They put in at Canarre, where Marotus had written the story of the big and little leagues, and, passing by way of Meden, Uti, Uden, and Gelasim (that is, in Greek, Nothing, Nothing, Nothing, and Laughable), they reach the Isles of the Fairies, where Gargantua must be. It isn't said that they bother to call on him. Finally they arrive in the port of Achoria (Homeless City) and rest before taking up arms. The fifth section is forty-six lines long, and in it reading-aloud-time and happening-time are the same—a matter of three or four minutes—since it consists of the words of Pantagruel and his four friends, reported verbatim in direct discourse. Their words make up a "gab," a ritual exchange of formalized boasts such as one finds in Old French epics and once in the prose *Lancelot*. Oddly enough, the longest, culminating speech is given by Carpalim (Rapidity), who might have seemed the palest of the four companions. He boasts that he passes so fast and lightly that he can walk over a wheat field without bending the stalks, "for," he says, "I am of the lineage of Camilla the Amazon." "Camille Amazone" is the last name in the chapter, its two last words. Carpalim is quoting the fourth book of the *Aeneid* in translation, the same book that tells of Aeneas's taking disloyal leave of Dido. We would have everything to gain from re-reading the whole chapter in that light and from thinking about women warriors, but we have to stop somewhere, so why not here?

I wonder about a couple of things. Why are the last words of Christ, which might be appropriate to Pantagruel's new situation without a father, transferred to the lady who writes them down? Why did Jesus borrow those words from the psalm of David? What is a quotation? Must the father be translated before we can consider the loves of the son? Does the son's forgetting and sudden remembering have anything to do with the father? Is there perhaps no such thing as written romance, only unwritten romance or invisibly written romance?

Works Consulted

Approaches to Romance. Ed. Peter Haidu. Yale French Studies 51 (1975).

Chrétien de Troyes. *Le Chevalier au Lion (Yvain).* Ed. Mario Roques. CFMA. Paris: Champion, 1960.

———. *Le Chevalier de la Charrette.* Ed. Mario Roques. CFMA. Paris: Champion, 1958.

Cioranescu, Alexandre. "Rabelais et les Iles Canaries." *Bibliothèque d'Humanisme et Renaissance* 25.1 (1963): 88–96.

Clement, Nemours H. *The Influence of the Arthurian Romances on the Five Books of Rabelais.* U of California Publications in Modern Philology 12. 3. Berkeley: U of California P, 1926.

Dauzat, Albert, and Charles Rostaing. *Dictionnaire étymologique des noms de lieux en France.* Paris: Larousse, 1963.

Derrida, Jacques. *De la Grammatologie.* Collection "Critique." Paris: Editions de Minuit, 1967.

Dragonetti, Roger. "Aux Frontières du Langage Poétique." *Romanica Gandensia* 9 (1961): 98ff.

———. *La Vie de la Lettre au Moyen Age.* Paris: Seuil, 1980.

Frye, Northrop. *Anatomy of Criticism: Four Essays.* Princeton: Princeton UP, 1957.

Glauser, Alfred. *Rabelais Créateur.* Paris: Nizet, 1966.

Les Grandes et Inestimables Cronicques du Grant et Enorme Geant Gargantua. Ed. Ch. Marty-Laveaux. Paris: Lemerre, 1881.

Hanning, Robert W. *The Individual in Twelfth-Century Romance.* New Haven: Yale UP, 1977.

Horrent, Jules. *Le Pèlerinage de Charlemagne: Essai d'Explication Littéraire avec des Notes de Critique Textuelle.* Bibliothèque de la Faculté de Philosophie et Lettres de L'Université de Liège. Paris: Belles Lettres, 1961.

Jakobson, Roman, and Linda Waugh. *The Sound Shape of Language.* Bloomington: Indiana UP, 1979.

Jameson, Fredric. "Magical Narratives: Romance as Genre." *New Literary History* 7 (1975): 135–63.

———. *The Political Unconscious: Narrative as a Socially Symbolic Act.* Ithaca, N.Y.: Cornell UP, 1981.

Kelly, F. Douglas. *Sens and Conjointure in the* Chevalier de la Charrette. The Hague: Mouton, 1966.

Ker, W. P. *Epic and Romance: Essays on Medieval Literature.* London: Macmillan, 1897.

Kurth, Godefroid. *Histoire Poétique des Mérovingiens.* Paris: Picard, 1893.

La Charité, Raymond C. "Chapter Division and Narrative Structure in Rabelais's *Pantagruel.*" *French Forum* 3 (1978): 263–71.

———. *Recreation, Reflection, and Re-creation: Perspectives on Rabelais's* Pantagruel. Lexington, Ky.: French Forum, 1980.

Lancelot: Roman en Prose du XIIIe siècle. Ed. A. Micha. Textes littéraires français. 9 vols. Genève: Droz, 1978–83.

Lancelot du Lac: The Non-cyclic Old French Prose Romance. 2 vols. Ed. Elspeth Kennedy. Oxford: Clarendon, 1980.

Lefranc, Abel. *Les Navigations de Pantagruel: Etude sur la Géographie Rabelaisienne.* Paris: Leclercq, 1905.

Lot, Ferdinand. *Etude sur le Lancelot en Prose.* Bibliothèque de l'Ecole des Hautes Etudes 226. Paris: Champion, 1918.

Loomis, Laura H. "Observations on the *Pèlerinage Charlemagne.*" *Modern Philology* 25 (1927–28): 331–49.

Masuccio Salernitano [Tommaso Guardati]. *Il Novellino.* Ed. Giorgi Petrocchi. Firenze: Sansoni, 1957.

Parker, Patricia. *Inescapable Romance: Studies in the Poetics of a Mode.* Princeton: Princeton UP, 1979.

Plato. *Dialogues.* Trans. B. Jowett. Oxford: Clarendon, 1871.

——. *Oeuvres Complètes.* 5.2: "Cratyle." Ed. and trans. L. Méridier. Collection des Universités de France. Paris: Belles Lettres, 1931.

Rabelais, François. *Oeuvres Complètes.* Ed. A. Lefranc et al. Paris: Champion. Vols. 1 and 2: *Gargantua,* 1913. Vols. 3 and 4: *Pantagruel,* 1922.

——. *Pantagruel. Edition de Lyon, Juste, 1533.* Réimprimé d'après l'exemplaire unique de la Bibliothèque royale de Dresde par P. Babeau, Jacques Boulanger, et H. Patry. Publication de la Société des Etudes Rabelaisiennes. Paris: Champion, 1904.

——. *Pantagruel.* Ed. V.-L. Saulnier. Paris: Droz, 1946.

Sainean, Lazare. *La Langue de Rabelais.* 2 vols. Paris: Bocard, 1922–23.

Tilley, Arthur. "Les Romans de Chevalerie en Prose." *Revue du Seizième Siècle* 6 (1919): 45–63.

Tory, Geofroy. *Champ Fleury.* Paris, 1529; facsimile rpt., N.Y.: Johnson Reprint Corp., 1970.

Toynbee, Paget. "Dante and the Lancelot Romance." *Dante Studies and Researches.* London: Methuen, 1902. 1–37.

Vinaver, Eugène. *The Rise of Romance.* Oxford: Clarendon, 1971.

Le Voyage de Charlemagne à Jerusalem et à Constantinople. Ed. P. Aebischer. Textes littéraires français. Genève: Droz, 1965.

The Vulgate Version of the Arthurian Romances. Ed. H. Oskar Sommer. Vols. 3–5: *Le Livre de Lancelot del Lac.* Washington, D.C.: Carnegie Institution of Washington, 1910–12.

White, Sarah Melhado. "Lancelot on the Gameboard: The Design of Chrétien's *Charrette.*" *French Forum* 2 (1977): 99–109.

Zumthor, Paul. *Essai de Poétique Médiévale.* Paris: Editions du Seuil, 1972.

THE BOAT OF ROMANCE
AND RENAISSANCE EPIC

David Quint

Two cases of intertextual allusion in Renaissance epic lead me to raise again the hoary subject of epic and romance. The first case involves cantos 14–16 of Tasso's *Gerusalemme liberata* and a discourse on Fortune that depends on several episodes in Boiardo's *Orlando innamorato.* The second concerns Milton's use of Camoes's *Os lusíadas* in book 2 of *Paradise Lost.*[1] Tasso's allusions to Boiardo involve the assimilation and transformation of romance adventure into a "higher" epic context which celebrates the Renaissance voyages of exploration. An opposite procedure, I shall argue, takes place in *Paradise Lost,* where Milton demotes from the ranks of epic the exploits of discovery celebrated by Camoes and recasts them into the pattern of adventure. The question of whether the romance adventure can be assimilated into epic terms becomes identical to the question of whether the voyage of discovery can be treated as an epic subject matter. Renaissance interpretations of the discoveries saw them alternatively as heroic acts of martial conquest or as commercial trading ventures, corresponding, respectively, to "aristocratic" and "bourgeois" points of view. Epic traditionally aligns itself with aristocratic values; when, in the context of the voyages of discovery, it casts romance as its alternative "other," it lends a mercantile cast to the romantic adventure. The generic split between epic and romance may in this instance yield an ideology of class distinction.

I

In cantos 7 and 8 of the *Rinaldo*,[2] the chivalric romance which Tasso composed at the age of eighteen, Rinaldo of Montalbano and his faithful sidekick Florindo take a trip in an enchanted boat that is called the "barca aventurosa" (7.73). Its purpose is to carry knights-errant to whatever adventure may be currently available to give them an opportunity to demonstrate their prowess. The enchanted boat, which travels without human guidance carrying the hero from episode to episode, is a common topos of chivalric romance. It is a close relative of that eternally wandering Odyssean ship which is for Borges and Northrop Frye the virtual emblem of romance itself.[3] More specifically, such ships embody the adventure principle that is a ubiquitous, perhaps essential feature of romance narrative: counterbalancing an equally constitutive quest principle, it accounts for all the digressions and subplots which delay the quest's conclusion and which come to acquire an attraction and validity of their own. Georg Simmel describes the adventure as an "island of life which determines its beginning and end according to its own formative power,"[4] and the romance boat often travels to a series of islands and discrete episodes. This series may be random. In epic narrative, which moves toward a predetermined end, the magic ship signals a digression from a central plot line, but the boat of romance, in its purest form, has no other destination than the adventure at hand. It cannot be said to be off course. New adventures crop up all the time, and the boat's travels describe a romance narrative that is open-ended and potentially endless.[5]

When the boat is encountered again in Tasso's writings, at the opening of canto 15 of the *Gerusalemme liberata,* it has become the boat of Fortune. Its pilot is an allegorical figure, whose description (15.4–5) recalls the character of the Fata Morgana in Boiardo's *Orlando innamorato* (2.8.43). Boiardo's version of Morgan le Fay personifies Fortuna (2.9.25) or Ventura (2.9.19). The etymological link suggests why the "barca aventurosa" should now belong to the province of Ventura-Fortuna; the chance of the moment bestows adventures, and the adventurer takes chancy risks. The iconography of Fortune and her boat is a Renaissance commonplace, part of a humanist conflation of the concepts of Fortune and Occasion (*kairos*) which redefines the experience of time; it transforms the contingent moment into an opportunity for human action and exploitation.[6] For Boiardo, the seizure of occasion—the forelock of Fortune which

dangles before Morgana's brow—is the ideological emblem of romance adventure itself. In Orlando's successful pursuit and mastery
of Morgana in the second book of the *Innamorato* (2.8–9, 13) he
allegorizes the triumph of heroic virtue over whatever adventures
Fortune or the romance narrative may present, adventures which are
Ventura's infinitely variable forms.[7] Similarly, the iconography of
Fortune's boat assimilates her with the ever-changing winds and
tides—contingent forces which man cannot control but which,
through foresight and exertion—the Renaissance virtues of prudence
and fortitude—he can learn to time properly and turn to his advantage.

But if Tasso assimilates the boat of romance adventure with Boiardo's figure of Fortune, the animating principle of such adventure,
he simultaneously transforms both Fortune and her boat into epic,
rather than romance, entities. Like Dante (*Inferno* 7.61–96), Tasso
represents Fortune as the minister of Providence (*Liberata* 9.57);
her apparently random actions in fact carry out a larger divine
plan for human history. Here she tames the seas in order to convey
the knights Carlo and Ubaldo on their divinely sanctioned mission
to rescue their comrade Rinaldo (no relation to the Rinaldo of the
Rinaldo) from the island of Armida, to bring him back to the First
Crusade where he is destined to lead the victorious final assault on
Jerusalem. Fortune's boat no longer sails into digressive romance adventures but has become an essential part of the epic machinery that
drives forward to the providential goal and narrative endpoint of
Tasso's poem.

Moreover, as her craft passes through the Gates of Hercules, Fortune prophesies the voyage of a future Atlantic sailor:

> Tu spiegherai, Colombo, a un novo polo
> lontane sì le fortunate antenne,
> ch'a pena seguirà con gli occhi il volo
> la fama c'ha mille occhi e mille penne.
> Canti ella Alcide e Bacco, e di te solo
> basti a i posteri tuoi ch'alquanto accenne:
> ché quel poco darà lunga memoria
> di poema dignissima e d'istoria. (15.32)

[You, Columbus, will extend your fortunate sails so far in the direction of a new world that Fame will scarcely be able to follow you
and keep you in sight, Fame with her thousand eyes and thousand
wings. Let her sing of Hercules and Bacchus, and let it suffice that

she give only a little mention of you to your posterity: that little will afford a long record of events worthy of poetry and history.]

The final epic transformation of Fortune's boat is into the ship of Columbus with its "fortunate antenne." The journey of Carlo and Ubaldo outside the Mediterranean world becomes the prototype for the Renaissance voyages of exploration and colonial expansion, voyages that could similarly transvalue romance adventure into the stuff of epic. The Age of Discovery provided real-life adventures that not only were the equal of fabled ones—Portuguese conquistadors in India compared their own exploits favorably with those of Amadís[8]—but also were seen to be chapters in historical plans that would bring Christianity to the newly discovered world and fulfill the destinies of various European nation-states. The enterprise of discovery and conquest afforded sixteenth-century epic poetry with one of its two great contemporary subjects, the other being the struggle between Christian Europe and the Ottoman Empire, the subject reflected in Tasso's fiction of the First Crusade. By Tasso's own literary theory, the subject that merits both poetic and historical treatments is by nature an epic one, and in the *Liberata* he elevates Columbus into an epic hero of undying fame. Columbus's voyage is placed within a providential scheme, the first step in evangelizing the peoples of the New World (15.29). Tasso thus transforms the boat of Fortune twice over into an epic ship: just as it receives a fixed course and destination in Tasso's plot, the boat prefigures future voyages of discovery that carry out God's plot for history. No longer the emblem of the fortuitous at all, the boat escapes the aimless pattern of romance wandering, of adventure for its own sake.

Such wandering into romance adventure is also depicted by the *Liberata*. While Carlo and Ubaldo travel to Armida's island on Fortune's boat, Rinaldo falls into Armida's clutches one canto earlier by entering a little skiff which he finds moored by the bank of the Orontes (14.57f.). This boat, which promises to take him to the greatest "meraviglie" the world has to offer—the marvels which sixteenth-century theorists and readers alike considered to be the chief pleasure of romances,[9] is a second version of the "barca aventurosa" of the *Rinaldo*. The Rinaldo of the *Liberata* has left the Crusader army to take up knight-errantry. He proposes a voyage of discovery of his own, a journey to the source of the Nile (5.52), and he enters the world of romance by sailing to the little enchanted island in the Orontes, an island of adventure. Presiding over this romance world is Armida, who takes the place of Boiardo's Fortuna; indeed, we are to see her as a version of that Fortune figure. The Orontes island where Armida first captures Rinaldo foreshadows her garden paradise in the Fortunate Islands (14.70, 15.37) or, as the Canaries are also known, the Happy Islands (15.35). The labyrinthine structure of Armida's palace (16.1.8) and the bas-reliefs on its doors (16.2–7) recall the reliefs of the labyrinth of Crete on the gates of the Fata Morgana's realm in *Orlando innamorato* (2.8.15–17), and the celebrated tableau of Armida gazing at her mirror (16.20) similarly echoes Boiardo's description of Morgana embracing her favorite Ziliante: "Mirando come un specchio nel bel viso" (2.13.22). These allusions cast the rescue of Rinaldo from Armida's palace as a rewriting of Orlando's rescue of Ziliante from an overly favorable Fortune.

Tasso's fiction thus contains and juxtaposes two versions of the boat of adventure, two versions of Boiardo's figure of Fortune—both the allegorical Fortune who pilots their ship and the fallacious maidens on Armida's island who address Carlo and Ubaldo as "fortunati" (15.6.62)—to distinguish the epic voyage from its romance double. Romance adventure draws Rinaldo away from his true historical mission into a world of Fortune. In such a world, where time is broken down into a series of contingent, unrelated moments, isolated from one another and from any larger historical or narrative plan, Boiardo's humanist imperative to exploit occasion shades into the *carpe diem* theme contained in the song of the rose recited by Armida's parrot (16.14–15), and the adventure becomes an end in itself. Tasso insists, however, that to live in a world of Fortune is to become her prisoner, and he portrays Rinaldo not as Boiardo's Orlando, the master of Morgana, but rather as Ziliante, her beloved captive. Escape from the romance prison—from an existence which is merely episodic—is offered by epic, which posits a goal that transcends the adventure of the moment and organizes what may seem otherwise random events into a coherent narrative. This epic teleology characteristically invokes a "higher" vertical dimension of synchronic meaning that proposes to explain the horizontal world of diachronic action in which the romance adventure is normally confined. Tasso's boat of Fortune is an emblem of the assimilation of romance into such epic structures of meaning. The boat and the actions to which it carries its passengers are no longer subject to Fortune the personification of chance and contingency but rather to Fortune the servant of Providence. In the epic world, nothing is left to chance.

II

The voyage to the Canaries in the *Gerusalemme liberata* is one of the many epic models to which Milton alludes in Satan's journey to

earth through Chaos in book 2 of *Paradise Lost,* a journey that is cast
as a sea voyage. Beelzebub describes earth as "the happy isle" (2.410)
and later Satan passes through stars that seem to be "happy isles, /
Like those Hesperian gardents famed of old, / Fortunate fields, and
groves and flowery vales, / Thrice happy isles" (3.567–571). But
while Milton's fiction recalls Tasso's and other earlier epic voyages—
those of Odysseus, Jason, Aeneas, and Spenser's Guyon—his principal subtext is the journey of Vasco da Gama around the Cape of
Good Hope to India in the *Os lusíadas* of Luis de Camões. Scholars
have noted how the initial comparison of the flying Satan to a fleet
returning from "Bengala, or the isles / of Ternate and Tidore"
(2.638–639) and heading for the Cape is balanced in book 4 (4.159–
65) by the simile which likens the archfiend outside Eden to "them
who sail / Beyond the Cape of Hope, and now are past / Mozambic."
These similes at either end of Satan's trip invoke the Indian Ocean
world of Camões's epic.[10] I should like to point out a further series
of recollections and direct echoes of the *Lusíadas*—more specifically
of Sir Richard Fanshawe's English translation of the poem published
in 1655—which constitute a whole pattern of Miltonic allusion.
Camões describes the palace of Neptune on the ocean floor; on its
doors are sculpted bas-reliefs (6.10–12) which depict first Chaos and
subsequently the four elements, evoking a traditional identification
between the ocean and the sources of material creation. Milton's
Chaos is described as a "dark / Illimitable ocean" (2.890–91), where
prime matter has not yet disposed itself into elemental form, "neither
sea, nor shore, nor air, nor fire" (2.912). On its way to India, da
Gama's fleet is caught in a terrible storm:

> The *thund'ring's* such, that there are now no hopes
>   But that HEAV'N's *Axles* will be streight unbuilt:
>   The ELEMENTS at one another tilt. (6.84)[11]

Milton's Chaos, a realm of incessant storms, is described in strikingly
similar terms. Its noise peals no less in Satan's ear

>   than if this frame
> Of heaven were falling, and these elements
> In mutiny had from her axle torn
> The steadfast earth. (2.924–27)

Later compared to a "weather-beaten vessel" (2.1043), Satan makes
his way through the gusts of Chaos to the court of Chaos himself.
When he asks this anarch for directions to get to earth, the action

parodies da Gama's visit to the King of Melinde from whom he seeks a pilot to guide him to India. His address to Chaos—

> I come no spy
> With purpose to explore or to disturb
> The secrets of your realm (2.970–72)

—has precedents in the *Odyssey* (2.71–74) and *Aeneid* (1.527–29), but these were in turn imitated by Camões in da Gama's speech to the Moslem king. Milton's choice of the word "spy," which has no counterpart in the classical epics, indicates that his model was indeed Fanshawe's translation:

> *We* are not Men, who spying a weak *Town*
> Or careless, as we pass along the shore,
> Murther the *Folks,* and burn the *Houses* down. (2.80)

Finally, the alliance which Satan forges with Chaos and Night, offering to turn over all the profits of his mission to earth to his partners—"Yours be the advantage all, mine the revenge" (987)—recalls and echoes another moment in Camões's poem, the similar proposition which da Gama offers the Zamorin of Calicut on behalf of his Portuguese King: *"His* shall be the *glory, thine* the *Gain* be found" (7.62).[12]

Like the voyage of Columbus, da Gama's expedition inaugurated the Age of Discovery. Tasso's encomium to Columbus celebrated the voyages of discovery as providential events; Milton's fiction, by recasting the events of the *Lusíadas* into Satan's journey, suggests that the voyages are the work of the devil. As da Gama opened up a route to the Indies for the trade and imperialism of Europe—particularly Catholic Europe—so Satan blazes a trail for Sin and Death to build their bridge by "art / Pontifical" from Hell to Earth (10.312–13). Adam and Eve, who after their fall don fig leaves which liken them both to the Indians of Malabar and to the native Americans whom "of late / Columbus found" (9.1099–118), assume the roles of innocent natives victimized by their European conquerors.

It is not surprising that the Puritan poet Milton should reject the providential interpretations of the exploits of Renaissance discovery advanced by Catholic epic poets such as Camões and Tasso. His criticism, moreover, runs along generic lines. For whereas Tasso had seen the voyages of discovery as events which raised the adventures of romance to the level of epic, Milton's fiction suggests a reverse process. When Satan enters Chaos where "high arbiter / Chance governs all" (2.909–10), he finds himself at the mercy of the warring elements.

> At last his sail-broad vans
> He spreads for flight, and in the surging smoke
> Uplifted spurns the ground, thence many a league
> As in a cloudy chair ascending rides
> Audacious, but that seat soon failing, meets
> A vast vacuity; all unawares
> Fluttering his pennons vain plumb down he drops
> Ten thousand fathom deep, and to this hour
> Down had been falling, had not by ill chance
> The strong rebuff of some tumultuous cloud
> Instinct with fire and nitre hurried him
> As many miles aloft: (2.927–38)

This passage is a tour de force both of science fiction space fantasy and of slapstick comedy. Satan's wings are like a ship's sails waiting to be filled by favoring winds. The phrase "Uplifted spurns the ground" wittily indicates that while Satan's trip may seem to be a haughty act of will, he is not in fact traveling under his own power but is rather swept off the ground by an updraft from Chaos. When these winds fail, moreover, the becalmed Satan plummets, flapping his useless wings, and still would be falling through the infinite reaches of space to this day if a chance explosion had not sent him hurtling back up into the air again. This cartoonlike reduction of the archfiend to a plaything of Chaos is highly comic, but it also presents a startling idea: that Satan would never have accomplished his journey to earth in order to seduce Adam and Eve but for a piece of very bad luck. Milton demonstrates that the evil will gives itself up to the play of chance, that its activities are ultimately random and fortuitous: there is only one coherent plan of action in the universe and it belongs to God.[18] Chaos is a realm of Fortune, hence a world of adventure, and Satan is transformed from epic voyager to a romance adventurer who takes advantage of, but is also depedent on, the occasions which chance brings his way; it is not surprising to hear the same Satan in *Paradise Regained* tempting Christ to seize "occasion's forelock" (3.173). It is as an "adventurer" that Satan returns from earth to Hell in book 10 (10.440, 10.468), and the devils who remained behind in book 2 on their own mission of reconnaissance through Hell, a "bold adventure to discover wide / That dismal world" (2.571–72), are similarly "adventurous" (2.615) explorers whose endeavors find "no rest" or final destination. The deflation of the epic deed into an adventure which has no more than a momentary significance not only undercuts the heroic posturings of Milton's devils but also represents his judgment on the enterprise of discovery as a literary subject matter. Other Renaissance poets may assert that the voyages of discovery serve higher ends and merit inclusion among the transcendent fictions of epic. For Milton those voyages accomplish merely temporal (hence Satanic) ends and accordingly belong exclusively to the world of time and chance. The flying Satan is figuratively a ship sailing through the seas of Fortune, a boat of romance.

III

There is a further argument latent in this same opposition between the epic voyage and romance adventure within the context of the Age of Discovery, an argument which depends on the allegiance of epic fictions to the class ideology of a martial aristocracy. The terms of this ideology are vividly spelled out in a passage of the *Lusíadas* which Milton chose to parody—the trading agreement which da Gama offers to the Zamorin of Calicut. India will receive the profits of their transaction; the King of Portugal will reap the glory: "De ti proveito, e dele glória ingente" (7.62) (*"His* shall be the *glory, thine* the *Gain* be found"). Camões's hero claims that Portugal's aim in opening up new trade routes, the general goal of all the voyages of discovery, is the acquisition not of the wealth which traders normally seek but of fame. The claim is on the face of it implausible. Yet it is central to the ethos of the *Lusíadas* and reflects a larger split in sixteenth- and seventeenth-century attitudes toward the enterprise of discovery.

Propaganda for the discoveries ran up against a time-honored aristocratic disdain for mercantile activities. This prejudice was institutionalized by sixteenth-century statutes in Spain and France which forbade noblemen from practicing trade.[14] The situation was somewhat different in Portugal. Conservative noblemen might complain that expansion in the Indies was causing their fellows to neglect their landed estates and turn merchant.[15] But the Portuguese nobility generally followed the lead of their king, investing and taking an active part in the lucrative Eastern ventures. The royal monopoly on the Indian trade, in fact, made commerce appear to be a patriotic duty. The Portuguese empire, moreover, was based on the tribute of conquest as well as on trade; it was gained and maintained through a series of wars with Moslem trading rivals.[16] If profit was a matter in which a gentleman was not supposed to take any interest, the Portuguese aristocracy could view its participation in the imperial enterprise primarily in terms of its traditional role as a military caste, in terms of personal honor, patriotism, and religious zeal.

These are the terms of the *Lusíadas,* and indeed they are the traditional terms of epic, a genre historically linked to aristocratic values. The overriding ethical imperative of Camões's poem is the acquisition of martial fame, both for oneself and for one's country. Missionary and crusading motives are also ascribed to da Gama's expedition; though important, they are decidedly secondary to the pursuit of fame. Camões's Portuguese hero disdains money and the gifts of Fortune (6.98). Greed and the desire for wealth are attributed instead to the Indian natives: the Zamorin's chief official is eventually won over by a bribe, occasioning the narrator's execration upon gold (8.96–99) at the very moment when da Gama's men gain access to the Indian markets—and to Portugal's European neighbors (7.11). Exchanging gain for glory, Camões provides a version of the Portuguese ventures in the East that plays down their commercial character, a version that was both consonant with epic norms of behavior and congenial to the self-image of a noble reader.

In England the gentry similarly persuaded themselves to invest in New World ventures by appealing to the idea of a glorious national destiny. They contrasted their nobler motives with those of their merchant partners, concerned primarily with the return on their investments.[17] Here, too, epic themes could come into play. Writing in 1577, Abraham Fleming laments the lack of a Homer to celebrate the return of Martin Frobisher, "our Ulysses," whose fame deserves to live forever:

> A right Heroicall heart of Britanne blood,
> Ulysses match in skill and Martiall might:
> For Princes fame, and countries speciall good,
> Through brackish seas (where Neptune reignes by right)
> Hath safely saild, in perils great despight:
> The Golden fleece (like Iason) hath he got,
> And rich returned, saunce losse or lucklesse lot.[18]

As a propagandist for empire, Fleming does not wish to dispense with the incentive of riches altogether, but they are an added incentive, mentioned after the primary motives of personal glory and patriotism. The English adventurer could think of himself less as a businessman, more as a soldier and epic hero. The notorious early experience of the Jamestown settlement, where idle gentlemen were found bowling in the streets while the colony faced starvation, is an example of how counterproductive such aristocratic attitudes could be when the adventurer arrived in the New World.[19]

The Renaissance voyage of discovery could be described as an epic voyage to distinguish it as an aristocratic rather than a mercantile pursuit. But voyages of seafaring epics might themselves need to be differentiated from commercial doubles or false twins. In the *Odyssey* the travels of Odysseus are carefully distinguished from less-heroic maritime activities. The prominence of Phoenician traders—"gnawers of other men's goods"—in the lying stories which Odysseus recounts about himself to Athena (13.255–87) and Eumaios (14.192–359), as well as in Eumaios's narration of his own life story (15.390–483), suggests a parallel between these masters of the sea and the poem's wandering hero. To prevent the reader from drawing such a parallel, Homer inserts a scene in book 8 where Odysseus declines to compete in the Phaiakians' athletic games and is consequently insulted by a young nobleman, Euryalos:

> "No, stranger, for I do not see that you are like one versed in contests, such as are now practiced much among people, but rather to one who plies his ways in his many-locked vessel, master over mariners who also are men of business, a man who, careful of his cargo and grasping for profits, goes carefully on his way. You do not resemble an athlete." (8.159–64)[20]

Odysseus promptly repudiates this slur by picking up the heaviest discus and throwing it farther than any of the Phaiakians' casts.[21] The episode is strategically placed, however, for it precedes Alkinoös's decision to ask all the men of Phaiakia to assemble gifts for Odysseus; in fact, the same Euryalos presents the hero with a special gift to make amends for his ill-measured words (8.396–411). This is the wealth with which Odysseus returns to Ithaca, more wealth, Poseidon will complain (13.134–38), than Odysseus could have attained had he brought back his share of the plunder of Troy—the normal means for an epic hero to acquire property. Homer takes pains to demonstrate that the Phaiakians' gifts are a tribute to Odysseus's heroism—to the fact that he is not a base merchant as Euryalos had charged—in order to distinguish his wealth from the profits of a trading expedition. Nonetheless, ancient critics noted the pecuniary motives of the heroes of the *Odyssey*. The second-century author Aelian wrote that Odysseus and Menelaus "traveiled from region to region, after the custome of the Marchantes of Phenicia, for they did hourde and heape up money lyke mountaines, the desire whereof spurred them forward, and imboldened them to attempt dangerous journeys by lande, and perilous voyages by sea."[22]

Similarly, Jason's quest for the golden fleece, the subject of the *Argonautica* of Apollonius Rhodius, was regarded in antiquity as a commercial venture: Juvenal (6.53) refers to this second voyager of classical epic as "mercantor Iason." In Fleming's verses, the golden fleece is equated with the riches brought back by Frobisher's expedition, and Spenser's *Faerie Queene* would later allegorize the Libyan Syrtes upon which the Argo is caught in the fourth book of the *Argonautica* (1228f.) as the "quicksand of Unthriftyhed," upon which merchants' ships are seen to founder (2.12.18–19).

When the actions of the *Odyssey* and the *Argonautica* are transferred to the sea, the domain of traders and sailors, epic fiction collides with social reality, and uncertainties arise about their heroes' motives and behavior. These uncertainties correspond to generic uncertainties about the poems themselves. If they claim relationship to the martial world of epic—Odysseus returns from the world of the *Iliad* and greets the hero of that poem in the underworld, Jason is the shipmate of the greatest of heroes, Hercules—the episodic wanderings of their heroes into a world of the marvelous indicates a turn toward romance. The *Odyssey* was regarded by Renaissance critics as the first *romanzo*—as it still seems to be regarded by Frye.[23] There is, I wish to argue, a link between the disposition to view the voyages of Odysseus and Jason as trading ventures and the resemblance of these voyages to romance adventures. This link is clearly visible in the most extended Renaissance rewriting of the Jason story in economic terms. We are brought back to the fiction of the *Orlando innamorato*.

In the first book of Boiardo's poem, Orlando accepts and overcomes the trials proposed to him by the Fata di Isola del Lago. These are the same obstacles which Jason faced at Colchis: the enchanted bulls, the dragon, and the armed men springing up from the dragon's teeth.[24] In canto 25, Orlando is rewarded with what he is told is the greatest "ventura" (4) for which a knight can hope: a little dog with which he can hunt down a marvelous stag with golden horns. The stag is Boiardo's version of the golden fleece, for it molts its horns six times a day and is guaranteed to make its capturer infinitely rich. Orlando, however, flatly refuses to have anything to do with this adventure. He does not regret having undergone the trials, for danger and toil are the source of chivalric honor (13). But the search for wealth, he declares, is an unending one, because the searcher is never satisfied.

Che qualunque n'ha più, più ne desia:
Adunque senza capo è questa via.

Senza capo è la strata ed infinita
De onore e di diletto al tutto priva. (1.25.14–15)

[For he who has more, desires more: therefore this road is without end. It is an endless and infinite road, totally lacking in honor and pleasure.]

Because, Orlando maintains, one can never have enough money, its pursuit will be as endless as it is inglorious. Without a final goal, such activity will bear a disturbing likeness to the open-ended structure of Boiardo's own romance narrative, to the apparently endless, loosely connected string of adventures upon which Orlando will himself embark. The likeness is reinforced by the episode's play on the word "ventura." Orlando voices his desire, "Dio me doni alta ventura" (1.25.2) ("God grant me a high adventure"), the characteristic desire of the knight-errant for some marvelous adventure. The phrase is very similar to formulas which recur, often as salutations, in the letters of a sixteenth-century Venetian merchant: "che'l Signor Dio li doni venttura . . . lo eterno Dio ve dono quelo dexideratte e a noi tan bien venttura . . . si che staremo alla vedetta et aspettar venttura che Idio la mandi . . . che'l nostro Signor Dio ne manda venttura"[25] ("The Lord God should grant him luck . . . the eternal God grant you what you desire and such good luck to us . . . so we are on the lookout and await opportunity, which God send us . . . our Lord God send us good luck"). The merchant prays for good fortune and the specific chance to make a fortune: such an opportunity is offered to Orlando in place of the adventure which he craves. But the knight rejects the offer of fabulous wealth. Like Homer, Boiardo finds it necessary to disassociate his hero from the economic activity which so closely resembles the hero's adventures in the realm of romance.

The enchanted stag, moreover, returns us to Boiardo's figure of Fortune, for the stag, first described at 1.17.57–58, is the property of the Fata Morgana, none other than Ventura herself. Like her stag, Morgana is also a kind of golden fleece, for her forelock, the forelock of occasion, is golden (2.8.58). The seizure of Fortune by her forelock, representing the humanist idea of man exploiting time to his advantage, can easily bear an economic interpretation: for the merchant, time is money. In one sense, the *Innamorato* may be said to disclose the social origins of its romance ideology, for the idea that fortune can be mastered through fortitude and prudence was developed by Florentine humanists who were either merchants themselves or closely associated with mercantile society, and their terms were drawn from a traditional mercantile vocabulary.[26] But the hero of the aristocratic poet Boiardo wants nothing to do with this aspect of Fortune, and Orlando's further encounters with Morgana contain two further rejections of wealth: first when he rebukes his cousin Rinaldo for trying to carry off some of the golden furnishings of Morgana's subterranean realm (2.9.33), later when he refuses Morgana's offer of riches and treasure, a bribe to prevent him from rescuing Ziliante from her clutches (2.13.23–24). Ziliante is the son of King Manodante, who has amassed more than half the wealth of the world (1.21.49, 2.11.46), and Boiardo's fiction allegorizes the dangers of being Fortune's favorite, of being the prisoner of one's own wealth and good fortune.[27] The tenor of all these episodes in the *Innamorato* is the same: the knight should grasp all opportunities to make a trial of his strength and virtue in the adventures which Fortune sends his way without turning into a grasping Fortune hunter. He should be a Jason who turns down the golden fleece.

IV

Boiardo's romance concedes, if only to forswear, a resemblance between its adventures and money-making ventures. This resemblance can enter into the generic distinction which epic draws between its closed form and the open-ended romance narrative. The higher, transcendent goals toward which epic narrative is directed correspond to the ethical goals by which a martial aristocracy claims to distinguish itself from social inferiors who—in the eyes of the aristocrat—care only for their day-to-day temporal needs and the accumulation of wealth. To the extent that the romance adventure remains autonomous from these goals—that it remains merely the adventure presently at hand, dealt out by an everchanging Fortune—it remains, from the perspective of epic, immersed in contingent time and inevitably directed toward temporal goods. The hierarchy of genres may thus reflect an ideology of social hierarchy.[28] When, moreover, Renaissance epic describes the recent voyages of discovery, this dichotomy between epic and romance finds a specific ideological application. It reflects the divergent interpretations of the voyages which ran along class lines. The enterprise of discovery could alternately be understood as a heroic endeavor in the epic, aristocratic mold or as a business expedition undertaken by adventurous mer-

chants in search of their fortunes. It is in this light that we may return to the fictions of Tasso and Milton.

Tasso's encomium of Columbus, whose ship of discovery is a future epic extension of the providential boat of Fortune of canto 15, is
juxtaposed with a repudiation of the romance Fortune figure Armida, who replays the role of Boiardo's Morgana, the "Fata del
Tesoro" (2.12.24) and dispenser of all worldly wealth. Her captive
Rinaldo takes the place of the rich heir Ziliante in the *Innamorato*.
In the immediate fiction of the *Liberata,* Armida tempts Rinaldo
with concupiscence, but in the play of allusion to Boiardo's poem
which produces two opposing figures and concepts of Fortune, the
temptations of her realm are all of Fortune's temporal gifts. The
celebration of Columbus juxtaposed with the rejection of this
worldly Fortune—which is also a generic rejection of the romance
adventure—and the implication that Columbus's voyage represents
an alternative to that Fortune fit into an ideological scheme that elevates the voyages of discovery into epic events by dissociating them
from economic pursuits. The symbolic geography which places Armida's garden in the Canaries, where Columbus provisioned before
sailing west in 1492, makes of Rinaldo a kind of Columbus *manqueé,*
one who got sidetracked along the way. The Canaries were a flourishing trading center by the sixteenth century, and the historical
Columbus had modeled his title and prerogatives as the Admiral of
the Ocean Sea on those of the Admiral of Castile, who controlled
shipping to the Canaries and was entitled to a one-third rake-off on
the profits.[29] There were indeed fortunes to be made on the Fortunate Isles.

In the figure of Ubaldo, the knight who journeys on the boat of
Fortune to rescue Rinaldo, there is a further hint that Tasso's rejection of romance is also a rejection of a mercantile interpretation of
the voyages of discovery. For Ubaldo is a former romance adventurer, chosen for this epic mission because of his wide travel experience in his youth, when he wandered through various countries and
regions of the earth. He is like a man "che virtute e senno *merchi*"
(14.28), one who trades in virtues and wisdom. His journeying makes
him an Odyssean figure,[30] particularly reminiscent of Dante's Ulysses, who told his men to follow "virtute e canoscenza" (*Inferno*
26.120); it is Ubaldo's curiosity about Atlantic navigation (15.24)
which prompts Fortune to discuss the earlier Dantesque Ulysses
(25), whose aimless wandering ended in shipwreck, before she goes
on to prophesy the future, providential voyage of Columbus. There
is a sense, then, in which Ubaldo, no less than the boat of Fortune

itself, is a piece of romance machinery which Tasso transforms and rehabilitates by placing it in an epic context and to which, in the figure of Ulysses, he opposes a demonic romance double.

Like Homer's Odysseus, moreover, Ubaldo in his earlier wanderings already possessed a commercial double, for trading in wisdom can resemble trade itself. Conversely, the Renaissance merchant could be praised for the wide experience of the world he acquired through his business ventures. In his *Suma de Tratos* of 1569, the Spaniard Tomás de Mercado asserts of merchants that

> conversing with many peoples, dwelling in different realms, trading with various nations, experiencing different customs, considering the differing governments and political institutions of peoples, they make themselves universal men, practiced and apt for whatever business ventures may offer themselves to them. They acquire and build up a great store of prudence and experience by which to guide and govern themselves, in particular circumstances as well as general ones. They are useful to the state because of their knowledge of the various things which they have seen and heard in their travels.[31]

The ideal merchant has become a universal Renaissance man and also an Odyssean man of many turns, and he is described in terms remarkably similar to those with which Tasso decribes Ubaldo. Ubaldo's wealth of experience is the kind sought by romance heroes such as Boiardo's Orlando, but, as was the case in the *Innamorato,* such wealth may be difficult to separate from the material, monetary wealth with which it seems to come hand in hand. Ubaldo's voyage to Armida's island is shown, however, to be a rejection of his former adventuring: romance adventure as an end in itself is figured in the fate of the drowned Ulysses, while the formerly wandering Ubaldo is placed on the formerly wandering boat of Fortune, and both are set upon a straight epic course—what will be the future course of Renaissance exploration. Tasso's depiction of the discoveries as epic events seems to require first the exorcism of a romance spirit of adventure, which, it is estimated, may be identical to the spirit of trade.

The effort to distinguish heroic from money-making pursuits may find a specific context in the ideology of Renaissance discovery, but it also conforms, as we have seen in the *Odyssey,* to a normative epic ethos. The verb "mercare," which describes Ubaldo's former activities, appears one more time in the *Liberata.* It is, in fact, the very last word spoken by a character in the poem. Just before Goffredo reaches the Holy Sepulchre he turns down the offer of a large ransom from the captured Altamoro, King of Samarkand. He spares Altamoro's life, but declares:

de la vita altrui prezzo non cerco:
guerreggio in Asia, e non vi cambio o merco. (20.142)

[I do not seek a price for another's life: I wage war in Asia, and do not change money or trade there.]

The passage recalls episodes in the *Iliad* (21.34–113) and the *Aeneid* (10.521–34) where Achilles and Aeneas refuse to spare suppliants who beg to ransom their lives; part of its purpose is to end the *Liberata* with an act of clemency amid the general massacre (143) of the Saracen army. But it also closes Tasso's epic with an assertion of a heroism untainted by baser desires for gain, with Goffredo's refusal to turn merchant.[32] The taking of ransoms and selling of prisoners were common features of sixteenth-century warfare, both between different European nations and between Europeans and the Ottoman Turks. The privateering Knight of Malta and the knights of Saint Stephen, the modern-day crusaders of Tasso's own time, combined warfare with business and were not likely to pass up offers of ransom from their Muslim captives in the manner of Goffredo.[33] Tasso may thus find both heroic arenas of his century—the exploits of discovery *and* the crusade against Islam—threatened by mercenary behavior inadmissible within the ethical code of epic. He closes his poem by reasserting epic's traditional class prejudice, its exclusion of money and trade from the heroic world.

Milton, in keeping with his general criticism of the earlier epic tradition, exposes as false the distinction which that tradition draws between martial heroism and mercantile activity. He accompanies his reduction of Satan from epic voyager to chance adventurer by depicting Satan as a commercial traveler:

As when far off at sea, a fleet descried
Hangs in the clouds, by equinoctial winds
Close sailing from Bengala, or the isles
of Ternate and Tidore, whence merchants bring
Their spicy drugs: they on the trading flood
Through the wide Ethiopian to the Cape
Ply stemming nightly toward the pole. So seemed
Far off the flying fiend: (2.636–43)

This simile is the first to develop the comparison between Satan's journey and a sea voyage. The voyage in question is a trading venture, engaged in bringing back the Eastern spices that were the initial goal of Renaissance discovery. The passage retrospectively lends a mercantile note to Beelzebub's earlier talk of "enterprise" (345)

and "some advantageous act" (363), and it colors the exchange between Satan and Chaos about "recompense" (981), "advantage"
(987), and "gain" (1009). If Satan and the devils are "adventurers,"
they are also Merchant Adventurers.[34] The conversation between
Satan and Chaos, I have already noted, is an ironic rewriting of the
moment in the *Lusíadas* where da Gama claims to seek a trading
agreement with Calicut for the sake of Portugal's glory rather than
her profit. Milton's fiction not only casts doubt upon da Gama's protestations of heroic disinterestedness, but in the character of Satan
the trader it reflects upon other heroes of maritime epic like Odysseus and Jason, long suspected of being merchants in disguise.

By the middle of the seventeenth century, the Portuguese monopoly on the Indian Ocean trade had long been broken by the Dutch
and British. These new commercial rivals had waged two wars by
the time *Paradise Lost* was first published in 1667, and a third was
fought before the second edition of the poem appeared in 1674.[35]
The focus of Milton's criticism constantly shifts between a revision
of the earlier epic tradition and an indictment of European expansion and colonialism that includes his own countrymen and contemporaries. Moreover, Milton may be aware of the implications for epic
poetry of the emergence of a merchant class whose interests had begun to shape the imperial destinies of the nation. The merchant not
only contested with the nobleman for power but also laid claim to
the nobleman's very nobility. In 1641, Lewis Roberts, merchant and
Captain of the City of London, argued in *The Treasure of Traffike*
that trade ennobled its practitioners:

> And if true Nobilitie should have taken its foundation, (as the Iudi-
> cious and Learned have observed heretofore) from the courage of men,
> and from their Valour, there is no vocation wherein there is so many
> usefull and principall parts of man required, as in these two, for they
> are not only to adventure and hazard theire owne persons, but also
> their estates, goods, and what ever they have, amongst men of all na-
> tions, and Customes, Lawes, and Religions, wheresoever they are in-
> habited.[36]

Roberts comments further in another passage:

> It is not our conquests, but our Commerce; it is not our swords, but
> our sayls, that first spred the English name in *Barbary,* and thence
> came into *Turkey, Armenia, Moscovia, Arabia, Persia, India, China,*
> and indeed over and about the world; it is the traffike of their Mer-
> chants, and the boundlesse desires of that nation to eternize the En-
> glish honour and name, that hath enduced them to saile, and seeke

into all the corners of the earth. What part is there unsearched, what place undiscovered, or what place lyes unattempted by their endeavors, and couragious undertakings?[37]

Roberts speaks proudly for a merchant class that asserts its self-worth by claiming the heroic virtues which had been heretofore the exclusive property of the aristocracy. The merchant shows as much if not more valor, courage, and patriotism in his ventures as the nobleman does in his soldierly profession. Moreover, trading exploits, rather than martial ones, are the source of England's national glory and her achievements in the enterprise of discovery. Insisting that the true heroes of exploration are merchants, Roberts provides an alternative to an aristocratic ideology which interprets the discoveries in terms of imperial conquest. While such a mercantile version of the voyages of discovery may preserve their heroic nature—at least in the merchant's eyes—it cannot be accommodated to epic terms, for epic does not celebrate bourgeois heroes, however heroic they may be. Milton's deflation of the epic voyager Satan into a representative of the East India Company suggests that the aristocratic ideology which animated earlier epic has by now become obsolete. Just as the leveling artillery in the War in Heaven reveals the uselessness of a warrior class—a lesson which was learned, as always imperfectly, by the Royalists during the Civil Wars—so the presence of traders on the oceans of the East suggests that a new social class has taken over the heroic arena that formerly belonged to the gentleman soldier.

V

Renaissance epic insists on the mercantile cast of the romance adventure in order, in Tasso's case, to distinguish the voyage of discovery from its false commercial twin or, in Milton's, to disclose the true economic nature of that voyage. This epic characterization of the adventure was in some ways prophetic of the future of romance. It points up the relative flexibility of romance's open forms vis-à-vis epic's more rigid classical structures and greater commitment to social hierarchy. This flexibility, which led Renaissance critics to consider romance the genre of innovation, allowed it to change to meet the demands of a new audience in ways that epic could not. The example of the voyages of discovery itself suggests the failure of aristocratic ideology and literary forms to describe a reality that was increasingly pervaded by early capitalism. As a bourgeois reading public began to command the literary marketplace, epic was doomed and romance had to adapt quickly to survive. A late flowering of courtly and pastoral prose romances proved to be a dead end. The future for romance, as epic had already intimated, lay with the new world of money and materiality[38]—and with the novel.

In chapter 29 of the second part of *Don Quijote,* Don Quijote and Sancho come across an oarless little boat on the river Ebro. The ingenious hidalgo concludes that some enchanter has placed the craft in his path to carry him to the aid of some other knight or important person in distress. Cervantes's probable source is an episode in *Palmerín de Inglaterra,* but it might just as well have been Tasso's "barca aventurosa." The knight and squire settle in this boat of romance and set it adrift. In spite of Sancho's protests that they have not traveled five yards from the river bank, Don Quijote believes that they have already been transported seven or eight hundred leagues, and he speculates whether they have crossed the equator: "according to those Spaniards and others who embark in Cádiz in order to go to the East Indies, one of the signs by which they know that they have passed the equinoctial line that I have spoken of is that the lice die on board the ship." Ordered to search his body, Sancho confirms that they have not yet reached the equator.[39]

Here again the romance boat of adventure has turned into the Renaissance ship of discovery, and we may speculate whether that ship is on a heroic epic voyage or just on a mercantile adventure.[40] But to do so is to remain inside Quijote's mad imagination where literary genres and other things are impossibly confused. The novel does not allow us to remain there long. A few moments later, the knight and squire collide with a water mill, their vessel is smashed to pieces, and its enraged former owner demands to be paid for its loss. The boat of romance turns out to be nothing more than a boat.

Notes

[1] Torquato Tasso, *Gerusalemme liberata,* vol. 3 of *Opere,* ed. Bruno Maier (Milan: Rizzoli, 1963); Matteo Boiardo, *Orlando innamorato,* ed. Aldo Scaglione (Turin: U.T.E.T., 1966); Luis de Camões, *Os lusíadas,* ed. Frank Pierce (Oxford: Clarendon, 1973); *The Lusiads,* trans. Sir Richard Fanshawe, ed. Geoffrey Bullough (1655; London: Centaur, 1963); John Milton, *Paradise Lost, The Poems of John Milton,* ed. John Carey and Alastair Fowler (London: Longmans, 1968).

[2] Torquato Tasso, *Rinaldo,* vol. 2 of *Opere,* ed. Bruno Maier (Milan: Rizzoli, 1963).

[3] Northrop Frye, *The Secular Scripture* (Cambridge, Mass., 1976) 15, 30.

[4] Georg Simmel, "The Adventurer," *Georg Simmel 1858–1918: A Collection of Essays,* trans. David Kettler, ed. Kurt H. Wolff (Columbus, Ohio: Ohio State UP, 1959) 244.

[5] On the magic boat as a digression from epic to romance, see James Nohrn-

berg, *The Analogy of the Faerie Queene* (Princeton: Princeton UP, 1976) 9–
11. For the dialectical structure of romance narrative, which both posits and
defers a point of closure, see Patricia Parker, *Inescapable Romance* (Princeton:
Princeton UP, 1979).

[6] See Frederick Kiefer, "The Conflation of Fortuna and Occasio in Renaissance Thought and Iconography," *Journal of Medieval and Renaissance Studies*
9 (1979): 1–27. See also Nohrnberg 309–11.

[7] I have discussed the generic and ideological implications of Boiardo's episode in "The Figure of Atlante: Ariosto and Boiardo's Poem," *MLN* 94
(1979): 77–91. See also Charles S. Ross, "Angelica and the Fata Morgana:
Boiardo's Allegory of Love," *MLN* 96 (1981): 12–22.

[8] James B. Mackenna, ed., *A Spaniard in the Portuguese Indies: The Narrative of Martín Fernández de Figueroa* (Cambridge: Harvard UP, 1967) 134–
37. Menéndez y Pelayo brings up an anecdote about an early-seventeenth-
century Portuguese soldier in India who believed in the literal truth of the
books of chivalry and sought to emulate the deeds of their heroes in his combat against the natives. *Orígenes de la Novela* 1, *Edición Nacional de las Obras
Completas de Menéndez y Pelayo* 13 (Madrid: C.S.I.C., 1943) 370–71n. This
story of a Don Quijote *avant la lettre* is also cited by Irving Leonard in his
study of the book trade to the Spanish New World, *Books of the Brave*
(Cambridge: Harvard UP, 1949) 26.

[9] See Tasso's own remarks in the first of the *Discorsi dell'Arte Poetica:*
"Poco dilettevole è veramente quel poema che non ha seco quelle meraviglie
che tanto muovono non solo l'animo de gl'ignoranti, ma de' giudiziosi ancora."
Torquato Tasso, *Prose,* ed. Ettore Mazzali (Milan: Ricciardi, 1959) 353.

Rinaldo plays the role of an Achilles who wrathfully departs from the crusader army not to sulk in his tent but to wander into the realm of romance
fortune. While Tasso's specific allusions are to the *Orlando innamorato,* these
are mediated by the poem which Tasso deeply criticizes in the *Discorsi:*
Giangiorgio Trissino's *L'Italia liberata da Gotti* (1547). Trissino's Achillean
hero Corsamonte leaves Belisario's army in canto 11.527ff., angered because
the general has not granted him his beloved Elpidia in marriage. He eventually travels to Monte Circeo, the dwelling of the blind fairy Plutina (761ff.).
Plutina, as her name implies, is a treasure demon and a Fortune figure,
reminiscent of Boiardo's Morgana. In canto 13.271ff., the magician Filodemo
divines Corsamonte's whereabouts and dispatches two knights, Trajano and
Ciro, in search of the absent champion. Here clearly is the literary precedent
for Tasso's Magus of Ascalon and for the mission of Carlo and Ubaldo. In
this scheme Armida plays the role of Plutina. But Armida also recalls another
of Trissino's demonic fairies, Acratia, who, together with her accomplice
Ligridonia, imprisons Corsamone earlier in cantos 4–5 of the *Italia liberata;*
Acratia is a figure of lust and concupiscence, modeled on Ariosto's Alcina.
Tasso models Armida on both Alcina and Morgana; his inspiration for this
conflation of Ariosto's and Boiardo's heroines was Trissino's poem. It is,
however, on Armida's symbolic nature as a Fortune figure that the model of
the *Italia liberata* primarily insists, a negative and potentially demonic Fortune
contrasted with the providential Fortune who serves divine ends. In Tasso's
later revision of his epic into the *Gerusalemme conquistata,* Fortune becomes
wholly and exclusively negative; the episode of the providential Fortune and

her boat is cut, and Fortune appears as a literal demon (18.70) of the sea and storms. This change is remarked upon by Guido Baldassarri in *"Inferno" e "cielo": Tipologia e funzione del "mervaglioso" nella Liberata* (Rome: Bulzoni, 1977) 34–35.

[10] See James H. Sims, "Camões' 'Lusiads' and Milton's 'Paradise Lost': Satan's Voyage to Eden," *Papers on Milton,* ed. Philip Mahone Griffith and Lester F. Zimmerman (Tulsa, Oklahoma, 1969) 36–46. Sims brilliantly relates (41) the second simile to Satan's farewell to Hope some fifty lines earlier, at 4.108–10. I intend here to fill out some of the details which confirm Sims's argument for the presence of the *Lusíadas* behind Satan's journey. See also two other pioneering studies by James H. Sims: "Christened Classicism in *Paradise Lost* and the *Lusiads,*" *Comparative Literature* 24 (1972): 338–56, and "The Epic Narrator's Mortal Voice in Camões and Milton," *Revue de Littérature Comparée* 51 (1977): 374–84.

[11] I have discussed in more detail the link between Milton's Chaos and Camões's description of Neptune's ocean palace in *Origin and Originality in Renaissance Literature: Versions of the Source* (New Haven: Yale UP, 1983) 208–09.

[12] Sims, "Christened Classicism" 348, argues that the conversation between Satan and Chaos recollects the descent of Camões's Bacchus to the palace of Neptune. The resemblance between Chaos and the primordial realm of Neptune (see n11) bears out his point. Milton has thus conflated three separate episodes of Camões's poem into one: da Gama and the King of Melinde (book 2), Bacchus and Neptune (book 6), and da Gama and the Zamorin of Calicut (book 7). One effect of this virtuoso display of allusion is to make da Gama inseparable from the demonic pagan god who tries to thwart his mission.

[13] See Milton 551, notes to v. 935.

[14] It hardly needs stressing that the Spanish nobility did nonetheless invest in mercantile ventures, particularly those to the New World. See Ruth Pike, *Aristocrats and Traders: Sevillian Society in the Sixteenth Century* (Ithaca, N.Y.: Cornell UP, 1972), and Richard Konetzke, "Entrepreneurial Activities of Spanish and Portuguese Noblemen in Medieval Times," *Explorations in Entrepreneurial History* 6 (1953–54): 115–20. The aristocratic prejudice against commercial activity could be reinforced by religio-juridical treatises which instructed the Renaissance merchant how to regulate his business on this side of usury. In a 1542 guide for merchants, Juan Sarabia de la Calle cites Cicero's condemnation of trade in *De Officiis* (1.42) and reminds his reader: "Y por ser la mercadería officio tan vil se cuenta por una de las siete artes mecánicas, e si algún caballero públicamente le usase por sí mismo pierde la honra de la caballería por la ley de Partida." *Instrucción de Mercaderes del Doctor Sarabia de la Calle* (Madrid: Joyas Bibliográficas, 1949) 24. A similar disapproval of merchants can be found in Tomás de Mercado, *Suma de Tratos y Contratos,* ed. Nicolás Sánchez-Albornoz (1569; Madrid: Inst. de Estudios Fiscales, 1977) 72. For a comment on marriages between noble and merchant families, see Mercado 63. Such scholastic treatises had, however, little to do with the merchant's real experience and should be carefully distinguished from the practical handbooks which taught arithmetic, accounting, and other business procedures. For discussions, see Henri Lapeyre, *Une famille de marchands:*

les Ruiz (Paris: Colin, 1955) 126–40, and Natalie Zemon Davis, "Sixteenth-Century French Arithmetics on the Business Life," *Journal of the History of Ideas* 21 (1960): 18–48. Davis sees in these handbooks an incipient attempt to give value and social dignity to the merchant's profession.

[15] R. Hookyaas, "Humanism and the Voyages of Discovery in 16th Century Portuguese Science and Letters," *Mededelingen der Koninklijke Nederlandse Akademie van Wetenschappen, Afd. Letterkunde* 42 (1979): 99–159, 33–37; Vitorino Magalhaes-Godinho, *L'économie de l'empire portugais aux XVe et XVIe siècles* (Paris: S.E.V.P.E.N., 1969) 833–35. On the low social position of merchants in Portugal, who were, in effect, squeezed out by royal monopolies, see C. R. Boxer, *The Portuguese Seaborne Empire, 1415–1825* (New York: Knopf, 1969) 318–39.

[16] See Boxer as well as Bailey W. Diffie and George D. Winius, *Foundations of the Portuguese Empire, 1415–1580* (Minneapolis: U. of Minnesota P, 1977). Carlo Cipolla, *Guns and Sails in the Early Phase of European Expansion, 1400–1700* (London: Collins, 1965) 132–38, suggests that the idea of a crusade allowed the Renaissance conquistadors to reconcile "the antithesis between business and religion that had plagued the conscience of medieval Europe."

[17] T. K. Rabb, *Enterprise and Empire: Merchant and Gentry Investment in the Expansion of England, 1575–1630* (Cambridge: Harvard UP, 1967) 33–55. See also T. K. Rabb, "The Expansion of Europe and the Spirit of Capitalism," *The Historical Journal* 17 (1974): 675–89.

[18] From Fleming's introduction in verse (a four-stanza "rythme decasyllabicall, upon this last luckie voyage of worthie Capteine Forbisher") to Dionyse Settle, *A true reporte of the last voyage into the west and northwest regions* (London, 1577), fol. Ai verso. This stanza is cited in John Parker, *Books to Build an Empire* (Amsterdam: N. Israel, 1965) 70.

[19] Edmund S. Morgan, "The Labor Problem in Jamestown, 1607–1618," *American Historical Review* 76 (1971): 595–611.

[20] *The Odyssey of Homer*, trans. Richmond Lattimore (1965; New York: Harper and Row, 1975) 125.

[21] This passage is discussed in M. I. Finley, *The World of Odysseus*, 2nd ed. (New York: Penguin, 1979) 69–71.

[22] Aelian, *Variae Historiae* 4.20. Aelianus, *A registrie of Hystories, containing Martial exploits of worthy warriours, Politique practice of Civil Magistrates . . .* , trans. Abraham Fleming (London: Woodcocke, 1576) 58. James Joyce followed Victor Bérard's theory that the *Odyssey* reflects the experience of ancient Phoenician sailors and made his modern-day Ulysses into a semitic commercial traveler; see Michael Seidel, *Epic Geography: James Joyce's Ulysses* (Princeton: Princeton UP, 1976).

[23] The first theorist of the romanzo, Giovanni Pigna, noted its resemblance to the *Odyssey*. See *I Romanzi di M. Giovan Battista Pigna* (Venice, 1554) 24. The idea soon became a commonplace among defenders of Ariosto. See Bernard Weinberg, *A History of Literary Criticism in the Italian Renaissance* (Chicago: U of Chicago P, 1961) 955, 970, 999. Northrop Frye, *Anatomy of Criticism* (Princeton: Princeton UP, 1957) 319.

[24] There is an earlier French treatment of the Jason story as a chivalric romance to which Boiardo may be indebted: Raoul Lefèvre, *L'Histoire de Jason,* ed. Gert Pinkernell (c. 1460; Frankfurt: Athenäum, 1971).

[25] *Lettres d'un marchand venitien Andrea Berengo (1553–1556)*, ed. Ugo Tucci (Paris: S.E.V.P.E.N., 1957) 176, 132, 143, 152.

[26] Christiane Bec, *Les marchands écrivains: Affaires et humanisme à Florence, 1375–1434* (Paris: Mouton, 1967) 301–30.

[27] See Ross (n7, above) for a discussion of Boiardo's allegory of riches, especially 13n4, 20–21.

[28] Erich Köhler, *L'aventure chevaleresque: Idéal et réalité dans le roman courtois*, trans. Elaine Kaufholz (1956; Paris: Gallimard, 1974), has argued that the origins of chivalric romance in the twelfth century reflect the aspirations of a lower nobility that sought to define its own ethos in opposition to the new central power of the crown, whose own ideology was expressed in the epic *chanson de geste*. The vestiges of this split between a strictly martial, nationalistic ethos and an ethos of aristocratic courtliness can still be found in the poems of Ariosto and Tasso, in the conflict between duty to a collective army and the individual pleasures, normally amorous, of knight-errantry. But in Renaissance epic this same conflict may also have begun to express a division between the nobility and the ethos of the merchant classes, the latter clothed in the forms of romance.

[29] Samuel Eliot Morison, *Admiral of the Ocean Sea: A Life of Christopher Columbus* (Boston: Little, Brown, 1942) 364–67.

[30] Ubaldo's Odyssean character is further reinforced by extended allusions in canto 16 (29, 32, 48) to the *Achilleid* (1.785–960) of Statius. In liberating Rinaldo from Armida, Ubaldo plays the role of Statius's Ulysses who, together with Diomede, draws the young Achilles out of his hiding place among the maidens of Scyros and away from his beloved Deidamia.

[31] Mercado 71–72: "porque conversando con muchas gentes, estando en distintos reinos, tratando con varias naciones, experimentando differentes costumbres, considerando el diverso gobierno y policía de los pueblos, se hacen hombres universales, cursados y ladinos para cualesquiera negocios que se le ofrezcan. Adquieren y aumentan una gran prudencia y experiencia para guidar y regirse, así en los sucesos particulares como generales. Son útiles a su república, por la gran noticia de varias cosas que han visto oído en su peregrinación." One can compare to these merchants and to Tasso's Ubaldo Francus, the hero of Ronsard's unfinished epic *La Franciade* (*Oeuvres complètes*, ed. Gustave Cohen [1572; Paris: Gallimard, 1950] 1: 663). Francus has been prepared for his present epic mission by having been sent on a Grand Tour, a kind of Odyssean preparation:

> En maint païs je l'ay fait voyager;
> Il a cognu maint peuple et maint danger,
> Cognu les moeurs des hommes pour se faire
> Guerrier pratiqu'en toute grande affaire. (1.498–501)

Here, too, the language suggests a confusion between Odyssean adventures in search of experience and business ventures. Francus the warrior seems also to be a man of affairs.

[32] The end of the *Liberata* thus coincides with its beginning, where God looks down on the Crusader army and compares the perfect zeal of Goffredo who "ogni mortale / gloria, imperio, tesor, mette in non cale" (1.8), with all the other Crusaders, each of whom possesses some impure motive or moral deficiency. In the third book of his *Discorsi del poema eroico*, published in

1594, Tasso follows Plato (*Republic* 3.390e) in condemning Achilles for having sold the body of Hector back to Priam in the last book of the *Iliad*. Goffredo's refusal of Altamoro's offer of ransom may thus also reflect a traditional criticism of Achilles's avarice. See Tasso, *Prose* 608–09.

[33] See Ferdinand Braudel, *The Mediterranean and the Mediterranean World in the Age of Philip II,* trans. Sian Reynolds (New York: Harper and Row, 1973) 873–80.

[34] The mercantile and colonialist dimensions of Satan's mission to earth which I am outlining here have also been discussed by J. Martin Evans in the commentary to his edition of *Paradise Lost: Books 9–10* (Cambridge: Cambridge UP, 1973) 46–47.

[35] See Holden Furber, *Rival Empires of Trade in the Orient, 1600–1800* (Minneapolis: U of Minnesota P, 1976).

[36] *Early English Tracts on Commerce,* ed. J. R. McCullough (Cambridge, Eng.: Economic History Society, 1952) 83.

[37] *Early English Tracts* 108.

[38] Today the aptly named *Fortune* magazine speaks of "the romance of big business."

[39] J. M. Cohen, trans., *The Adventures of Don Quixote* (Hammondsworth: Penguin, 1977) 658.

[40] In the captive's tale in part 1, Cervantes appears to locate ventures to the Indies squarely in the sphere of commerce. The captive and his two brothers are offered careers in the "Iglesia, mar, o casa real" (39). The sea represents "el arte de la mercancía," and the brother who chooses this profession and becomes rich in Peru (42) is pointedly contrasted with the captive, whose participation at Lepanto and the Goletta have placed him in the epic world of the sixteenth century; he is said to be of "más altos pensamientos" than his wealthy brothers. The captive returns penniless to Spain, confirming his father's words that although war "no dé muchas riquezas, suele dar mucho valor y mucha fama." Cervantes seems to suggest a kind of sibling rivalry between epic and the romance of the Indies, and he appears to subscribe to the epic ideology this essay has described. See also the opening of *El Celoso Extremeño,* where the title character successfully voyages to the Indies to recoup his fortune.

THE ROMANCE
OF CHIVALRY IN SPAIN
From Rodríguez de Montalvo to Cervantes

Harry Sieber

At the beginning of the sixteenth century, Rodríguez de Montalvo popularized the reading of romances of chivalry. In the first decade of the seventeenth century, Cervantes satirized the readers of those romances. I would like to consider what happened in between, examining the Spanish chivalric romance from a slightly different perspective. Traditionally, critics have simply accepted the Cervantine view. Hispanic literary history has bracketed the genre as prelude, as fiction used to fill printed pages and keep readers entertained while the world awaited the opening of the main attraction—that flourishing of Spanish letters between 1550 and 1650 which we now refer to as the Golden Age. I ask my reader to forget this preconception, to ignore traditional periodization and categories.[1] Instead, we will put on pre-Cervantine spectacles and examine the career of the genre in sixteenth-century Spain or, more precisely, between the publication of Montalvo's *Amadís de Gaula* in 1508 and the appearance of Cervantes's *Don Quijote* in 1605. I propose to look first at the texts themselves and then beyond the texts, to a changing *mentalité* which was incompatible with the romance as presented by Montalvo and elaborated by his successors. Finally, I will mention briefly Cervantes's rewriting of the sixteenth-century romance in a form which succeeded where others failed, namely in his accommodation and/or reconciliation of the romance as a genre and the changed attitudes of its reading public.

With regard to the texts, Martín de Riquer states my case very concisely: "the prose *Lancelot* is the primary model of the *Amadís of Gaul,* and because the *Amadís* is the father of the Spanish romances of chivalry, these are presented to us as the Spanish interpretations of the chivalric romance of adventures created by Chrétien de Troyes."[2] But the *Amadís,* as the priest tells us in his examination of Don Quijote's library, was itself a thing of mystery. What was not mysterious about it, however, is that *Amadís* the book fathered a monstrous progeny. Montalvo's four-book *refundición* and continuation are based on a much earlier three-book Spanish text that was known in the mid-fourteenth century. It was Montalvo's version that touched a waiting, sensitized audience. After its publication in Zaragoza in 1508, reprints were taken from the presses in 1511, 1519, 1521, 1526, 1531, 1535, 1539, 1545, 1547, 1551, 1552, 1563, 1575, 1580, and 1586.[3] Moreover, if Amadís's adventures were unavailable during the years when new imprints failed to appear, his readers could survive on the fifth book of the cycle, the adventures of his son, *Las sergas de Esplandián:* 1510, 1521, 1525, 1526, 1542, 1549, 1587, and 1588; or on the seventh book of the cycle, the adventures of his grandson, *Lisuarte de Grecia:* 1514, 1525, 1534, 1539, 1543, 1548, 1550, 1564, and 1587. Henry Thomas clarifies the bibliographical panorama: "During the hundred years that followed the publication of the *Amadís of Gaul,* fifty romances of chivalry appeared in Spain and Portugal. They were published at the rate of almost one per year between 1508 and 1550; to these were added nine more between 1550 and . . . [1588]; and three more appeared before the publication of *Don Quijote.*"[4] The characters, themes, and structures of many of these books were linked together through the genealogical bonds created by the *Amadís,* often acknowledging the influence and control of the father, whose power was strengthened by his ubiquitous presence for more than eighty years. And even when no specific family relationship existed, the names and the adventures of the characters echo one another and can often be traced back to the *Amadís* itself. The *Palmerín* cycle, for instance, became a worthy competitor of the *Amadís* from its first appearance in 1511. But the name of Palmerín's mother, Griana, is little more than a rearrangement of Oriana, heroine of the *Amadís.* In the case of Diego Ortúñez de Calahorra's *Espejo de príncipes y caballeros (Mirror of Princes and Knights;* Zaragoza, 1555)— a book to which I will return—the fair Briana stands for Oriana in the adventures of the Caballero del Febo (Knight of the Sun).[5]

The real mystery of the *Amadís* is what it means both in its own right and in terms of literary history. Montalvo's reworking is a stated fact. He tells us in the prologue: "And I, . . . desiring that some vestige of remembrance of me might remain, and not daring to set my feeble talents at that with which the wisest learned men have been concerned, have sought to join the latest ones to write about the most trivial and insubstantial matters on account of their being most in keeping with the weakness of my talents; namely, by correcting these three Books of *Amadís,* which through the fault of poor scribes or revisers were read in corrupt and defective versions; and by translating and emending the fourth Book, together with the *Exploits of Esplandián* its offspring, which up to now within no one's memory has been seen, for very fortunately it came to light in a stone tomb discovered underground below a hermitage near Constantinople and was brought to this part of Spain by a Hungarian merchant."[6] What is meant by this statement has been the subject of dispute and speculation. How much did he write and rewrite? What were his contributions and how can they be understood to have founded the genre in Spain? Much of this particular mystery has been clarified in the studies of Grace Williams, María Rosa Lida de Malkiel, Armando Durán, and, more recently, Frank Pierce and James Fogelquist.[7]

Williams, after a careful comparison of geography, names, and structure, was certain that the *Amadís* derived in great part from the *Table Ronde* and the *Roman de Tristan,* with scattered indebtedness to *Merlin* and the Spanish *Gran conquista de Ultramar.* Lida de Malkiel supported this thesis but added that many of the names in the *Amadís* not found in Arthurian sources do exist in the *Roman de Troie* or in the Spanish *Crónica troyana.* More important is Lida de Malkiel's analysis of the so-called *Amadís primitivo,* the primary subject of her study, in which she argued that Montalvo radically changed the romance's original ending. In the primitive version Esplandián kills his father; his mother, Oriana, commits suicide after hearing the news. Montalvo refers to this outcome in the romance itself but gives it an allegorical interpretation rather than a literal one; he keeps Amadís and Oriana alive so that they can be publicly married in book 4, the section of the romance invented by Montalvo himself. The original *Amadís* reflected the death of Ulysses in the Trojan cycle, particularly in Leomarte's *Sumas de historia troyana,*[8] an outcome set aside so that Amadís could fight more battles in other continuations. The greatest change effected by Montalvo, according to James Fogelquist, would distance the *Amadís* from some of its Arthurian ancestors in a special way. The lovers do not live in "fear of the angry jealousy of the woman's husband, but rather under a sense of honor and justice of the woman's father."[9] Amadís swears his love to Oriana when he is twelve years old; even though their love is consummated before their public marriage, Amadís's constancy and faithfulness are put to the test as he resists extramarital temptation. Montalvo's elimination of adultery, together with his addition of moral commentary, set the tone which would characterize a number of continuations.

These hurried references to the *Amadís* are sufficient to indicate that some changes took place as a result of Montalvo's intervention. It may be worthwhile, however, to look more closely at the book itself to assess some of its main features in terms of my later comments on the *Espejo de príncipes* and to provide some sense of its structural and thematic pattern for those who may not recall its detail:

> The story begins not many years after Our Lord's Passion, with the arrival of King Perión of Gaul in Little Britain, whose Christian King, Garínter, he had come to see. When Perión meets Garínter's younger daughter Elisena, he falls in love with her, and with the help of her servant, their love is consummated. Their union is presented as one of true love and tokens and promises are given; thus we have the first example of the marriage of vows, or secret marriage. Perión leaves Little Britain and Elisena gives birth secretly to Amadís, whom she is compelled with equal secrecy to dispatch in a chest on the open sea, but with the ring Perión gave her and his sword, together with a letter . . . identifying him as a king's son. Amadís is rescued . . . [and] is later presented at Court [by a Scottish knight] where he meets Oriana, the daughter of Lisuarte, king of Great Britain. They fall in love and he is made a knight by Perión, his unknown father. Amadís's first adventures establish his skill and valor, for which Urganda, a great enchantress, gives him a lance. Amadís's brother, Galaor, carried off by a giant and given to a hermit, learns that he too is a king's son. Meanwhile Oriana rejoins her father in London. Amadís and his cousin Agrajes arrive at Perión's court, and the three knights defeat Abiés, king of Ireland. Amadís then receives a letter from Oriana to join her and now, recognized by his parents, he sets out to become a knight at Lisuarte's court. On the way he dubs his own brother a knight without knowing who he is, and later when Galaor disappears, he searches for him only to be enchanted by an evil magician, Arcaláus. The news of Amadís's false death reaches the court. He is finally freed, however, and united with his brother, they join Lisuarte and make their way to London, where all the knights swear to protect ladies and damsels. Later Lisuarte and his retinue are treacherously captured and imprisoned by Arcaláus, who hopes to make Barsinán of

Sansueña King of Great Britain. Amadís defeats Arcaláus, frees Oriana and the young couple consummate their love.

Amadís, accompanied by Galaor and Agrajes, then fulfills his promise to avenge Queen Briolanja of Sobradisa by defeating her father's murderers and restoring her to her kingdom. This causes the beginnings of deep jealousy in Oriana since Briolanja falls in love with Amadís. Amadís and his companions defeat Abíseos, the usurper, and his sons.[10]

This much-reduced view of book 1 of the *Amadís* contains the major structural and thematic elements that will epitomize later romances: the remote times in which it takes place; the secrecy surrounding the origins and birth of the hero; the presence of a stepfather and of an unknown brother; the intervention of good and evil enchanters; signs of identity in the form of letters, tokens, and weapons; the introduction into the court of a foreign king; the swearing of political and marital—if not moral—allegiances; separations of hero from heroine, kings from their kingdoms. Books 2, 3, and 4 carry on the same pace. In book 2, Amadís receives a letter from Oriana in which she accuses him of falling in love with Briolanja. Amadís reacts by turning into a hermit to do penance. The couple is reunited, and all is forgiven, just in time for Amadís to have a falling out with Oriana's father, Lisuarte. Lisuarte plans for his daughter to marry the emperor of Rome in book 3; Amadís defeats the Roman fleet, rescues Oriana, and decides that it is his Christian obligation to achieve peace with Lisuarte. But Lisuarte rejects his efforts; a major battle ensues, which Amadís wins. Lisuarte then recognizes Amadís as his son-in-law, after which they all travel to Amadís's kingdom, the Insola Firme, where a great festival takes place. This would be the logical ending of the romance,[11] but Montalvo extends it for several chapters in order to push Esplandián to the forefront in preparation for book 5. Urganda foretells the great future of Esplandián whose glory, she says, will far exceed his father's. The romance closes with Amadís and his followers on the Insola Firme to help King Lisuarte if further troubles develop.

I have given more detail than necessary for my immediate purpose, which is to cut through the variety of plots to some essential features of the *Amadís* as a whole. One window through which a basic design can be perceived has been opened by James Fogelquist. By concentrating on the prophetic passages in the romance, Fogelquist's attention was drawn to what he considers to be the text's thirteen major events:

1. Amadís's birth and separation from his mother.
2. The recognition of Amadís by his parents.
3. The first encounter between Amadís and his brother, Galaor, during which Amadís dubs him a knight without recognizing him.
4. The second encounter between Amadís and Galaor, in which they battle each other before recognizing one another.
5. Amadís's refuge on the Peña Pobre as a result of Oriana's jealousy.
6. Their reunion and reconciliation in Miraflores.
7. The battle between the hundred knights of Lisuarte and those of Cildadán of Ireland, a battle won by Britain with three blows from Amadís's sword.
8. The break in the friendship between Amadís and Lisuarte.
9. Oriana's rescue by Amadís from the clutches of the Romans who take her to marry Patín (emperor of Rome).
10. The great battle between the armies of Lisuarte and Amadís.
11. The attempt of King Arábigo to take over Great Britain while Amadís and Lisuarte are at war.
12. The reconciliation of Amadís and Lisuarte.
13. Esplandián's completion of the adventures on the Peña de la Doncella Encantadora, which occurs in Montalvo's *Sergas*.[12]

Fogelquist further states that "these events, taken together with the sequence of Amadís's prophetic dreams, serve to mark off the beginnings and endings of distinct segments of Amadís's adventures, that is, the central thread of the narrative" (128). Fogelquist uses his enumeration in support of his main thesis, namely that the narrative structure of the romance "follows . . . the most elemental form of the chronicle" (129). His list, however, is more important because it reveals a very distinct structural pattern: birth and separation are followed by confrontation, recognition, and reconciliation. Taken in sequence, and discarding the final event because it actually belongs to book 5, these narrative segments fall into three equal parts: 1–4, 5–8, and 9–12, with some overlapping between the first and second parts concerning the love relationship between Amadís and Oriana. Amadís's separation from his mother and his identity as the Doncel del Mar in the first event are repeated—with a significant difference—in event five, with his separation from Oriana and his identity as Beltenebrós on the Peña Pobre. Event two—Amadís's reunion with his parents—is echoed in event six with his reunion with Oriana in Miraflores. At this point the pattern undergoes a slight reversal: Amadís is separated from Oriana; his friendship with her father takes a turn for the worse; and their secret marriage is threatened when her father plans to marry her in a public ceremony to the emperor of Rome. This plot reversal, which questions the order of the romance itself, is ultimately turned around and leads again to the established pattern: confrontation, recognition, and reconciliation— Amadís and Lisuarte engage in a major battle, Amadís wins, and Lisuarte recognizes his daughter's marriage to Amadís and the consequent legitimacy of his grandson, Esplandían. A new alliance is formed through the reconciliation of son and father-in-law; the resulting dynasty augurs an optimistic future. In one sense, Montalvo has returned his readers to the prologue, written sometime between 1492 and 1504, that is, after the military conquest of Granada, the expulsion of the Jews, and the consolidation of the peninsula under Christian domination. Ferdinand and Isabella are still alive, a new world has been discovered beyond the horizon, and justifiable optimism rules the day.

There is no beginning, middle, and end to the structure of the *Amadís;* rather it is a constant and repetitious process of separation, confrontation, recogntion, and reconciliation. The reduction of its great variety, a variety exemplified in the adventures of an accumulating number of characters, to a poetic unity that would have been recognizable by Cervantes did not come until Tasso composed his own *Amadigi,* finished by 1557 but not published until 1560.[13] But to return to Spain. Did the manifest popularity and success of the *Amadís* establish it as a model for other chivalric romances in the peninsula? A look at Ortúñez de Calahorra's *Espejo de príncipes* will provide us with at least one answer.

Calahorra's romance in many ways is an excessive response to Montalvo's *Amadís.* In Eisenberg's recent edition, the first part alone, published in 1555, fills six volumes and more than 1700 pages.[14] A brief résumé will serve as a guide to my comparison:

> Trebacio's election as emperor of Greece provokes the invasion of a Hungarian king, Tiberio, who claims the throne. Tiberio offers his daughter, Briana, to the English prince Teoduardo in exchange for military support of his invasion. Trebacio, however, defeats Hungary, hears of Briana's beauty, and falls in love with her without having seen her. Trebacio kills Teoduardo, assumes his identity and marries Briana, who bears him two children: the Caballero del Febo and his twin brother, Rosicler.
>
> Trebacio is soon carried away by a magical boat to the Island of Lindaraja, where an enchantment forces him to fall in love with the island's namesake: they have a daughter also called Lindaraja. In the meantime, Febo and his brother, who are said to be the sons of a local

villager, are taken to a monastery where they are cared for by their true mother. (Let us recall that Trebacio and Briana are secretly married.) The young Febo, like his missing father, is carried away in a small boat; he, however, is found by a friendly king, Florión, who has also come across another lost prince, Claberindo of France. Florión's own son, Brandizel, and the two princes are sent to the court of Florión's uncle, the sultan of Babylon. At this point, and at a still tender age, Febo begins to display the feats of arms for which he will become famous: he kills the giant who threatens the sultan and his daughter. Somewhat later, he kills the imperialist Africano, who attempts to take over Babylon, and returns the kingdom of Persia to Florión. Febo again is taken away in a magic boat to an unknown destination.

Meanwhile, Rosicler too leaves home in search of adventures, but of his own will: he saves a young boy from the claws of a wild bear and kills the evil Argión who had terrorized the Valley of the Mountains by demanding his usual quota of virgins. Later Rosicler makes his way to England, where he falls in love with Olivia, the daughter of King Oliverio. Rosicler's rustic origins make him unfit for the princess of a major kingdom, and until his true identity is made known a few chapters later, he suffers the humiliation of her rejection. Olivia discovers her error, but too late, because Rosicler leaves for the Island of Candramante, where, with the help of his brother, he kills Candramante's two sons and their vassals. Before Rosicler can discover that it was his brother who helped him, Febo is carried away by a magic boat to the island of Lindajara, where he frees Trebacio—his unknown father—from a deep enchantment. Father and son then kidnap Briana and carry her to Greece.

Trebacio and Briana, happily reunited, secretly leave the monastery where she has been living, and make their way to Constantinople. Rosicler in the meantime has gone to Russia in search of adventures. After killing several evil-doers, he sails to Alexandria, but ends up in Phoenicia because of bad weather. He saves the King of Antioch and promises him that he will restore him to his kingdom. The Caballero del Febo, meanwhile, travels through Greece when he meets Lindabrides and her brother Meridián; he defeats Meridián and in so doing, wins the hand of Lindabrides and the Kingdom of Tartaria. His love-life becomes complicated when Claridiana, seeing his portrait, falls in love with him, and heads for Constantinople to see him in the flesh. He falls in love with her during a jousting tournament, in which he fights his own brother without knowing it. Neither wins the joust—since both are equally strong—but they do finally recognize one another; moreover, they both are reunited with their parents, Trebacio and Briana, and all celebrate their extraordinary good fortune.[15]

I have given a reduced summary of the first book and of the first thirty-six chapters of the second, but this suffices to allow us to draw some immediate conclusions with regard to the *Espejo de príncipes* and a few of its structural and thematic relationships to the *Amadís.* The characters in the *Espejo* at least exist within a recognizable sixteenth-century Spanish world: the Mediterranean basin with some sidetrips to the north. But they also move in a recognizable plot: secret sexual encounters and marriages lead to secret births; repetitious separations conclude in predictable reunions; mistaken identities create momentary confusion for the characters—and for the readers—but are clarified in recognition scenes; threatened kingdoms determine political alliances and allegiances. And, yes, the Caballero del Febo and Claridiana—like Amadís and Oriana before them—promise to marry and do so in the final book, quickly, the narrator tells us, "so that should she be pregnant, their error would not be discovered."[16] But Calahorra is not finished. He allows his protagonists less than an hour of sexual horseplay, because, after all, they are on horses, before interrupting them with the sounds of another battle, in which the Caballero del Febo and his wife ride off to defeat the pagan Bramarante.

In this instance, military might, not sexual satisfaction, is the knight's first pleasure. The love motif, worked well into the construction of the *Amadís,* often functions in the *Espejo* as titillating ornamentation. The initial love trysts of King Perión of Gaul and Elisena and of King Trebacio and Briana will serve as "control" examples. The narrative purpose of these scenes is the same: they account for the biological origins of our respective heroes. In the *Amadís* the future parents encounter one another at night in Perión's room; in the *Espejo* Trebacio surprises Briana in her garden in the late afternoon. Montalvo is straightforward: "The king remained alone with his mistress, whom he gazed at by the light of the three candles that were in the chamber. As he looked at her it seemed to him that all the beauty in the world was united in her, considering himself very fortunate that God had brought him to such a connubial state. And thus embracing they went to bed" (Montalvo 1: 30–31). By contrast, Calahorra draws out the meeting between Trebacio and Briana by adding luxuriant detail: "A great variety of trees, intertwined with fragrant jazmin, encircled them so that they could not be seen; the sweet sound of flowing water splashed over the shaped stones [of the fountain] in harmonious accord with the sweet melody of a great variety of harp-tongued birds nestled among the green branches, in such a way that together they increased the emperor's desire. Thinking how he could carry out his plan, his tongue was already too confused to speak to her and his ability to understand her failed, and all of his limbs were trembling so that his intention, understood by the princess, placed her in great danger. And wanting to leave that place, the emperor took her in his arms. And without being strong enough to deny satisfying his desires, nor she strong enough to defend herself from him, and just as Phoebus's radiant rays began to thin out and to form golden points, and the lanterns of the Last Firmament were losing their glow with the coming of darkness, and [with] the influences of the fortunate planets concurring, and through the wishes of the Universal Maker, the Caballero del Febo and Rosicler were engendered, whose rays of chivalry extended so far beyond them that all the great deeds of their ancestors and of their contemporaries were forgotten . . ." (1: 60–62; translation mine). Perión takes Elisena to bed with him; Trebacio takes not only Briana but the entire universe as well; Perión's three-candle night light is transformed into Trebacio's golden sun and the fading lanterns of the heavens; Perión's sparse room is replaced with Trebacio's garden of delights, including a crystalline fountain, Nature's melodious song, and perfumed air. Montalvo presents a black and white photo while Calahorra focuses his color movie projector first on the lush surroundings, then on a darkening fade-out of the sky with an obligatory voice-over from the narrator. Montalvo's following moral commentary on Elisena's loss of virginity stands in stark contrast to Calahorra's exulting prediction of future fame and glory for the twins.

It is tempting to label the *Amadís* a type A romance and the *Espejo* a type B, but this would wrongly call attention to their differences when what seems to make them recognizably different is the increased variety found in the *Espejo* and in other, later-sixteenth-century romances. Multiplication of plots within plots introduces more characters, more examples of love and valor, and, as we have seen, more description. But in the end the characters, stories, and examples are much the same; only their names, locations, and associates change. Amplification and repetition relate one romance to another in structural and thematic terms; variety helps to sustain their illusion of uniqueness.

Thus, the chivalric romance in Spain is a genre rooted in literary cannibalism, a cannibalism apparently sanctioned by an insatiable audience. Throughout the first half of the sixteenth century, each romance fed off its predecessor and was, in turn, devoured by hungry readers. Mysteriously, however, the popularity of romance waned after the mid-sixteenth century. In the thirty-three-year period between the abdication of Charles V (1555) and the defeat of the Armada (1588), the flood of romances was reduced to a trickle, and other types of prose fiction gradually dominated the marketplace. There is a temptation—indeed, some literary historians have been more than tempted—to ascribe this basic change in literary taste to the influence of these great political events. However, to do so is both naive and misleading.[17] What twentieth-century observers view as major historical watersheds were rarely so perceived by the broader society of Philip II's Spain. To understand shifts in reader demand, one must examine the many less significant, often forgotten, incidents and events which had a far more significant impact on the preferences and tastes of readers than did a few isolated, though well-publicized, major happenings.

First, one must attempt to define "the reader." I offer only a few suggestions on a topic which continues to baffle historians and critics alike.[18] The reading of chivalric romances was not the exclusive prerogative of feudal lords or confined, as one recent study asserts, to "a noble class turned sedentary after the conclusion of the reconquest."[19] Neither, however, can we assume that these works were enjoyed by peasants resting from their labors in the fields, as critics who draw their evidence from Cervantes's fiction would have us believe.[20] Of sixteenth-century readers we can say only two things: (1) they were literate, in a society where as much as 80 percent of the population could not read;[21] and (2) they had access to books, in a world without lending libraries or mass production or an extensive publishers' distribution network. Readers, therefore, can be assumed to have been educated; reasonably affluent, or connected to someone with sufficient capital to afford books; and resident in, or free to travel to, some urban center where books were available. These qualifications did not exclude as much of the population as one might at first suspect.

During the sixteenth century, Spain experienced an educational revolution. In 1470, there were six universities; by the early seventeenth century that number had grown to thirty-three.[22] Most graduates were trained in law and were absorbed into Spain's expanding bureaucracy. Thus to the traditional literate elite, there was added a growing pool of legal professionals, urbanized legal professionals, who resided in the administrative centers of Castile, the Americas, and the European imperial possessions of the Spanish crown. This new audience usually found printers ready to supply their needs. Twenty-three Spanish towns had printers in 1501. When the first press was established at Madrid in 1566, the new capital became the forty-sixth Spanish publishing center.[23] The product these shops supplied was not prohibitively expensive. For example, when the romance *Lepolemo* first appeared in 1521, its price was roughly equivalent to the wages received for three days' work by a laborer in Old Castile.[24]

Alterations in the composition of the reading public were part of broader changes occurring in Castilian society as a whole in the sixteenth century. Demographic expansion and accelerating urbanization created concerns that were new to the Iberian peninsula. In the first half of the century alone, it has been calculated that more than a million inhabitants were added to the population, with a 15 percent increase in the peninsula as a whole.[25] Even more significant was the shift in migration patterns within the country itself. Most Spanish cities doubled or tripled in size, while Madrid experienced a 900 percent increase. This process accelerated in the 1570s and 1580s as agriculture declined and populations were increasingly displaced from lands in northern Castile, settling in urban centers such as Madrid or Seville in search of work and/or charity.[26] Urban concentration produced urban crisis. Food supplies were uncertain, housing space was restricted, and city dwellers faced a threat to property and life as never before from crowded and unsanitary conditions. For much of Castilian society, changes in the later sixteenth century altered the basic conditions of life. Throughout the Middle Ages, energy had been directed toward the establishment of urban nuclei and the repopulation of newly conquered territory; in the early sixteenth century Castile faced the same problem and utilized the same methods in establishing colonial centers in the Indies. However, in the 1550s, there were no new frontiers available for conquest. Castilian society faced more immediate issues—the need to supply shelter and sustenance, employment and justice—for an increasingly concentrated population. It should not surprise us, therefore, that a different audience—one with altered expectations and attitudes, facing new issues which demanded immediate solutions—should demand different kinds of fiction.

One condition appears, on the surface, to have remained constant. Spain continued to make war in Europe.[27] If the chivalric enterprise was centered on honor, valor, strength in battle, and defense of king and kingdom, why did not the military operations of Philip II precipitate a new wave of interest in the romances of chivalry? Even Don Quijote, for instance, reminds us that a knight's horse comes before his lady. However, Geoffrey Parker has demonstrated the changes which combat underwent in the course of the sixteenth century, stating that "the eclipse of cavalry by infantry meant that victory in war . . . came to depend not on the quality of the combatants nor on the excellence of their armament, but on their numbers. A government bent on war had now to mobilize and equip every man who could be found" (Parker 5). Massive formations and not individual combat became the rule of the day. Men on horses were no match for pikemen, and by the 1570s in Holland all heavy Spanish cavalry were paid off and regrouped only when unfortified towns and pitched battles were foreseen (Parker 11). Heroic confrontations were a thing of the past in the world of new military realities: victory over fortified redoubts and brick and rubble constructions would come only with lengthy sieges, blockades, and starvation of the enemy (Parker 10). This was hardly a situation that favored individual prowess, and, perhaps more significantly, not the kind of scene that could be viewed by the knight's lady; the only "ladies" present were most likely the camp followers.

Those Spanish soldiers who read romances of chivalry—and according to Croce, there were many—were precisely the recruits so difficult to come by in the 1570s. "As early as 1575 an attempt to raise 2,500 men for service in Italy produced only 1,750 . . . (70 per cent of the quota)," (Parker 42), and obviously not all of these were literate. The problem was almost as bad for the army in Flanders. In 1567 the Duke of Alba was extremely pleased that "a large number of *particulares* [gentlemen] had volunteered to serve in the Spanish infantry which he led to the Netherlands" (Parker 40–41), but by the 1590s—the time of plague and famine in Castile—they were difficult to find. It may not be a coincidence that not one new romance was published during this decade and that only four old ones were reprinted, according to Maxime Chevalier.[28]

The romance by its very nature could not change to accommodate a changing society, whose growing awareness of immediate issues began to push aside the remote worlds of the chivalric experience. Variety came to be interpreted as confusion; the supernatural and the extraordinary—reflected in magic, enchantment, giants, dwarfs, over-endowed men and women—as unlifelike; secret births, marriages and sexual encounters as morally reprehensible; and the reading of such material as dangerous to one's soul and, in at least one case, to one's sanity.

In the very shadow of the romance, new literary tastes emerged and were satisfied by a new literature of immediacy. Though I would not suggest a cause-and-effect relationship, the first picaresque novel, *Lazarillo de Tormes,* appeared in 1554, just as interest in the romance began to wane. It was a harbinger of things to come, but it remained generically isolated until the publication of *Guzmán de Alfarache* at the end of the century. The picaresque novel, like the romance of chivalry, is pseudobiographical, but there is one critical reversal. The romances create an illusion of authorship by some unknown, past historian whose work has been rediscovered, translated, edited, and/or revised by some contemporary writer such as Montalvo or Calahorra. The picaresque novel is presented as a contemporary *auto*biography whose episodes have been selected and controlled by a fictional author. Thus there is a shift in narrative authority from distant source to immediate one. Implicit are temporal and spatial transformations as well. The new fiction was set not in a remote land and the distant past but in contemporary urban centers—Seville, Toledo, Madrid—with recognizable geographical landmarks and street names. Readers were invited to observe adventures—and misadventures—which were close at hand and to explore unfamiliar urban locations: the beggars' lodging, the brothel, the hangman's house. If the romance portrayed heroes whose visage could only be imagined, the picaresque novel revealed scars and deformities, and the lives and manners of characters who could be encountered in the marketplace and on the street.

For readers who retained their taste for the heroic, the Renaissance epic and the Moorish tale celebrated the deeds of Spanish historical figures and events in the 1550s and 1560s (Ercilla, *La Araucana,* 1569, 1579, 1584; Rufo, *Austríada,* 1584; *El Abencerraje y la hermosa Jarifa,* 1559). Spanish balladry also concentrated on the great deeds or the anecdotal adventures of Castilian heroes and of others who were deemed to be so, and while the *romances* seemed to be popular in the first half of the century, there was no extensive demand for them in collected form until the 1550s, when multiple editions began to appear (*Cancionero sin año,* 1550, 1555; *Primera parte de la Silva de varios romances,* 1550; *Romancero general,* 1600). The increasing demand to be related directly to a collective past found its most authoritative expression in the growing number of histories and historical compendia: the relatively uncritical *Los cuarenta libros del*

Compendio historial of Garibay (1571) culminated in the relatively judicious *Historiae de rebus Hispaniae* of Mariana (1592). Because of its language, Mariana's Latin work was intended for an educated elite, but the author seemed to recognize the existence of a much wider demand and translated it into Castilian six years later.

But even the relatively immediate past was too remote for much of the new audience. The here-and-now became a central issue. The establishment of permanent theaters in major cities in the 1560s (Barcelona, 1560) and 1570s (*corrales* in Seville, Valladolid, and Madrid, 1575) reflected the most immediate literary experience possible: live action. While Lope de Vega's invention of a national theater might have begun with the heroes of the *romancero* or of sixteenth-century chronicles, it changed its emphasis to fill the popular demand of its growing audience. The *comedia de capa y espada* (the cloak and dagger play) was set in contemporary society and dealt with current patterns of behavior, even though much of that behavior was based on chivalric codes. It is especially clear regarding the Spanish theater that demographic changes, urban growth, and a new audience were centrally involved in the foundation and development of fiction as immediacy.

Viewed from this perspective, Cervantes brought the chivalric romance into contemporary focus by making it part of the new literature of immediacy. Don Quijote is a knight-errant who comes from central Spain, not from Greece or Hungary. His adventures take place at the end of the sixteenth century, not in early Christian times or the Middle Ages. Roadside inns are his castles, peasant women his damsels in distress, and windmills his giants. It is commonplace to say that the figure of Don Quijote is the "word made flesh" of the sixteenth-century Spanish romance of chivalry. Cervantes's choice of an old man to fill the role of a knight-errant, however ridiculous it seemed at the time, is strangely emblematic of the end of the genre's career. The romance, already on its deathbed by the 1590s, was resuscitated one more time to undertake what turned out to be its most problematic mission, namely the accommodation of adventure and imagination to the new awareness of immediacy felt by its reading public. Historiography, theater, and the picaresque—not to mention more weighty material such as the sociological treatise of Pérez de Herrera or the innumerable *Memoriales* of the time[29]—reflected an attitude of self-absorption in which imagination and adventure had no place. Don Quijote too was self-absorbed, but his self-absorption was mediated by another world, a world that provided unpredictable

variety, freedom from the mundane, and an unending source of rec-
reational pleasure. Cervantes, in writing one more romance, wrote
the last "medieval" romance. But literary historians have no right to
lament its passing, for how else could we account for the origins of
the modern novel?

Notes

[1] Cf. Daniel Eisenberg, *Romances of Chivalry in the Spanish Golden Age*
(Newark, Del.: Juan de la Cuesta, 1982) xvii.

[2] Martín de Riquer, "Introducción," Eisenberg ix.

[3] This and the following bibliographical information is taken from Henry
Thomas, *Las novelas de caballerías españolas y portuguesas,* trans. Esteban
Pujals (Madrid: C.S.I.C., 1952), and from Daniel Eisenberg, *Castilian Ro-
mances of Chivalry in the Sixteenth Century,* Research Bibliographies and
Checklists (London: Grant and Cutler, 1979).

[4] Thomas 113–14.

[5] Thomas was the first to note the similarity in the names (69).

[6] Rodríguez de Montalvo, *Amadís of Gaul,* trans. E. B. Place, 2 vols. (Lexington, Ky.: U of Kentucky P, 1974) 1: 19–20.

[7] Grace Williams, "The *Amadís* Question," *Revue Hispanique* 21 (1909):
1–167; María Rosa Lida de Malkiel, "El desenlace del *Amadís* primitivo,"
Romance Philology 6 (1952–53): 283–89; Frank Pierce, *Amadís de Gaula*
(Boston: Twayne, 1976); Armando Durán, *Estructura y técnicas de la novela
sentimental y caballeresca* (Madrid: Gredos, 1973); James Fogelquist, *El
Amadís y el género de la historia fingida* (Madrid: Porrúa, 1982).

[8] Lida de Malkiel 289.

[9] Fogelquist 103. Cf. R. S. Loomis, ed., *Arthurian Literature in the Middle
Ages: A Collaborative History* (Oxford: Oxford UP, 1959), where Lida de
Malkiel summarizes the views of Bohigas Balaguer: "the central plot of *Amadís* coincides with that of *Lancelot.* In both an unknown youth of royal descent is accepted at the court of a king, whom he serves loyally, except that he
falls in love with the sovereign's wife or daughter. There are two main vicissitudes in the course of the love-affair: first, the knight rescues the lady from
an abductor, thus earning her love or promise of love; second, the lady,
jealous on account of a false report, rejects the knight, who loses (or comes
close to losing) his mind and lives in solitude. The chief accomplishment of
both heroes is the conquest of a marvellous abode—the Joyeuse Garden or
the Insula Firme—to which they take their ladies in moments of peril" (415).

[10] This slightly edited quotation of the plot summary is taken from Pierce
27–29.

[11] According to Lida De Malkiel, "La vida de Amadís, que se abría así con
el motivo popular de la exposición del héroe recién nacido, se cerraba así con
el motivo popular de la muerte del héroe en armas contra su hijo desconocido"
(286).

[12] Fogelquist 127–28; translation mine.

[13] See Franceso Foffano, *Il poema cavalleresco* (Milano: F. Villardi, 1904):
"Parimenti, il Tasso lascia aparte episodi che non hanno stretta attinenza coll'

azione principale, e che ne attarderebbero senza ragione lo svolgimento; egli vuol dare al poema la maggiore unità possible, e far si che le avventure disparate, possano . . . raggrapparsi intorno a pochi personaggi principali: cerca insomma nella varietà l'unità" (177–78).

[14] Diego Ortúñez de Calahorra, *Espejo de príncipes y cavalleros*, ed. Daniel Eisenberg, 6 vols. (Madrid: Espasa Calpe, 1975).

[15] This plot summary is essentially a translation, with several omissions and modifications, from Eisenberg, Introducción, xix–xxix.

[16] Ortúñez de Calahorra 6: 246.

[17] Here I must refer to Eisenberg's *Romances of Chivalry,* a book which has served me well up to this point: "But certainly one of the principal causes, if not the single most important cause, of the decline in composition of new romances was the abdication of Carlos V in favor of his son Felipe II. That Carlos' reign ended in 1555 is no coincidence" (48). See also p. 104 for statements that hedge even less.

[18] Maxime Chevalier, *Lectura y lectores en la España del siglo XVI y XVII* (Madrid: Ediciones Turner, 1976), esp. ch. 1, pp. 65–103: "El público de las novelas de caballerías"; and Daniel Eisenberg, "Who Read the Romances of Chivalry?" *Romances* 89–118.

[19] Eisenberg, *Romances* 120.

[20] See, for instance, Alban Forcione, *Cervantes, Aristotle, and the* Persiles (Princeton: Princeton UP, 1970) 13; Eisenberg, *Romances,* cites a list of examples, including Forcione's.

[21] Chevalier 19.

[22] Richard L. Lagan, *Students and Society in Early Modern Spain* (Baltimore: Johns Hopkins UP, 1974) 63.

[23] Francisco Vindel, *Manual de conocimientos técnicos y culturales para profesionales del libro* (Madrid: Góngora, 1948) 130–32, 144–46.

[24] The book sold for 95 *maravedís* (for this and the prices of several other romances, see Eisenberg, *Romances* 99). A laborer received 29 *maravedís* per day in 1521; see Earl J. Hamilton, *American Treasure and the Price Revolution in Spain, 1501–1650* (Cambridge: Harvard UP, 1934) 395, for money wages in Old Castile-León.

[25] J. Vicens Vives et al., *Historia de España y América* (Barcelona: Ed. Vicens Vives, 1961) 3: 14–15.

[26] Noël Salomon, *La vida rural castellana en tiempos de Felipe II,* trans. Francesc Espinet Burunat (Barcelona: Editorial Planeta, 1973).

[27] Geoffrey Parker, *The Army of Flanders and the Spanish Road, 1567–1659* (Cambridge: Cambridge UP, 1972).

[28] See Chevalier, between pp. 64 and 65.

[29] Cristóbal Pérez de Herrera, *Discursos del amparo de los legítimos pobres y reducción de los fingidos* (Madrid: L. Sanchez, 1598); for the *Memoriales* see Evaristo Correa Calderón, *Registro de arbitristas, economistas y reformadores españoles (1500–1936)* (Madrid: Fundación Universitaria Española, 1981).

CERVANTES AS READER
OF ARIOSTO

Marina Scordilis Brownlee

Many of the major preoccupations of modern literary theory
(issues of reader response, genre theory, the ontological status of the
text, and so on) have their origins to a large extent in sixteenth-
century Italy. For it was in the first half of that century that Aristotle's *Poetics* was rediscovered and translated into Italian.[1] The second half of the century was dominated by numerous attempts to
apply Aristotle's aesthetic principles to Renaissance literature, particularly to the genre of romance which, of course, had no Aristotelian paradigm.

The extended controversy which resulted from this rediscovery involved two theoretical schools represented on the one hand by the
so-called Ancients and on the other by the Moderns. The basis of the
argument waged in the literary academies had to do with four interrelated principles of composition: (1) unity of plot (a single plot
with a single hero), (2) verisimilitude, (3) character decorum, and
(4) exemplarity.[2]

The sixteenth-century Ancients found the romance form to be de-
ficient in each category. It is important to note, moreover, that
Ariosto's *Orlando Furioso* was the prime object of this neo-Aristotelian controversy—because of its monumentality, its artistic ingenuity
and its immense popularity as entertainment literature.[3]

In terms of unity, the critics argued, the *Furioso* fails from the start
since, as the first verse of the poem ("Le donne, i cavallier, l'arme,

gli amori, / le cortesie, l'audaci imprese io canto" [1.1, 1–2]) (I sing
of knights and ladies, of love and arms) attests, romance and epic
subjects are combined.[4] While there are numerous plots, there are
also numerous principal heroes. Orlando is one of the heroes (although he is off-stage for thirty-one of the forty-six cantos of the
poem). Ruggiero—ancestor of Ippolito d'Este, Ariosto's patron—is
another principal hero, for it is the founding of the House of Este
which is celebrated at the conclusion of the poem with his marriage,
not Orlando's. Astolfo, who goes on a Dantean journey from Hell
to the Earthly Paradise to the Moon (where St. John the Evangelist
explains human nature to him), is yet another candidate for principal hero. Similarly, the obtrusive narrator himself is one of the
principal heroes of the work, carrying on an extra-diegetic discourse
addressed to his patron or his reading public in general in each of
the cantos, dwelling on his own love affair, and the like. The forty-
sixth (and final) canto begins, moreover, with an elaborate description of Ariosto's own ship reaching the safe harbor at the end of his
lengthy poetic voyage, greeted by the most illustrious poets and
scholars of his day, replete with the triumphal pealing of bells and
blaring of trumpets.

Verisimilitude, the believability necessary for a work to be enjoy-
able, according to the neo-Aristotelian critics, is grossly violated by
Ariosto as well. Magical armor, flying horses, monsters, and necro-
mancers abound. Imaginary geography exists in tandem with real
geography. And, finally, the chronological time line is collapsed so
that Ariosto's narrator moves effortlessly from the time of the Trojan War to eighth-century Carolingian France to twelfth-century
Arthurian France to sixteenth-century Italy. In terms of character
decorum, the neo-Aristotelians deplored the depiction of a wise and
noble warrior (Orlando) gone mad as a result of his infatuation
with a woman (Angelica). In terms of exemplarity also, the *Furioso*
was considered unacceptable. Orlando's behavior is clearly not an example to be imitated. To make matters worse, the narrator himself
is mad, as he explicitly admits to his readers in the second stanza of
the poem.[5]

Upholding the Aristotelian precept of literature as imitation of
actions worthy of emulation, the Ancients called for the replacement
of romance by epic, invoking Virgil as their model. The Moderns
sought to reconcile Aristotelian theory with Renaissance romance
practice, to purify constructively the "flaws" of the romance genre—
recognizing on the one hand its importance as entertainment litera-

ture and on the other the need to change with the times. Tasso was the spokesman of the latter group, as was Cervantes's Canon of Toledo at the end of part 1 of the *Quijote*.[6]

Cervantes's initial assertion that he is writing the *Quijote* to discredit the romances of chivalry, his attacks on the Spanish national theater, his criticism of the *vulgo* (to whom both the romances and Lope de Vega's plays appealed greatly), his adherence to the neo-Aristotelian precepts espoused by the Canon in the *Persiles,* his very last work—all have contributed to the assumption that Cervantes himself was a rather staunch advocate of neo-Aristotelian theory and practice.

By extension, Cervantists have tended to minimize the importance of Ariosto for Cervantes. As Maxime Chevalier's *L'Arioste en Espagne* reveals, comparative analyses of the two texts have confined themselves largely to isolated and ungenerative source studies of particular characters or episodes of the *Furioso* which appear in the *Quijote,* of which there are many. Basing his work on a lengthy review of previous scholarship, Chevalier concludes that no programmatic transformation of the *Furioso* exists in the Cervantine text: "les efforts déployés en ce sens on été plus tenaces que fructueux."[7]

Despite this normative neo-Aristotelian side of Cervantes's aesthetic theory, there exists at the same time an unmistakable voice of skepticism on the matter. As Alban Forcione explains, "the polarity marking [Cervantes's] attitude toward nearly every province of human experience is also present in his attitude toward art."[8] It is this skeptical countercurrent which is the object of this essay—as expressed in generic, structural, and characterological parallels shared by the *Furioso* and the *Quijote*.

Textual evidence exposes Cervantes's skeptical presentation of this literary debate over the relative merits of the Ancients and the Moderns. The Canon of Toledo himself, we recall, is the author of an unfinished romance. Although he has written more than one hundred pages of this manuscript, however, he cannot bring himself to finish it because he knows that his "ideal readers"—the cultivated few who will understand and appreciate his "purified romance" in accord with neo-Aristotelian doctrine—constitute a very small group indeed.[9] Don Quijote's syllogistic reasoning ultimately succeeds in undermining the Canon's position on the primacy of verisimilitude. (The Canon, for example, is willing to believe in the existence of a wooden horse which flies through the air.) The outcome of this debate is, as Forcione observes, that "belief depends ultimately on the will of the individual reader, and attempts to define sharply the limits of the truth which the reader will tolerate are idle.[10]

In true Cervantine fashion, what links the discussion between the Canon and the priest to the ensuing discussion between Don Quijote and the Canon is a parodic reworking of the substance of this discussion. Sancho, adopting the stance of an uncompromising classicist, attempts to reveal the absurdity of his master's belief that he is enchanted by subjecting it to the scrutiny demanded by the Canon's principle of verisimilitude. Don Quijote responds in the manner of the Moderns—invoking their perennial argument that "contra el uso de los tiempos no hay que argüir" (492) (customs change with the changing times). An enchanted person, Sancho points out, neither eats nor sleeps, nor does he need to relieve himself of bodily wastes.

> —Verdad dices, Sancho—respondió don Quijote—; pero ya te he dicho que hay muchas maneras de encantamentos. y podría ser que con el tiempo se hubiesen mudado de unos en otros, y que agora se use que los encantados hagan todo lo que yo hago, aunque antes no lo hacían. De manera, que contra el uso de los tiempos no hay que argüir ni de qué hacer consecuencias. Yo sé y tengo para mí que voy encantado y esto me basta para la seguridad de mi conciencia. (491–92)

["You are quite right," replied Don Quijote, "but I have told you already that there are many kinds of enchantments; and time may have changed the fashion from one kind to another. It may be usual now for people under a spell to do all that I do, although they did not before; so there is no argument or drawing conclusions against the usage of the times. I most certainly know that I am enchanted, and that is sufficient to ease my conscience." (433–34)]

This scatological interlude thus deflates the very valid aesthetic principle of custom itself—and, by extension, the entire controversy of Ancients versus Moderns.[11]

The academic debating of artistic freedom per se is, as we see, parodically undermined at the end of part 1 of the *Quijote*. However, the parody extends even further, for the first part of the work ends, significantly, with a series of mock-academic sonnets—all written by academicians—eulogizing Don Quijote, Dulcinea, Sancho, and Rocinante. Further, they present Don Quijote and Rocinante as having surpassed their Ariostan counterparts.[12] At the end of the presentation of the sonnets, we read:

> Estos fueron los versos que se pudieron leer; los demás, por estar carcomida la letra, se entregaron a un académico para que por conjeturas

los declarase. Tiénese noticia que lo ha hecho, a costa de muchas vigilias y mucho trabajo, y que tiene intención de sacallos a luz, con esperanza de la tercera salida de don Quijote. (523)

[These were such verses as could be deciphered. The rest, as the characters were worm-eaten, were entrusted to a university scholar to guess their meaning. We are informed that he has done so, at the cost of many nights of study and much labor, and that he intends to publish them, which gives us hope of a third expedition of Don Quijote. (461)]

What follows this definitive deflation of academic discourse are the words "Forsi altro canterà con miglior plectio"—a mongrel, hispanicized version of verse 8, stanza 16, canto 30 of the *Furioso:* "Forse altri canterà con miglior plettro" (Perhaps someone else will sing [this song] with a better plectrum).

Cervantes's choice of this Ariostan verse is highly significant for several interrelated reasons. The passage is traditionally interpreted as nothing more than an example of the well-known romance construct of continuation—witness Chrétien de Troyes, Guillaume de Lorris, and the like. Cervantes is, therefore, seen as adopting the pose of the romancer who invites continuation. Yet more is at issue here.

First, this verse (one of a total of 38,736) does not come at a structurally significant point in the *Furioso.* Rather it is the eighth verse of the sixteenth stanza of a canto containing a total of ninety-five stanzas. Its significance is instead thematic.

In the *Furioso* this verse functions to indicate officially that the love intrigue of Angelica (the cause for Orlando's madness) will no longer be pursued. She takes a young African soldier as her lover; thus she can no longer serve as the ineffable ideal maiden worthy of absolute devotion as she had been for Orlando. Ariosto chooses to leave behind that narrative thread of Orlando's wish-fulfillment fantasy[13] for a different subject matter—a more problematized view of love and human nature in general, culminating in the theme of universal madness.

Cervantes understood this verse in the Ariostan context and included it in the *Quijote* not merely to signify a lack of poetic closure for part 1 but also to indicate his emulation of Ariosto in altering his own course. The point is made more explicitly at the beginning of part 2, ch. 1, when Don Quijote himself repeats the seminal verse of the *Furioso,* this time no longer in a mongrelized hispano-Italian, but in perfect Spanish ("quizá otro cantará con mejor plectro" (555), glossing its meaning thereafter. Ariosto did not continue Angelica's

story, in Don Quijote's own opinion, because of its sordid nature
and her generally base comportment. Don Quijote further remarks
that

> sin duda que esto fue como profecía; que los poetas también se llaman
> *vates,* que quiere decir *adivinos.* Véese esta verdad clara, porque des-
> pués acá un famoso poeta andaluz lloró y cantó sus lágrimas, y otro
> famoso y único poeta castellano cantó su hermosura. (551)

[no doubt [Ariosto's invitation] was a kind of prophecy; for poets
are called *vates,* which means diviners. The truth is plain to see, for
since then a famous Andalusian poet has wept and sung her tears,
and another famous and unique poet has sung her beauty. (408)]

These are Barahona de Soto and Lope de Vega respectively. They
chose to follow out the path which Ariosto rejected for a better one.

The implicit irony of Ariosto's invitation was clearly understood
by Cervantes. Indeed, from the very beginning of the *Quijote*—in
the prefatory verses—Cervantes establishes none other than himself
as the true continuator whom Ariosto prophesied. The first laudatory
poem (addressed by Urganda the Unknown to the *Quijote* itself)
identifies the subject of the work in the third stanza by citing the
first verse of the *Furioso,* "[de] damas, armas, caballe—" (28) (Of
ladies, arms and cavaliers),—that is, precisely the same commingled
romance and epic subject matters as the Italian text, with the same
lack of unity of plot for which the earlier text was so severely criticized by the neo-Aristotelians. Two verses later, moreover, Don
Quijote is referred to as a "new Orlando."[14] Shortly thereafter, Orlando himself offers a dedicatory sonnet to Don Quijote, saying, "No
puedo ser su igual; que este decoro / se debe a tus proezas y a tu
fama, / puesto que, como yo, perdiste el seso. / . . . / iguales en
amor con mal suceso" (33) (I cannot be thy rival, for thy fame /
And prowess rise above all rivalry, / Albeit both bereft of wits we
go . . . Love binds us in a fellowship of woe).[15]

These multiple linkings of the *Quijote* to the *Furioso* are further
strengthened in part 1, ch. 6, during the inquisition of Don Quijote's
library. The priest, in speaking of Ariosto and his Spanish adaptors
says, "si aquí le hallo, y que habla en otra lengua que la suya, no le
guardaré respeto alguno; pero si habla en su idioma, le pondré sobre
mi cabeza" (70) (If I find [Ariosto] here speaking any language but
his own [Italian], I shall show him no respect. [He will be con-
signed to the flames.] But if he speaks his own tongue, I will wear
him next [to] my heart" [59]).

By choosing the Ariostan verse both to end part 1 of the *Quijote* and to begin part 2, after having clearly discredited all previous Spanish continuators, Cervantes is implicitly, yet unmistakably, establishing the *Furioso* as a programmatic subtext for the *Quijote*. The transition of this verse from a mongrel hispanicized Italian to pure Spanish is, I suggest, an indication that Cervantes presents his own work as the authentic Spanish continuation of Ariosto. Having established and deflated the neo-Aristotelian controversy between Ancients and Moderns in part 1, Cervantes offers the literary text (first the *Furioso,* then the *Quijote*) to speak for itself.

This self-presentation by Cervantes is corroborated by the fact that the vast majority of allusions to the *Furioso* found in the *Quijote* are taken from part 1 of the *Furioso* and, in addition, most occur in part 1 of the *Quijote*.[16] Furthermore, Don Quijote and Orlando are both mad in the first parts of their respective works and are cured in the second parts. In addition, part 1 of each text transpires in eight months' time (as we are told near the very end of each first part).[17] Part 1 in each case offers a particular example of individual madness, part 2 an image of universal madness.

Broadly speaking, both first parts are concerned with presenting various generic constructs and deflating them thereafter. In Ariosto, to take only a few of the numerous examples which he offers, we see Ginevra's faithful lover Ariodante deciding to commit suicide by hurling himself off a precipice into the sea (having believed the false rumors that his lady has been unfaithful). He takes the tragic plunge, as so many lovers have done. Yet he changes his mind in midstream, as it were, and swims to shore, being reunited with Ginevra and marrying her immediately thereafter (6.4, 6.14–15). Similarly, Angelica finds herself at the mercy of a lecherous old monk who drugs her so that she will be unable to resist his sexual assaults. However, when the longed-for moment arrives, he finds himself to be impotent (8.50). In another case we see Orlando, who had been an illustrious defender of the Christian cause, abandon Charlemagne's camp to search for Angelica. He disguises himself in Moorish dress so as to move undetected among the Infidel, and, moreover, he speaks Arabic so fluently that he is taken for a native (9.2–5). Likewise, Ruggiero, when on the verge of raping Angelica, cannot unhook the many buttons and snaps of his armor quickly enough, and she escapes (10.114).

On the one hand, each of these episodes offers an unanticipated development by departing from the generic norm. Yet in addition, each departure is an example of the so-called confrontation of life and literature consistently ascribed to the *Quijote,* that is, reality intruding on fiction. Any literary genre, as both authors sought to illustrate, offers only a selective, partial presentation of reality. And in their respective texts they repeatedly demonstrate the selectivity of any given genre. Ariosto employs the generic traditions of epic and romance, consistently setting up one construct after another, raising the reader's "generic expectations" and then deflating them. Cervantes employs the same type of generic manipulation in part 1 of the *Quijote;* however, in addition to epic and chivalric romance he treats virtually all other major (and several minor) genres: pastoral romance, Greek romance, picaresque, Italianate novella, theater, historical novel, mariological miracle narrative, as well as several others.

Although Cervantes clearly broadened the scope of generic manipulation to include more literary forms than epic and romance, the net effect is the same. In each case man is liberated from mythic paradigms; he does not conform to predetermined types. In other words, both authors explode the neo-Aristotelian notion of character decorum—the belief that young men, for example, are impetuous, old men cautious, slaves sneaky, young women passive, gullible, and inarticulate.

This liberation from mythic paradigms as represented by the various genres, which corresponds to a liberation from transcendent views, was essential before the novel could emerge. In each case, a critique of literature is the necessary point of departure for a critique of reality itself.

A consensus seems to exist that part 2 of the *Furioso* is qualitatively different from part 1, by virtue of its noticeably more somber tone. Nonetheless, in terms of its generic identity several different interpretations exist.

Eugenio Donato, in his Girardian analysis of the text, views the second part as being, like the first, romance in nature. He concludes his analysis by affirming that "the referential aspect of Ariosto's narrative is simply the indefinite realm of other narratives."[18]

David Quint, on the other hand, avers that "with the destruction of Atlante's palace [at the very midpoint of the poem, canto 23] the *Furioso* jettisons romance midway in order to proceed to an epic closure."[19] More precisely, the fundamental difference which Quint finds between parts 1 and 2 has to do with the treatment of time. As he observes, part 1 of the poem takes place in a timeless realm. Knights do battle, pursue damsels, are manipulated by sorcerers, and have seemingly endless, nearly fatal adventures. Yet their mortality, it seems, is perpetually deferred. Indeed, the first major character to perish—Pinabello (an avatar of Pinabel in the *Chanson de Roland*)—does not do so until the end of part 1 (22.96). This artificial universe, protected from time and its contingencies, is, moreover, referred to explicitly by the African necromancer Atlante, tutor and guardian of Ruggiero. We learn in canto 12 (sts. 21, 22) that Atlante's principal goal is to prevent Ruggiero from dying, for he wishes to perpetuate the romance world:

> Questo era un nuovo e disusato incanto
> ch'avea composto Atlante di Carena,
> perché Ruggier fosse occupato tanto
> in quel travaglio, in quella dolce pena,
> che 'l mal' influsso n'andasse da canto,
> l'influsso ch'a morir giovene il mena.
> Dopo il castel d'acciar, che nulla giova.
> e dopo Alcina, Atlante ancor fa pruova.
>
> Non pur costui, ma tutti gli altri ancora,
> che di valore in Francia han maggior fama,
> acciò che di lor man Ruggier non mora,
> condurre Atlante in questo incanto trama.
> E mentre fa lor far quivi dimora,
> perché di cibo non patischin brama,
> sì ben fornito avea tutto il palagio,
> che donne e cavallier vi stanno ad agio. (12.21–22)

[This was a new and unusual piece of magic devised by the wizard Atlas, who meant thus to keep Ruggiero so preoccupied with this bittersweet love-quest of his that the evil influence would pass him by—the influence appointing him to an early death. The steel-girt castle had proved useless, so had Alcina; here he was, trying something else. / It was not only Ruggiero whom Atlas plotted to draw in this magic trap, but anyone else in France who enjoyed the highest reputation for valor—these he lured in lest Ruggiero die at their hands. And while he condemned them to this enforced residence, he had left the palace so abundantly provided that knights and ladies could dwell there in comfort and eat their fill. (118)]

Nonetheless, despite Atlante's efforts, his palace is ultimately destroyed by the Book of Reason which Logistilla had given to Astolfo (22.23). As a result, the disenchanted former prisoners became subject to time and history.

Yet, although time does finally intrude on these characters in a way in which it had not done during the first half of the poem, it does not alter the concern for romance subject matter, it does not in fact move from romance in part 1 to epic in part 2. The timeless yearnings of the characters are largely the same, the principal difference being that in part 2 they often meet with disillusionment and unfulfillment.

Speaking of the treatment of love in the second part of the *Furioso,* C. P. Brand explains: "A more serious, sad and even bitter note characterizes several of the later stories and we are conscious of an overall change or development of tone from the uncomplicated pursuit of Angelica in the early cantos to the earnest and murky passions of the later ones. It is noteworthy also that whereas the love stories in the first half of the poem are largely concerned with bachelor knights and unwed maidens, or at least with wooing, falling in love and the first flush of love or desire, the later cantos present us with a succession of married women and especially men, no longer concerned to win their lovers but preoccupied with keeping those incipient horns from their worried heads."[20]

Rather than being epic in nature, as Quint maintains, I would suggest that part 2 of the *Furioso,* while continuing the admixture of romance and epic matters, offers a more novelistic approach to its characters.

René Girard observes that the novel implies a linear development which, as Donato explains, "has to take into account both the journey of the character through the domain of desire and at the end his distancing from it to establish the epistemological privilege of the subject's claim to hold a discourse which is not a discourse of desire but a discourse about desire and about the [disenchanting] truth of desire."[21] This kind of shift is (*pace* Donato) precisely what we see in part 2 of the *Furioso.* In addition to anguished individuals who dwell on their imperfect love lives, we see Ariosto employing perspectivism; several characters are responding to the same circumstances in markedly different ways—the novelistic concern for how something is in all its human complexity, as opposed to the idealized romance depiction of how it should be.

In other words, there is a proliferation of doubles in part 2 of the *Furioso* (as there is in part 2 of the *Quijote*). To take one example of the many which Ariosto offers, Rinaldo is disenchanted in terms of Angelica (who, we recall, has cast her lot with Medoro, the African soldier). Rinaldo is pursued by a monster (Jealousy personified) and is rescued by Scorn personified. He is cured by drinking at a magic fountain whose water has the effect of making him hate Angelica. Shortly thereafter he meets a knight who promises that he will reveal whether Rinaldo's wife is chaste if Rinaldo is willing to drink from a special goblet (an episode which is recalled by Cervantes in the Tale of Foolish Curiosity, 1.33–34). If she is chaste, none of the wine will spill onto Rinaldo's chest. Rinaldo refuses the test because he realizes the need to have faith in his mate, the need at any rate to maintain the illusion of fidelity. He tells the knight:

> Gli è questo creder mio, com'io l'avessi
> ben certo, e poco accrescer lo potrei:
> sì che, s'al paragon mi succedessi,
> poco il meglio saria ch'io ne trarrei;
> ma non già poco il mal, quando vedessi
> quel di Clarice mia, ch'io non vorrei.
> Metter saria mille contra uno a giuoco;
> che perder si può molto e acquistar poco. (43.66)

[My belief in my wife amounts to a certainty—I could add little to it. Therefore, had I succeeded in the test, I should have derived little advantage from it; but I should have done myself no little harm, had I discovered in my Clarice that which I had rather not. It would have been a wager of one thousand to one, with a great deal to lose and little to gain. (516)]

The knight who offers him the goblet himself had taken the test, realized his wife's infidelity, and been miserable ever since. Giocondo and King Astolfo, on the other hand, when they realize their wives' infidelity, retaliate by sleeping with thousands of women throughout Europe (27.73). When they find not one faithful wife anywhere, they happily return to their own wives, realizing that such is the standard behavior in women. Immediately thereafter, a mature man who is not identified by name speaks in defense of women and against the double standard by which men behave. The very next canto (29), by contrast, presents Isabella allowing herself to be beheaded by Rodomonte in her unassailable constancy to the deceased Zerbino rather than submitting to Rodomonte's amorous advances.

We thus see the metaphysical and epistemological reasons for the multiple threads of Ariosto's verbal tapestry: human nature defies categorization according to the idealizing genres of epic and romance. What Ariosto offers instead is a vision of man in all his novelistic complexity.

The treatment of epic in the second part of the *Furioso* is, significantly, analogous to the problematization of romance. For one thing, we find the horrors of war repeatedly juxtaposed with chivalric ideals. In canto 36, st. 5, in fact, it is none other than Ipollito himself, Ariosto's patron, who is rebuked for his "unchivalrous" deployment of artillery.

A further example of the problematizing of the epic matter of part 2 of the *Furioso* is evidenced by Ruggiero's dilemma throughout much of the second half of the poem. He and Marfisa, as we learn thanks to Atlante's revelation in Canto 36, sts. 59, 66, are not only brother and sister, twins in fact, but also descended from Christians (st. 73).

This information complicates Ruggiero's life tremendously for, although he is now for the first time aware of his Christian heritage and does, in fact, become baptized, he still feels a real debt of gratitude to Agramonte, commander in chief of the Infidel forces:

> Oh come a quel parlar leva la faccia
> la bella Bradamante, e ne gioisce!
> E conforta Ruggier, che così faccia,
> come Marfisa sua ben l'ammonisce;
> e venga a Carlo e conoscer si faccia,
> che tanto onora, lauda e riverisce
> del suo padre Ruggier la chiara fama,
> ch'ancor guerrier senza alcun par lo chiama.
>   Ruggiero accortamente le rispose
> che da principio questo far dovea;
> ma per non bene aver note le cose,
> come ebbe poi, tardato troppo avea.
> Ora, essendo Agramante che gli pose
> la spada al fianco, farebbe opra rea
> dandogli morte, e saria traditore;
> che già tolto l'avea per suo signore. (36.79–80)

[[Bradamante] encouraged Ruggiero to do as Marfisa admonished him. He should come and present himself to Charlemagne, she said, who paid such honor, adulation, and respect to the bright name of his father, Ruggiero, and even now called him a peerless champion. / Ruggiero was quick to aver that this indeed is what he should have done at the outset; but that, not having well understood the facts as he afterwards did, he had left it too late: as it was Agramant who had buckled on his sword, it would be a crime to slay him, and he would be a traitor, for he had accepted him as his liege lord.]

These verses illustrate both the complications inherent in the epic world per se and the difference between the values of the epic world and those of romance—a key theme throughout the *Furioso* as a whole. They reflect the complexities of life which neither genre by itself can adequately communicate, as Ariosto took pains to illustrate.

Whereas part 1 offered the uncomplicated (and unrealistic) yearnings and actions of its unreflective characters, part 2 offers substantially more reflective characters—time and its contingencies, failed quests. The move from idealistic action to realistic reflection also characterizes the two parts of the *Quijote*.

In part 1 we see Don Quijote energetically embarking on one romance quest after another. In part 2, he is reflective and largely the recipient of the actions of others. Indeed, the first adventure initiated by him in part 2 does not occur until chapter 29 (the Enchanted Boat sequence). It is, moreover, the first time Don Quijote gives up a quest, realizing its illusory nature.[22] Significant also is the fact that much of the action of part 2 takes place at night. The seemingly endless circular time of part 1 (when Don Quijote appeared to be for the most part unaffected by his failures) has given way to the linear time of his progressive disenchantment in part 2. This move from the circular time of romance to the linear time of the novel thus parallels the Ariostan progression from the first to the second part of the *Furioso*.

Similarly, both Cervantes's and Ariosto's second parts contain voyages of ascent and descent—the traditional loci of illumination in romance. In Ariosto the voyage to the Moon (34) represents the aerial journey, while in the *Quijote* it is the trip on Clavileño (2.41). The underworld, oracular cave construct is represented by Astolfo's journey to Hell (34), which corresponds to Don Quijote's experience in the Cave of Montesinos (2.22).

Don Quijote, we remember, does not believe Sancho's account of his aerial voyage on Clavileño, just as Sancho doubts the Cave episode. The outcome of this mutual skepticism is Don Quijote's remark in chapter 41: "llegándose don Quijote a Sancho, al oído le dijo:—Sancho, pues vos queréis que se os crea lo que habéis visto en el cielo, yo quiero que vos me creáis a mi lo que vi en la cueva de Montesinos. Y no os digo más" (837) (Don Quijote went up to Sancho and whispered in his ear: "Sancho, if you want me to believe what you saw in the sky, I wish you to accept my account of what I saw in the Cave of Montesinos. I say no more" [735]).

In Ariosto's text it is important to note that Astolfo, Orlando's English cousin, not Orlando, is entrusted with the extraterrestrial journey. As we learn, Astolfo has been predestined to go to the Moon to regain Orlando's lost wits for him. St. John the Evangelist, his guide, explains to Astolfo that whatever we lose on Earth (empires, treasure, fame, unfulfilled desires, lost moments—in short, everything imaginable, both tangible and intangible) is deposited on the Moon. There is, however, one notable exception, namely lunacy, madness, which remains perpetually on Earth: "sol la pazzia non v'è poca né assai; / che sta qua giù, né se ne parte mai" (34.81, 7-8) Folly . . . whatever its degree, is missing from [the Moon]: it stays down here [on earth] and never leaves us).

Astolfo recovers Orlando's wits (which have been preserved in a bottle), as well as "a good portion of his own [wits]" (34.84, 3)— much to his amazement. He inhales his wits and is told by St. John, in a very Erasmian moment, that madness is universal:

> Altri in amar lo perde, altri in onori,
> altri in cercar, scorrendo il mar, richezze;
> altri ne le speranze de' signori,
> altri dietro alle magiche sciocchezze;
> altri in gemme, altri in opre di pittori,
> et altri in altro che più d'altro aprezze.
> Di sofisti e d'astrologhi raccolto,
> e di poeti ancor ve n'era molto.
>   Astolfo tolse il suo; che gliel concesse
> lo Scrittor de l'oscura Apocalisse.
> l'ampolla in ch'era al naso sol si messe,
> e par che quello al luogo suo ne gisse:
> e che Turpin da indi in qua confesse
> ch'Astolfo lungo tempo saggio visse;
> ma ch'uno error che fece poi, fu quello
> ch'un'altra volta gli levò il cervello. (34.85-86)

[Some lose their wits in loving, some in seeking honours, some in scouring the seas in search of wealth, some in hopes placed in princes, some in cultivating magical baubles; some lose them over jewels, some over paintings, and some over other objects which they value above all else. Here the wits of sophists, astrologers, and poets abound.

Astolfo collected his, for the author of the mysterious Apocalypse permitted him. He held to his nose the phial containing his wits and they just seemed to make their way back into place. Turpin asserts, it seems, that from there on Astolfo lived sensibly for a long time, until a subsequent caprice of his lost him his wits a second time. (420-21)]

Despite this privileged moment of illumination, then, we see that Astolfo remains a backslider. Nonetheless, he fulfills his task, returning to Earth, where he presents Orlando with his wits in a bottle, which the latter inhales according to St. John's instructions. He is instantly cured of his love madness, no longer possessed by mad love for Angelica. In fact, Orlando appears to be indifferent to women for the remainder of the poem.

The manner of Orlando's cure, as well as Astolfo's, is strikingly artificial, mechanical. There are, however, other characters whom we encounter, as discussed above, who do grow psychologically as a result of their various confrontations with adversity.

What differentiates the *Quijote* from the *Furioso* in this regard is the fact that Ariosto has multiple heroes, some of whom are mechanically cured (Orlando, Astolfo), whereas others (including the narrator) are not.[23] From this clear disparity of presentation the question which arises in the reader's mind is one of hierarchy, namely, How does one make sense out of these multiple progressions? The poem requires, as Robert Durling explains, "an act of mind that integrates all the complexities of tone and event."[24] It is the reader himself who must wade through the mad narrator's polymorphous text—this *lucido intervallo,* a brief "lucid interval" in the face of universal madness, as Ariosto describes his poem (24.3). Unlike Cervantes, Ariosto does not entrust his larger meanings to one or two characters, such as Don Quijote and Sancho. The Ariostan reader must order the text for himself, retrospectively deciding just what its larger implications are. He has total freedom to read and interpret the first-person narrative of this madman as he chooses.

Cervantes, I suggest, encapsulates Ariosto's mad narrator into the person of Don Quijote—inscribing him within the text, giving him a rational audience of readers who serve to anchor his subjective madness in the world of objective empirical reality.[25] The first-person Ariostan narrator becomes the third-person madman, Don Quijote— a literary madman whose madness (like that of Ariosto's narrator figure) stems from Ovidian, Carolingian, and Arthurian literature. The fantastic landscapes, monsters, and enchantments of Ariosto's mad narrator are equally the subject of Don Quijote's deranged mental energies. The collapsed time line of Ariosto's narrator (offering a steady counterpoint between the literary past and his contemporary society) are analogous to Don Quijote's mental divagations between that same literary past and his contemporary society.

Finally, Cervantes turns Ariosto's first-person narrator into a third-person character for a very particular reason, namely, to clarify further his literary response to the neo-Aristotelians, which constitutes a valorization of the *Furioso* per se. By casting this figure into a third-person voice that interacts with a multitude of other inscribed readers who react to him in a variety of ways, Cervantes illustrates that objectivity is in large measure in the eye of the beholder. In this way he reasserts the fact that one cannot predict or prescribe reader response—in direct defiance of Ancients and Moderns alike. As such, Cervantes exploits the *Furioso* to impose the primacy of the text itself and hence the freedom of the artist.

Notes

[1] Aristotle's *Poetics* was translated from Greek into Latin in 1498 by Giorgio Valla. However, it was not until Robortello's commentary, the *Explicationes* (1546), that the *Poetics* became the focus of literary theoreticians. One year later, in 1549, Bernardo Segni published the first vernacular translation of the *Poetics*, entitled *Rettorica et poetica d'Aristotile*.

[2] "The Quarrel of the Ancients and the Moderns . . . had its roots in [the] very matter of new precepts for the new genres. It arose because certain theorists thought that new poetic forms might be practised in new ways, independent of or widely divergent from the old ways, and that the poems so written could be equal in quality—if not superior—to those of classical antiquity, whereas other theorists insisted that any departure from classical norms was in a way heretical and must lead only to inferior and illegitimate works." Bernard Weinberg, *A History of Literary Criticism in the Italian Renaissance*, 2 vols. (Chicago: U of Chicago P, 1961) 2: 808.

[3] The dispute over Ariosto began in 1549 with Simone Fornari's commentary on the *Furioso*, which is preceded by a defense of the text entitled "Apologia brieve sopra tutto l'*Orlando Furioso*." This was followed in 1554 by a pamphlet containing the epistolary dialogue of Giovanni Pigna and Giovambattista Giraldi Cintio concerning the merits of the *Furioso* (Weinberg 2: 957ff.).

[4] This and all subsequent quotations from the *Furioso* are from Santorre Debenedetti and Cesare Segre, eds. (Bologna: Commissione per i testi di lingua, 1960). Translations are from Guido Waldman, trans., *Orlando Furioso* (Oxford: Oxford UP, 1974).

[5] "Dirò d'Orlando in un medesmo tratto / cosa non detta in prosa mai, né in rima: / che per amor venne in furore e matto, / d'uom che sì saggio era stimato prima; / se da colei che tal quasi m'ha fatto, / che 'l poco ingegno ad or ad or mi lima, / me ne sarà però tanto concesso, / che mi basti a finir quanto ho promesso" (1.2).

[6] ". . . siendo esto hecho con apacibilidad de estilo y con ingeniosa invención, que tire lo más que fuere posible a la verdad, sin duda compondrá una tela de varios y hermosos lazos tejida . . . la escritura desatada destos libros da lugar a que el autor pueda mostrarse épico, lírico, trágico, cómico, con todas aquellas partes que encierran en sí las dulcísimas y agradables ciencias de la poesía y de la oratoria; que la épica también puede escrebirse en prosa como en verso" (483). This and all subsequent quotations from the *Quijote* are from Martín de Riquer, ed., *Don Quijote de la Mancha*, 2 vols. (Barcelona:

Editorial Juventud, 1965). Translations are from J. M. Cohen, trans., *The Adventures of Don Quixote* (Hammondsworth: Penguin, 1977), unless otherwise indicated.

[7] Maxime Chevalier, *L'Arioste en Espagne* (Bordeaux: Féret, 1966) 455.

[8] Alban Forcione, *Cervantes, Aristotle and the* Persiles (Princeton: Princeton UP, 1970) 126.

[9] Likening the "purified" drama to the "purified" romance (of which, he confesses, he had written a manuscript of more than one hundred pages before abandoning the enterprise), he reasons: "las [comedias] que llevan traza y siguen la fábula como el arte pide, no sirven sino para cuatro discretos que las entienden, y todos los demás se quedan ayunos de entender su artificio, y que a ellos les está mejor ganar de comer con los muchos, que no opinión con los pocos, deste modo vendrá a ser un libro, al cabo de haberme quemado las cejas por guardar los preceptos referidos, y vendré a ser el sastre del cantillo" (484–85).

[10] Forcione 106.

[11] Cervantes, in fact, prepares us for this deflationary treatment of the quarrel between Ancients and Moderns in the prologue to part 1, when the unnamed "friend" assures the author figure that, in the last analysis, he need not worry about the citations, marginalia, and commentaries which occupied the neo-Aristotelians, for one very simple reason: "este vuestro libro no tiene necesidad de ninguna otra cosa de aquellas que vos decís que le falta, porque todo él es una invectiva contra los libros de caballerías, de quien nunca se acordó Aristóteles" (24). Also see Forcione 104–07.

[12] The poems at issue are sonnets 1 and 3. In the first, Don Quijote is described as having gained fame from Cathay to Gaeta (Orlando's territory); and in the third, Rocinante is said to be far braver than Brilladoro and Bayardo, the horses of Orlando and Rinaldo (Riquer 519–21).

[13] Orlando has no right to expect Angelica's devotion since she has never declared reciprocal love for Orlando.

[14] "De un noble hidalgo manche- / contarás las aventu- / a quien ociosas letu- / trastornaron la cabe-: / damas, armas, caballe-, / le provocaron de mo-, / que cual Orlando furio-, / templado a lo enamora-, / alcanzó a fuerza de bra-/ a Dulcinea del Tobo-" (28).

[15] Joseph R. Jones, ed., John Ormsby, trans., *Don Quixote* (New York: Norton, 1981) 19.

[16] The following allusions are made to the *Furioso* in the *Quijote* on the following pages in Riquer: Agramonte, 251, 462, 463, 467; Angelica, 32, 101, 237, 251, 551, 552; Ariosto, 70, 551; Astolfo, 241; Bayardo, 521; Bradamante, 241; Brillardo, 521, 824; Brunello, 566, 738; Carlomagno, 486, 496, 714, 730, 734–36; Carlos V, 401, 593; Frontino, 241, 824; Hippogryph, 241; Mambrino, 100, 191, 192, 238, 239, 457, 458, 466; Marsilio, 731, 733–36, 739; Medoro, 237, 251, 551; Orlando, 28, 32, 122, 238, 550, 824; Prester John, 22, 481; Rinaldo, 38, 70, 77, 334, 548, 550, 773, 824; Rodomonte, 548; Roldán, 38, 122, 238, 239, 250, 251, 497, 548, 550–52, 596, 778, 1019; Ruggiero, 548, 824; Sacripante, 100, 551–52, 566, 738; Sobrino, 463, 548; Turpin, 70, 76, 498, 548.

[17] The narrator of the *Furioso* informs us in canto 22, st. 72, v. 1, that eight months have passed since Pinabello and Bradamante met in canto 2. In part 1 (Riquer 515), Sancho reveals that he has been serving Don Quijote for eight months.

[18] Eugenio Donato, " 'Per Selve e Boscherecci Laberinti': Desire and Narrative Structure in Ariosto's *Orlando Furioso*," *Barroco* 4 (1972): 32.

[19] David Quint, "The Figure of Atlante: Arioso and Boiardo's Poem," *MLN* 94 (1979): 87.

[20] C. P. Brand, *Ludovico Ariosto: A Preface to the* Orlando Furioso (Edinburgh: Edinburgh UP, 1973) 78.

[21] Donato 31.

[22] "Dios lo remedie; que todo este mundo es máquinas y trazas, contrarias unas de otras. Yo no puedo más" (755).

[23] In canto 35, sts. 1–2, the narrator asserts that his madness can be cured only if his lady will look upon him favorably.

[24] Robert Durling, *The Figure of the Poet in the Renaissance* (Cambridge: Harvard UP, 1965) 180.

[25] For two recent and differing appraisals of the problem of madness for Don Quijote and Orlando, see Manuel Durán, "Cervantes and Ariosto: Once More with Feeling," *Estudios literarios de hispanistas norteamericanos dedicados a Helmut Hatzfeld con motivo de su 80 aniversario,* ed. Josep M. Solá-Solé, Alessandro Crisafulli, and Bruno M. Damiani (Barcelona: Ed. Hispam, 1974) 87–101, and Martín de Riquer, "Ariosto y España," *Convegno internazionale Ludovico Ariosto,* Atti dei Covegni Lincei 6 (Rome: Accademia Nazionale dei Lincei, 1975) 319–29.

THE TRUTH OF THE MATTER
The Place of Romance in the Works of Cervantes

Ruth S. El Saffar

What I propose is based far more on my study of Cervantes—about which I can speak with considerably more authority—than on my knowledge of romance.[1] Following a favorite either/or tradition of whose weaknesses he is nonetheless thoroughly aware, Northrop Frye has ventured that all critics are of either the Iliad or the Odyssey variety.[2] He counts himself among the latter, and I, who hadn't thought about it in that way, found on reflection that I too am probably an Odyssey critic, which may be why I spent so many years carrying around books by Frye.

Being an Odyssey critic is not something one is free to admit or even to know about oneself. Like Twinkies aficionados in a health food store, we tend, around our colleagues, to keep our proclivities for romance to ourselves. In Cervantes's time the culprits—universally censored by the reigning moralists and literary critics, who were nearly all neo-Aristotelians—were the chivalric and pastoral romances. Today's version of pure fantasy unburdened by moral or social concerns is far more accessible and more commonly indulged in. It is turned out at half- and full-hour intervals throughout the day and night on the television sets virtually everyone owns and sits in turnstiles and magazine counters in every drugstore, grocery, and airport.

I speak here of something different, however, though I will confess to an evening or two with *Dallas* and *Fantasy Island*. (Frye, of a more erudite cast, admitted to Sir Walter Scott in his confession— and that, at the urging of Richard Blackmur and only in airports.) My interest in romance in Cervantes originated in something quite other than the nonreflective pleasures of prime-time television. In fact, I became involved in such unread and underrated Cervantine works as *La señora Cornelia, Las dos doncellas, La española inglesa, La gitanilla,* and most especially the *Persiles* despite an initial distaste for them.[3]

The weight of empirical and rational academic traditions work to all but stifle understanding of what have frequently been called Cervantes's idealistic *novelas*. So heavy is the burden of our intellectualism that for many years I studied those neglected works of Cervantes—amounting to more than half of all the prose fiction he wrote—against the current of my own prejudices. Reading the *Persiles* is nothing like watching *Quincy,* I can assure you. What really attracted me, since it wasn't easy pleasure, has taken me years to appreciate. I consulted Frye a lot because he seemed least persuaded, among contemporary critics, of the innate superiority of the novel over romance and, by extension, of the intellect over the imagination. Indeed, he found the late romances of Shakespeare to be the "genuine culmination" of the playwright's work,[4] just as I have argued that the *Persiles* and *La española inglesa* were the crowning achievement of Cervante's lifetime as a writer, and not the hack works they have so often been taken to be.

Frye's great contribution to the problem of romance has been his insistence on its integrity. Representing romance as the "structural core of all fiction"[5] whose essence is only disguised or displaced, not altered, when it is hooked on to the matter of everyday experience, Frye has allowed us to break with our fascination with realistic fiction and to see the novel in fact as a subtype of romance, built on a parodic or deflationary attitude that nonetheless betrays its dependence on the form against which it is reacting.

Maurice Z. Schroder has also shown the symbiotic relation of novel to the romance form it seems to spurn. Although he basically looks at romance as an escapist genre, an "enchanted world of triumphant adventure,"[6] he also understands the novel's dialectical relation to that genre, noting that the great age of the novel coincided with the period in which romanticism was at its height. The difference is that Schroder privileges "knowledge of the world as it is," while Frye gives priority to the structure of the imagination, which is, for him, independent of time and place.

What I have not found clearly made by anyone is a distinction which I discovered I needed to make sense out of the development of Cervantes's career as a writer. Very briefly I will describe the two categories, "escapist" and "quest," that I will use. Escapist romance plunges the reader directly into fantasy without providing a link that connects the characters in any meaningful way with the everyday world. Quest romance, on the other hand, leads a character into and back out of fantasy—demonic or paradisal or both—thereby throwing the emphasis on the character and the transformation he undergoes during his experience in the dream world. Escapist romance, of which the pastoral, the chivalric, and present-day soap operas are examples, is basically sensationalist. The pleasure it offers comes from the strange and forbidden nature of the world into which it leads the reader and the sense it gives him or her of being momentarily off-limits and free from the normal constraints of life. Escapist romance, in other words, is essentially social-centered, offering its pleasures as excursions which, while seeming to be an escape from, actually reinforce the established order. Quest romances are more radical and potentially more dangerous. They say, in essence, that the established order has flaws that can be healed only by going out of it into an asocial world, the experience of which is, or can be, redemptive. Escapist romance has no natural ending. Quest romance, on the other hand, has a structure that clearly marks its beginning and end.

The two types variously called "romance," depending on the critic, therefore differ radically from one another in their structure and in the conceptions out of which they arise. They have in common only a stock of conventions (indomitable heroes, menaced virgins, catastrophes, and coincidental encounters) which give them superficial similarity.

In *Don Quijote,* part 1, Cervantes, having tried his hand twenty years earlier at a pastoral romance, seems convinced that escapist romance—pastoral and chivalric—was a severely flawed genre. He made an impact on literary history by throwing an unvarnished example of fantasy into the arena of "the world as it is" and documenting the consequences of the ensuing struggle. There can be no doubt that Cervantes intended with his novel to attack the romances of chivalry and to illustrate, through Don Quijote, the damaging effects "the enchanted world of triumphant adventure" can have on the reader. But we make a mistake, we show our rationalistic bias and render the whole of Cervantes inaccessible to us, if we imagine that Cervantes's goal even in *Don Quijote,* part 1, was to dispense with romance. Romance obviously gave him pleasure. He had to have read a lot of chivalric and pastoral fantasies to have parodied them as subtly as he did. His problem was to find a literary form that would preserve that pleasure in the fact of an active critical intelligence.

In chapters 48–50 of *Don Quijote,* part 1, Cervantes stages a literary debate between a spokesman for neo-Aristotelian literary theory, the Canon of Toledo, and an unregenerate spokesman for romance, Don Quijote. The two arguments intersect on so few points that any hope of compromise between positions must be abandoned. The question which is so important for the Canon—to distinguish what is true from what is not in the romances of chivalry—simply does not concern Don Quijote. Who cares whether the heroes of romance lived? For Don Quijote's purposes they are all equally dead and equally alive. What most concerns him is the question of pleasure, a pleasure very closely connected with fantasies of sex and violence—a pleasure which refers to the senses and which is very little affected by minor difficulties of a rationalist nature.[7]

The main point is that sensual and intellectual pleasure in literature—though they both reflect the material world from which they are derived—have no common ground. It is that—the chasm between reason and sensuality, and not the possible superiority of one or the other—that bothers Cervantes. What I think is key to an understanding of *Don Quijote,* part 1, and to Cervantes's whole opus is that Cervantes's underlying metaphysics is unitary. Everything comes into place if we understand that the struggle throughout his works is to bring into harmony those things which—in literature and in life—are traditionally held asunder.

The most damaging aspect of escapist romance, in the form of the chivalric and pastoral idylls which Cervantes came to attack in his middle period (1598–1606), had ultimately less to do with his mad gentleman than with the world in which escapist romance was the preferred form of literary entertainment. An early episode in the *Coloquio de los perros,* a short novel about which I will say more later, makes the case clearly. The dog Berganza has just escaped the murderous, tumultuous, adulterous world of the butchery, fully expecting to find in the countryside to which he runs the peace and harmony so lacking in the city. His surprise at finding coarse, illiterate, atonal, not to say thieving shepherds in what was supposed to be his safe haven came about because at the butchery the corrupt mistress of one of his masters used to entertain herself by reading pastoral romances.

Far more important than Berganza's disillusion with the shepherds is that the idyllic pastoral romances served as entertainment in a world marked by degradation and depravity. Escapist literature not only wastes time and falsely dresses up reality, we are forced to conclude. It actually serves as the handmaiden of corruption and violence by siphoning off the reader's natural and deep-seated desire for a more beautiful world and emptying those instincts into repositories safely removed from everyday life. Having satisfied the fantasy of romantic love, the reader can then close the book and resume life as usual among the butchers. So separate become the worlds of "fantasy" and "reality" that the victim of such a dichotomy feels justified, finally, in assigning all that is good, just, and proper to never-never land. "Oh, that only happens in novels (or romances)," becomes the stock response to a promising situation.

Escapist literature, then, takes part in a kind of Manicheism which perpetrates stagnation, hopelessness, and cynicism. Both Don Quijote and the Canon, the two participants in the inconclusive debate over literature in chapters 48–50, have in common a desire to bring back into one the separated worlds of fantasy and reality. Don Quijote attempts the feat by jumping into the world carrying his dream with him and seeking to impose it on everyone he sees. His lost teeth, battered ribs, torn ear, and final caging argue effectively against the merits of that particular method. The Canon, though more circumspect, is no more successful. He confesses to having written some one hundred pages of a story he was unable to complete whose chief aim was to "marry the false fables to the intelligence of those who read them" (ch. 47).[8]

The desired marriage of the imagination and the intellect, of fantasy and reality, fails as much for the Canon as for Don Quijote. It fails in literature and it fails in life. It also fails for Cervantes, who manages in part 1 of *Don Quijote* to juxtapose and to alternate the two worlds but not to integrate them.

The nature of the dialectic in which *Don Quijote,* part 1, is caught can be nicely seen in the story of the galley slave Ginés de Pasamonte, whom Don Quijote frees from his chains in chapter 22. Life distributes itself, for Ginés, between two moments, each feeding on and creating the possibility for the other, in an endlessly repeated and never-transcended cycle. Ginés is either busy at his game of thieving and conniving or clapped behind the bars of his jail cell. The thieving portion of the cycle, he says, provides the narrative material for the subsequent period of imprisonment. In that second phase, thief turns author, writing of the exploits that landed him in jail. When will his book be finished? When his life is. There is no possibility of rising above the line, of transforming its linearity into something more resembling a spiral, from which glimpses of an earlier time could be made with new insight, greater perspective.

It is just such a linear, untranscended vision of literature and life that threatens *Don Quijote*, part 1, and that determines its episodic, apparently unplanned character and its lack of a genuine ending. The capture of Don Quijote at the end of part 1 is just another adventure for Don Quijote, another event in the series. From his point of view, the ending is arbitrary, even false. It is an occasion, as captivity is for Ginés de Pasamonte, for consolidating his adventures and planning his escape, not an opportunity for repentance.

What must be remembered is that Cervantes, though he is obviously making fun of romance in part 1, is also embracing it. There is clearly a nostalgia on Cervantes's part, beneath the scoffing and disillusion, for the same Golden Age that Don Quijote would like to restore by the force of his arms. The error, both for Don Quijote and for his author, has been to take an aggressive attitude toward whatever seems to stand in the way of that dreamed-of place. The aggressive approach emphasizes the obstacle rather than the goal, fomenting the illusion and chaos of which the famous windmills are only one example.[9]

A major obstacle to a full understanding of Cervantes's achievement as a writer has been to see *Don Quijote* as a single novel. Part 1, which we have been discussing so far, came out in 1605. Part 2 came out in 1615, two years after the publication of the *Exemplary Novels* and one year before Cervantes's death and the publication of the *Persiles*. The many differences between the two parts of *Don Quijote*—differences that affect the characters, the narrator, the structure, the ending, and the nature of the hero's journey—are all reflections of a major shift in orientation on Cervantes's part that will allow, in the *Persiles,* the marriage of opposites that Don Quijote and the Canon dreamed of in *Don Quijote,* part 1.

The shift in orientation that takes place between the two parts of *Don Quijote* is from a concern with an *out there* with which the hero must do battle to an *in here* where the only significant struggle can take place. Don Quijote makes the point early in part 2 when he tells Sancho, just as they are leaving home for their third sally:

It is for us to slay pride by slaying giants, to slay envy by our generosity and nobility; anger by calmness of mind, and serenity of disposition; gluttony and drowsiness by eating little and watching late into the night. (2.8, 518)[10]

The movement inward of which Don Quijote speaks is captured topographically in part 2 through the succession of interiors to which Don Quijote repairs. In part 1 there were occasional inns where knight and squire stayed, but they were rare and were places of confusion and loss of consciousness. Part 2, on the other hand, is full of resting places, which Don Quijote often seeks out. They are his principal places of learning and he spends many hours alone in them. The 1615 Don Quijote goes to caves and spends quiet nights in houses of such notables as Don Diego, the Duke and Duchess, and Don Antonio, always as an invited guest. The topographical reiterations of inner space have their psychological correlation in the melancholy which is Don Quijote's dominant mood. Don Quijote in part 2 is locked into the question of his identity as he never was in part 1.

The signs of inward-turning are also represented in the temporal-spatial disposition of the work, which is organized on a pattern of concentric circles, of planned journeys with clear destinations, whose widest circle embraces Don Quijote's trip from home to ocean and back home again. The return, however, no longer belongs, as it did in part 1, to an alternating cycle of success and failure. Return at the end of part 2 signifies both the hero's recovery of himself and his transformation. Don Quijote goes home in chapter 73 to become Alonso Quijano the Good. His reconciliation with his destiny marks the end of the illusion which is the product of the escapist impulse. When Don Quijote releases his invented self, all the antagonisms that characterized his life in fiction fall away, including his bitter though scarcely conscious struggle against his fictional Arab scribe Cide Hamete.[11]

Don Quijote, part 2, I submit, is not the antithesis of the more obvious work of romance, the *Persiles.* It is, on the contrary, its natural prelude. The shift to which I referred earlier from an externally oriented, episodic, adventure-centered tale to one that is focused on the development of the character takes place sometime between 1605, when *Don Quijote,* part 1, was published, and 1615–16, when *Don Quijote,* part 2, and the *Persiles* came out. I cannot give positive proof of dates, but I have good reason to suspect that the *Casamiento engañoso* and the *Coloquio de los perros,* the double *novela* that ends Cervantes's collection of short stories (1613), not only was written in but actually captures the moment of turnaround that made romance—quest romance—the preferred form for all of Cervantes's subsequent fiction.

The two *novelas* make one of the richest works Cervantes wrote, addressing successfully for the first time the vexing problem of the split between fiction and reality and of the relation of the author to his work—problems that were evident even in his earliest writings. Since I am more concerned here with romance with relation to Cervantes's entire opus than with specific manifestations of it in his work, it is necessary to undertake a brief discussion of the *Casamiento-Coloquio*.

The first story, the *Casamiento engañoso,* serves as a frame for the second. The *Casamiento* is told by an impoverished former lieutenant called Campuzano. Campuzano has just come out of the hospital, having undergone a cure for syphilis. He encounters his friend Peralta, to whom he tells the story of his disgrace. His downfall, as he narrates it, came through his pursuit of a deceitful lady who, having attracted him by her apparent wealth, turned out to have faked hers in order to win his. Since both were up to the same tricks, neither wound up with what he wanted. The lady, Estefanía, made off with Campuzano's chest of false gold. He came out of the deal homeless and diseased.

In the hospital to which he surrenders what remains of him, Campuzano overhears a conversation between two dogs which takes place on the last two nights of his stay. The dogs, Berganza and Cipión, develop the theme that Campuzano has already introduced in his tale of deceitful marriage. Berganza's life story, which is the subject of the first night's conversation, bears all the earmarks of a picaresque tale. Berganza is the classic servant of many masters, and the story of his life touches on all sectors of society, from butchers and shepherds to constables and magistrates, from the poorest to the richest, from the people in the inner circles of power to the gypsies and Moors on its periphery.

But it becomes clear very early that the story is not so much about those masters and their corruption as it is about how to tell such a story. The story, the dogs agree, must be told in a straightforward manner—no affectations or digressions will be tolerated. Furthermore, Berganza must tell his story without indulging in slander or in abstraction, despite the fact that he complains "I've only got to open my mouth a few times to find words rushing to my tongue like flies to wine, all full of malice and slander. And so I say again what

I've said before: that we inherit the tendency to do and speak evil from our first parents and absorb it with our mother's milk" (208).[12]

The rules of this particular storytelling game require no slight amount of self-discipline, and the reader comes to suspect, as the temptations to fall into cynicism mount, that the very act of telling has something of a rite of purification about it. The exercise becomes the more poignant as we realize that it is done for its own sake, as an act of sheer faith. Berganza, exasperated at his friend Cipión's constant admonitions, and the added requirement that he bite his tongue whenever he is caught in cynicism and slander, explodes, "Let the devil bite himself, but I don't want to bite myself or do my good deeds behind a mat, where I can't be seen by anybody who can praise my honest intention" (214).

The shift of emphasis away from the social ills of an obviously destructive society toward the one who appears to be their victim not only refocuses the work toward the author and toward itself as literature but has a transforming effect on the speaker and his unknown listener, the woebegone "victim" Campuzano. The exercise of stopping the proliferation of victims, of catching the victim in the act of becoming in his turn, through malice, resentment, slander and hypocrisy, a victimizer, releases, as if by magic, the character/author/ listener from the cycle of ups and downs that dominated the action of *Don Quijote,* part 1. Not only does the *Coloquio* turn the picaresque upside down, it also asserts the possibility that the demonic, instead of being a world in itself, inexorably sealed off from paradise, is in fact the very passageway to the paradisal, a passageway so essential that if avoided, it will always stand as a block to the desired goal. With Berganza's guided tour through the hell of murderers, butchers, thieving shepherds, constables, false prophets, and empty-minded playwrights, we are carried, unawares, into the realm of quest romance.

The tour through the demonic, in other words, is not being carried on for its own sake. Because of the layering of narrators and listeners at two levels of the story, the emphasis shifts toward the act of rendering and receiving and away from the events that are its ostensible subject. The same self-reflexivity that Don Quijote demonstrates in part 2 becomes a factor in Berganza's would-be picaresque tale. The effect, however, is not so much to alter that tale as to turn it upside down.

Let us call Frye back for a moment, just to make sure we are on track. In his chapter "Themes of Descent" in *The Secular Scripture,*

Frye makes reference to the "Earth-mother at the bottom of the world." She is "a beautiful and sinister female ruler, buried in the depths of a dark continent, who is much involved with various archetypes of death and rebirth" (114). He also writes, not too many pages later, still plumbing the dark side of romance, of Apuleius's *Golden Ass,* to which the dogs make explicit reference in their colloquy. "In Apuleius," Frye says, "the nadir . . . of the main action of the story comes at a point when a woman is condemned as a whore, and . . . the ass [Lucius] is ordered to have public intercourse with her" (118).

The center of Berganza's story combines both images—that of the sinister female ruler and that of public intercourse with a whore. The incident appears to be just another in the series, but in fact it opens up to the dogs the whole mystery of their origin and their destiny. The witch whom Berganza meets threatens him with an infinite regress of fantasy, telling him, while they are alone at night in the secrecy of her hut, that he is a witch's child, transformed by malice into a dog. Berganza is then left to keep watch over the witch while she covers herself with ointment and goes into a trance. Out of fear, he drags her possessed, naked body out into the central plaza, subjecting both her and himself to public outrage when they are found together the next morning.

It is in that fantasy within a fantasy within a fantasy that the first possibility of transformation is introduced, however. For the witch assures Berganza—the sleeping Campuzano's demonic projection of himself—that he can be released from enchantment "When . . . the mighty / are speedily brought down / and the humble exalted / by that hand which has power to perform it" (230–31).

From the witch, the most infernal of the creatures he meets and the one who exposes him to the most personal fear and public humiliation, Berganza, and through him Campuzano, learns that there is a bottom to the pit, though the turning point is just as mysterious as Dante found it to be when he reached the base of his inferno.

Berganza and Cipión come out on the other side of their experiences of the world's corruption deciding to spend the remainder of their years in the service of the good alms collector Mahudes, who lives at and works for the very Hospital of the Resurrection where Campuzano has come for his cure. When Campuzano, having come out of his own kind of hell, leaves the hospital, he has experienced, himself, a resurrection. Having heard and copied down the dogs' conversation, he is no longer the unrepentant soldier, caught up in the vainglory of handsome uniforms and false gold chains. His new intent is to be a writer whose method, like that of Berganza, entails close but disinterested concern to render faithfully the experiences of his life.

Campuzano tells his friend Peralta of the colloquy he overheard:

> Since I was listening so attentively, my mind was in a delicate state, and my memory was also delicate. . . . I learnt it off by heart and wrote it down the next day in almost the same words in which I had heard it, without looking for rhetorical colours to adorn it, nor adding or subtracting anything to make it pleasing. . . . I put it in the form of a colloquy to avoid the "Scipio said," and "Berganza replied," which stretches out the narrative. (192–93)

Like Berganza, Campuzano takes responsibility for his experiences, however difficult they are for him to accept, and he renders them carefully, leaving them as free as possible from the contamination of his own wishes and fears. He says, "many times since I have heard them, I have been unwilling to believe myself, and have preferred to take as something I dreamed what in fact . . . I heard." He even adds, "I should be an animal too if I didn't believe what I heard, and what I saw, and what I shall dare to swear" (192).

Campuzano's apprenticeship as a writer involves taking seriously the world of the dream, not disparaging it as the narrator of *Don Quijote,* part 1, was inclined to do. In Campuzano's careful exercise of rendering the dream correctly, he is engaging his intelligence in the service of the imagination, producing thereby a marriage based on acceptance rather than on conquest.

I bring the term "marriage," which the Canon of Toledo used metaphorically, back now into the discussion to explore it thematically. For what we will see, turning to the late *novelas* and the *Persiles,* is that the central theme for all of them is love surrendered to the discipline of marriage. In all of the late *novelas* Cervantes's characters are put through a training program by which they learn, like Campuzano, to place their material powers and impulses—their intelligence, their wealth, their social standing and their sexual desires—at the service of eros, which figures as the structural equivalent of the imagination.

In escapist romance, whether pastoral or chivalric, the operation is reversed. It is eros that serves the structure of the world as it is, becoming the instrument of ritualized rebellion rather than of true transformation. The escapist romance, like adultery, which it often portrays, highlights the short-lived pleasures that derive their delight from the illicit.

The quest romance pattern that I have called characteristic of Cervantes's late works is subject to great variation in its details. Sometimes, as in *La española inglesa* and *La ilustre fregona,* the emphasis falls on the descent from and return to society by a young man whose unconscious task it is to redeem, through the woman, the transgressions perpetrated on her by his father. In others, such as *La señora Cornelia, Las dos doncellas,* and *La fuerza de la sangre,* the redemptive work is carried on by the female character, whose job it is to retrieve her "unwedded husband" from the world of escapist romance to which he flees after having seduced her.

What does not vary, in all the late works, however, is the overall process, which begins inevitably in desire and ends when the victim of that initially rebellious and sometimes even violent expression of passion takes responsibility for it. The process, expressed thematically as a movement from love to marriage, gives the work an opening and closing that earlier works of fiction by Cervantes lacked. It gives shape and identity to the work and confers on it the desired metaphorical marriage the Canon spoke of, by allowing a wedding of the author's imagined universe with the reality of day-to-day experience.

Eros functions in Cervantes's works, when once it is liberated from the terrifying, blocking image of the great whore, as a redemptive force, bringing harmony to the individual, to the couple, and to the society from which they were initially ejected. From the literary point of view eros works as the dream—that locus of activity both above and below the functioning of everyday life. The hero within fiction, like the author outside, finds his way out of and back into society by faithfully following the lead of that dream, as we saw in the case of Campuzano.

At the beginning of this essay I suggested that what was bothering Cervantes in *Don Quixote,* part 1, far more than the problem of which was better, the intellect or the imagination, or any of the other terms in opposition that can be found in his 1605 novel, was that he couldn't see how to structure an imaginative universe in which the opposites could complement each other. The difficulty had theoretical, characterizational, structural, and thematic expressions, only some of which I mentioned. My idea was that Cervantes's goal from the beginning of his career—and space does not allow me to show how it works out in the 1585 *Galatea,* but it does—was to perform the wedding, literary, thematic, and psychological, that his unconscious metaphysics of unity sensed could be made. His whole opus is best understood as a struggle to get past the dualism that separates heaven and earth, male and female, literature and life, highborn and lowborn.

One of the primary underlying images for a metaphysics of unity is the androgyne, which, along with the idea of an earthly paradise, suggests a return to the first creation story in Genesis. Another essay in this volume shows how the androgyne can be deflated into transvestism and be employed as evasion in the literature of escape.[13] But the androgyne had and has another role to play when it is interpreted spiritually, as it often was in the Renaissance.[14] My feeling is that the image of the androgyne will arise naturally when the other processes of overturning and rebirth have taken place.

It is far too late in this essay to consider the *Persiles* in any depth. Suffice it to say that Cervantes's last work traces a very clear movement from alienation to integration on the part of both male and female main characters and that that process is mirrored structurally within the work. Gone is the distanced, ironic narrator, the lack of beginning and ending, the poor integration of plot and episode, and the ambiguous nature of the role of the hero that characterized Cervantes's earliest works. The *Persiles,* patterned after Heliodorus's *Ethiopic History,* separates radically the strands of story and discourse and, from a thematic point of view, those of male and female protagonists, threatening them throughout with disjunction but leading them just as surely to union. The marriage at the end of the *Persiles* is as thoroughly structural as it is thematic, drawing together into one great *summa* all the loose strands and bringing, finally, the beginning together with the end, suggesting an eternity reached through the complex peripeties of the temporal.

The *Persiles* also has both descent and ascent motifs and many representations of the cycle of death and rebirth. Its involvement in the cycle of nature is represented in its participation in the seasons—from winter to summer—and in its movement from north to south, both with the idea of return implied. Its identification with the mother goddess is represented in the hidden but all-important action of the queen mother, whose inspiration to follow the lead of the heart initiates the heroes' actions and totally undermines the patriarchal authority vested in the hero's older brother. The work contains several images of the androgyne, the most graphic and striking being that of the hero and heroine, in their first embrace at the beginning of the book after years of separation, each dressed in the clothes of the other. That external image of assimilation of the contrasexual becomes internalized across the course of the narration and is reified in the marriage which finally takes place on the last page of the work.

I see the transformations in Cervantes's works—from pastoral romance to parody romance to quest romance—as landmarks in a fundamental shift taking place gradually over the period of Cervantes's career as a writer. Each work represents a stage in the process of moving out of the formulae of dualism, where sensation and intellect dominate, and into those of unity, which depend on the priority but not the primacy of spirit. What makes Cervantes fascinating is that he has shown the path that leads from eros to spirit. When that path is followed to its end, the novel is no longer possible, nor is escapist romance. What we have observed, to borrow from Kevin Brownlee's essay, is the shift that places *songe* in opposition not to truth but to *mensonge,* locating dream, all of a sudden, with the realm of truth.[15] I submit here that when the truth of the matter becomes its permeation of spirit and not its alienation from or even domination of it, then a new genre emerges, a genre with structural and thematic characteristics that require their own equally distinctive critical approach. So long as we are caught in the dichotomies that entangled the Cervantes of 1605, we will not be able to read his late romances. But I think we are arriving at a time when that will be possible.

Being an Odyssey critic is a tricky thing, it turns out. You have to have that secret hankering for the fantasy stuff, but you also have to like to see things wrapped up at the end, to be assured that underneath it all there is a pattern. By way of conclusion, I would like to affirm, quite simply, that this is my case.

Notes

[1] Hispanists have been slow to insist on the romance/novel distinction that has flourished in Anglo-American criticism for more than a century. Spanish lacks an equivalent of the English term *romance,* making discussion awkward, especially since the Spanish term *romance* has other literary significations. E. C. Riley, "Teoría literaria," *Suma cervantina* (London: Tamesis, 1973), acknowledges the importance of the distinction for discussing Cervantes's work, something he did not do in his earlier *Cervantes' Theory of the Novel* (Oxford: Clarendon, 1961). For a good discussion of the problem of romance in Spanish letters, see Alan Deyermond, "The Lost Genre of Medieval Spanish Literature," *Hispanic Review* 43 (1975): 231-59.

[2] Northrop Frye, *A Natural Perspective* (New York: Harcourt, 1965) 1.

[3] *La señora Cornelia, Las dos doncellas, La española inglesa,* and *La Gitanilla* are *novelas* that appeared together in a collection of twelve works under the title *Novelas ejemplares* (1613). The full title of the *Persiles* is *Los trabajos de Persiles y Sigismunda, historia setentrional,* published in 1617, a few months after Cervantes's death. I set out to show, in *Novel to Romance* (Baltimore:

Johns Hopkins UP, 1974), that all the above-named *novelas* were written, like the *Persiles,* in the last several years of Cervantes's life.

[4] Frye 7.

[5] Northrop Frye, *The Secular Scripture* (Cambridge: Harvard UP, 1976) 15.

[6] Maurice Z. Schroder, "The Novel as Genre," *The Theory of the Novel,* ed. Philip Stevick (New York: Free P, 1967) 21.

[7] For an excellent reading of the Canon's literary debate with Don Quixote, see Alban Forcione, *Cervantes, Aristotle, and the* Persiles (Princeton: Princeton UP, 1971) 91–130.

[8] I have used my own translation here, since the Cohen translation, to which I will turn for all subsequent quotations, renders this passage too loosely to make my point.

[9] For a full discussion of Cervantes's unconscious participation in Don Quijote's folly, see Cesáreo Bandera, "Cervantes frente a don Quijote," *Mimesis conflictiva* (Madrid: Taurus, 1975).

[10] References are to part, chapter, and page number in J. M. Cohen, trans., *The Adventures of Don Quixote* (Baltimore: Penguin, 1950).

[11] I refer here to the famous statement, addressed by Cide Hamete to his pen, on the closing pages of *Don Quixote,* part 2: "For me alone Don Quixote was born and I for him. His was the power of action, mine of writing. Only we two are one" (Cohen 2.74, 940).

[12] Page references here and throughout the discussion of the *Casamiento-Coloquio* are to C. A. Jones, trans., *Exemplary Stories* (Baltimore: Penguin, 1972).

[13] Louise Horowitz, "Where Have All the 'Old Knights' Gone?: *L'Astrée,*" in this book.

[14] Ian Maclean, *The Renaissance Notion of Woman: A Study in the Fortunes of Scholasticism and Medical Science in European Intellectual Life* (Cambridge: Cambridge UP, 1980), says, "One theory of the creation of woman, that Adam was androgynous, and that his female half was separated from his during sleep, is refuted in Augustine and all subsequent orthodox commentators, although it must have held a strong appeal for Renaissance neoplatonists. It would necessarily imply . . . that God was also androgynous; this idea, gnostic in origin, reappears in the work of Paracelsus and even in marginal theology" (12). The relation of the androgyne to love is developed in the work of Leone Hebreo, whose *Dialoghi d'Amore* is a work Cervantes drew from extensively in *La Galatea.*

[15] Kevin Brownlee, "Jean de Meun and the Limits of Romance: Genius as Rewriter of Guillaume de Lorris," in this book.

WHERE HAVE ALL
THE "OLD KNIGHTS" GONE?
L'Astrée

Louise K. Horowitz

Nostalgia for the "knights of old" is a traditional convention of Renaissance romance, which, like the knights on horseback themselves (long an anachronism by existing martial standards), allowed for the integration of one literary tradition into and by another. "Oh gran bontà de' cavallieri antiqui" (Oh the great goodness of the knights of old), sighs Ariosto in the *Furioso*.[1] "Old," of course, has no historical meaning whatsoever. Rather, it provides a loaded allusion to old texts, to earlier literary production, which over the centuries had been successfully transmitted from book to book, from country to country.

Likewise, in the second volume of d'Urfé's massive opus *L'Astrée*, the narrator, addressing the principal male character, Céladon, exhorts him not to fear loving and living as did once "les chevaliers de la Table ronde."[2] Arthur's knights reappear occasionally in d'Urfé's four volumes, as fleeting references, thereby conveying metonymically an entire paradigm or system of behavior. The courtly allusions, moreover, mesh harmoniously with d'Urfé's use of the term "honnête amitié," which appears in the work's full title: *L'Astrée de Messire Honoré d'Urfé . . . ou par plusieurs histoires et sous personnes de bergers et d'autres sont déduits les divers effets de l'honneste amitié*. Like the fleeting references to courtly standards, the summoning up of "honnête amitié" in the title and elsewhere throughout the long work creates a codified conventional base for d'Urfé's fiction. Both concepts, which in *L'Astrée* are virtually interpenetrable, convey in brief fashion extensive moral systems of an idealistic nature.

Were that all d'Urfé offered in *L'Astrée*—metonymic allusions— we would have enough to situate the romance's ideological base. As it turns out, however, he provides much more. I wish to focus on a few major episodes of *L'Astrée* in an effort to demonstrate, first, the disintegration under romance conditioning of an elaborate ethical structure, which ostensibly governs the text and, second, the exploitation of romance conventions themselves to establish a polyvalent sexual, textual experience. It should then be possible to supply an answer to my query "Where have all the 'old knights' gone?" Briefly, I think they and their "old love" have been swallowed up, consumed by a writing experience that converts them, for a second time, into "new" characters. Their initial transformation had been class and socially based. Once knights, now shepherds (their ancestors having quit the ways of the court for the so-called gentler pastoral ways), they additionally will lose their sexual identity through tricky technical, textual toying. Once knights, then shepherds, now transvestites—so goes the movement of the principal episodes in *L'Astrée*. Indeed, almost all of the primary tale—the love story between Céladon and Astrée—occurs "in drag." While disguise is most assuredly a romance convention, and particularly a cherished Renaissance convention, and while, as Edward Turk has observed, it is a technique that inevitably invites transvestism, for Honoré d'Urfé it is basically the whole of the primary episode.[3] Travesty turning toward transvestism is not only functional: in the Astrée-Céladon episode, it is the major focus, perhaps even the *raison d'être* of the whole story. As such, disguise allows for the genesis of a wholly textual sexuality, the evocation of eroticism across gender, without gender, and therefore purely essential, the perfect matching of writing itself to the wish fulfillment inherent to romance as text and to romantic love.

Such analysis should allow us to grasp in terms of Honoré d'Urfé what Karl Uitti has called "generic intent."[4] For in *L'Astrée,* two movements occur. Through the meticulous and studied creation of essential, gender-free sexuality, d'Urfé offers, first, an alternate text to the otherwise pervasive theoretical base (in keeping perhaps with late Renaissance tradition). Second, he twists the most obvious conventions—which he presents unambiguously in his text—in favor of a writing experiment at once dependent on and yet fully transcending romance norms.

That d'Urfé exploited romance conventions is unquestionable. Northrop Frye's useful summary of the romance medium in *The Secular Scripture* allows us to see how obvious was d'Urfé's use of the traditional techniques. Downward plunges to lost identity and revery; foolish, inattentive father figures; a double heroine, split between virginity and love-marriage; metamorphosis through disguise and name change; an erotic, dreamlike existence, close to the level of unconscious fantasy; magic fountains; oracles; nymphs—all coexist in d'Urfé's book, particularly in the major episodes spanning his four volumes, to create the seemingly perfect romance structure.[5] Thus, on the one hand, this romance typology flies in the face of the work's dominant idealistic base. Some romance texts clearly may be seen as efforts to portray a gap between discourse and act. Uitti has shown how behavioral patterns contrast very early in *Yvain* with courtly strictures, and Myriam Jehenson, in a recently published study of Renaissance pastoral romance, offers a similar comparison, in this case between Neoplatonic dogma and "real-life" standards in Sidney's *New Arcadia* and *L'Astrée*.[6] As regards Honoré d'Urfé's text, the theoretical, idealistic framework is extremely complex, an amalgam of the aforementioned "old" courtly practices; of the Neoplatonic abstractions espoused in Italy (and translated quickly into French) by writers such as Hebreo, Varchi, and Ficino; of traditional pastoral norms of *otium* and innocence; of Petrarchan suffering; and of neo-Stoic reliance on the primacy of reason as a vital governing source. It is impossible to sort out or through these diverse currents as they appear in *L'Astrée,* for they consistently blend and commingle. At stake ultimately is one vast abstract discourse, articulated by different characters but predominantly by Adamas, a druidic priest, and Silvandre, a shepherd companion to Céladon.

What happens, however, in the work's multifold tales stands in striking contrast to this elaborate structure of cerebral, idealized approaches to love. Both secondary and primary tales contradict "honnête amitié," or any of its cultural variations, opposing through sex and violence the verbose explanations of pure love based on duty, service, fidelity, discretion, goodness, and reason. Two texts simply coexist: the one, a conveyer of past and present ideals, striving toward a morally uplifting view of the emotions and, concomitantly, of literature; the other, a rampantly erotic text designed to subvert the very principles so eloquently held aloft throughout d'Urfé's four long volumes. This undercutting of theory has been signaled by diverse contemporary critics who, in one fashion or another, focus on d'Urfé's deconstruction of his carefully orchestrated dogma.[7] One text—romance—thus parallels yet does not destroy another—metaphysical and ideal—just as the opening lines of *Yvain* rebuff the courtly assumptions at its base (only for them to reappear in later Chrétien texts) and just as the final parts of the *New Arcadia* offer an ironic jab at the Platonic model of the first two books, yet never wholly canceling it out.

This is the basic structure, then, of *L'Astrée,* labeled pastoral romance as it weds *bergerie* and *chevalerie* and wavers between idealistic theory and passion, between discourse and act. It is all held together in what Clifton Cherpak has called an "inconsistent compound."[8] But this opposing of two tones is in itself a limited aspect of *L'Astrée*. For once understood, the issue begs for a more precise reading. What d'Urfé chooses to do with the stuff of romance is how we may truly grasp his "generic intent." I believe he offered his readers the most obvious romance signs, charging them to do little more than act as the mark of romance, in order to work through material leading him to an original presentation of the one romance convention he is fascinated by: disguise. The voyeurism, travesty, and transvestism and the erotic fantasies they sustain and engender are not new to literature, of course. D'Urfé's contribution, however, is to have fabricated a text not only where they are predominant but whereby writing itself, grammar itself, transmits an erotic fantasy allowing for an androgynous, but intense, sexuality to be generated through the manipulation of form.

Before testing the full implications of these assumptions, let me briefly discuss the appearance of other romance conventions in *L'Astrée*. D'Urfé's method is clear: to "sign" his work as romance, to display prominently romance conventions, thereby permitting him to explore minutely the text as romance and life as romance. Hence, there *is* a double heroine in *L'Astrée,* actually a triple one. The love-marriage theme is incarnated by Astrée and her cousin Phillis; the virgin, the cold female, whom Frye has shown is the other significant female participant in romance, occurs in the person of a character named, not too unexpectedly, Diane.[9] Of course, for d'Urfé the choice was perfect: he had his conventionally cold virgin as well as the emblem of his wife, Diane de Châteaumorand. And he had also the assurance of contemporary literary reference and continuity, for Diana is the heroine and the title of Montemayor's work, which was greatly admired by the French. In all ways, the name could not be more emblematic: like references to the knights of the Round Table, it tells all. Similarly, the book's unifying water symbol, the Fontaine

de Vérité d'Amour, is obviously conventional. It fails to inspire ele-
mentally, its mythological base is no longer effective, and, above all,
the fountain is absurd in its premise of revealing to lovers whether
or not their ardor is mutual. Its unique talent is acceptable only
within the confines of romance. The fountain, like the selection of
the name Diane, is the sign that L'Astrée is self-consciously romance.

Disguise, too, of course, is a traditional romance convention. The
Greeks had used it, and in d'Urfé's era, travesty was commonly relied on to create a tantalizing discomfort to be righted by the work's
end. Ariosto, Shakespeare, and Sidney were intrigued by the plot
complexities arising from situations of disguise, particularly across
gender, where the possibilities of mistaken identity in love matters
are at once humorous and potentially alarming, if left uncorrected,
which they never are. Sidney, for example, does not even wait until
the tale's end in the New Arcadia to rupture the erotic potential resulting from confused identity. He allows only certain characters to
be baffled by Pyrocles's disguise—Basilius and a few lightheads—
while Gynecia figures out Pyrocles's ruse immediately, and Philoclea
quickly learns that the so-called Amazon is indeed a man.[10] Thus,
the erotic limits of the disguise motif are held in check, even though
the plot functionally depends on Pyrocles disguising himself as an
Amazon. In a similar fashion Sidney chooses to label Pyrocles as
"she" the whole time he is disguised, but this too works as a functional device, a romance formality.[11] In L'Astrée, however, travesty
and name change, or the shifting of masculine and feminine pronouns, are not merely devices allowing the plot to progress. Rather,
the formal procedures become above all the means to a radical exploration of romance and romantic love.

Disguise runs rampant throughout L'Astrée, in both secondary and
primary tales. In the secondary material, however, it is almost always
tactical and momentary and rarely allows for sexual play. The traves-
ties which occur in the principal episodes, that is, in those tales involving the work's major characters, pass quickly beyond tactic to
essence. Such episodes offer the premise of sexual inversion which
d'Urfé twists and turns to create simultaneous, multiple meanings.
The premise behind these convoluted sections is clear and clean, for
Neoplatonism sanctions friendship and close bonding between
women. D'Urfé accepts this tradition and creates rich emotional ties
between women in a world where the male is often rapacious.

Yet the charms of female bonding are not where d'Urfé is ultimately headed. He merely exploits the convention of female friend-

ship to allow for the simultaneous filtering of both heterosexual and homosexual patterns, which in turn dissolve into an essential, gender-free sexuality. D'Urfé's intent was not to portray lesbianism along with heterosexual union, pitting one against the other. Instead, his goal appears to be an erotic production creating, momentarily, both types of love while denying the signal importance of either. Gender, character, identity all fade before the obsessive voice of passion and fantasy pleasure.

There is space here to explore only the Astrée-Céladon passages while alluding briefly to two disguise episodes centering on Diane. In both of the Diane tales, the convention of female friendship is stretched to the limit. Initially, she is wooed by a man, Filandre, disguised as his own sister, Callirée. D'Urfé, maintaining that their conversation is like that between two women, nonetheless depicts stereotypical "courtois" scenes of a male declaring himself to a female, the perfect mime of heterosexual courtship rites. The textual disclaimer of "womanly" talk thus coexists with male comportment in the reader's mind.

In a second episode, Silvandre, a shepherd, and Phillis, a shepherdess, engage in a wager to determine who may best "serve" their "mistress" Diane. Phillis's clothing remains undisguised here: her travesty is one of pure mimicry, and this peculiar situation works, initially and superficially, because of the codes sanctioned by Renaissance Platonic doctrine. D'Urfé plays with words: "Phillis fait si bien la passionnée qu'il n'y a berger qui s'en sceust mieux acquitter" (Phillis knows so well how to feign a woman ardently in love that no shepherd could have pulled it off any better) (2: 293). It is the curious word interchange of "la passionnée" with "le berger" that permits the veiled surfacing of the suggested sexual inversion. The entire odd episode, vacillating between a "male" and "female" image allows ultimately for a polyvalent relationship to surface. Yet no authorial intervention of a systematic type ever intrudes to allow us to reach such a conclusion. Rather, d'Urfé is silent, allowing the formal manipulation of terms to work for itself. We see Phillis as female, undisguised, yet we hear male-typed language and view male-linked acts. All three levels of relating—female friendship, heterosexual courtship, and homosexual bonding—coexist in the narrative, none allowed full fruition, yet none denied textual status. The question, I should add, is never whether Phillis is "only" feigning. What she "truly" feels has no meaning in an absurd situation acceptable only within the limitations of romance. I believe that a legitimate reading will view d'Urfé experimenting with the limits of his prose, striving for that point in writing where a pure eroticism, independent of sexual distinction and act, may be generated.

Thus, Diane, withdrawn virgin by mythological, cultural, and literary standards, in *L'Astrée* is repeatedly caught up in the most equivocal situations. No obviously erotic act ever occurs: it need not, for the verbal exchanges and fetishistic practices are entirely enough. Diane, for example, presents a bracelet made of her hair to Phillis and thereby successfully imitates traditional heterosexual practices. "Traditional" not only because we normally associate such gift-giving with male-female situations but because even within the confines of *L'Astrée,* d'Urfé sets up the model for us. Earlier in the work Astrée had also given such a bracelet to Céladon.

Nonetheless, all of the Diane material stops short of its full erotic potential. D'Urfé creates and then restrains the gender-confused, and thus identity-confused, implications of his writing. When, however, the book turns to the love story between Céladon and Astrée, he allows the situation to develop explosively. Céladon spends most of his time in *L'Astrée* disguised as a female. On three separate occasions he dons women's clothes and fools everyone. Escaping from Galathée, the nymph princess who, passionately in love, has kept him imprisoned in her palace, he becomes one "Lucinde" and is able to liberate himself successfully. This passage, tactical, momentary, and functional, nonetheless serves another purpose in terms of the work's readership: it establishes Céladon as a female presence, no small matter since, for so much of *L'Astrée,* he appears "in drag."

In a second example of travesty, now bordering on transvestism, Céladon dresses up as Orithie, a female who, as tradition has it, will act out the role of Paris in judging the most beautiful naked shepherdess. The levels of gender confusion are substantial, for Céladon is assuming Orithie's identity, that is, the identity of a fictional female, who in turn is to play the role of a male, Paris. How are we to read the scene? How does Astrée read it? With considerable difficulty, for if Orithie is presumed to be female, the convention of female bonding assumes a new, more intense coloration, for Astrée herself is disturbed. If, on the other hand, she perceives, subconsciously or otherwise, Céladon's presence behind the disguise, or any male presence (since Orithie is to pretend to be a Paris figure), a voyeuristic heterosexuality surfaces, pleasurable to both onlooker and victim. What emerges is nothing less than titillating, for Céladon and Astrée, and for readers as well since they also are participating as onlookers. It is as if d'Urfé is seizing here on the very heart, on the sheer momentum of reading romance: voyeuristic participation. Such unchecked voyeurism is scarcely original. Earlier pastoral fiction, particularly Italian, had allowed for "spy" scenes with an erotic base: typically the lover watches his mistress as she bathes or sleeps. D'Urfé, however, goes beyond the conventional format by refusing to relate sexuality to gender. Any attempt to separate and compartmentalize is inherently doomed. Céladon, as we read the episode, is at once himself, Orithie, and Paris, living his fantasy, and perhaps ours, at the "zero degree."

Thus it is that by the time we arrive at the tale's central episode—Céladon disguised now as Alexis, a druidic princess—we are no longer astonished by the ruse. Quite the opposite: we have come to expect and accept it, as perhaps has Astrée, who, for her peace of mind, may even subliminally require it. As with Diane, the most ardent expressions of passion are acceptable, even desirable, provided they emanate from a so-called female. Similar signs coming from a male are rebuffed and censored. Slowly, fear of heterosexual coupling surfaces in the text. Once the threat of male involvement is removed, the female comfortably partakes in the most intimate exchanges.

This new subterfuge, Céladon disguised as the druidic princess Alexis, is formulated by Adamas, the high priest (whose function in *L'Astrée* is clearly as much that of a matchmaker as a counselor of spiritual wisdom), and acceded to by Céladon. Since Astrée has banished Céladon from her sight during a quarrel, this ruse becomes the sole means for Céladon to be near her once more. The casuistry is supremely obvious. States Adamas: "That you are Céladon, there is no doubt . . . but it is not because of this that you will defy her order, for she didn't command you to cease being Céladon, but only to cease showing her this Céladon. And she will not be seeing you, but Alexis" (2: 398). It is apparent that the ambiguous situation contrived by Adamas completely undercuts his elaborate metaphysical speculation whose roots are the Neoplatonism so familiar to sixteenth- and early-seventeenth-century Europeans. All the long-winded exposés on beauty, goodness, and reason, culminating in "honnête amitié," which serve to nullify sexually based passion, are completely ruptured by this erotic projection.

The Alexis-Astrée episode, which begins in the second volume and continues through the fourth, extends the sense of folly that was apparent in the Filandre-Silvandre-Diane episodes. The wordy discourse between Alexis and Astrée duplicates the traditional and courtly expressions of male-female relationships and, at the same time, transfers such language to bonding between females. The masquerade viewed literally, as Jacques Ehrmann wrote, is at least marginally suggestive of a homosexual relationship, as the creation of Alexis negates codified male discourse.[12] But negation is really not the correct term. Rather, the two levels join, forming thereby a double, simultaneous image. The teasing thrust of homosexuality, and of a world gone completely awry, is brought home humorously, furthermore, when Hylas, the book's ardent womanizer, falls passionately in love with the disguised-as-Alexis Céladon, thus maintaining the sense of folly inherent in all the travesty episodes.

Since Alexis-Céladon and Astrée now cohabit, much of their time is spent dressing, undressing, and sleeping. Pastoral romance had given d'Urfé, no doubt, the idea of such voyeuristic living. But by converting Céladon into a female character, he doubles his fantasy. From volume 2 on, Céladon is called simply Alexis by d'Urfé in those passages dependent on act: touches, kisses, embraces. Only when the character occasionally reflects on this odd lifestyle does the narrator allow him his real name. Thus, subtly, Céladon becomes a woman, through the continued textual presence of the female name. Yet, behind the costume, behind the linguistic mask, one feels the presence of the male figure. Such confusion is increased when pronouns replace names, for identity then further vacillates. "Elle" replaces "il" in the most ardent passages. Grammar alone creates and sustains the hermaphroditic feeling of the text. Ultimately, neither heterosexuality nor homosexuality can predominate: they cancel each other out, while a gender-free experience, perhaps the very essence of romance, surfaces. Ultimately, sexual identity, and hence identity, are lost in a purely erotic mass.

But this loss of identity, characterization, and character is not limited to a situation depicting a simple, if radical, alteration. Pursuing his fantasy, Céladon seeks to become not only Alexis but Astrée herself! Certainly, the transformation of self into the beloved, the linking of two souls such that the lover is metamorphosed into his mistress, whose will he embraces and assumes—these idealized concepts are elaborated by Céladon and Adamas throughout L'Astrée, in their interpretation of Neoplatonic thought. However, Céladon's wish to become Astrée in the Alexis episode is a far cry from the exalted spiritual union lauded in the doctrinal passages of the work. As Céladon clothes himself in Astrée's robes, he is sensually charmed, and these feelings are duplicated and again isolated from gender when Astrée in turn dons Alexis's own garb. Thus, as Céladon is transformed now into Astrée, giving up his identity for hers, the whole fantasy (which still allows for the parallel subliminal perception of both Alexis and Céladon) turns autoerotic. No partner is needed, the ultimate projection of fulfillment in a solitary, nonthreatening bond. This sense of solitary pleasure is extended, yet paradoxically reinvigorated with a multiple dimension, when the newly fused self splits, atomizes, as Céladon, in drag as Astrée, contemplates the sleeping female—Astrée?—at his side. Who desires whom? And what?

As Honoré d'Urfé weaves his tale, the original Céladon-Astrée link, which is the diegetic premise, is canceled in favor of a character- and gender-free eroticism. Ehrmann, in his quasi-existential study, focused on this relational gap, which creates in *L'Astrée* what he sees as an identity crisis. In a valueless world, exempt from standards save the crushing one of Love, the self withers, vacillates, and becomes lost unto itself.[13] Particularly Céladon undergoes a debilitating crisis, alienated not only from the social unit but also from himself. However, the rather metaphysical identity crisis portrayed by Ehrmann seems misplaced here. While he is correct in stating that identity is denied in the the travesty-transvestite scenes, he sidesteps the basic loss which occurs. If identity is nullified in the major disguise episodes, it is neither character nor personality that is denied (these have never been especially clear in *L'Astrée*), but rather gender. All the principal disguise episodes take place in a potentially explosive sexual atmosphere, and if identity vacillates, if the self is uprooted, it is in reaction to the difficult demands of sex. Schizophrenic, the Alexis episode is a fantasy. Whose, however, is not clear: Céladon's, or perhaps Astrée's own, for she appears to require his disguise and has just maybe created it for herself. As in Luis Buñuel's film *Belle de Jour,* we are never sure if the erotic projection is the wife's or the "boy scout" husband's. Or the viewer's. In that film, as in *L'Astrée,* all appear to share in its generation; all certainly sustain it.

We have come a long way from the "knights of old," or, for that matter, from "honnête amitié." Yvain's hermitlike retreat led to a gaining or regaining of a moral base; Céladon's solitary retreat to the woods leads to masquerade. And it never leads out. D'Urfé failed to finish his work. Such incompletion is typical of his era. And, of course, he died before he had completed his task. Nonetheless, death cannot explain all, since he had had four very long parts to close and did not. The ascending movement described by Frye, the regaining of lost identity, an impending marriage—none of this oc-

curs in d'Urfé's *L'Astrée*. His secretary Baro did it all for him, in a
fifth part, nullifying slowly the Alexis persona by referring to the
disguised character as Céladon, by maintaining intact the masculine
pronoun. Fantasy is thus denied, while Baro creates a fictional universe sanitized by Neoplatonism. Identity is resumed, alienation dis-
pensed with, and "all's well that ends well." To read Baro's text is to
feel keenly the enormous gap between his generic intent and that
of Honoré d'Urfé. Baro sought to demystify, to normalize a world
gone awry. Why didn't d'Urfé, finally, do the same in a concluding
section? I believe the answer lies precisely in the concept of intent.
For d'Urfé, the romance medium had moved beyond the telling of
a good love story, beyond the traditional obstacles, beyond magic,
beyond the preservation of virginity (which is only technically maintained in *L'Astrée*), beyond loss of identity per se and its resump-
tion. His goal was to wed the living of romance as presented in a
text to the reading of that text. As Karl Uitti has aptly remarked concerning the lovers of *Cligés:* "Chrétien stresses that they are living a
romance, perhaps, in fact, that to a degree all such lovers live a
romance and that love, so conceived, is 'romantic.' "[14] Something like
this occurs also in *L'Astrée,* although d'Urfé pushes further, exploits
more fully than Chrétien the implications of romance as both genre
and romantically conceived love. For him, the essential romantic structure is erotic, in all its possible connotations. Desire is ambiguous,
linked neither to character nor to gender, a floating, undifferentiated
mass. It sustains fantasy projections uncensored by conscious dicta and,
as such, the purest, freest erotic reveries. Céladon's cohabitation with
Astrée, while he is disguised as Alexis, is the written, textual exploration of these essential yearnings, yearning of an androgynous nature
which transcend the more limited Western notion of heterosexual
romance, of one man and one woman forever. Céladon has it all. He
exists simultaneously as himself, as Alexis, and as Astrée, and in
doing so he harmonizes the diverse levels of sexual tension in one
perfect and complete dream. Romantic indeed, in the fullest sense of
the term. No wonder d'Urfé left off where he did, unable or unwilling to conclude. Who would want to give up such a dream for mere
"true" identity? Romance, after all, is the willing, if momentary, sus-
pension of such integrity.[15]

Notes

[1] See C. P. Brand, *Ariosto* (Edinburgh: Edinburgh UP, 1974) 98–99.
[2] Honoré d'Urfé, *L'Astrée,* ed. Hugues Vaganay (Geneva: Slatkine, 1966)
2: 4.

[3] Edward Baron Turk, *Baroque Fiction-Making: A Study of Gomberville's Polexandre*, North Carolina Studies in the Romance Languages and Literatures (Chapel Hill: U of North Carolina P, 1978) 129.

[4] Karl D. Uitti, *Story, Myth, and Celebration in Old French Narrative Poetry, 1050–1200* (Princeton: Princeton UP, 1973) 156.

[5] Northrop Frye, *The Secular Scripture* (Cambridge: Harvard UP, 1976).

[6] Uitti 155–56; Myriam Yvonne Jehenson, *The Golden World of the Pastoral* (Ravenna, Italy: Longo, 1981).

[7] In addition to Jehenson, see particularly Gérard Genette's introduction to the 10/18 excerpted edition of *L'Astrée*, "Le Serpent dans la Bergerie" (Paris, 1964) 7–22.

[8] Clifton Cherpack, "Form and Ideas in *L'Astrée*," *Studies in Philology* 69 (July 1972): 332–33.

[9] Frye 83.

[10] Jehenson 141.

[11] Jehenson 143.

[12] Jacques Ehrmann, *Un Paradis désespéré: L'amour et l'illusion dans* L'Astrée (New Haven: Yale UP, 1963) 80–81.

[13] Ehrmann 55–56.

[14] Uitti 171.

[15] I have analyzed in greater detail d'Urfé's use of the convention of disguise. See *Honoré d'Urfé*, Twayne's World Authors Series (Boston: Hall, 1984).

AFTERWORD
The Problems of Generic Transformation

Ralph Cohen

I begin by asking your indulgence. I have been so deeply involved in the subject of genre that I found I was, in the writing of these remarks, turning from the genre into which I was slotted to one in which I feel more familiar, from the afterword to a theory of the afterword. It was an act of will, and an act that reasserted what we all know: the problematics of genre are problems of our own making. I do not mean by this that we would have no such problems if we followed some approved answers for solving them. I mean that genre problems are made by poets, writers, and scholars like us even though we have at times attributed such formulations to forces outside ourselves—to God, the muses, society, and the devil.

It is particularly relevant, I think, to inquire in a volume on genre why critics consider genre a viable explanatory tool. After all, the alternatives to genre dominate contemporary criticism whether in the practice of interpreting a work without dependence on generic theory or in the analysis of *écriture* as a substitute for genre or in the preference for modes of discourse. Michel Foucault in explaining his abandonment of genre attributes the concept to categories that have lost their validity for us:

> Can one accept, as such, the distinction between the major types of discourse, or that between such forms or genres as science, literature, philosophy, religion, history, fiction, etc., and which tend to create certain

great historical individualities? We are not even sure of ourselves when we use these distinctions in our own world of discourse, let alone when we are analyzing groups of statements which, when first formulated, were distributed, divided, and characterized in a quite different way.[1]

In this quotation, the use of "literature," "fiction," and "science" as "genres" indicates the aberrant uses to which the term has been put. Without pursuing the critical fortunes of genre theories, I can point to some general reasons for rethinking genre theory. The first is that contemporary genre theory is rooted in problems of continuity and discontinuity especially significant for a period such as our own. Any theory of genre ought to explain why and how genres originate and the reasons for their variations, interrelations, and discontinuance. Second, a contemporary genre theory ought to assume that a text is a hierarchical network, a system that is linked with other texts in a larger system to form a generic hierarchy. Thus some forms, like tragedy, or epic, or satire, or lyric, are dominant at one time and recessive or subordinate at others. A genre theory provides us with a comprehensive system to study all texts as a family of forms. It is thus possible to select from these all such texts as have been identified as literary. Again, a genre theory can provide us with analyzable features that interconnect and interrelate genres while permitting each text in which they appear to retain its generic identity. For example, some genres, like proverbs or the epigram or the maxim, are not only independent but tend to form parts of other forms. Bakhtin, for instance, declares that the novel is the genre that is especially distinguished by multiple voices and the multiple dimensionality of languages:

> Diversity of voices and heteroglossia enter the novel and organize themselves within it into a structured artistic system. This constitutes the distinguishing feature of the novel as a genre.[2]

And, finally, a genre system is valuable to us because it brings to our attention a body of texts the variety of which has only too frequently been ignored in literary study.

Genre systems have had various functions in a history beginning with Aristotle's explanation of the structure, aim, and effect of tragedy as a dominant form of artistic education in a community. There have, since Aristotle, been numerous genre theories with somewhat different aims for classifying texts, relating them, and analyzing aspects of their structure. And each of these theories advocates or supports certain values of literary study for the audiences they address.

Maria Corti, for example, points out that up to the present, theories of genre have generally belonged to one of two categories: "those of an abstract, atemporal, deductive nature and those of a historic, diachronic, inductive nature."[3] She has serious objections to both categories and offers her own historical-inductive approach, complemented and corroborated by structuralist methods. Her approach "poses the problem of the transformation of literary genres and of their functions" and "relates genres to the universe of senders and addressees," procedures that have as their social aim a contribution "to our understanding of literary communication and of the relations between literature and society."[4]

The very term "genre" contains, in the various meanings given to it, some of the problems of genre. Is genre a text or a discourse, a product or a process, or both? Is it a member of a class or is it a class? Within a class, what changes does it undergo without losing its membership? Can a genre be a member of more than one class? Under what conditions does one genre become transformed into another? What is the relation between a literary genre and society? The term has its source in the Latin *genus,* which refers to "kind" or "sort" or "species" or "class." Its root terms are *genere, gignere*—to beget and (in the passive) to be born. In this latter sense it can refer both to a class and to an individual. And it is of course derived from the same root terms as "gender."

I have said that there were important reasons for rethinking genre theory in our time, but perhaps the most interesting is our own sense of the widespread exemplification of generic change and our realization that a genre theory is analogous to social and scientific theories which seek to explain changes in matter, man, and society. In ancient and modern written texts, we note the pervasiveness of kinds and their transformation. Biblical Genesis narrates the earliest generic transformations by describing the origin of the heavens and the earth and of man and woman.

> In the beginning God created the heaven and
> the earth.
> And the earth was without form, and void;
> and darkness was upon the face of the
> deep. . . .
> And God said, "Let there be light," and there
> was light.
> And God saw the light, that it was good: and
> God divided the light from the darkness.
> (Gen. 1:1–4)

God created light from darkness, man from the dust of the ground: "And the Lord God formed man of the dust of the ground, and breathed into his nostrils the breath of life; and man became a living soul" (Gen. 2:7). The transformation of earth into a living soul is an elemental transformation; but it is transformation because it implies a continuity, for man returns to the dust from which he came. Dust to dust: for something to be transformed it must retain some features, aspects, or elements that permit us to recognize that we have, indeed, a *trans*formation, not a completely new object. Something in the form needs to be transferred in order for something to be transformed. In some way, a transformation must be reconstituted so that its form change is not totally disconnected from that which has been changed. Robert Nisbet puts it this way: "Change is a succession of differences in time in a persisting identity." And he goes on to say that "only when the succession of differences in time may be seen to relate to some object, entity or being the identity of which persists through all the successive differences, can change be said to have occurred."[5] The crucial term here is "identity."

Consider the problem of identity and form change in mythological stories. Zeus, Hera, and other Greek gods and goddesses are constantly changing shape. Such form change, whatever its aim, is governed by a consciousness of the god's power and the god's knowledge that whether he becomes a bird or a beast, he can return to his original form. In other words, the language, soul, or spirit retains an identity. We can see this clearly in Apuleius's story (written in the second century) of Lucius, who is transformed into an ass though he continues to think in the language of a human being: "though I was no longer Lucius, and to all appearances a complete ass, a mere beast of burden, I still retained my mental faculties."[6] Or consider the famous twentieth-century story which begins "As Gregor Samsa awoke one morning from uneasy dreams he found himself transformed in his bed into a giant insect."[7] Gregor's shape changed but he continued to think in human language and to be concerned about his human affairs. Such transformation, such continuity and discontinuity, creates moral, conceptual, and self-identity problems. In a theory of genres the principle of identity is more complex. The critic constructs such identity knowing full well that each instance of a genre is in some way different from all previous instances. He must accept the openness of a class, and it is not always clear that a work belongs only to one genre. The very multidimensionality of language makes texts candidates for more than one genre. It is as though every text is endowed with an ambiguous identity whether by author, critic, or both.

Oral and written discourse proceed by linguistic transformations regardless of whether the speaker or writer accepts or denies a theory of genre. The reason for this is that language characteristically converts nonlinguistic behavior into language. Language is, at least in this respect, transformational, and any attempt to narrate another's discourse by retelling, revising, or reconstructing it necessarily involves a process of construction. Within language we can see that figures of speech like metaphor and personification are transformational figures. In metaphor, two different kinds—for example, a woman and a rose, a river and poetry—are joined by relating certain common features and implying a continuity within discontinuity. Metaphor, therefore, operates by demonstrating that what may appear to be two distinct and unrelated identities can be understood as a transformation. Personification, too, can be understood as revealing a universe in which nonhuman objects and beings possess the gestures, features, languages of human beings and are thus characterized by transformations. I do not equate metaphor or personification with genre, but I wish to indicate that genre theory is part of a larger explanatory enterprise concerned with understanding identity and change. And this enterprise applies not merely to literary forms but to the world of matter as well. Matter undergoes change, and the language that describes it is ambiguously generic: a seed *becomes* a seedling, a caterpillar *becomes* a butterfly. A theory of genre, therefore, attempts to characterize the processes of continuity and discontinuity, and its language is inevitably ambiguous.

Any instance of a genre is analyzable as pointing backward to its diachronic ancestry, forward to its alteration of this inheritance. Any text, therefore, in a theory of genre can be understood as being at a point of intersection between past and present, in which it is revising, supporting, supplementing, undermining the class in which it is placed. This is what I meant when I said that every text is a process and a product. The language of genre is metaphoric, and genre theories pursue different aspects of the generative metaphor. But we should not forget that such pursuits of theoretical explanation form a genre of their own with their own distortion mechanisms. Inquiries into the classifications of writing, into the structure of these classifications—their interrelations with norms and values—make the various generic theories continuous while they also alter our notion of what a literary theory is.

To put it paradoxically, a theory of genre seeks to explain the continuity that governs discontinuity and the discontinuity that governs continuity. A theory of "genre," whether it refers to tragedy or epic or epigram, is a construct of criticism; it is, as I said above, a theory of our own making. If we grant the value of a genre theory, which theory should we embrace? Do we wish a theory which takes for granted that its subject matter is the forms in which authors write, or shall we proceed by extrapolating from the writings an ideal story or form such as "narrative" or "romance"?

I am aware that "narrative" and "romance" can be interpreted as empirical generic forms. Genette wavers between considering "narrative" as an abstraction to be found in numerous genres—that is, as a "mode" of writing—and "narrative" as a synonym for novel. So, too, "romance" can be a particular literary form, the "romance," or a mode of writing that is a feature of comedy, tragedy, novel, poem, and other genres or subgenres. It is the confusion of mode with genre that I wish to examine, a confusion that conflates the abstract with the empirical.

Narrative has become one of the more salable and assailable theories of genre. No one familiar with contemporary theory is unaware of the valuable distinctions pertinent to the structure of narrative. There is *story,* "a sequence of actions or events conceived as independent of their manifestation in discourse," and *discourse,* "the discursive presentation or narration of events."[8] There are points of view, author, implied author, reader, implied reader, rhetorical distinctions such as prolepsis, analepsis, and so forth. By concentrating on distinctions between story and discourse, critics have been able to introduce important distinctions in explaining the devices and procedures of narrative structure. Yet narrative critics disagree even about these elementary distinctions. And if we regard narrative as a genre theory, there are two major dilemmas that it faces: the first is that a drama, a painting, or a novel can have a narrative and that the theory provides no procedure for distinguishing and evaluating the nonnarrative elements from the narrative. The second is that writers do not produce narratives; they write stories, poems, novels, dramas, but not narratives. The narrative is an extrapolation from a drama, as in Jonathan Culler's discussion of Sophocles's *Oedipus Rex:* "The analysis of narrative would identify the sequence of events that constitutes the action of the story."[9]

But in this play there are several other narratives; for example, the second messenger describes in detail the death of Jocasta. What we have here is another narrative that cannot be distinguished from the first by reference to discourse. For the discourse of the first narrative is that of the critic, not of the dramatist. The theoretical entanglements that this creates result from the separation of genre theory from the kinds of writing that actually exist. The drama as a symbolic, ritualized performance may function differently at different times, but its role as a genre cannot be deciphered without some historical understanding. A genre like the drama or epic has a social function which audience or listeners grant, and it cannot be analyzed in disregard of these.

We can see the difficulties that will arise if we study "romance" as a genre in the manner in which critics have discussed "narrative." When Northrop Frye refers to "romance," he refers to Schiller's two terms—"naive" and "sentimental." Naive romance is "a kind of story that is found in collections of folk tales and *märchen,* like Grimm's Fairy Tales"; sentimental romance is a "more extended and literary development of the formulas of naive romance." He wants the reader to see "romance" in early and modern times as primarily "prose narrative" of a certain type. But this is not the view of narrative structure. Romance, he points out, has recurrent structures such as two types of narrative linkage, and heroes and villains who "exist primarily to symbolize a contrast between two worlds, one above the level of ordinary experience, the other below it."[10] His concept of structure is subtle and provocative, but it is committed to the view that its features, however drawn from different times, are divisible into the basic structure.

But such a theory does not seek to answer why such different actual genres arise as tragedy, comedy, history, pastoral, pastoral-comical, historical pastoral, tragical historical—indeed why the whole Polonian classification should arise. Such a theory is not interested in explaining why literary conventions arise or decline, why genres are constituted as they are, when they are.

If, however, we consider such questions as appropriate, then the process of naming the genre to which a work belongs steers us to a view of artistic structure, its literary and philosophical ramifications.

Henry Fielding calls *Joseph Andrews* "a comic romance," which he defines as a "comic epic poem in prose; differing from comedy as the serious epic from tragedy: its action being more extended and comprehensive; containing a much larger circle of incidents, and introducing a greater variety of characters."[11] This definition, relying on epic, comedy, and romance, indicates that for the author the work

possessed features from all three genres that were combined in imitation of *Don Quijote*. The text therefore was, for the author, a combination of structures from several different genres.

If *Joseph Andrews* is a romance, it also includes authorial commentaries that are not romantic structural features. It includes inter-
polated narratives in which the heroes become listeners and minor
characters become narrators. It includes a fragmentary narrative as
well as a long digression on the *Iliad*. It is, in fact, an example of the
multidimensionality and multitemporality of a text, since many of
the procedures are borrowed from Cervantes and others contain allusions to biblical and later texts.

I have been noting the author's generic identification of *Joseph
Andrews,* but you are all aware that such identification is also made
by critics in transaction with the text. The author's identification is
surely pertinent, but it is not final, especially in the cases of a genre
name such as the "novel," which was not in currency in Fielding's
time. It is evident that in a transaction genre critics might locate the
novel in the subgroups of romance; it might be considered within
the novelistic genres that mix fact with fiction. But it would not be
considered an epistolary novel or a comic epic poem in prose which
is a genre without members.

But, more important, its generic identification would be determined
by the works to which it is related, for example, as a parody of
Pamela or as a work with a romance conclusion in which the true
identities of hero and heroine are discovered, and they live happily
ever after, or, indeed, a romance ending that provides a fantasy that
steers the reader away from the attack on the vanity and hypocrisy
of most of the characters in the novel.

Whatever the generic identification of *Joseph Andrews,* it is a text
that is part of a continuing generic process. As such, its structure will
inevitably be somewhat changed from prior instances of the genre,
supplementing, supporting, questioning, parodying it. It is to this
process of genre change that I now wish to turn.

Thus far I have dealt with the reasons for a genre theory, the
nature of genre theory in relation to change in matter, man, and
society, the manner in which a text might be constituted for genre
theory, and some of the dilemmas that involve narrative and romance
theories. I use as a test case a story that exists as a poem, a prose fiction, a drama, and a novel.

In 1624 there was published "The Ballad of George Barnwell," a
poem about a merchant's apprentice who fell in love with a prostitute, was seduced by her, and was persuaded to rob his master and

murder his uncle. The prostitute was tried and hanged, and Barn-well escaped to Poland where he too was hanged, but for a murder he claimed he did not commit. This story with some revisions was made into a prose fiction that was published in 1700. It formed the basis for George Lillo's *The London Merchant,* produced in 1731, and it was revised as a ballad by Bishop Percy in 1765 and became part of a novel called *Barnwell* by Thomas Skinner Surr in 1798.

My aim here is to examine the ballad, the play, and the revision and to bring to the fore some of the problems pertinent to genre transformation and to distinguish these from other genre changes. To begin, the ballad falls within a genre that is sung, and this ballad was set to the same music as Thomas Deloney's "The Rich Merchant Man." Its subject matter, while dealing with a merchant's apprentice, contrasted with the noble merchant of the earlier ballad. The poem is narrated in the first person by Barnwell but is con- cluded by a third-person narrator. Within the poem there are sev-eral inexplicable narrator shifts. The poem begins with an address to "all youths of fair England" and concludes with a warning to beware of harlots.

The poem presents a picture of debauched innocence and of the gross pleasures of the flesh and their consequences. The characters are of low descent, the diction often vulgar, but among the more interesting aspects of the ballad is its computational imagery, reflect-ing the merchandising and accounting characteristic of the appren-tice's task.

When the ballad was converted into a tragedy, a number of changes took place that throw light on genre as a shaping of artistic force. The eighteenth-century tragedy was still considered a dominant form, and it was still reserved for conflicts among princes, kings, and their followers. To convert a vulgar ballad into a tragedy demanded that the characters be elevated and that the problems become affairs of state. What takes place in *The London Merchant* is the elevation of the merchant—not a character in the ballad—to the status of a gentle-man who deals in political matters and sees his role as a moral model. The subject matter of the play becomes the typical subject matter of heroic drama: a conflict between love and duty, Barnwell's love for the prostitute and his duty toward his master. And Barnwell, who is no more than a youth, compares himself, as a betrayer of trust, to no less than Satan, "the grand apostate, when first he lost his purity; like me, disconsolate he wandered, and while in heaven, had all his future hell about him."[12]

If we examine an elementary change in which a passage narrated by Barnwell in the ballad is spoken by the prostitute in the drama, we can see that there is an ideological shift. The ballad refers to a "dainty gallant dame," indicating the readiness of the speaker to succumb to temptation. By shifting the speech to the woman, it is she who forces the meeting and designs the seduction. In the ballad, Barnwell states:

> As I upon a day was walking through the street
> About my master's business, I did a wanton meet:
> A dainty gallant Dame, and sumptuous in attire,
> With smiling looks she greeted me and did my name require.[13]

In the drama, the prostitute declares:

> Having long had a design on him, and meeting him yesterday, I made a full stop, and gazing wishfully on his face, ask'd him his name; he flush'd, and bowing very low, answer'd, George Barnwell. I beg'd his pardon for the freedom I had taken, and told him, that he was the person I had long wish'd to see, and to whom I had an affair of importance to communicate, at a proper time and place. He nam'd a tavern; I talk'd of honour and reputation, and invited him to my house; he swallow'd the bait, promis'd to come, and this is the time I expect him.[14]

The dramatic form provides a different structure of character from that of the ballad. Millwood addresses a servant who she believes shares her values and, in the tradition of the drama, informs the audience of her motives and manipulation of Barnwell. The ballad provides no such information but resorts frequently to repetition, especially in the rhyme, as one would expect in an oral performance. The tragedy requires a conflict that introduces two families, two sets of values, two households. It provides a local habitation and a fictitious past to justify its significance.

The two genres have different conceptions of the nature of character. The tragedy, however, unlike the ballad, is concerned with redemption and punishment. Female viciousness brings atheism along with it, but Barnwell is redeemed by biblical instruction and goes patiently to his death.

These additions bring in the merchant and his daughter and a trustworthy apprentice to counter Barnwell, as well as bringing servants into the prostitute's household who first support her values and cater to her needs but turn against her when she urges Barnwell to become a murderer. But the point of the additions, contrasts, and character transformations is to establish moral principles to underlie the conflict and to show the extent to which principles can be bent without being broken.

The tragedy is conceptually different from the ballad. The latter is governed by mutual guilt; the former lays out the difference between venial and fatal crimes. The tragedy focuses on class changes and the moral responsibility that accompanies such changes; the ballad outlines the consequences of sensual indulgence. We have here two different sets of values rather than a transformation of one set into another.

My use of this hypothesis of genre change is meant to support two points. The first is that if we fail to attend to the actual written form, the ballad or tragedy, we overlook the control that the genre exercises on narrative material. The music of the ballad, for example, acts as generic bonding with other ballads; other features of the poem, such as imagery, diction, and character become subordinated when the story is transposed into a quite different genre. My second point is that generic control requires an awareness of historical connections for adequate understanding.

If *The London Merchant* is an example of a transposition of some ballad features into a tragedy, what would a transformation be? I have tried to suggest that transformation involves continuity and that examples of it might be revisions or alterations that result in modifying a genre or in providing it with a different concept. The term "transformation" is used by critics to refer to two quite different categories. It refers to the variations a genre undergoes that do not involve a conceptual change and to genre modifications that do. This seems a simple enough distinction, but if a text is itself a system and part of other systems, how do we distinguish concept changes from surface variations? If Tzvetan Todorov is right in urging that new genres are formed from old, how can we determine which variation merely supports, which defends, or which supplements a concept and which overturns it?

Is *The London Merchant* a transformation of a narrative found in "The Ballad of George Barnwell"? Of course it is, but I doubt the usefulness of considering narrative a genre. As a structural feature of a ballad, it is transformed, but the ballad itself does not become a tragedy. Some of its features such as characters can be included in the drama; particular sentences can be identified. But most of the generic features of the ballad, its poetry, its song, its narration are not transformed and do not lead to the tragedy.

If we adhere to some kind of historical inductive theory, we still need adequate explanatory principles, but we will not assume that a ballad can be transformed into a drama. It can, as in the ballad opera, become a component, a feature of a dramatic form, it can be absorbed into a more comprehensive structure so that some novels contain ballads, but we need to distinguish this process from a gradual movement within a form. The simplest example of a transformation is the ballad revision of 1765. In it the poulter's measure is turned into four-line quatrains, the diction smoothed, the narrator made consistent, the repetitions reduced. Thus, the original lines.

> Quo' she, "thou art a paltry Jack, to charge me in this sort,
> Being a woman of credit good, and known of good report

become

> Quoth she, Thou art a knave
>   To charge me in this sort,
> Being a woman of credit fair
>   And known of good report.[15]

Bishop Percy, who made the revision, retained the second half of the lines in this passage and made his revisions in the first half, displacing the vulgar "paltry Jack" with the colloquial "knave" and removing the repetition of "good." These are, however, part of a systematic attempt to refine the vulgarity, ungrammaticalness, and discontinuity of the original. There is an attempt to remove the ballad from its common origins and to locate it in the realm of contemporary balladry. We can thus see, if we examine the many aspects of his transformation, that they include omissions, diction shifts, repetition removals, stanzaic alteration, and narrator manipulation.

These add up to conceptual change, even though much of the original ballad is retained. The shift in concept might be put this way: the original structure accepted versification and metrics that permitted vulgarity, discontinuity, unevenness. The revision sought to refine the language and the rhyme scheme and remove irregularities and repetitions. It transformed the ballad into an eighteenth-century artistic achievement. This is the transformation that Pope wrought when he "versified" Donne's satires. It is a process governed by a concept of refinement addressed to a literate audience rather than the populace at large.

But the study of revision seems an easy and not very usable example. The more difficult project is to undertake an explanation of a transformation in which one genre seems to lead into another.

Here the explanatory principle is to trace the steps in the transformation with sufficient care so that no gap is too broad for leaping. One of the most eminent examples of this effort is M. H. Abrams's explanation of the transformation of the georgic descriptive poem into what he calls the "greater Romantic lyric." He declares "that the most characteristic Romantic lyric [poems like Coleridge's "Frost at Midnight," Wordsworth's "Tintern Abbey," Shelley's "Ode to the West Wind," and Keats's "Ode to a Nightingale"] developed directly out of the most stable and widely employed of all the classic kinds."[16] He selects features from John Denham's *Coopers Hill* and from Gray's "Ode on a Distant Prospect of Eton College" and finds these to be variations of the neoclassic norm; finally he turns to William Bowles's sonnets and finds there the conceptual transformation he has been seeking. Its structure includes above all "a determinate speaker, whom we are invited to identify with the author himself, whose responses to the local scene are a spontaneous overflow of feeling and displace the landscape as the center of poetic interest."[17]

Despite the care with which Abrams moves from features in a georgic-descriptive poem to a sonnet that lyricizes them, there remain questions about the relations between the two forms. There is no doubt that features can change their function and that functional change may be associated with conceptual change. But is it likely that this is the case here? Poets from Dryden to Johnson eschewed the sonnet as genre. They did so because its structure seemed inhospitable to their antithetical poetic structures, to the heroic couplet as a norm, to the segmental sense that the couplet provided. From Denham onward the couplet became for neoclassic writers a favored poetic verse, one that Dryden and later Pope recognized as consolidating the social and moral values they were intent on promoting. The sonnet, constructed on cyclical or other principles, did not lend itself to these values or, at the very least, the poets thought it did not.

The theoretical issue is whether a return to a form rarely used by one's predecessors constitutes a revolutionary change, that is, a conceptual change, or whether such a form, when eventually used, is made to function within eighteenth-century concepts—whether these imply a Lockean empiricism, a Hartleyan associationism, a segmented, additive poetic world. In other words, its external change conceals an internal acceptance. The techniques of resistance with acceptance can include renewed older forms that function as do the contemporary ones, additions that exaggerate the principles they are supplementing, the introduction of a new diction that does not undo but does subdue the force of the received concepts.

In an article entitled "The Structure of Romantic Nature Imagery" (1954), written before Abrams's article (1965), William Wimsatt analyzed Bowles's sonnet "To the River Itchin" (1789) and compared it with Coleridge's imitation "To the River Otter" (1796). He found that the Bowles sonnet provided a flat announcement of Hartleyan association, where as Coleridge's sonnet showed him to be concerned "with the more complex ontological grounds of association (the various levels of sameness, of correspondence and analogy) where mental activity transcends mere 'associative response.' "[18] Wimsatt recognized a continuity between Bowles's sonnets and Coleridge's; the difference lay in a shift of intensity which affected and enacted the structure of nature imagery. The criterion for conceptual change was, for him, intensity or depth, a romantic "dramatization of the spiritual through the use of the faint, the shifting, the least tangible and most mysterious parts of nature—a poetic counterpart of the several theories of spirit as subtle matter current in the eighteenth century, Newton's 'electric and elastic' active principle, Hartley's 'infinitesimal elementary body.' "[19]

What Wimsatt sought to do was to trace within the same form a transformation of values. The sonnet possesses a rather rigid external form, and he sought to show a change in its construction of metaphor, in its move from the tangible aspects of nature to the intangible. Concepts in poetry—ways of knowing and thinking—can be found in any of its structural features. Wimsatt found them in the imagery, but they can be found in the versification, in the meter, in the form itself. We need to understand that genre transformation can be traced through these structural elements. The subject matter itself is no necessary indication of the concepts that a work is enacting.

What seems valuable in Wimsatt's presentation is the recognition of the multidimensionality of Bowles's sonnet so that its imagery of nature is future-related and its associationism is past-related. Wimsatt does not raise the question of the sonnet as a genre nor does he inquire whether it functions symbolically to resist or supplant the values of the georgic poem. He does argue, I believe correctly, that features of nature imagery reveal epistemological and moral hypotheses.

What signals conceptual change other than intensity of imagery, shifts in versification or diction? One important indicator is parody of a norm or form, as in Keats's first stanza of "Ode on Melancholy" followed by stanzas that offer a contrary norm. We can see this in Coleridge's parody of the sonnet and his own practice as an alternative. Another indicator is a poet's use of a verse form that is later rejected because it represents values he no longer shares. This is the case with Wordsworth, who begins with the couplets of "An Evening Walk" and "Descriptive Sketches" and turns from them to the lyrical, autobiographical poem. Or we can observe the shift in function of a form as in Blake's use of a hymn form in "London," which in the violence of the diction and the synaesthetic imagery undermines the form and converts it from a peaceful support of social and religious values to a violent attack on them.

It has not been my aim in this essay to solve the problems of generic transformation but to show their complexity and to offer some possible solutions. I said at the opening of this essay that we construct the problems of genre, and I have tried to explain why we wish to do so. The problems of genre and generic transformations are not insoluble. Their solutions will help us resolve other issues such as those of periodization and the relation of generic change to social and scientific change. But our success lies in so formulating our problems that they are soluble and that the solutions do lead us to enhanced understanding of our subject and our society. I assure you, however, that I have kept before me the memory of such an exercise in one of my classes. I invited the students to construct their own examination by posing to themselves a set of questions that I would have to approve. I did, in fact, approve the set to which I refer. They seemed to me difficult but provocative. The day before the examination, the student came to see me. "I cannot," she said, "answer the questions I set myself. What shall I do?"

"You face," I said, "a serious dilemma."

Notes

[1] Michel Foucault, "What Is an Author?" *Textual Strategies,* ed. Josué V. Harari (Ithaca: Cornell UP, 1979) 143.

[2] Mikhail Bakhtin, *The Dialogic Imagination: Four Essays,* trans. Caryl Emerson and Michael Holquist, ed. Michael Holquist (Austin: U of Texas P, 1981) 231.

[3] Maria Corti, *An Introduction to Literary Semiotics* (Bloomington: Indiana UP, 1978) 115.

[4] Corti 117.

[5] Robert Nisbet, *Social Change and History* (London: Oxford UP, 1969) 168.

⁶ Robert Graves, trans., *The Golden Ass* (New York: Farrar, 1951) 72.

⁷ Stanley Korngold, trans., *The Metamorphosis* (New York: Bantam, 1981) 3.

⁸ Jonathan Culler, *Structuralist Poetics* (Ithaca: Cornell UP, 1975) 169–70.

⁹ Culler 172.

¹⁰ Northrop Frye, *The Secular Scripture* (Cambridge: Harvard UP, 1976) 53.

¹¹ Henry Fielding, *Joseph Andrews,* ed. Martin Battestin (Middletown, Ct.: Wesleyan UP, 1967) 4.

¹² George Lillo, *The London Merchant* (Boston: Heath, 1906) 31.

¹³ Thomas Percy, "The Ballad of George Barnwell," *Reliques of Ancient English Poetry* (London: Lewis, 1906) 3: 306.

¹⁴ Lillo 47.

¹⁵ Percy 315.

¹⁶ M. H. Abrams, "Structure and Style in Greater Romantic Lyric," *From Sensibility to Romanticism,* ed. F. W. Hilles and Harold Bloom (London: Oxford UP, 1965) 208.

¹⁷ Abrams 217.

¹⁸ William Wimsatt, "The Structure of Romantic Nature Imagery," *The Age of Johnson* (New Haven: Yale UP, 1950) 295.

¹⁹ Wimsatt 299.

CONTRIBUTORS

Kevin Brownlee, associate professor of French and Italian at Dartmouth College, specializes in medieval French literature and Dante studies. He is the author of *Poetic Identity in Guillaume de Machaut* and is currently completing a book on Jean de Meun's poetics.

Marina Scordilis Brownlee is associate professor of Spanish and Comparative Literature at Dartmouth College. She has published *The Poetics of Literary Theory: Lope de Vega's* Novelas a Marcia Leonarda *and Their Cervantine Context* and *The Status of the Reading Subject in the* Libro de buen amor.

Ralph Cohen, William R. Kenan Professor of English at the University of Virginia, has written extensively on English literature and on critical theory. He is the author of *The Art of Discrimination* and *The Unfolding of the Seasons* and the editor of *New Literary History.*

Nancy Freeman-Regalado, Professor of French at New York University, has published *Poetic Patterns in Rutebeuf: A Study of Noncourtly Poetic Modes of the Thirteenth Century.* She has recently completed a book entitled *Reading Villon's "Testament."*

Louise K. Horowitz is associate professor of French at Rutgers University at Camden. She is the author of *Love and Language: A Study of the Classical French Moralist Writers* and *Honoré d'Urfé* as well as a variety of articles on other aspects of seventeenth-century French literature.

Douglas Kelly, professor of French at the University of Wisconsin at Madison, includes among his recent book publications *The Medieval Imagination: Rhetoric and the Poetry of Courtly Love* and *The Romances of Chrétien de Troyes,* a collection of essays which he edited.

Edward Morris is professor of French at Cornell University. His research interests center on the French Renaissance and on the interrelationship of literature and music. He is currently working on the aesthetics and semantics of rhythm in Rabelais.

Stephen G. Nichols is professor of Romance Languages at the University of Pennsylvania. His most recent book publications are *Romanesque Signs: Early Medieval Narrative and Iconography* and *Mimesis: From Mirror to Method, Augustine to Descartes,* which he coedited with John Lyons.

David Quint is associate professor of comparative literature at Princeton University. He is the author of *Origin and Originality in Renaissance Literature* in addition to articles on Boiardo and Ariosto and a translation of Poliziano's *Stanze.*

Ruth El Saffar is professor of Spanish at the University of Illinois at Chicago. She has written *Novel to Romance: A Study of Cervantes's* Novelas Ejemplares, *Distance and Control in* Don Quijote, *and Beyond Fiction: The Recovery of the Feminine in the Novels of Cervantes.*

Cesare Segre, professor of Romance philology at the University of Pavia, has published widely on medieval and Renaissance Romance literatures as well as on literary theory. Among his major works in English are *Semiotics and Literary Criticism* and *Structures and Time.*

Harry Sieber, professor of Romance languages at Johns Hopkins University, is the author of *The Picaresque* and *Language and Society in* Lazarillo de Tormes. He has edited Cervantes's *Novelas Ejemplares* and written a variety of articles on such Renaissance authors as Gómez Manrique, Quevedo, and Calderón.

Karl D. Uitti is the John N. Woodhull Professor of Modern Languages at Princeton University and writes on medieval French literature. His books include *Linguistics and Literary Theory* and *Story, Myth, and Celebration in Old French Narrative Poetry.* Among his most recent publications are essays on Chrétien de Troyes, Marie de France, and medieval historiography.

INDEX

INDEX